ENGLISH G

LIGHTHOUSE

Lehrerfassung

6

Vokabeltrainer-App

Verfügbar für: iOS, Android und Windows Phone

Cornelsen

English G · Lighthouse · Band 6

Lehrerfassung

Im Auftrag des Verlages herausgegeben von
Wolfgang Biederstädt, Köln
Frank Donoghue, Nenagh, Irland

Konzepterarbeitung von
Susan Abbey, Nenagh, Irland
Wolfgang Biederstädt, Köln
Frank Donoghue, Nenagh, Irland

Erarbeitet von
Susan Abbey, Nenagh, Irland
Frank Donoghue, Nenagh, Irland

unter Mitarbeit von
Joachim Blombach, Herford
Annette Bondzio-Abbit, Bielefeld
Hartmut Bondzio, Bielefeld
Uta Franke, Leipzig
Marc Proulx, Berlin
Martina Schroeder, Stedtlingen
Udo Wagner, Voerde
Herbert Willms, Herford

in Zusammenarbeit mit der Englischredaktion
Klaus Unger (Projektleitung); Annegret Hauser (koordinierende Redakteurin); Doreen Arnold; Jutta Seuren, Kathrin Spiegelberg, Silvia Wiedemann *sowie beratend* Irja Fröhling, Mara Leibowitz, Olivia Wintgens; Franziska Gross (bildrechtliche Unterstützung)

Vokabelanhänge
Ingrid Raspe, Düsseldorf; Uwe Tröger

Beratende Mitwirkung
Birgit Estabillo, Berlin; Verena Flocke, Düren; Alexander Kraft, Guldental; Jürgen Lohmann, Dinslaken; Jörg Rademacher, Mannheim; Andrea Rohoff, Hannover; Dr. Daniela Schirmer, Kiel; Berit Schaarschmidt, Aschaffenburg; Konstanze Stöckermann-Borst, Leimen; Herbert Willms, Herford sowie Ulrike Rath, Aachen

Layoutkonzept und technische Umsetzung
Klein & Halm Grafikdesign, Berlin

Umschlaggestaltung
Cornelsen Verlag Design unter Verwendung der Entwürfe von Klein & Halm Grafikdesign, Berlin, und kleiner & bold, Berlin

www.cornelsen.de

Druck: Firmengruppe APPL, aprinta Druck, Wemding

1. Auflage, 1. Druck 2017
ISBN 978-3-06-032715-7

ISBN 978-3-06-033980-8 – E-Book

PEFC
PEFC/04-32-0928

PEFC zertifiziert
Dieses Produkt stammt aus nachhaltig bewirtschafteten Wäldern und kontrollierten Quellen.

www.pefc.de

Dein Englischbuch enthält folgende Teile:

Unit 1–3	Die drei Kapitel des Buches
Diff-Bank	Weitere Aufgaben – unterschiedlich schwer
Wordbank	Zusätzliche Wörter und Wendungen zu bestimmten Themen
Text file	Interessante Texte, passend zu den Units
Exam file	Aufgaben zur Vorbereitung auf die Abschlussprüfung
Language file	Zusammenfassung wichtiger Sprachregeln
Skills file	Beschreibung wichtiger Lern- und Arbeitstechniken
Vocabulary	Wörterverzeichnis zum Lernen der neuen Wörter
Dictionary	Alphabetisches Wörterverzeichnis (*English-German*)

Die Units bestehen aus diesen Teilen:

Lead-in	Einstieg in die neue Unit
Theme 1 / Theme 2	Neue Themen mit vielen Aktivitäten und Übungen
Focus on language	Entdecken von Regeln und Üben wichtiger Strukturen
Text	Eine Geschichte zum Lesen
Skills training	*Listening – Reading – Speaking – Writing – Mediation – Viewing*
STOP! CHECK! GO!	Üben, Vertiefen, Lernfortschritte feststellen (Von deiner Lehrperson kannst du ein Lösungsblatt erhalten. Hörtexte findest du auf der Audio-CD im Workbook.)
MORE CHALLENGE	Üben und Vertiefen mit höherem Schwierigkeitsgrad

In den Units findest du diese Symbole:

	Partnerarbeit / Gruppenarbeit
	Nur auf CD / Auf CD und im Schülerbuch
	Filme auf der DVD
○	Leichtere Übungen
●	Schwierigere Übungen
○ // ● p. 104	Parallelaufgaben: die leichtere in der Unit – die schwierigere in der Diff-Bank
More help p. 102	Hilfen zu einer Aufgabe in der Diff-Bank
More practice 3 p. 104	Weitere Übungen in der Diff-Bank
More challenge 4 p. 107	Weitere Übungen mit höherem Schwierigkeitsgrad

INHALT

	Lerninhalte	Your task (Lernaufgabe)	Texte	
English around the world 	· die Bedeutung des Englischen als *lingua franca* und für sich selbst erschließen · Lebenswelten in einigen englischsprachigen Ländern kennen lernen			
Unit 1 Embrace diversity 	· Aspekte der Gegenwart und Geschichte Südafrikas kennen lernen · über Vielfalt in einer multikulturellen Gesellschaft sprechen · vier jungen *Born Frees* begegnen · Ideen für eine Südafrika-Reise diskutieren · Karikaturen beschreiben · Alltagsgespräche als Tourist/in führen · ein *work & travel programme* kennen lernen · einen indischen *teen* in seinem Alltag begleiten	**Where to go?** mögliche Urlaubsaktivitäten in Südafrika planen und diskutieren (p. 15) 	**Short texts** *Diversity in South Africa* (pp. 10–11) **Articles** *The dreams and reality of the* Born frees (p. 12) *South African English is lekker!* (p. 16) **Advert** *An adventure around every corner!* (p. 14) **Internet forum / Website** *Where to go?* (p. 15) *Volunteer in India …* (p. 24) **Cartoons** (p. 17) **Narrative text** *adapted from the novel* **Scarred lions** (pp. 19–21, *easier version* pp. 106–107)	
*MORE CHALLENGE Hunting the hunters	· einen Artikel über Wilderei in Südafrika erschließen · *discourse markers* verstehen und nutzen		**Article** *The Lion Queens* (p. 30)	
Unit 2 Take a stand! 	· über politisches Engagement Jugendlicher sprechen · Beispiele erfolgreicher Online-Kampagnen diskutieren · Nachrichten verstehen · Konsumverhalten reflektieren · stereotype Menschen- und Berufsbilder identifizieren, Alternativen entwickeln	**Young people and politics** in Gruppenarbeit eine Befragung vorbereiten, durchführen, auswerten sowie die Ergebnisse präsentieren (p. 37) 	**Online articles and comments** *Digital activism* (p. 34) *#ILookLikeAnEngineer* (p. 46) *Earth Hour …* (p. 50) **Poem / Song** *It's your future* (p. 36) **Narrative text** *adapted from the novel* **Face** (pp. 41–43, *easier version* pp. 121–122)	
*MORE CHALLENGE Doing the right thing	· einen authentischen Blogeintrag zu einem Handlungsdilemma erschließen · eigene Verhaltensoptionen reflektieren		**Blog entry** 'My shameful dilemma', by Jon Snow (p. 52)	

Kompetenzen	Sprache	Seite
Listening: interviews: *Around the world* (p. 8) **Speaking:** Mehrsprachigkeit und insbesondere die Bedeutung des Englischen im eigenen Leben diskutieren (p. 103)		8
Listening: Travel talk (p. 22); *Two young volunteers* (p. 29) **Speaking:** über eine Tourismuswerbung diskutieren (p. 14); role-plays *Pickpockets?, Holiday plans* (p. 23); a short talk *A volunteer project for me?* (p. 29) **Reading:** article *The dreams and reality of the* Born frees (p. 12) **Writing:** Karikaturen beschreiben (p. 17); typische Fehler korrigieren (p. 18); den eigenen Alltag beschreiben und mit einem Dokumentarfilmporträt vergleichen (p. 25); article *A must-see in Germany* (p. 28) **Mediation course (1)** ***Everyone can do something*** (p. 24); *Tourist attractions* (p. 28) **Study skills:** Arbeiten mit einer Fehlersammlung (p. 18) **Viewing:** *Braai Day* (p. 13); *Amar* (p. 25)	**Wortschatz** und **Strukturen** *talking about diversity and a difficult history; analysing adverts; describing cartoons; characterizing literary figures; talking about work and holiday plans* **using present tenses** revision: ***simple present***, ***present progressive*** (pp. 16–17) **more on relative clauses (defining and non-defining,** p. 110**)** ***STOP! CHECK! GO!** (pp. 26–29) Üben und vertiefen; Lernfortschritte erkennen	10
Reading: einen Sachtext analysieren (p. 30) **Speaking | Writing:** themenneutrale Redemittel verwenden	**Wortschatz** und **Strukturen** *analysing a non-fictional text* **using discourse markers** (pp. 31, 135)	30
Listening: story *Digital citizens* (p. 33); podcast *A campaign to keep students safe* (p. 35); poem *It's your future* (p. 36); news reports (pp. 38, 45) **Speaking:** eine Bilderfolge als *story* erzählen (pp. 32–33); über das Interesse an Politik und aktuelle Themen sprechen (p. 36); passende Geschenke diskutieren (p. 45); *Typically German things* beschreiben (pp. 51, 101) **Reading:** online articles (pp. 34, 46, 50); poem (p. 36) **Writing:** Kommentare (pp. 35, 43); typische Fehler korrigieren (pp. 40, 49); blog entry (p. 51) **Mediation course (2)** ***At the market*** (p. 44); announcements (p. 51) **Viewing:** *Digital citizens* (pp. 32–33); *It's your future* (p. 36); *Walk or fly* (p. 47)	**Wortschatz** und **Strukturen** *telling a story from pictures; talking about activism and online campaigns; analysing a poem; doing and presenting a survey; analysing a film* **using past tenses** revision: ***simple past***, ***present perfect***, ***past progressive***, ***past perfect*** (pp. 38–39) **more on past tenses:** ***present perfect progressive*** (p. 120) ***STOP! CHECK! GO!** (pp. 48–51) Üben und vertiefen; Lernfortschritte erkennen	32
Reading: blog entry (p. 52) **Speaking:** Handlungsoptionen abwägen, eigene Haltungen reflektieren (pp. 52, 53) **Study skills:** Wortfelder rezeptiv und produktiv nutzen (p. 53)	**Wortschatz** und **Strukturen** *talking about attitudes and options; improving the style of texts* **using synonyms** (p. 53)	52

	Lerninhalte	Your task (Lernaufgabe)	Texte
Unit 3 Future visions 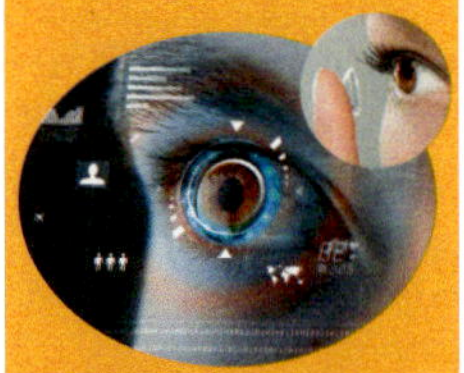	· über futuristische Technologien diskutieren · Chancen und Nachteile neuer Medientechnologien abwägen · Aspekte nachhaltiger Lebensweisen kennen lernen und erörtern · erfolgreiche Reklamationen und Beschwerden verfassen	**Wearable technology and me** einen Kommentar zum persönlichen Nutzungsverhalten verfassen und in einer Geschichte fortführen (p. 57) 	**Story** *Emma's world* (pp. 56–57) **Online article and comments** *Will we ever live on Mars?* (p. 60) **Formal complaints** (p. 67) **Narrative text** *adapted from the novel* **Floodland** (pp. 63–65, easier version pp. 130–131)
***MORE CHALLENGE** Goodbye and good luck	· eine Rede vorbereiten und halten		**Speech** (Hörtext p. 74)
***Exam file B1 and A2** 	· Musteraufgaben zur Vorbereitung der Abschlussprüfung bearbeiten: wahlweise auf dem **Niveau B1** (pp. 76–91) oder **A2/A2+** (pp. 92–99)		**Articles** *I'm a European* (**B1** p. 79, **A2** p. 94) *School in different places* (**B1** p. 82) **Narrative texts** *The Bracelet* (**B1** pp. 80–81, **A2** pp. 95–96); *Principals and principles* (**B1** p. 86) **Advert** *Climate Change Challenge Weekend* (**B1** p. 84, **A2** p. 97) **Email** (**B1** p. 87, **A2** p. 98)

Anhang

PARTNER-B-Seiten	100
DIFF-BANK	103
***WORDBANK** Discourse markers	135
***WORDBANK** Talking about texts	153
***TEXT FILE**	
TF 1 PROJECT Around the world (Unit 1)	136
TF 2 USA: a balance of powers (Unit 2, Bilinguales Modul *Social Studies*)	140
TF 3 The Question *(a play)* (Unit 1)	142
TF 4 Searching for a two-way street *(a poem)* (Unit 1)	146
TF 5 Currents *(a short story)* (Unit 3)	151
TF 6 English for jobs (Unit 1)	154

SKILLS FILE		
SF 1–5	STUDY AND LANGUAGE SKILLS	160
SF 6	Listening	165
SF 7	READING COURSE	166
SF 8	Reading literature	168
SF 9	SPEAKING COURSE	170
SF 10	WRITING COURSE	172
SF 11	Talking about visuals	179
SF 12	MEDIATION COURSE	182
SF 13	VIEWING SKILLS	184
LANGUAGE FILE		
LF 1–2	TALKING ABOUT THE PRESENT	185
LF 3–8	TALKING ABOUT THE PAST	187
LF 9–14	TALKING ABOUT THE FUTURE	190
LF 15–16	Word order	192

Kompetenzen	Sprache	Seite
Listening: interviews *The opinions of a futurologist* (p. 55), *My generation makes a difference* (p. 72); presentation *A student's talk on sustainable living* (p. 58); podcast *Robots for the home* (p. 66) **Speaking:** über neue Technologien, ihre Chancen und Nachteile diskutieren (pp. 54–55, p. 66); über Pläne sprechen (p. 61); *Is it better to recycle or buy new?* (p. 73) **Reading:** *Emma's world* (pp. 56–57) **Writing:** comment, story (p. 57); typische Fehler korrigieren (p. 62); *A message in a bottle* (p. 65); formal complaints (p. 67); *You and superheroes* (p. 69) **Mediation course (3)** ***Passing on information*** (p. 68); *An online chat with Eino* (p. 73) **Study skills:** Unbekannte Wörter erschließen, Arbeiten mit dem Wörterbuch (pp. 62, 71) **Viewing:** *Sorry* (p. 59); *The Red Thunder* (p. 69)	**Wortschatz** und **Strukturen** *describing and discussing new technologies and media; talking about ways of sustainable living; complaining effectively* **using future tenses** revision: ***will*-future**, ***going to*-future** (p. 61) **more on future tenses:** ***simple present, present progressive*** *(with future meaning);* ***future perfect, future progressive*** (p. 129) ***STOP! CHECK! GO!** (pp. 70–73) Üben und vertiefen; Lernfortschritte erkennen	54
Listening: *Maya's speech* (p. 74) **Speaking:** *Making a graduation speech* (p. 74)	**Wortschatz** und **Strukturen** *giving a speech;* **using passive structures and expressions** (p. 75)	74
Listening: **B1** pp. 76–78, **A2** pp. 92–93 **Reading:** **B1** pp. 79–83, **A2** pp. 94–96 **Mediation:** **B1** pp. 84–85, **A2** p. 97 **Writing:** **B1** pp. 86–88, **A2** p. 98 **Speaking:** **B1** pp. 89–91, **A2** p. 99	**B1** **A2**	76 92

LF 17–18	Questions	193
LF 19–22	Adjectives, Adverbs	194
LF 23	Indirect speech	196
LF 24	Modal verbs and their substitutes	198
LF 25–27	Conditional sentences (types 1,2,3)	199
LF 28–29	Relative and contact clauses	201
LF 30	*Participle clauses instead of subclauses	202
LF 31	Reflexive pronouns	203
LF 32	The *-ing* form (gerund)	203
LF 33	The passive	205
LF 34	Question tags	207
LF 35	*The definite and indefinite article	207
LF 36	*Countable and uncountable nouns	208
GRAMMATICAL TERMS		208

VOCABULARY	210
DICTIONARY (English–German)	239
ENGLISH SOUNDS · THE ENGLISH ALPHABET	272
IRREGULAR VERBS	273
LIST OF NAMES	275
COUNTRIES AND CONTINENTS	276
QUELLENVERZEICHNIS	278
TYPICAL EXAM INSTRUCTIONS	280

Die Angebote des Schülerbuches sind nicht obligatorisch abzuarbeiten. Die Auswahl richtet sich nach dem schulinternen Curriculum.

(*) = optionale Angebote

English around the world

▸ *KV 0* ▸ *DFF 1.1* ▸ *INKL pp. 8–9*

1 Around the world

a) Can you identify the five countries in the photos?

1.01 b) Listen to the five young people. Check your answers to a).

1.01 c) Listen again and complete this table.

Name	*How many languages?*	*English at home?*	*English is used: Where? Why?*
...	...	...	...

d) Can you name any of the other countries in green?

More practice 1 | p. 103

▸ Text file 1, PROJECT Around the world, pp. 136–137

Unit 1 Embrace diversity

▸ KV 1 ▸ INKL pp. 10–11

1 Diversity in South Africa

▸ Skills file 7.2, p. 166

a) South Africa is a very diverse country. Scan the texts and list examples of diversity.

b) Compare your list with other students.

Multicultural South Africa

South Africa is known as the *Rainbow Nation* because of the great diversity of people who live there. The first people came from different parts of Africa. In the 1600s the Dutch colonized South Africa, followed by the British in the 1800s. When diamonds and gold were discovered in the 1850s, people came from lots of places, especially Asia (e.g. India and China). Today South Africa's mix of cultures, skin colours, languages, religions and food is as colourful as a rainbow.

Find out more: *What language did the Dutch people bring to South Africa? What's it called today?*

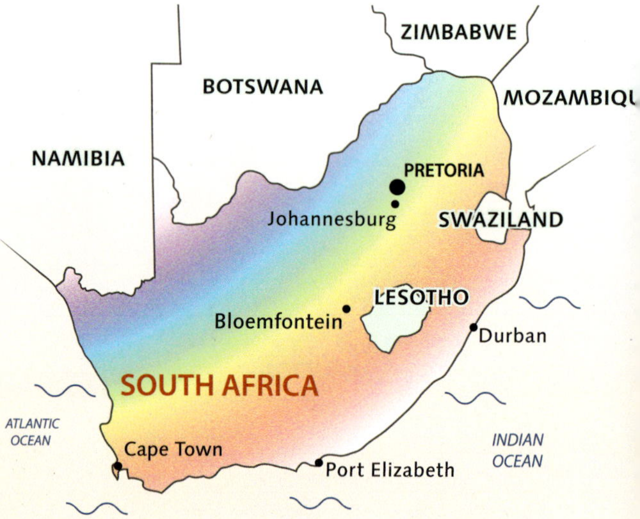

A world in one country

South Africa has many different landscapes – huge °corn fields, °grasslands, desert, high mountains and thousands of kilometres of coast – a world in one country. Some people say that a good time to visit is between May and August, when there isn't too much rain and it isn't too hot. It's winter in South Africa then and there isn't so much °vegetation, so you can see the wildlife better. Also it's the low season, so the prices are low.

Find out more: *What's the biggest city in South Africa? And what currency do they use?*

2 What have you learned?

a) Read the texts again. Note down important facts about South Africa in a table.

b) Pick some *Find out more* questions from pp. 10–11. Do some internet research. Add information to your table.

▸ Skills file 5, p. 164

► KV 1 ► INKL pp. 10–11

The "Big Five"

South Africa is famous for its diverse wildlife. It has many kinds of wild animals. But the ones everybody wants to see are the *Big Five*. They are the African elephant, the African °rhino, the African °leopard, the African lion and the Cape buffalo. They're called the *Big Five* not because they're the biggest animals, but because they can be the most dangerous.

***Find out more:** What other wild animals can you find in South Africa?*

Apartheid – a difficult history

Before 1994 people were segregated in South Africa. For example, non-white people had to live outside towns and cities in poor areas called townships. People were segregated in places like stadiums, parks, public toilets, and on buses and trains. They also had to go to different schools. It was difficult for non-white people to get good jobs, and many were poor. This racist system was called apartheid. More and more people protested against it. Some, like Nelson Mandela, were sent to prison for a long time. In 1990 Mandela was released from prison. Apartheid was ended, and in 1994 he became President of South Africa.

***Find out more:** How long was Nelson Mandela in prison? Who's the President of South Africa today?*

Students protesting against apartheid, Johannesburg 1987

Languages in South Africa

Many different languages are spoken in South Africa. There are 11 official languages, including African languages like isiZulu, isiXhosa. There's also Afrikaans and of course English. Lots of South Africans are multilingual – they speak two or more languages.

***Find out more:** What are the most popular languages in South Africa?*

3 Diversity and you

a) What kinds of diversity are there in your area? Find as many examples as you can.

b) Write a short text: 'Diversity and me'. More help p. 103 More challenge 1 p. 103

► Workbook 1, p. 3

▸ INKL pp. 12–13

Born Frees

1 READING South Africa – then and now

Read and make notes about these questions:
- What was life like for black people in South Africa during apartheid?
- Is it different now? If yes, how? More help p.103 ▸ *Skills file 7, pp. 166–167*

The dreams and reality of the *Born Frees*

In 1994, South Africans elected their first black president – Nelson Mandela. This was the end of apartheid. Today the South Africans who were born after 1994 are called *Born Frees*. They have no memory of apartheid. They don't know what it was like to be segregated and for black people to have no access to good schools and well-paid jobs. Today things are better, but there's still violence, poverty and unemployment.

Asandiswa lives in a township in Cape Town and wants to become a teacher. "A lot has changed since apartheid because back then black people weren't allowed to go to white schools. Women had to sit at home, to look after babies and cook. Now black women can get good jobs and black kids can go to white schools."

Brode lives with his mother in a suburb of Cape Town. He wants to be a baker and a surfer. "My parents were able to walk around freely at night. Now we don't have the same freedom, it's too dangerous."

Akhia was born to parents of different races. Her father is white and her mother is black. During apartheid this relationship would have been illegal. Akhia lives with her parents in a suburb of Johannesburg. "In apartheid I wouldn't have been born and I would never have met my boyfriend because he's white. Now I think we have a lot of freedom."

Teboho lives in Soweto with his grandmother. "I'm totally free. I can go anywhere I want, be anyone I want, date anyone I want, skateboard anywhere I want. Our opportunities are a lot better than our parents' were. Box: Voc., p. 211 I want to travel the world and be a professional skateboarder."

Lindokuhle lives in a township outside Johannesburg. He takes lots of photos of life there. "I have been documenting the drug problems in my township. Of course I feel free, but there are lots of challenges, like drugs and fighting."

▸ KV 2 ▸ DFF 1.2 ▸ INKL pp. 12–13

2 Working with the text

a) Complete these sentences with words and phrases from the text (lines 1–6):

1 *Born Frees* are ...
2 During apartheid black people were often poor because they had ...
3 But even after apartheid things aren't perfect because you still see ...

b) Match the sentence parts (look at lines 7–37):

1 Asandiswa is happy now because ...
2 Brode is the only one who says that ...
3 Akhia feels it's important that now ...
4 Teboho says that today things are better ...
5 Lindokuhle worries about problems ...

A for him than they were for his parents.
B you can date people from other races.
C some things were better before.
D that people in the townships still have.
E black women have more opportunities.

c) Find words or phrases in the text that mean more or less the same as:

1 the leader of a country or state (lines 1–6)
2 the South African political system that segregated people of different races (l. 1–6)
3 fighting (l. 1–6)
4 an area outside the city centre (l. 13–17)
5 against the law (l. 18–26)
6 to go out with a girl or boy (l. 27–33)
7 problems (l. 34–37)

More practice 1 p. 104
More challenge 2 p. 104

3 VIEWING Braai Day

South Africans celebrate their diversity on September 24th. It's a national holiday, so people often get together for a barbecue (*braai* in Afrikaans). That's why some people call it *Braai Day*.

a) Pick one of the tasks 1–4. Then watch the video and make notes.

1 Listen to the **song**:
- What's the mood of the song?
- What words and phrases can you hear?

2 Watch the **people** in the video.
- What kind of people do you see?
- What kind of activities are they doing?

3 Look at the **settings** in the video.
- What different settings can you see?
- What's the weather like in the video?

4 Look at the °use of **colour** in the video.
- What scenes are in black and white?
- What scenes are in colour?

b) Discuss: What is the message of this video? Talk about the following questions. Watch again if you need to.
- What's the mood of the video?
- Does it show South Africa in a good or bad light? Give examples.
- What's the message about segregation?
- How can South Africans be happy together?
- What does the video promise for South Africa's future?

▸ Workbook 2–3, p. 4 ▸ Skills file 13, p. 184

South African adventures

An adventure around every corner!

Everybody knows that South Africa is full of game parks where you can go on safari and see amazing wild animals. Thanks to the work of these parks you can still see rhinos and elephants in the wild in spite of °poachers who hunt and kill them. But there's more. South Africa has a great diversity of unique activities for adventure lovers. If you're looking for something different, you'll find it here.

Shark diving

See 5 – 20 sharks on a 30-minute dive. The boat trip includes shark watching and informative talks on sharks and conservation. The whole trip takes about two and a half hours. If you don't see any sharks, you'll get your money back.

Bungee jumping

This bungee jump drops an awesome 216 metres into the °picture-perfect Bloukrans River Valley below. Make sure someone is filming as you step off the edge of the highest bungee jumping platform in the world.

Ostrich riding

For a truly unique South African adventure try ostrich riding! These are the fastest birds on land and have been known to run up to 70°kph! So if you enjoy adventure (and weigh 75°kg or less), this is for you!

1 A South African ad

Think about these questions. Then discuss your ideas with a partner. More help p.104

1 Who do you think the ad is aimed at?

2 What is its message?

3 Is the ad effective? Give reasons.

4 How do you personally react to the ad?

▸ Skills file 7.5, p. 167

▸ KV 41 ▸ INKL pp. 14–15

2 YOUR TASK Where to go?

a) Scan this internet forum. Make a list of things to do in South Africa.

b) Make notes about the pros and cons of the different suggestions.

Baz: Looking for ideas for a two-week trip to South Africa
I'm from Australia and my family is planning a two-week trip to South Africa. We'd like to know what other travellers think are ***must-dos***. We'd like to get out and do stuff rather than just sit in a car. Thanks in advance for your help.

↓ Replies:

Box: Voc., p. 213

AP: Top of my list would be a visit to a national park – preferably Kruger National Park – to see the amazing wildlife. You can't leave without seeing a lion or an elephant!

Capetowngirl: Cape Town is a must. Things to do: Go up Table Mountain in a cable car. Walk among °penguins on Boulders Beach. If you're feeling brave, go shark diving.

Vulu: You should find out something about South Africa's past. I recommend Robben Island, where Nelson Mandela spent 18 of his 27 years in prison.

Stef: What about a tour around a township? If you want to be active, take a cycle tour.

Baz: Thanks to everyone for their ideas. We definitely want to do a safari, and Cape Town is also on our route. Diving with sharks?? Is that safe? Not sure how I feel about township tours. Isn't it a bit strange to go around looking at places where poor people live?

↓ Replies:

Capetowngirl: Shark diving means that you go down in a cage and the sharks come and look at you. It's very exciting and quite safe.

Stef: The best township tours include contact with local people. The tours bring money into the townships. And they give visitors an insight into what it's like to live there.
Personally, I'm not so sure about shark diving. The sharks come because food is put out for them. Will they start going to other places where humans are – e.g. beaches – and expect food? If they do, people will get worried and say that they must be killed. ☹

Capetowngirl: When people see the sharks close up, they realize what amazing creatures they are. Then they want to protect them. That's very good for sharks!

c) Imagine you're planning a trip to South Africa. Choose at least one activity from pp. 14–15. Give a short talk (at least one minute). Describe the activity and explain your choice.

d) Listen to other talks and comment on other people's choices. More help p. 105 More practice 2 p. 105

▸ Workbook 4–5, pp. 5–6

1 English in South Africa

a) Before you read the article, look at the chart. What information does it show?

b) Read the article. Then answer questions 1–4 below.

South African English is lekker!

Box: Voc., p. 213

South African English has some colourful words and phrases. For example, when you meet someone, they might say "Howzit!", instead of "Hello, how's it going?" Traffic lights in South Africa are called "°robots", and "lekker" means nice. English speakers from other countries are sometimes confused when a South African says "I'll do it just now". That doesn't mean that they'll do it now, or even soon. It actually means they might do it sometime in the future.

Languages of South Africa

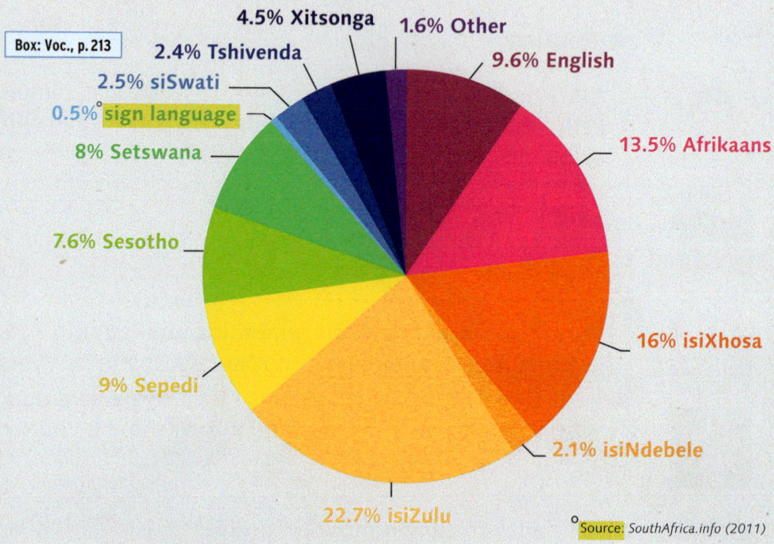

°Source: *SouthAfrica.info (2011)*

As the chart clearly shows, most South Africans don't speak English as their first (or home) language. In fact, English is the first language of only 9.6% of South Africans, which is about 5 million people. The majority of the population speak African languages, such as isiZulu and isiXhosa, at home. Also many speak Afrikaans, the language brought by settlers from Holland in the 17th century.

However, the number of English speakers is growing, and more people are learning English. Because so many languages are spoken in South Africa, people need a *lingua franca* – in other words, one language that most people understand. Although English isn't the first language of the majority, it has become the *lingua franca* in education, the media, business and also the government. As a result, more and more young people are choosing English as their second language.

1 What does the title of the article mean?

2 Which language is spoken as a first language by the biggest number of South Africans?

3 Explain the difference between a first language and a second language.

4 Why do you think South Africans prefer to use English as a *lingua franca*?

▸ *Skills file 7.4, p. 167; 11.3, p. 181*

2 Using present tenses

FOCUS

1 You use the ***simple present*** to talk about things that usually (*always, often, sometimes, never*) happen or about something permanent. Example: "Lekker" means "nice". ▸ *Language file 1, p. 185*

2 You use the ***present progressive*** to say what is happening at the moment and to describe pictures or cartoons. Example: The number of English speakers is growing. ▸ *Language file 2, p. 186*

3 **NEW** Some verbs are **not** usually used in the ***progressive*** form.
Example: ~~I'm understanding~~ → I understand
Similar verbs: *be, believe, know, like, mean, need, seem, want* ▸ *Language file 2, p. 186*

Find examples of the ***simple present*** and the ***present progressive*** in the article on p. 16.

3 A South African cartoon

Complete the sentences. Use the ***simple present*** or the ***present progressive***. // ● p. 105

1 In this cartoon a boy *is asking* (ask) a man for directions while his parents ... (wait) in their car.
2 They are probably from England because the boy ... (wear) a T-shirt with the British flag.
3 There's a sign for the Lion Park on the left, and that's what the tourists ... (look for). Box: Voc., p. 213
4 The boy looks confused and question marks show that he ... (not understand) what the man ... (say).
5 The cartoon is only funny if you ... (know) that some South African English words are different to British English.
6 The British boy ... (not know) that in South Africa when people talk about a robot, they ... (mean) a traffic light.

4 Describing a cartoon

Write about this cartoon. Then read out your description to a partner. More help p. 105

1 Describe what you can see in the cartoon: first the picture, then the words (if there are any).
2 What do you think the cartoon is about?
3 Explain what you think the artist wants to say.
4 What do you think of the cartoon?
▸ *Skills file 11.2, p. 180*

▸ KV 6 ▸ DFF 1.4

5 Improve your English: typical mistakes

a) Read the tips and correct the text. Compare with a partner.

1 In German you say 'Es gibt', but you don't say this in English. Check in a dictionary.

3 In German you say 'mehr als', but in English you say *more …* Check in a dictionary.

5 Instead of the adjective *good* you need an adverb here. Why? ▸ *Language file 20, p. 195*

English – a world language

English is spoken as a first language by most people in the US, the UK, Canada, Australia, Ireland and New Zealand. ~~It gives~~ also many other countries around the world where English an important second language ~~is~~.
Examples are South Africa and India. In fact more people speak English in India ~~as~~ in any other country in the world.
In Europe more and more people ~~learn~~ English. For example in Sweden 80 % of the people say that they speak English ~~good~~, and in Germany 50 % say the same. ~~Also~~ it's very important to improve your English.

2 Remember the correct word order in English sentences (S-V-O, ▸ *Language file 16, p. 192*). In English you don't put the verb at the end of a sentence.

4 To describe things that are happening at the moment you use the … … (→ p. 17, ex. 2).

6 'Also' in German 'doesn't mean the same as *also* in English. It's a ***false friend***. Instead use *To sum up / In other words / This means / So*.

b) Collect your own typical mistakes in a list like this. ▸ *Skills file 1 and 3, pp. 160 and 162*

Typical vocabulary mistakes	*Typical grammar mistakes*
1) ***Different phrases in German and English***, e.g.: "Es gibt" → There is/are, "mehr als" → more than, …	1) ***Word order***: S-V-O in English statements, e.g.: There are many countries where English is important. (≠ German word order: "…, wo Englisch wichtig ist.") More challenge 3 p. 110
2) ***False friends***: similar words in English and German but they mean something different: e.g.: also (= "auch"), become (= "werden"), … ▸ Skills file 1, p. 160	2) ***Adjectives*** → describe nouns, e.g.: They speak good English. Their English is good. ! ***Adverbs*** → describe verbs, adjectives, participles, e.g.: They speak English well. I like well-spoken English.
…	…

c) Complete the table.

German	*English*	*German*	*English*
auch	also	also	…
…	become	bekommen	…
…	meaning	Meinung	…
…	strong	streng	…
…	hear	zuhören	…
…	kind	Kind	…

d) Choose the right word.

1 I (mean / think) that learning English is fun.
2 It's important to (become / get) good (marks / notes) in English.
3 I prefer (strong / strict) teachers.
4 It was very (interested / interesting).
5 (Hear / Listen to) me!

▸ Workbook 11–12, p. 9

1 The blurb

First look at the blurb from the °back cover. What do you learn about …
- the main character?
- the setting?
- the plot?

Now read the text below. You can read an easier version of the story on pp. 106–107.

Buyisiwe (Buyi) feels like a stranger in London, where he grew up. Then he gets some terrible news: his mother can't take care of him any more. He has to join the father he has never met, in Africa. What is his new life in Africa going to be like? How will he feel in his new home?

1.02

Returned (°adapted from the novel °*Scarred Lions* by Fanie Viljoen)

Trouble in the air

There was trouble in the air. I just knew it. For days I could feel it – in the crowded trains in the London Underground, in the school classrooms, in the streets. And it made me scared.

I felt hunted …

It was late in the afternoon. Friday. I took the escalator and finally stepped out of the °musty underground °tunnels. The morning rain °lined the streets. Everybody wanted to get home as soon as possible. Grey clouds °covered the sky. It would rain again very soon. Trouble, I thought again. There was trouble in the air. So I walked quicker – I felt hunted like an animal.

I caught a °sudden °glimpse of myself in a shop window. Black face, frightened eyes, the cut on my lip. And I felt like a stranger. Box: Voc., p. 214

How could this be? I had lived in London all my life. I lived here with my mum in a two-bedroomed council flat above the street. I went to a state school here. But somehow I was a stranger. Was that my problem?

Buyisiwe. My name °echoed in my head. A stranger's name. Why not James, Chris or Peter? Or even Jonathan? Why not any other name, like most of the boys in school? Buyisiwe. That is what they called me. A Zulu name that meant – 'returned'.

This is my home

The rain was coming down as I got nearer to our flat. I °hurried home. My clothes were cold and wet when I reached the front door. Inside it felt warm. Safe. I pushed back my cap and took the stairs to the second floor. Shouting voices came from one of the flats. I ignored it like I always did. I didn't know any of the people living around us. I saw their faces °every now and again. But I didn't know their names. They °certainly didn't know mine. They didn't care, °and neither did I.

Mum wasn't home yet. I switched on the TV on my way to the kitchen. In the kitchen I °gulped down some milk °straight from the °carton. If mum could see me now … "How many times do I have to tell you to use a glass?" That's what she would say. Sometimes I do it just to °piss her off.

There was some °leftover pizza in the fridge. The cheese had °turned a °dull yellow in a sea of °olives, °pineapple and some kind of meat. I heated it in the microwave and went back into the living room. I made myself comfortable on the couch. My mind °drifted back to the fight I'd had at school with Jonathan.

"Zulu!" his voice still rang in my ear. "What are you doing here, Zulu? Why don't you go live with your people?"

Your people! This is my home. I don't know any other place.

A difficult decision

Mum °sighed as she came in through the front door. Her eyes had dark °rings under them, her face was °paler than usual, her blond hair was a mess.

"Don't just lie there, Buyi, come and help me."

"What, pizza again? We had pizza last night."

"I'm tired. I'm not going to cook. °Besides, you like pizza."

"Yeah, but not every day."

"You could have cleaned up a bit, you know."

I looked at the °dirty °dishes, the full °dustbin, the untidy flat …

"I'm also tired. It's Friday. Who works on a Friday evening?"

Mum sighed again. There were tears in her eyes.

"You don't make life any easier for me, you know, Buyi. You don't help me in the house. I °struggle to keep food on the table, to keep a roof over our heads. I'm tired of it all! So I've made a decision."

"What decision?" The °fear returned.

Something was different about mum. She was like an animal trapped in a cage, trying to get out. She °turned away. Tears were °streaming down her face now. Her shoulders were °shaking. I wanted to put my arms around her, but I couldn't. There was a wall between us.

"This is probably the most difficult decision I have ever made."

"Mum?" I now whispered.

"After what happened at school today, I know what I have to do."

"So you found out about it?"

"The school phoned me, Buyi." Her face was sad.

"Mrs Fletcher told me about the fight. It wasn't your first fight … And now I know that the time has finally come."

Mum fell silent for a moment. Things were about to change, I knew it.

"You are fourteen now, Buyi. It's time for you to meet your father. I've phoned him a couple of times. I told him about our °financial °difficulties. We °talked things over …"

"Mum?"

"I know he hasn't been here for you when you were growing up. But that will change now. He … he has agreed to look after you from now on."

"What?" I cried. °Terror filled my voice.

Mum nodded. "Buyi, you're going to live with your father in South Africa."

Departure

I couldn't sleep for days after my talk with Mum. Africa? °Where the hell is Africa, °anyway? Why do I have to go to Africa? Just because I got into a fight? For not fitting in? For being different?

I couldn't sleep …

I really didn't know if I wanted to meet my dad. Why should I suddenly want to meet this man who has been ignoring me all my life?

Mum had planned everything. She got me a passport, got my father to pay for the ticket, packed my bags … and one day °off we went to Heathrow Airport.

South Africa, I thought, what would it be like living there? I have seen °bits on °television. Not much, though. It's the place where Nelson Mandela comes from. And they've got wild animals down there. Would the animals be walking in the streets? °Do they even have streets and shopping malls? Do people there live like people in London?

"I love you, Mum," I said before I went to the departure hall. I don't think I had ever said that before.

"And I love you too, Buyi," she said and hugged me. I wished I could have stayed with Mum °forever. But the time had come to leave.

2 O Working with the text

Find out which words are missing. Choose the best answer from the table below.

Buyi lives in London with his mum, but he doesn't … (1) there. This Friday was a very … (2) day. We learn that Buyi has problems … (3). We find out that his mum has problems too – she seems very … (4). Now she has decided that Buyi's dad should look after his … (5). So the boy is going to … (6) South Africa. Buyi is very … (7) when he hears this news. He actually knows … (8) about the country of his father.

1	*go to school*	*feel at home*	*work hard*	*want to stay*
2	*wet*	*windy*	*freezing*	*sunny*
3	*with his father*	*at school*	*in the underground*	*at home*
4	*stressed*	*excited*	*happy*	*sleepy*
5	*friend*	*daughter*	*wife*	*son*
6	*visit*	*move to*	*leave*	*think about*
7	*stressed*	*bored*	*worried*	*happy*
8	*nothing*	*a lot*	*only a little*	*everything*

More practice 3 p. 110

3 Characterization

a) Scan the text for information about the character of Buyi. ▸ *Skills file 7.2, p. 166*
What lines give you the information? Make notes in a table.
Use headings like: ***age***, ***home***, ***personality***, ***appearance***, ***feelings***, ***relationships***, … More help p. 111

b) Write a short text about Buyi (about 80 words). Use your notes from the table in a).

4 Your response to the text

Choose a) or b). Write a short text.

a) Imagine you're Buyi in the departure hall. Say how you're feeling, what you think your new life will be like, what you're looking forward to, what you'll miss …

b) ● Having roots in two cultures has advantages and disadvantages. What do you think they are? Give reasons and examples. ▸ *Skills file 10.7, p. 177* More challenge 4 p. 111 More practice 4 p. 111

! You can read part 2 of *Returned* on pp. 108–109.

FIT FOR EXAMS

1 LISTENING Travel talk

a) Travel plans Simon is telling his friend Sienna about his plans.
1.05 Complete the sentences while you are listening. You'll hear the text twice.

1 Simon has won (A) a radio (B) a trip (C) money.
2 It's going to be (A) spring (B) summer (C) winter in South Africa when Simon is there.
3 He especially wants to see (A) elephants (B) giraffes (C) lions.
4 He's going to go to Cape Town by ...
5 Robben Island is famous because ...
6 Sienna is disappointed because ...

FIT FOR EXAMS

Before you start, read the task:
- What exactly do you have to do (e.g. answer questions, fill in gaps, ...)?
- How many times will you hear the text?
- What is the text about? Look at the title.
- What kind of text is it (e.g. a dialogue, an advert, a phone call, an announcement)?
- Is there a picture? What can it tell you?

▸ Skills file 6, p. 165

b) Phoning a hostel Listen twice to the phone
1.06 call and fill in the missing information.

Hostel name?	Blue Moon Hostel
City?	...
Price for the room?	...
What kind of breakfast? How much is it?	...
Is there Wi-fi? Where?	...
Check-in time?	...
Other facilities at the hostel? Name two.	

c) At a station You'll hear two announcements only once. Pick the correct option.
1.07
1 Which train is the announcement about?

(1) **London Liverpool Street to Cambridge**
Platform 19
Time: 14.28

(2) **Cambridge to London Liverpool Street**
Platform 9
Time: 14.18

(3) **London Liverpool Street to Cambridge**
Platform 9
Time: 14.38

2 What's the problem?

(A) **Lockers** are now available in the station on the ground floor.

(B) **Please mind your bags.** Thieves are operating in the station.

(C) **Security Notice** Unattended bags in the station will be removed immediately and may be destroyed.

▸ Workbook 16–17, p. 11

2 SPEAKING Pickpockets?

a) Act out this conversation with a partner.

Partner A:
You're a tourist at a train station in Norway. You've just noticed that your wallet is missing.
- Tell the police officer about your problem (e.g. somebody stole your wallet / you left your wallet somewhere ...).
- What was in your wallet (e.g. ID, credit card, student card, money, etc.)?
- Ask the police officer for help.
- Answer the police officer's questions.

Partner B:
You're a police officer at a train station in Norway. A young German tourist has a problem. Try to help.
- Ask the tourist what was in the wallet.
- Ask how much money was in it.
- Ask if a passport is missing.
- Ask the tourist for some details: name, where from, where staying, alone or with friends, enough money to get a train ...

b) Talk about these questions:
1 Have you (or a friend) ever lost something / or was something stolen from you?
2 Did you (or he / she) report it to the police?
3 Did you (he / she) get it back? How?
4 How can you be careful in shops / stations?

FIT FOR EXAMS
Listen carefully to your partner.
Answer all your partner's questions.
If you don't understand, you can ask:
Can you please repeat that?

3 SPEAKING Holiday plans

Partner B: Go to p. 100.
Partner A:
a) You're planning your summer holidays.
You've found this idea – Interrail.
Read the ad and answer your partner's questions.

b) Then ask your partner about his / her idea. Ask questions like:
- What kind of holiday?
- Where?
- How long?
- Cost / Pay?
- What job / duties?
- Live where?
- Languages?

c) Agree with your partner which of the two holidays you should go on and why.

Discover Europe with an Interrail Pass

Want to find out everything Europe has to offer? With an Interrail pass you have the freedom to go °wherever you want. This is a fun way to explore Europe's best places. You can travel by train to 30 countries.

Special prices if you buy now!

°*Duration*	*Youth*
5 days	190 euros
10 days	280 euros

Start where you like, stop where you like, finish where you like. You can see all the sights of Europe.

Here's a beach tour you can do:
Go from Portugal to northern Spain along the south coast of France into Italy, to Croatia and then to Greece.

▸ DFF 1.6 ▸ INKL p. 22

4 MEDIATION Everyone can do something

a) You're planning to do some volunteering work in India in the summer holidays. Read the information on this website.

Volunteer in India – summer programme

Delhi, the capital city of India, is famous for its °bazaars, historical monuments, religious buildings, amazing food ... and a lot more. But the city is also well known for its poverty and street children. By joining our summer programme in Delhi this summer you can get to know this great world city – and you can make a difference. "Everyone can do something," Mother Teresa once said.

The Jama Mashid Market, New Delhi

Travel:	Volunteers book their own tickets to Delhi. They are picked up from the Indira Gandhi International Airport in Delhi by our local staff and brought to their accommodation in the city.
Accommodation:	This is provided in the volunteer house in Delhi. Here volunteers have Wi-fi internet access and modern facilities. Accommodation is free.
Meals:	Volunteers are served two Indian meals daily (breakfast and dinner). Typical meals include dal (°lentils), °curry, °rice, vegetables, salad and roti (Indian bread). Volunteers can buy bottled water at local markets.
Duties:	1) School work and fun activities at °day care centres for street children, **or** 2) Work at the 'Elephant village', feeding the elephants, cleaning the °premises, bathing the elephants.
Highlights:	Get to know the city of Delhi and its people. Visit local bazaars and street markets. Take a free trip to the city of Agra and the famous Taj Mahal palace.
Minimum age:	17 years or younger if you are °accompanied by an adult
Dates:	*Arrival in Delhi:* June 27th *Departure:* July 20th
Costs:	$1199 + $225 °administration fee (US dollars)

b) Your parents have some questions. Answer them in German.

1 Wohin willst du? Und wie kommst du dorthin?
2 Wie lange wirst du dort bleiben?
3 Und was für Arbeit ist das?
4 Wieviel verdienst du?
5 Wie bist du untergebracht?
6 Was ist mit dem Essen?
7 Geht das mit unter 18 Jahren überhaupt?
8 Welche Argumente sprechen dafür?

FIT FOR EXAMS
- Think about who you are mediating for, what they need to know, and why.
- Choose the information that you need – don't translate everything.
- Don't translate word for word.

▸ Skills file 12, pp. 182–183

▸ Workbook 19, p. 14 ▸ Text file 6 English for jobs, pp. 154–159

5 VIEWING Amar (all great achievements °require time)

a) Before you watch

Read this description of a film by film-maker Andrew Hinton about an Indian boy, Amar.

If a film-maker decided to make a 10-minute film about your daily routine, what do you think he / she would want to film? Discuss.

Amar is 14 and at the top of his class. Some day he'd like to be a professional °cricketer, but for now he has two jobs and also goes to school in the afternoons. This short documentary is a simple journey with Amar through his daily routine.

b) Your first reactions

Watch the film. Then talk about your first reactions to it in class.

- What surprised / impressed / shocked you about Amar's day? Why?
- Which scenes stick in your mind? Why?

c) The film-maker's technique

Watch the film again, and make notes about these things:

1 What do you hear (e.g. music, dialogue, voice-over, sounds, an interviewer)?
2 What do we see Amar doing?
3 What kind of places do we see in the film?
4 When do we hear Amar talking?
5 Where does the title come from?

d) Partner B: Go to p. 100.

Partner A: Describe your still to partner B and listen to him / her. Find out what's the same and what's different in your stills.

- What time of day is it?
- Why is Amar there?
- Do we see Amar in a close-up, a medium shot or a long shot? What effect does that have on the viewer?

Think of a caption for your still.

More practice 5 p. 112 | More challenge 5 p. 112

6 WRITING About the film

Describe your day in detail and compare it to Amar's day.

- Think about your daily routine, your home, your school, and other places you go on a normal day.
- Would you like to swap places with Amar for a day? Why (not)?

Write 120–150 words. You can put your text in your °DOSSIER.

More practice 6 p. 112

► Skills file 13, p. 184

▸ *KV 8* ▸ *DFF 1.3* ▸ *INKL pp. 24–27* ▸ *INKL pp. 80–83*

1 LANGUAGE Sharks

a) O Complete the text. Use the ***present progressive***.

It's a warm, sunny day at False °Bay, Cape Town. Lots of tourists ... (1 enjoy) the beach. A °shark spotter ... (2 stand) on the hill behind the beach and another one is on the beach. They ... (3 look for) sharks. The people on the beach know that it is safe for them to go swimming because a green flag ... (4 fly).

What do the flags mean?

Green flag: Spotters ... (5 watch) the bay and there are no sharks.

Red flag: A shark has been seen, but it is a long way from people and it ... (7 move) away from the area.

Black flag: The weather ... (6 make) it difficult for the spotters to see sharks.

White flag: Sharks ... (8 swim) near to the beach and the beach is closed.

b) Complete the text with verbs from the box. Use the ***simple present***.

not °attack • grow • be scared • feel (?) • say • die • swim • look • know (?)

How ... you ... (1) when you see a photo of a shark? Most people ... (2) of them because they see news stories about shark attacks. In fact there are more than 400 types of shark and most of them ... (3) people. Experts ... (4) that sharks can be dangerous, but also that all over the world only about 12 people ... (5) from shark attacks each year. So how much ... you ... (6) about sharks? The largest is the big, friendly whale shark which ... (7) to the size of a bus (5–10m).

The most dangerous shark is the famous great white. °Sand tiger sharks ... (8) as aggressive as great whites, but in fact, they are shy and ... (9) away from people.

c) Complete the text. Use the ***simple present*** or the ***present progressive***. // ● p. 113

1 Three sharks ... around a surfer, but he doesn't see them. (swim)
2 People are waving at the surfer because they ... to warn him. (want)
3 A boy is talking on his mobile phone and ... at the sharks. He is °horrified because he ... that there will be an accident. (point, think)
4 A girl ... up a white flag that has a black shark on it. (put)
5 Swimmers are running out of the water because they ... the meaning of the flag. (know)
6 A man ... at the flag and it ... that he doesn't understand what it means. (look, seem)
7 Some surfers ... on the beach with their boards. They ... to go back into the water because they know that sharks ... usually in the bay for long. (stand, wait, not stay)

▸ *Language file 2, p. 186*

▸ KV 6 ▸ KV 8 ▸ DFF 1.4 ▸ INKL pp. 24–27 ▸ INKL pp. 80–83

2 WORDS False friends

a) Choose the correct words.
Use a dictionary if necessary.

1 Mrs Diel is a ... (strong / strict) teacher. What's your ... (meaning / opinion) of her?
2 Can I use your ... (°handy / mobile)? I need to phone my ... (bank / °bench).
3 Let's rest on that ... (bench / bank) for a minute.
4 My friend has a great ... (receipt / recipe) for healthy cupcakes.
5 Here's your °change. Would you like a ... (receipt / recipe)?
6 You will get bad ... (notes / °marks) if you don't take ... (notes / marks) when you're reading.

b) Copy the table and add the missing words. Use a dictionary if necessary.

German	English	English	German
(Sitz-) Bank	*bench*	bank	...
Flur	...	floor	...
Handy	...	handy	...
Note (Zensur)		note	...
Rezept		receipt	

c) Make sentences for your partner like the ones in a). Use words from b).

More challenge 6 p. 113

3 LANGUAGE Word order

a) Put the words in brackets in the right order to complete these sentences.

1 South Africans like the °waterfront in Cape Town because (they • there • can • lots of activities • do). *They* ...
2 On Robben Island you can visit the prison where (almost 20 years • Nelson Mandela • spent).
3 You get a great view of Cape Town if (of Table Mountain • you • to the top • go).
4 If (tourists • quickly • a lot of places • want to visit), they should go on a bus tour.
5 The Two Oceans Aquarium is a must if (interested in • you • sea animals • are).

b) Put the phrases in brackets in the right place. Sometimes there is more than one possible solution.

Nelson Mandela was born (on 18 July 1918 • in Mvezo). He went (in the early 40s • to university). He joined the ANC to fight the terrible apartheid system (during that time). He became the leader of the ANC (soon). Mandela was put (for 27 years • in 1962 • into prison). He became a symbol of the anti-apartheid movement (during his time in prison • quickly). Nelson Mandela was famous (by the end of the 1980s • all over the world). Although he felt °desperate (during that time • often), he gave up hope (never). He left prison thanks to international pressure (in 1990). F.W. de Klerk, the last white president, worked with Mandela to end apartheid. They both got the Nobel °Peace Prize (in 1993 • for their achievements). All races were allowed to vote (one year later • for the first time). Nelson Mandela became the first black president (in the same year). He gave up his °presidency (finally • at the age of 81 • in 1999). Mandela died (on 5 December 2013 • in Johannesburg).

▸ *Language file 15, p. 192*

4 MEDIATION Tourist attractions

a) Your grandparents want to know more about the Capilano Suspension Bridge Park. Read the text and explain to them what people can do there.

Capilano Suspension Bridge Park: Discover Vancouver's must-see attraction. Visitors can enjoy °thrilling °canyon views, °breathtaking °lookouts and unforgettable adventures. The park has °thrilled travellers from all over the world since 1889. For many, it is an °act of courage just to walk over the world-famous suspension bridge. You can also do the heart-stopping °cliff walk and experience the amazing Treetops Adventure that takes you 110 feet (33 m) above the °forest floor. You can explore the park °on your own or join a free tour to learn the secrets of the rainforest.

b) Explain the park rules to your grandparents.

ATTENTION

- Stay on the walkways.
- Walkways may be slippery when wet.
- Parents / Guardians must take care of their children.
- If you drop something, do not try to get it back yourself. Tell a member of staff.

ON THE BRIDGE, TREETOPS ADVENTURE AND CLIFF WALK

- No running or jumping!
- Do not try to make the bridges swing from side to side!
- Not suitable for wheelchairs or crutches.
- Hold small children by the hand.

5 WRITING A must-see in Germany

Your partner school would like to know more about your home town. Write an article for their school website (at least 150 words). Say which special place or attraction you recommend and why.

A must-see in Germany
- Where?
- What can you see?
- °Opening hours?
- Any personal experience there?
- Why is it a must-see?
- What can you do?
- Name?

▸ KV 7 ▸ DFF 1.1 ▸ INKL pp. 24–27 ▸ INKL pp. 80–83

6 LISTENING Two young volunteers

1.08

Listen to the two young people who both volunteered °abroad.
Take notes about their experiences in a table like the one below.

	Shane	Tess
1 Place		
2 For how long?		
3 Kind of project		
4 What activities? (at least two)		
5 Best things (at least one)		
6 °Difficulties (at least one)		
7 Reasons for volunteering (at least two)		

7 SPEAKING A volunteer project for me?

Do some research and make notes about a volunteer project that °interests you.
Then give a short talk about it. These questions can help you:

- What is the project about? Where is it?
- What is special about the work or the place?
- What kind of activities do volunteers do?
- What do / don't you like about the project?
- Do you think it is a good / bad thing for young people to do? Why?
- Is there anything that might be difficult?

▸ Skills file 5, p. 164; 9.1, p. 170

Hunting the hunters

Wichtigen Wortschatz von diesen Seiten findest du im Vocabulary auf S. 236–237.

1 What's it all about?

Skim the text 'The Lion Queens' and guess what it's about. Talk about your ideas.

The Lion Queens

by Kate Wills, *The Independent*

°Poaching in South Africa's national parks °is at record levels. °As a consequence, °certain animals, °notably rhinos, are at risk of °extinction. However, a new °anti-poaching unit, known as the Black Mambas, are now hunting the hunters.

A full °moon over the Balule °Game Reserve in South Africa means two things – poachers are out °on the hunt, as are the Black Mambas. No, not the fastest and deadliest snakes in the world, but a specially trained team of rangers – nearly all of them young women – who police the parks night and day to protect the animals from illegal hunting. And they are very successful.

Photographer Julia Gunther spent a week documenting the Black Mambas as part of her project – 'Proud Women of Africa'. This unit is made up of twenty-four women and two men from villages °surrounding the park. The women, who are all in their twenties and early thirties, spend long days °tracking humans and animals. However, °since they are °unarmed, they don't °confront the poachers. Instead, they call in the °armed unit.

The Balule Game Reserve is home to leopards, lions, °cheetahs, °hippos, elephants and rhinos. Although these are protected animals, a huge number of rhinos are killed every year in South Africa, as their horns are sold for use in traditional Asian medicine.

The Black Mambas started °patrolling in 2013 and as a result the number of rhinos killed in Balule since then has dropped to only three. For Lukie, 26, that's three too many. As well as °tackling the poachers, these women are also challenging gender stereotypes in South Africa. "I'm proud to be a Black Mamba," says Winnie, 22. "Many people don't know that women can do this job. We will show them that we can do it." As Leitah, also 22, °puts it, "I am strong, I am a woman – and I bite like a mamba!"

The Black °Mambas

Box: Voc., p. 237

There is a lot of unemployment in this part of South Africa. °Therefore, these young women are happy to have jobs. They work in the park for three weeks °at a time. Then they return to their families for ten days. Of course, the life of a Black Mamba is dangerous. But °despite this danger, they really like their work.

► Skills file 6, pp. 166–167

▸ DFF 1.8

2 Working with the text

a) Text type:

1 Do you think 'The Lion Queens' is a °fictional or a non-fictional text? Give reasons.

2 Find out more about these types of non-fictional texts: ***news story***, ***magazine article***, ***travel °feature***, ***interview***.

3 Now identify the text type of 'The Lion Queens' and give reasons for your choice.

b) °Attitude: Attitude means what the writer thinks about a subject.

1 Describe the writer's attitude to the Black Mambas and their work. Support your view with °quotes from the text.

2 The writer quotes what some Black Mambas say. What do the quotes tell you about the writer's attitude to these women?

Qolile, a proud Black Mamba

c) °Purpose: What do you think is the main purpose (aim) of the text? Pick the best statement and explain your choice.

1 It supports wildlife in the Balule Game Reserve.

2 It criticizes poaching in national parks in South Africa.

3 It °promotes the role that women can play in South African society.

d) Argument: The writer uses °***discourse markers*** that help you to understand the points and arguments of the article. For example, *As a consequence* (line 3) and *However* (line 6).

1 Find more words and phrases like this in the text.

2 What do these phrases mean in German?

▸ *Wordbank, p. 135*

3 Improve your style

a) Use the discourse markers in brackets and make these sentences clearer.

> ! With these ***discourse markers***, do you need to use one sentence or two? Check how the markers are used in the text.

1 There's a lot of poaching in the national parks of South Africa. Some animals might soon be extinct. (as a consequence)

2 The job of the Black Mambas is dangerous. They are unarmed. (although)

3 Many of the Black Mambas have young families. They spend three weeks away from home – in the park. (however)

4 Jobs like this are seen by many people as men's work. The Black Mambas are challenging such stereotypes. (therefore)

5 New Mambas are being hired. They have been so successful. (since)

b) Finish these sentences about the text in any way you like.

1 As well as the danger of meeting wild animals, the *Black Mambas* have to ...

2 Despite the great heat, these rangers ...

3 Instead of staying unemployed, women like Lukie, Winnie, Leitah and Qolile prefer to ...

4 The armed unit is often called in as the poachers ...

Unit 2

Take a stand!

▸ *INKL pp. 28–29*

► KV 9 ► INKL pp. 28–29

9

10

11

12

13

14

1 Digital citizens

a) With a partner, work out the story in the pictures. Use your imagination. More help p. 114

> This story is about three teenagers ...

> Yes, I think they live in a warm country ...

> I think you're right – maybe somewhere in Africa ...

> They're sitting ...

b) Think of a good slogan for the end of your story.

c) Tell your story to your group or class and end with your slogan.

1.09 **d)** Watch the film or listen to the story. Was your story the same or different? What were the differences?

More practice 1 p. 114 More challenge 1 p. 114

► Workbook 1–2, p. 21 ► Skills file 13, p. 184

Make a difference

1 READING **Digital activism**

a) Before you read: What can people do when they want to take a stand? Make a list.
b) Then read the article and add to your list.

Julia Bluhm (middle) with other activists at a *Seventeen* magazine protest

airbrushing a photo

1 In the past people went on demonstrations and protests if they were unhappy about something. These days young people turn to the internet first.

2 Julia Bluhm from Maine in the US was 14 when she decided that she didn't like the way teen magazines airbrush photos of girls. She created an online petition on *Change.org*, and she soon had over 80,000 signatures. She and a group of other teens then took the petition to *Seventeen* magazine in New York, and they very quickly agreed to change their policy. Result!

3 This is just one example of young people using the power of the internet. It's estimated that two in five young adults use the internet in this way. They get involved in social issues using tweets, °reblogs, *likes*, °status updates, memes and photo series. Box: Voc., p. 219

4 Sometimes the older generation doesn't realize just how effective this online activity can be. (Can't you just hear them °scratching their heads, wondering what a meme is ... Look it up, guys!)

5 Online activists point out that they also go on protests – Julia actually went to the offices of *Seventeen* with her petition. But some say that protests like these stay local. Via the internet you can contact the world and make it a better place.

Comments

> **AJ** Don't you think that it's very easy to just *like* something online and feel good about yourself. Go out and do something! Don't just sit in front of a screen!

> **HahaGirl** I respect people who put their views online. But be careful. There are internet trolls who make horrible comments. That can be very hurtful.

> **NinaH** I agree, AJ! There are loads of ideas at *DoSomething.org* – if you want to, well, do something. And HahaGirl, don't let the trolls stop you. That's what they want!

▸ Skills file 7.3, p. 166

► KV 10 ► DFF 2.1 ► DFF 2.2 ► INKL pp. 30–31

2 Working with the text

a) Match one heading to each paragraph (1–5). There are two more than you need.

A Different types of online activity
B Older people often don't know what you can do on the internet
C 20% of young people aren't interested in social issues
D *Seventeen* magazine online
E An example of a teen activist
F One advantage of online activism
G Young people have new ways of protesting

b) Explain <u>two</u> of the following in complete sentences.

1 demonstration (paragraph 1)
2 airbrush photos (paragraph 2)
3 petition (paragraph 2)
4 internet trolls (comments)

c) Julia Bluhm is doing an online question and answer session. Ask her three questions about her work as an online activist.

3 LISTENING A campaign to keep students safe

1.10

You're going to hear a report about a campaign organized by students at a secondary school to keep students safe.

a) Before you listen, speculate: What kind of things do you think the students were worried about? Then listen to the report and find out if you were right.

b) Listen again and complete the sentences:

1 The problem at the boys' school was ...
2 First they collected ideas on a ...
3 Some drama students made ...
4 They also had a competition to design ...
5 One student had a great idea to ...
6 The students didn't completely solve the problem, but there were two positive results:
- The police and the council ...
- The students didn't feel so ...

4 WRITING Now you

Choose a) or b) and write a text (80–120 words).

a) Comment on Julia Bluhm's campaign to stop teen magazines airbrushing photos of girls. Would you support a campaign like that? Why (not)? Explain your views.

b) "Young people need to be very careful when they post their views online." Describe the kind of things that people should think about before they get involved in an online campaign so that they stay safe online.

More challenge 2 p. 114

► Workbook 3, p. 22

Do you care?

1 Does anybody care?

Box: Voc., p. 220

a) Talk in class about these questions:

- Who is the chancellor of Germany? Do you care? Why (not)?
- What about other countries? Who are the prime ministers or presidents of Turkey, the US, Russia, France, Britain? Does it matter? Why (not)?
- Do you care about politics? What are the most important topics in the news at the moment?

b) Skim these three verses of Gary Turk's poem. Does the poet think people should care about politics? ► *Skills file 6, pp. 166–167*

Gary Turk

IT'S YOUR FUTURE

When I was 18, politics was boring.

I didn't go and vote, I didn't pay attention,
I didn't really care at what age people got their pension.
That seemed ages away, I was just °starting out,
I really had no interest in what politics was about.
(...)
So prove them all wrong, prove you have a voice,
Do the unexpected and accept you have a choice.
And vote, but first find out the truth,
Look at their policies and how it °affects the youth.
(...)
You have a say, that needs to be respected,
People are dying for the right to have a leader that's elected.
So °register to vote, be a part of democracy,
Doing nothing and complaining is °outright °hypocrisy.

2 Working with the text

a) Now read the verses in detail and complete these notes.

Lines 2–6: How did Gary Turk feel about politics when he was younger? Find three examples.

Lines 7–10: What does Gary Turk think young people should do? Find two things.

Lines 11–14: What does Gary Turk think people shouldn't do? Find two things.

b) True, false or not in the text?

1 Gary Turk is under 18 now.
2 He tells us that some people have to fight for the right to vote.
3 Gary Turk says that everybody should support democracy.
4 He says that it's OK if people don't vote.
5 He thinks that most young people just complain about everything.

c) Look at the title of the poem. Is it a good title? Why (not)? Talk to a partner.

More challenge 3 | p. 114

▸ KV 11 ▸ KV 12 ▸ INKL pp. 32–33

3 It's your future

1.11

Now watch the film of (or listen to) Gary Turk's poem. You'll hear more verses and you won't understand everything. But that doesn't matter – you only need to understand the message.

a) Pick the right words. // p. 115

1 Gary Turk says that when he was young he had no interest in (A) sport. (B) politics.

2 He says that politicians are old men in old (A) buildings. (B) clothes.

3 He thinks that we should stand up for (A) what we believe in. (B) more money.

4 The people who fight the wars are the (A) old. (B) young.

5 We should be a part of (A) the government. (B) democracy.

6 If we want to make a difference, we have to (A) grow up. (B) complain.

b) What's the main message of the poem? More practice 2 p. 115

4 YOUR TASK Young people and politics

A recent survey by students in schools in Ireland found that most young people between 15 and 19 years don't trust politicians. They say that most politicians don't care about young people. But the majority of young people say that they think politics is very important.

So what do young people in Germany think about politics and politicians?
Do a survey and find out. Work in small groups (3–4 students).

Step 1: Get ready: Think of questions that you want to ask. Agree on 5–10 questions. More help p. 116
Then decide who you want to ask – classmates, other classes, friends, etc.

Step 2: Do the survey: Ask as many people as you can. Note down their answers.

Step 3: Analyse the results: Write down how many people said what.

Step 4: Present the results to the class: Give a short talk – about 2 minutes. More help p. 116

Step 5: Write a report about your survey (100–160 words). More help p. 117

1 Teens in the news

Teens simply ignored robber

When a man walked into a store and demanded money, the young shop assistants ignored him until he went away. Police have praised the teens, but they have also given them a warning.

Teen changed racist graffiti

When a Birmingham teenager came across graffiti at his local bus stop, he decided that he had to do something about it.

Young refugees share their stories

Young refugees, students at a Sydney high school, told their stories of survival in a remarkable stage performance.

First read the short news reports above.

1.12 Then listen to the full stories and choose the right statements below.

News item 1

1 When the man walked into the store, the two young shop assistants ...
- A had just finished their shift.
- B were chatting together.
- C were both getting ready to go home.

2 The police have told the shop assistants ...
- A that it's important to be polite to customers.
- B that it's important to stay safe.
- C that they are real heroes.

News item 2

3 Luke was worried that someone might ...
- A be hurt by the graffiti.
- B think he wrote the graffiti.
- C spot him at the bus stop.

4 After Luke had added to the graffiti, ...
- A somebody reported him to the police.
- B he cleaned off the graffiti.
- C he reported the graffiti.

News item 3 Box: Voc., p. 221

5 Many of the performers ...
- A have been living in Sydney for years.
- B haven't been in Australia for long.
- C were born in Australia.

6 The performance was ...
- A very short.
- B very successful.
- C often interrupted by cheering.

▸ Workbook 6, p. 24

► KV 13 ► DFF 2.4 ► INKL p. 37

2 REVISION Talking about the past

FOCUS

1 When you are talking or writing about the past, the tense that you use most is the ***simple past***. It's often used with words like *yesterday*, *last week*, *two years ago*, ...
Example: At about 6 o'clock yesterday a robber walked into the shop.

► *Language file 3, p. 187* More practice 3+4 pp. 117, 118

2 You use the ***present perfect*** if the time when something happened is not important. It's often used with words like *just*, *already*, *ever*, *never*, *not ... yet*, *recently*, *since then*, *so far*, ...
Example: The police haven't found the robber yet.

► *Language file 5, p. 188*

3 You will come across other ways of talking about the past.
a) The two teens were chatting when the robber walked into the shop.
The ***past progressive*** shows that an action was in progress (i.e. they were chatting).
Then something interrupted it (i.e. the robber walked in, ***simple past***).
b) One of the teens had just finished his shift when the robber walked in.
The ***past perfect*** shows that one action (i.e. he had finished his shift) happened before the other (i.e. the robber walked in, ***simple past***).

► *Language files 4; 7* More practice 5 p. 118

3 From the local news

// p. 119

Complete the reports. Use the **simple past** or the **present perfect**.

a) There *was* (1 be) a big concert in the town centre last night, and John Young ... (2 come) into town to enjoy the music. He ... (3 start) the evening with a group of friends, but he ... (4 not stay) with them. His parents are now worried because their son hasn't come home yet. They have spoken to all his friends, but nobody knows where he is.

b) Everybody was very surprised last Friday when the new sports shop in the high street closed without warning. The shop workers are angry because all of them ... (1 lose) their jobs. They ... (2 organize) a protest, and it will take place on Tuesday outside the shop. So far they ... (3 not hear) anything from shop owners.

c) Many local students ... (1 do) their final school exams in April. They ... (2 wait) nervously since then for their results. At the local high school students ... (3 get) their results at 10 o'clock this morning. Some students are excited because they ... (4 do) well. But a few are quiet because they ... (5 not get) the results they were hoping for.

4 Have you ever won something? What did you win?

Have you ever ...
- won something?
- had a part-time job?
- taken part in a performance?
- raised money for charity?
- lived somewhere different?

Walk around: Ask other students questions from the orange box. When someone answers yes, ask follow-up questions like the ones in the blue box.

When did you ...? How did you feel?
How much ...? What ...? Where ...? Why ...?

More help p. 119
More challenge 4 p. 120

5 Improve your English: typical mistakes

a) Read the comments and improve this student's report.

Cakes, cakes and more cakes!
I have never seen so many yummy cakes in one place! Last Friday morning we ~~have~~ organized our Monster Cake Competition at school. Students and teachers brought cakes that they had made ~~himself~~. All the cakes were very good, but Miriam from class 7 won first prize. She made a ~~very~~ wonderful house out of gingerbread. Mr Schmidt's chocolate cake was also amazing. His cake wasn't as beautiful ~~like~~ Miriam's cake, but ~~he~~ was really delicious and he ~~became~~ second prize. After the competition we sold the cakes and made over €400 for a local homeless charity. A big thank you to everybody who ~~taked~~ part!

1 You need the ***simple past*** here. Why? ► Focus box, p. 39

2 They had made the cakes them... (***reflexive pronoun***) ► Language file 31, p. 203

3 'Wonderful' means 'very very good', so you can't use 'very' here.

4 'as beautiful ...' What comes next in this ***comparison***? ► Language file 19, p. 194

5 In English you don't use 'he' or 'she' for things.

6 ***False friend***! What's *bekommen* in English? Check in a dictionary.

7 'Take' is an irregular verb. ► Irregular verbs, pp. 273–274

b) Complete the report with the best answers from the table below.

Teen hero in pyjamas

Two days ... (1) 19-year-old Martin Smith was ... (2) to music in his bedroom when he ... (3) a noise. Martin said, "When I went downstairs, ... (4) two men in the kitchen. They didn't see me because they had ... (5) backs to the door. One guy had my mobile in ... (6) hand. I wanted to frighten them, ... (7), I shouted, and they both ran out of the house." ... (8) Martin was only wearing his pyjamas, he followed them. However, the robbers were faster ... (9) Martin, and he didn't ... (10) them. Afterwards Martin said, "It was a stupid idea to ... (11) them. But the guy dropped my phone, so I ... (12) my phone back. That was ... (13) brilliant!"

	A	B	C
1	before	ago	later
2	hearing	listening	playing
3	heard	has heard	hears
4	were	there were	there was
5	their	there	they're
6	my	their	his
7	but	also	so
8	However	Although	But
9	than	as	how
10	caught	got	catch
11	chase	chased	escape
12	became	become	got
13	very	really	a bit

More practice 6 p. 117

► Workbook 12–13, p. 27

▸ KV 14 ▸ KV 15 ▸ INKL pp. 34–36

1 The blurb

First look at the blurb from the back cover.

a) What do we learn about the main character?

b) Do you think this is a funny story or a serious story?

Now read the text below. If you want to read a simpler version of the story, go to pages 121–122.

> This is a story about Martin and his two friends, Mark and Matthew. They call themselves the 'Gang of Three'. During the school holidays they go around their area of London, looking for fun. Martin is the leader. He's cool, funny and he has a girlfriend. He seems to have it all. But one night something happens and Martin's life changes forever.

Face (adapted from the novel by Benjamin Zephaniah)

1.13

1 Walking around town

Martin, Mark, Matthew and Natalie °headed down the street in silence. When they arrived at the top of Natalie's street, Mark and Matthew waited at the corner while Martin °walked her to her door. He had to make sure she got home safe, but he also had to make sure he got his good night kiss.

The Gang of Three decided to °cut through a °housing estate. It used to be a nice place to live, but it wasn't any more. One of the °high-rise buildings had no doors on the front or the back, so the gang just walked through. Inside the back door, there were used needles everywhere on the floor.

2 Friends should stick together

As they walked through the estate, they could hear the sound of °screeching tyres, the sound of a car being raced. The sound was coming their way. Out of the dark they saw headlights °approaching. The °lights were on full beam, so they couldn't see the car or the driver, and it was coming fast. The car went past them, then turned back towards them. It °pulled up beside the Gang of Three. A shout came from the front passenger seat,

ox: Voc., p.222

"Martin, man. It's me, Pete."

It was Peter Mosley. He used to go to Martin's school. But now he was a member of a gang, known for their crazy activities. The car was a red Ford. Martin didn't know the driver, who looked older.

Pete shouted, "Come on, let's go riding."

"Nah, we're going home," Martin replied.

"Come on, man," Pete tried to °persuade the three to get into the car. "We'll just take you home."

"So you'll just give us a lift home," Martin said as he opened the back door of the car.

Matthew was °furious. "Are you really going? You're mad!" He walked away.

Martin and Mark got into the car.

Matthew shouted to his two friends in the car, "What kind of friends are you two? I thought we °were supposed to stick together."

He turned and headed home.

3 Dangerous driving

Martin and Mark were excited. They had never been in a fast car like this before. They were °speeding over °speed humps, driving on the wrong side of the road, going on the pavement. They went down one big road – the wrong way! When Martin realized this, he shouted, "Pete, let's go back, man! What's your °mate's name?"

The driver looked about twenty. He had long black hair, four teeth were missing and he had a °scar on his face.

"My name's Apache," he said.

"How long have you had the wheels?" Martin asked.

Apache began to laugh. "Twenty minutes, man. I got this car twenty minutes ago."
"What do you mean, you °nicked it?" Martin asked.
Both Pete and Apache laughed. Martin and Mark looked at each other. They were scared.
"Just leave us here," Mark said.

4 The car chase

Pete shouted, "Cops behind us."
The police flashed their headlights to get the boys to stop. But Apache °put his foot down, speeding forward. The police car stayed °right behind them.
Martin shouted angrily, "You °bastards, STOP!"
Apache wasn't listening. His plan was to drive to East Ham, a part of the city that he knew best, where he could °lose the police in the back streets. Pete threw a small packet out of the window.
"What's that?" Martin shouted.
"I'll show you in five minutes. When we get rid of the cops, we'll come back for it," Pete answered.
The police put on their sirens and flashing lights. Apache and Pete seemed to love the excitement. They sped through a red traffic light.
"Let us out," Martin said. "STOP THE °BLOODY CAR!" he shouted.
Apache and Pete only looked at each other and laughed.

5 The crash

As they approached a °junction, they could see more police cars, crossing the road. Then they crashed into one of the police cars. The red Ford rolled over, throwing Pete out of the front window. The car landed on the other side of the road, upside down. There was a moment of silence.

Box: Voc., p. 223

The police came over. Apache climbed out of the front window and tried to run, °straight into the arms of a police officer.
Mark climbed out of his side window and screamed, "Help, Martin's in there. My mate's in there."
He tried to open Martin's door, but it was too °damaged. Martin was °unconscious. His head was °bloody. A police officer °grabbed Mark and began to take him away.
"That's my mate. I'm trying to help my mate," he protested.
"We'll deal with him," the officer said and put Mark in the back of a police car, next to Apache.
Ambulances, more police cars and a fire engine arrived. Then there was a loud explosion and there was fire in the car. Martin was quickly pulled out through the broken side window. The °paramedics put him on a °stretcher, into an ambulance and °rushed him away.
From the back of the police car Mark shouted, "That's my mate Martin. I want to go with him."
But nobody listened to him.

6 No tears

Twenty-four hours later Martin's parents were sitting on chairs on each side of the bed. They had both had a °sleepless night. They were silent. They sat looking at Martin. Martin had been given a small room in the Burns Unit of the hospital, the same hospital where he had been born fifteen years before. He began to wake up and he opened his eyes very slowly. He began to feel the pains of the accident. His body felt hot. He tried to move.
"Martin, °love, °take it easy," his mother said. "Don't try to move too much."
His father left the room. His mother couldn't find words.
"Don't worry, love, the doctor will be here soon and she'll explain everything to you. Just °lie back and relax."
When his father came back, a °nurse and a doctor were with him. The doctor looked at Martin.
"Hello, Martin," she said. "You have had a very °serious accident, you know. You have some cuts, lots of °bruises, but no broken °bones. That's good. But you have some burns on your face. Sooner or later you will see these burns, so you must prepare yourself for this. But don't be too alarmed. Over time we can improve things. Have you any questions?"

Martin didn't reply. The doctor continued. "A hospital °counsellor will come to visit you soon. He is here to help you – you can talk to him about anything. We are all here for you if you need us."

Martin could only say "Thank you" to the doctor. For the first time in his life he wanted to cry, but he didn't have any tears.

2 Understanding the text

Find the parts (1–6) that match the following descriptions.

Description	Part
A In this part Martin and Mark realize that they have made a mistake.	
B In this part we get an idea of the area where the teenagers live.	
C In this part we learn that Martin's life has changed – probably forever.	
D Here we learn that Matthew is a strong character.	
E In this part we see the dangers of 'joyriding'.	
F Here we learn that Pete and his friend aren't afraid of the police.	

3 Working with the text

Part 1: This area of London isn't a nice place to live.
Scan part 1 and find at least two °quotes that tell you this.

Part 2: This story happened at night.
Find a quote in part 2 that shows you this.

Part 3: Martin and Mark changed their minds about being in the car.
Prove this with examples from part 3 of the text.

Part 4: How were Apache and Pete horrible to Martin and Mark?
Answer according to part 4 of the text.

Part 5: Find the mistakes in these sentences and correct them (according to part 5):
'When the car crashed, Apache tried to help Mark. He pulled him from the car before the explosion. Then an officer put Martin in a police car.'

Part 6: Describe Martin's situation in part 6 of the text, in your own words.
How do you think he was feeling?

4 WRITING A comment

Choose a), b) or c) and write a comment (80–120 words).

a) We can learn a lot from Martin's story.

b) Good friends should stick together.

c) You should always be able to say 'no'.

More practice 7 p.120

▸ DFF 2.7 ▸ INKL p. 38

1 MEDIATION At the market

2.01 **a)** **Part 1:** Vanessa is showing a visitor, Adana, around her home town. Listen to part 1 of their conversation and find out:

1 Where is Vanessa from?
2 Where is Adana from?
3 Why are they speaking English?
4 What does Adana want to find out?
5 What differences between their two countries do the girls discover?

2.02 **b)** **Part 2:** Adana sees this poster. What do you think it's about? Talk about it with a partner in English. Then listen to part 2 – were you right?

2.02 **c)** Listen to **part 2** again and think about these questions:

1 Does Vanessa mediate everything?
2 What does Vanessa do when she doesn't know the English word for *Minimalist*?

FIT FOR EXAMS

Decide **what information** your partner needs.
Only mediate the **most important information**.
If you don't know a word, **paraphrase**.
▸ *Skills file 12, pp. 182–183*

2.03 **d)** **Part 3:** How would you mediate here? Practise with a partner. Then listen to Vanessa and compare.

Adana	Can you tell us more about the *Kauf-Nix-Tag*? What other activities do people do?
Vanessa	...
Man	Ach, man kann vieles tun. Zum Beispiel rausgehen und die Natur genießen. Weit weg von den Läden, in den Park oder raus aus der Stadt, aufs Land.
Vanessa	...
Man	Oder einfach zu Hause bleiben, mit Freunden oder mit der Familie ... zum Beispiel zusammen kochen, ... nur nichts kaufen.
Vanessa	...
Adana	OK, but what about fun activities? Can you do anything exciting on *Buy-nothing-day*?
Vanessa	...
Man	Oh ja – es gibt den *Zombie walk*. Also, man schminkt sich wie ein Zombie ... ihr wisst schon ... weiß im Gesicht, rot oder schwarz um die Augen ..., und man geht in die großen Läden und läuft herum, ganz ruhig und friedlich ... wie ein Zombie. Du kaufst nichts, läufst nur herum, und die Leute sprechen dich an. Dann kannst du erklären, warum du nichts kaufst. So kommst du gut ins Gespräch.
Vanessa	...
Adana	Sounds interesting – but maybe not for everybody! Hey, thanks for talking to us.

More practice 8+9 p. 120

▸ Workbook 16–17, p. 29

▸ DFF 2.8 ▸ INKL p. 39

2 LISTENING Fashion Revolution

2.05 **a) A news report:** Listen to the news report. Which phrases complete the sentences best?

1 In the Rana Plaza disaster ...
- A nearly one thousand people were killed.
- B more than one thousand people died.
- C nobody was hurt.
- D nobody was killed.

2 *Fashion Revolution* wants ...
- A better wages for British workers.
- B cheaper clothes for shoppers in the West.
- C better quality clothes for everybody.
- D better working conditions for workers in the clothes industry.

3 Shoppers should think more about ...
- A how much they spend.
- B what they wear.
- C who makes their clothes.
- D if they need more clothes.

FIT FOR EXAMS

You won't understand everything. Just **don't panic**. While you're listening, **keep an eye on the tasks**.

▸ Skills file 6, p. 165

2.06 **b) A discussion:** You will hear a discussion between four teenagers: Anita, Jeff, Shiva and Alex. While listening, decide which of the statements are true or false.

1 The new department store sells mostly expensive, high quality clothes.
2 Sweatshops are factories where the employees work very hard and don't get a lot of money.
3 It's impossible to find out where clothes are made and who makes them.
4 By wearing your clothes inside out for a day, you show that you're against sweatshops.
5 The four teenagers decide to take part in *Inside Out*.

3 SPEAKING Picking the right present

It's your friend Jake's birthday soon. He's interested in fashion, films and music. He also likes reading. But he isn't a very active person. You want to buy him a present.

a) Discuss the pros and cons of each present idea below. ▸ Skills file 9.4, p. 172

b) Agree on one present for Jake. Think about these things:
- Which present do you think he'd like best?
- How much money do you want to spend?

▸ Workbook 18, pp. 30–31

▸ INKL p. 40

FIT FOR EXAMS

4 READING #ILookLikeAnEngineer

These billboards were part of a recruitment campaign run by a software company in San Francisco. The company was looking for new workers and asked members of staff to say how they felt about working for them. Their quotes were put up beside their photos in San Francisco underground stations. There was a huge reaction to the ads – but not one that was expected. The young female software engineer who was featured in the ad campaign received a lot of comments, some positive, but some very negative. Some people just didn't believe that she could be an engineer because – to them – she didn't look like one.

So what does an engineer look like? The engineer, I.A. Wenger, started a hashtag *#ILookLikeAnEngineer*, and encouraged other engineers to post photos of themselves to answer that question. The idea was a big hit and thousands of people posted pictures, and they are all so different! Their photos prove that engineers are definitely not just young white males in hoodies. That's just a stereotype. Although women and people of colour are still in the minority in STEM (science, technology, engineering, maths) careers, Wenger's campaign shows that engineers can be any gender or race and just about any age. The question is: Can campaigns like this change the stereotypes?

a) According to the article, which of the people A–D is most like the stereotype of an engineer? And which of them could actually be an engineer? Explain.
You can use words from the text.
Example:
The article says that the stereotype of an engineer is ... (line 24). So that means that the person in picture ... is most like that stereotype. However, ...

b) Can Wenger's campaign change stereotypes? Answer with examples from the text and give your own opinion.

More help p. 123 More challenge 5 p. 123

FIT FOR EXAMS

First find the **relevant information**.
It might be in different places in the text.
Then come to your own conclusions.
▸ *Skills file 7.5, p. 167*

▸ Workbook 19–20, p. 32

5 VIEWING Walk or fly

a) Watch the film and discuss these questions.

1 What do you learn about the life of the main character?
- What's his name? - Where does he live?
- Friends? - Family?
- Personality? - What makes him special?

2 What do you think is the turning point of the film?

3 Is it a happy or sad film? Give reasons.

b) Make four expert groups. Read the instructions for your group and watch the film again. Then talk about your results in your expert groups.

Group A – Location

The location is where a film is made.

1 What different locations do you see in this film? List them. Example: *a school yard, ...*

2 What do the locations tell you about Mark and his life?

Group B – Characters

1 What characters have speaking roles in this film? List them. Example: *the school principal, ...*

2 Describe their relationship with Mark.

Group C – Plot (storyline)

1 Summarize the plot of the film.

2 There are some flashbacks when the film goes back in time. What do they add to the story?

Group D – Script

1 Who says these things in the film?
- *What are you supposed to be?*
- *He doesn't bite. He may try to rescue you from a burning building!*
- *Just be cool. I'm wearing tights. How can I be cool?*
- *Do good!*
- *How do you °wee?*
- *It was daddy's job to keep people safe from °bombs.*
- *How do you want to get to this party – walk or fly?*

2 Are these lines important? Why (not)?

3 What do they tell us about Mark's story?

4 Identify other lines in the film that you think are important. Explain why.

c) Now make new groups of four, with at least one expert (A, B, C and D) in each group. Tell your new group what you've learned.

d) In *Walk or fly* Hannah says, "Most people want to be the same as everyone else." Comment on this idea. Do you agree? Give examples. What happens if you aren't the same as everyone else?

More challenge 6 p. 123

▸ Skills file 13, p. 185

2 STOP! CHECK! GO!

▸ KV 16 ▸ DFF 2.4 ▸ INKL pp. 42–45 ▸ INKL pp. 84–87

1 LANGUAGE The European Parliament

Complete this chat between Ralf, a German student on a class trip in Brussels, and Cathy, his Australian friend. Use the ***simple past*** or ***present perfect***. // ● p.123 ▸ Language file 5, p. 188

Ralf — I'm in Brussels. My friends and I ... (1 just leave) the European Parliament. What an interesting place!

Cathy — Really? I ... (2 not visit) Brussels yet but I'd like to go there one day. I'm interested in European politics.

Ralf — I think politics is important. My class ...(3 do) a survey last year and we ... (4 find) that most young people didn't vote in the last European °elections. I think that's terrible.

Cathy — Maybe people don't know about the advantages of the EU – like the euro. That makes it easier for people to travel, doesn't it? How long have you had the euro?

Ralf — In Germany we ... (5 get) the euro in 2002.

Cathy — Does the EU make a difference to your life in other ways?

Ralf — Yes, it does. For example, the EU °Parliament ... (6 recently °pass) a law to make mobile calls to other EU countries cheaper.

Cathy — So you think the EU is a good thing?

Ralf — I do. But this morning I ... (7 go) to a discussion about "Rules against °misuse of °trade secrets". I ... (8 never listen to) to such a boring discussion!

Cathy — OK, so politics is important, but sometimes it isn't very interesting.

2 LANGUAGE A week to remember

Complete this report about a Year 10 trip.
Use the ***past progressive*** or ***past perfect***. ▸ Language files 4; 7

We started to plan our class trip about a year ago. After we ... (1 discuss) lots of different °destinations, our teacher suggested Jersey, one of the small islands between France and the UK. We ... (2 not think) of going there until he told us about it. When we ... (3 do) some research, we found out that it is a good place for a holiday.
Everything went well until we arrived in Jersey. Just as we ... (4 leave) the airport, the bus drivers started a four-hour °strike. The next day when we ... (5 have) breakfast in our hostel, the °electricity °went off. On day two it rained all day, but luckily we ... (6 plan) some °indoor activities. While we ... (7 watch) the rain, some of us began to have °doubts about the holiday. But after the rain ... (8 stop), we met some other students and had fun on the beach with them. We even had problems on the journey home: While we ... (9 wait) for °take-off, an announcement said that our flight would be late because they ... (10 not finish) °loading our bags yet. In the end, although a lot of things went wrong, we all enjoyed ourselves on our trip to Jersey.

▸ KV 16 ▸ DFF 2.5 ▸ DFF 2.6 ▸ INKL pp. 42–45 ▸ INKL pp. 84–87

3 WORDS Find the words

a) For each verb (1–7), find three matching words (A, B, C or D).

1 make ...	A money	B attention	C a decision	D a difference
2 create ...	A a petition	B a campaign	C a say	D a website
3 take ...	A a stand	B place	C part	D a protest
4 sign ...	A a stereotype	B a petition	C a document	D a contract
5 do ...	A an activity	B a prize	C something	D nothing
6 get ...	A a pension	B attention	C involved	D graffiti
7 post ... online	A photos	B videos	C wars	D comments

b) For each word that doesn't go with a verb in a), find a matching verb from the box below.

change • have • go on • win • clean off • fight • pay

c) Complete the text about a new skatepark in Highdown. Use words from a).

A new skatepark for Highdown

Last year the old skatepark in Highdown closed because it was no longer safe. The BMX °riders and skateboarders who used to spend time in the skatepark turned to the internet. They started a website and lots of people ... (1) their comments and ideas online. Here are a few of them:

SK: Let's ... (2) an online petition and ask people to ... (3) the petition.
Sk8erboy: A petition is a great idea. If you get lots of signatures, maybe local politicians will get ... (4). They should ... (5) a stand and support your campaign.
RobinG: Don't just sit in front of your screens. Get out there and do ... (6) to make ... (7).

d) Correct the mistakes in this article about the new skatepark.

Our campaign for a new skatepark ~~made~~ (1) a lot of hard work! First we started a website ~~in~~ (2) the internet. ~~Than~~ (3) we organized an online petition and more ~~as~~ (4) 80 % of the people living near the park signed it. With the signatures we turned to local politicians and asked for ~~there~~ (5) support. The ~~difficultest~~ (6) task was raising the money to pay for the new skatepark. But in the end we did it! Now visitors to Highdown Park ~~become~~ (7) a nice surprise. ~~It gives there~~ (8) a big, modern, new skatepark.

4 READING *Earth Hour:* °Shine a light on climate action

Use a dictionary if you need help with the tasks. Don't worry if you don't understand everything.

Every year, hundreds of millions of people around the world switch off their lights for one °particular hour to °demonstrate their support for fighting °climate change. *Earth Hour* takes place every year near the end of March at 8:30 pm local time. During this time individuals, businesses and world leaders °join together in a °symbolic lights-out event.

Earth Hour was °launched in Sydney, Australia in 2007, with more than 2 million homes and businesses. Today the event °engages more than 172 countries and territories and millions of people around the world.

Taking part in *Earth Hour* is easy:

- See the *Earth Hour* website for the °precise date of the next *Earth Hour.*
- °Turn off all non-°essential lights at 8:30 pm local time and let us know you are taking part.
- Stand up for the °planet and celebrate with your friends, family, community, or at school. You could °host an indoor °candlelit dinner party with friends, have an outdoor picnic, create a °lantern flashmob, or post photos of °darkened °landmarks on social media using *#earthhour.*
- Tell all your friends that *Earth Hour* is on its way to becoming the world's largest movement for climate change action ever. Let's change climate change together!

a) Choose the summary that fits the text best (A, B, C or D).

A The text explains how people can take part in an environmental project in Australia.
B The text explains how people can save money by switching off lights.
C The text explains how millions of people waste electricity.
D The text is about how people can easily take a stand for the °environment.

b) Decide whether the statements are right, wrong, or not in the text.

1 The first *Earth Hour* took place in Sydney.
2 The event takes place in spring every year.
3 People switch off their lights at half past nine.
4 Even famous politicians take part in the event.

c) Complete each sentence with a suitable word from the text.

1 During *Earth Hour* millions of people show their ... for stopping climate change.
2 You can find the ... date on the internet.
3 Some people take photos of ... sights and post them on the internet.

d) Replace the word in orange with a word from the text.

1 a special hour 2 unnecessary lights 3 to organize a candlelit dinner

▸ Skills files 7.3 and 7.4, p. 166

5 WRITING Switch off your light, and switch on your social power!

Choose A, B or C and write a blog entry. Write about 80 words.

A Imagine you have just taken part in *Earth Hour* with your best friends. What did you do? How did you feel? Write about it.

B Do you care about the future of the planet? How can you make a difference? Write about your ideas and suggestions.

C ● Some people °criticize the symbolic character of *Earth Hour*. They say instead of celebrating one special hour in a year, we should care about the planet every day. What do you think about social actions like *Earth Hour*? Are they effective and helpful? Why (not)?

6 MEDIATION Announcements at the station and the airport

2.07

a) Listen to the five train station announcements in German. Help the tourists in English.

Tourist	Excuse me. Can you help me, please? I'm going to °Cologne. Is there a problem with the train?
You	*Yes, there is. The train to Cologne will be …*
Tourist	…
You	…
…	

2.08

b) Listen to the five airport announcements in English and help the tourists in German.

Tourist	Entschuldigung, was wurde gerade gesagt? Betrifft das den Flug nach München?
You	*Ja. Der Flug hat 2 Stunden Verspätung, weil …*
Tourist	…
You	…
…	

7 SPEAKING Typically German

a) Partner B: Go to p. 101.

Partner A: Describe these things to your partner without using the German word. Then listen to your partner. Which typically German things is he/she describing?

1

Schultüte

2

Strandkorb

3

Rosenmontagsumzug

b) Think of more examples of typically German things. Describe them to your partner without saying the German words. Can he/she guess what they are?

More challenge 7 | p. 124

Doing the right thing

Wichtigen Wortschatz von diesen Seiten findest du im Vocabulary auf S. 237–238.

1 What happened?

Jon Snow is a well-known British journalist and television presenter.
He is best known in Britain as a presenter of TV news. He was cycling to work one day when something happened. He wrote about it in his blog.

Jon Snow riding his °bicycle in London

a) Read Jon Snow's post and find out what happened.

My °shameful dilemma

Cycling along a reasonably °well-heeled street in the Camden area of north London, my °attention is drawn to an argument between a young man and a young woman on my left. Then I suddenly see him hitting her in the face.

I hear her screams and the man's shouts, and by the time my bicycle is °abreast of them, she is in tears, her face badly marked.

I °instinctively °intervene and ask if she needs help. The man is in a °hyper-paranoid, violent °state, and turns fast and °menacingly on me, shouting and °cursing, and I °take to my bike in °flight.

I pause °further down the road and look back, and there seem to be more people °about. I cycle back towards the group, seriously °concerned for the young woman's °welfare. And it seems to me the man is standing close to a °motorcycle.

Box: Voc., p. 238

The road is °straight and somehow °enclosed, with few escape points, and I °conclude very quickly that °if he were to °give chase, he'd get me. I °retreat, and I think about calling the police. But for some °inexplicable reason, I didn't.

Even now, I don't really know why not. Somehow I feel that they wouldn't have taken me seriously and that by the time it was all explained, the °incident would have °passed and there would only be my °account of it.

I don't often see °that sort of thing, and it's left me with a lot of °misgivings.

b) Summarize the main events in the text in a few sentences. ► Skills file 10.4, p. 175
Compare your summary with other students' summaries.

c) Discuss: If you had been Jon Snow, how would you have acted?
Would you have done something? What? Or would you have just kept going? Give reasons.

2 Looking at the language

a) The language in Jon Snow's post is rich and interesting. Let's find out why.
Find the words and phrases that Jon Snow uses for the underlined words below.

1 I'm cycling along a street in a rich part of London. (line 1)
2 I notice that a young man and woman are having an argument. (line 2)
3 She's crying. (line 6)
4 I stop for a minute. (line 10)
5 I'm very worried about the young woman. (line 11)
6 ... I quickly see that ... (line 13)
7 I move back. (line 14)
8 For a reason I can't explain ... (line 15)

> **!** You can improve and °enrich your style by collecting interesting phrases. Find out what they mean and how formal they are.
> Start by collecting good alternatives for the common word *say* in Jon Snow's post.

b) Use verbs from the box to enrich the language of these sentences.

1 "Get out of my house now," the woman said.
2 "I'm sorry I hurt you. I won't do that again," the boy said.
3 "I love you," he said, and left the room quietly.
4 "Let's go for a nice walk," her dad said.
5 "I don't feel well, please don't make me go to school," he said.
6 "We also think she's very nice," they said.
7 "Germany has a good team. But the English team is better," she said.
8 "It's very cold in this classroom," the teacher said.

> add • agree • answer • call • complain • cry • demand • joke • laugh • promise • remember • shout • smile • suggest • warn • whisper • wonder

c) Compare your sentences with different partners.
Discuss: How do the different verbs (synonyms) change the sentences?

3 WRITING More dilemmas

Pick one of these scenarios (A or B) and continue the text to describe a dilemma.
Did you intervene, or just keep going? **Or**: Write about another situation with a dilemma.

A

I was on my way home from school one day when I saw something terrible. My best friend Alice was talking to a man. I could hear them talking. "How much?" Alice asked. "£25," the man answered. Then Alice gave him some money and the man gave her something. I was very worried. At first I didn't know what to do. I was in a dilemma. Then I decided to ...

B

"Don't talk to Andrew," Beth whispered. "Don't message him, don't look at him .... or there'll be trouble," she warned. I had a problem. You see, Andrew was a good friend. But Beth was one of the most popular girls in class. Everybody admired her, me too! Some people were even afraid of her! I found myself in a real dilemma – what should I do? So I decided to ...

Unit 3 Future visions

▸ KV 17 ▸ INKL pp. 46–47

A

Exoskeletons

They can be used to help people who have lost the use of their arms or legs. They can also be used by firefighters or rescue workers in dangerous situations.

B

Delivering pizzas by drone

Pizzas, parcels and medicines can be delivered by drone to your door.

E

Active contact lenses

These 3-D contact lenses can let you read text messages and watch TV and movies using your eyes as a screen.

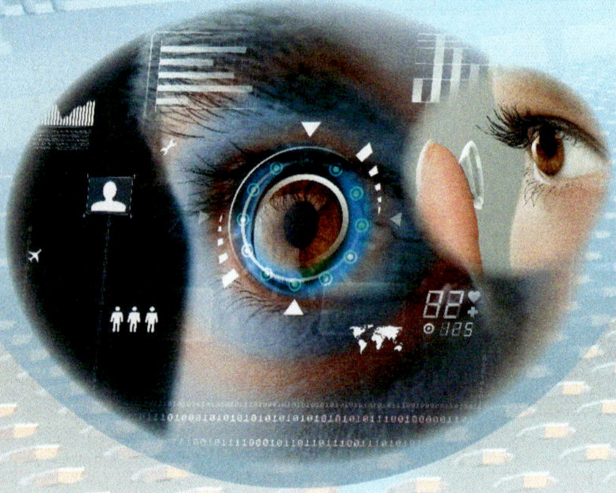

F

°Piezoelectric power

The players make the power for the electric lights when they run on this football field in Brazil.

1 Dreams or reality?

a) Think: Skim the headlines and pictures and ask yourself these questions:
- Which of these products do you think are available today?
- Which is a realistic plan for the near future?
- Which is just a dream – it'll never happen?

b) Pair: Now talk about these questions with a partner. Give reasons for your answers.

c) Share: Discuss the questions in class. Agree on one thing that's available today, one thing that's a plan and one thing that's just a dream.

More practice 1 p. 124

C

Hi-tech pillows

They read your dreams, send them to a computer, show them on a screen and then help you to understand them.

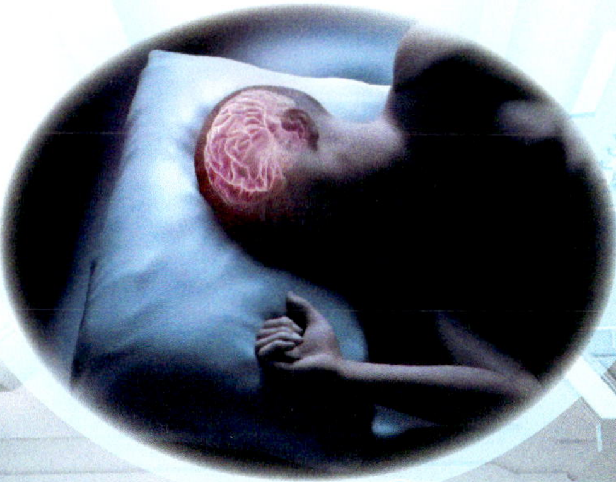

D

The first driverless vehicle

With special cameras and °radar technology, the first driverless truck drives 16,000 km on a test road in Germany.

G

Weather control

Scientists discover ways of controlling the weather. They can start or stop rain and they can stop hurricanes too.

H

Smart paint

You can change the colour of your house by choosing from a screen.

2.09

2 The opinions of a °futurologist

a) Are these eight products dreams or reality? Listen to the programme and take notes.

b) Listen again and take notes on the advantages and disadvantages of the products.
Partner A: Listen for the products on p. 54. Partner B: Listen for the products on p. 55.
Then talk about your notes.

c) Discuss these questions in small groups.
- Which of these products do you think would be the most useful and the least useful? Why?
- Do you think that any of these ideas or products are risky or dangerous?
- What other new ideas or products could change our world in the future?

▸ Workbook 1, p. 39

▸ KV 18 ▸ INKL pp. 48–49

A better world

1 READING Emma's world

a) Scan the two parts of the text and find some examples of technology. ▸ *Skills file 7.2, p. 166*

b) Then make two lists: (1) wearable technology; (2) °non-wearable technology.

2.10

Part 1 Just a normal Monday

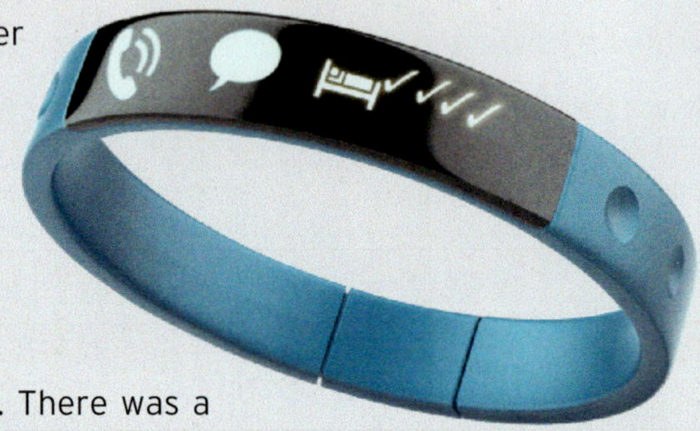

Emma opened her eyes and checked her smart watch. It told her that she had just had a perfect night (four hours of light sleep and nearly four hours of deep sleep). So she felt fit and ready for the day. She touched the glass screen on her desk.

"Good morning, Emma," it greeted her. "You slept well." Her school timetable for the day came up. There was a flashing message beside German: "Emma, you finished most of your homework. But remember to study for your German vocabulary test." "Oh yes, I nearly forgot," she said to herself. "I'll do it on the way to school."

Downstairs a fruit smoothie was waiting for her on the table. Her dad had received a report on the fridge computer that Emma needed to eat more fruit. She hadn't had her 'seven a day' yesterday. "Good old dad," Emma thought. He had already gone to work.

The journey to school was quicker now. People's wearable devices sent messages about where the traffic was bad and the driverless school bus could take a different route. So Emma had just enough time to learn her German words. She put on her wireless headphones and listened to her German vocabulary from the school network.

Box: Voc., p. 228

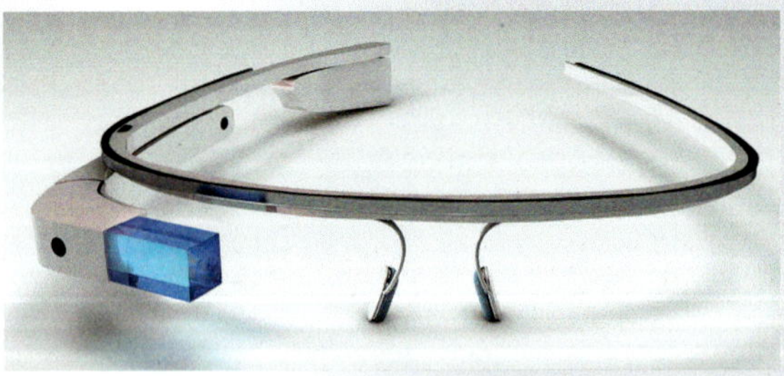

Emma moved quickly from class to class. Lessons were only 20 minutes long, because students didn't need time to open their bags, get their books out, etc. Emma remembered the bad old days when she had had to carry her heavy bag everywhere. Now she just put on her smart glasses. They saved the information that the teachers put on the smart boards. After school, she could study it all again on her computer at home. She could even watch the lesson again if she wanted to. But she didn't often do that.

After school Emma went to the home gym for an hour. Her PE teacher had checked Emma's data on his computer and he told her that she wasn't getting enough exercise. He also warned her not to eat any more fast food this week. He saw that she had eaten a burger on Saturday. So this evening Emma would only have a healthy salad for her dinner.

▸ KV 18 ▸ DFF 3.2 ▸ INKL pp. 48–49

2.11

Part 2 6742 more steps!

Emma sat with her friends in a cafe in town. They came here most Saturdays. They sent messages to each other and looked at people coming and going in the cafe. Emma liked people-watching. And she liked the donuts here too - especially with °caramel smoothies! The °alarm of Emma's fitness tracker buzzed. "Oh no. It says I have too much °glucose in my blood. I shouldn't finish this donut," she said to her friends. But nobody was listening. Emma's tablet buzzed. There was a message from her mum: "You've been in the Pink Elephant cafe for almost three hours. You said you were going to play football!!!" Emma groaned - she knew that she was in trouble.

On the way home, the girls passed the *Johnny Rocket Club*. There was a big red sign outside: **Cocktails half price from 5 to 7 pm.** "Let's go in," one of the girls said. But as they passed the door, there was a loud buzzing noise and a scanner flashed:

UNDER 18! NO ENTRY! - UNDER 18! NO ENTRY! - UNDER 18! NO ENTRY!

At home in her bedroom Emma put on her head-mounted display to watch a film. For a moment she thought about the old days when the whole family watched TV together. But now the TV was gone and the living room was the home gym.
Emma's smart phone buzzed. It told her that she still had a lot of homework to do and that she hadn't had enough exercise today - she still had to do 6742 more steps before she went to bed. Emma groaned, put on her smart shirt and went to the home gym.

2 Working with the text

a) Read the text. Which part is more positive about modern technology? Give reasons.

b) The other part shows a more negative side of technology. Prove this with at least two examples from the text.

c) Explain these words from the two parts of the text in complete sentences.

1 *watch* (line 3)
2 *wearable devices* (line 17)
3 *wireless headphones* (lines 19–20)
4 *people-watching* (line 39)
5 *groaned* (lines 44 and 56)
6 *head-mounted display* (line 49)

More practice 2 p. 125

3 YOUR TASK Wearable technology and me

a) Write a comment (about 60–80 words). Do you have a wearable device?
- If yes, what do you have? When do you use it? Is it good? Why (not)?
- If not, would you like any wearable devices? Why (not)? What would you like? ▸ Skills file 10.2, p. 174

b) Write a story (about 120–150 words). Start like this: *When I opened my birthday present, I got a great surprise. It was a ... My world was about to change forever ..."*

More challenge 1 p. 125

▸ Skills file 10.1, pp. 172–173

► *INKL pp. 50–51*

Can we keep on like this?

Box: Voc., p. 229

1 LISTENING A student's talk on sustainable living

a) Before you listen: Look at the slides A–E. What do you think each one shows? Is it a photo, a chart, a drawing, a logo, ...? Make notes.

Compare with a partner.

2.12 **b)** Listen to the talk. Put the slides in the right order.

A

B

C

D

E

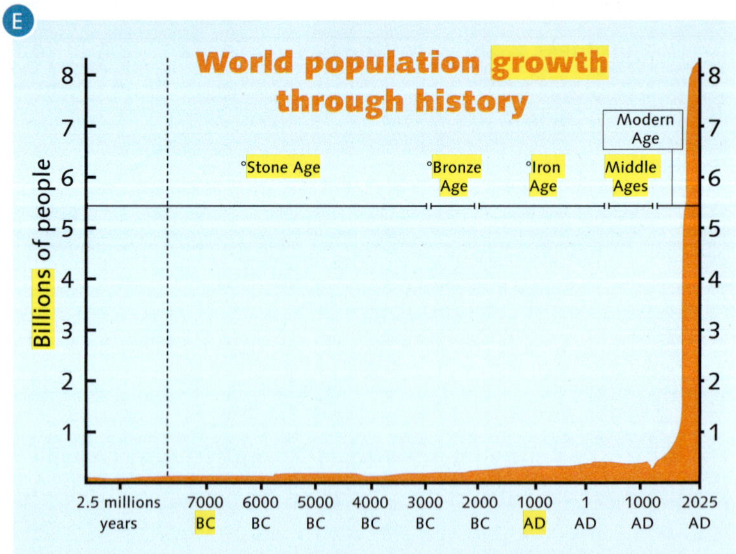

Source: Population Reference Bureau, Washington D.C.

▸ KV 19 ▸ DFF 3.3 ▸ DFF 3.4 ▸ INKL pp. 50–51

2.12

c) Read the questions. Then listen again and take notes. Answer the questions in a few words.

1 Why does the speaker think that sustainable living has become a big topic recently?
2 What does the speaker think is most interesting about the graph?
3 What is the population of the world now and what could it be in 2050?
4 Why isn't the speaker pessimistic about the future?

d) Choose one of the slides and prepare a short talk for the class. First describe the slide. Then comment on it. ▸ *Skills file 11.1, p. 179* More challenge 2 p. 125

2 VIEWING *Sorry*

a) Watch this video by activist Prince Ea. Don't worry if you don't understand everything. Write down three words to sum up the video.

b) Work in groups. Explain the three words you have chosen to your group.

c) Watch again and make notes about these things. Compare notes in your group.

1 Who exactly is Prince Ea saying *sorry* to?
2 He lists mistakes that his generation has made. Note down at least three.
3 Who can correct the mistakes, according to Prince Ea?
4 At the end, Prince Ea lists a number of big issues. But what is the most important issue according to him?
5 Is it a pessimistic or an optimistic message, in your view? Explain.

d) Prince Ea suggests everybody can help save the planet. What things can students like you do to help? Discuss in your group or in a written discussion. More practice 3 p. 126

► KV 20

1 New frontiers

a) Read the article and the comments. Then decide: Who are you most like – DrSpock or Spacecadet? Explain your answer.

Will we ever live on Mars?

Humans have always been fascinated by Mars, and we still are, according to the success of the film *The Martian*. In this film a °mission to Mars goes wrong and the main character is left behind on the red planet.

So will humans really go to Mars? This is a controversial question, but there are predictions that the first °spacecraft could arrive there by 2030 at the latest.

So what will life on Mars be like? Remember that the average temperature is -63°C; °gravity is only about 38 per cent as strong as the Earth's; and there is almost no °oxygen there. The optimists don't think this will be a problem. In spite of all the difficulties, they expect that the space pioneers will create a °habitat where they will be able to live and grow food.

There is another problem though. We might be able to get to Mars, but it's very unlikely we'll be able to get home again. However, this won't stop the real enthusiasts. Hundreds of would-be settlers signed up for a programme called *Mars One* °even though the organizers clearly said that they could only offer one-way tickets.

Replies:

DrSpock: I recommend the film. But I'm not going to sign up for a one-way ticket to Mars!

Spacecadet: The film sounds really interesting. I'm definitely going to watch it. I'd love to be a space pioneer. When I'm eighteen, I'm going to sign up for a Mars mission.

DrSpock: You're crazy ☺ I'm going to concentrate on improving life on Earth.

b) Make appointments with at least two partners and talk about some of these questions:

1 Do you like this kind of film? Why (not)?
2 Can you imagine being a space pioneer? What would you find most difficult?
3 Why do you think people want to get to Mars? Are you personally interested in space?
4 Is space travel important or should we be more worried about other things on earth?

c) Report the most interesting answers that you heard to the class.

2 REVISION Using future tenses

FOCUS

1 You use the ***will*-future** to talk about predictions.
It's often used with phrases *like I'm sure …, I think…, I believe …, I expect that, It's likely / unlikely that …, It's possible / probable that …*
Example: I'm sure that humans will live on Mars sometime in the future. But I don't think that it will happen by 2030. Will I go to Mars? No, I definitely won't!

2 You use the ***going to*-future** for plans.
Example: I've heard that the film *The Martian* is good. I'm going to watch it tonight.

► *Language file 9–10, p. 190*

3 What do you think?

p. 127

Complete the dialogue with suitable forms of the ***will*-future**.

DrSpock I don't think humans … (1 ever, get) to Mars. What about you?
Spacecadet Well, I believe that it … (2 happen) one day. Maybe it … (3 not happen) by 2030, but I'm sure that the scientists … (4 succeed) sometime in the future.
DrSpock Let's say they make it. How long … (5 it, take) to get there?
Spacecadet It's likely that the trip … (6 take) 8 months. It's a long way!
DrSpock What do you think life … (7 be) like on Mars?
Spacecadet It … (8 be) really difficult. The space pioneers … (9 not, be able to) go outside without special suits. They … (10 have to) wear them all the time as it's so cold. And there's the deadly °radiation. If they stay outside without a suit, they … (11 die).
DrSpock Where … they … (12 live) then?
Spacecadet They … (13 have to) live under the ground at first. But I expect that later they … (14 create) new habitats. I think it … (15 be) brilliant.
DrSpock Humans have made a big mess here on earth. I'm sure they … (16 make) the same mistakes if they go somewhere else.
Spacecadet Maybe you're right, but it's possible that we … (17 do) better next time!

More practice 4 p. 127

4 Talking about plans

a) Complete the answers. Use the ***going to*-future**. Then say what your plans are.

1 Have you thought about what job you're going to do in the future?
Amy Yes, I know exactly what I … (do). I … (train) as an engineer and I … (apply) to work for NASA in Huntsville, AL.
Jamilia I don't know what job I … (have). I … (not study) science. I prefer music.
You …

2 What are your plans for the weekend?
Amy On Saturday I … (finish) my homework. On Sunday … (prepare) for my exams.
Jamilia I … (be) busy! On Saturday we … (have) a lovely breakfast together. On Sunday I … (perform) with my choir.
You …

b) Continue these sentences. Write as much as you can. Use the ***going to*-future**.

1 It's my birthday next week, so …
2 We don't have homework tonight, so …
3 We have exams soon, so …
4 I have some plans for the holidays. I …

More practice 5 p. 127 More challenge 3 p. 128

► KV 21 ► DFF 3.5 ► INKL p. 55

5 Dealing with new words

a) The underlined words are all new.
What similar words do you already know?

b) Guess what these words mean.

1 The end of the film was very <u>predictable</u>.
2 Many parts of the world will become <u>over-populated</u>.
3 Some people have a <u>fascination</u> with Mars.
4 This film uses some very <u>futuristic-looking</u> technology.
5 Until recently most experts <u>rubbished</u> the idea that humans could live on Mars.
6 Humans will never live on another planet. That's just <u>wishful thinking</u>.
7 A lot of <u>pioneering</u> work has already been done.

> **!** You know the word *prediction*, and you know other words that end in *-able*. That can help you understand the new word *predictable*.
> ► *Skills file 1, p. 160*

6 Improve your English: typical mistakes

a) Read the comments and improve this student's text.

Space – the new tourist destination?

I hope that space is the new tourist destination I'd love to be a space tourist! I don't expect that I'll have the chance to go. But if I ~~will be~~ lucky, I'll go. I don't really believe it will happen because it simply so expensive ~~is~~ and I'm not sure that it will ever be cheap enough for normal people like me. But as soon as prices come down, I will on the first spacecraft. I'd really love to go into space for several reasons. First, I'd love to look down on the Earth from up there. Secondly, I'd love to explore new planets. A space pioneer's life must be so ~~excited~~! ~~So~~ I hope that space will be a tourist destination in the future. But unfortunately it's unlikely that I'll ever be a space tourist. ~~A shame~~!

1 Join these two short sentences with a linking phrase. ► *Skills file 10.1, p. 173*

2 You don't use *will* in the *if*-clause. ► *Language file 25, p. 199*

3 Word order (*S-V-O*)! Put the verb *is* in the correct place. ► *Language file 15, p. 192*

4 *Will* is right, but something is missing.

5 Wrong word – think of the difference between *bored* and *boring*.

6 Find a better phrase to start your conclusion. ► *Skills file 10.2, p. 174*

7 Nearly right – but not quite. Look up *shame* in a dictionary and find the right phrase.

b) Space – the new tourist destination?
Write a comment (80–100 words) on the question.

► Workbook 9–10, p. 45

▸ INKL pp. 52–54

1 The blurb

a) First read the blurb from the back cover of the book. Answer these questions:
- Do you think this could be a true story? Why (not)?
- Do you think it takes place in the past, the present or the future?
- What's *global warming*? Can you explain it? Check in a dictionary.

Global warming has caused the seas to rise and now a lot of Britain is under water. Some cities, like Norwich, have become islands. Zoe Black has been left behind on Norwich by accident, when her parents escaped in the last ship. There is little food and water on the island and people are starting to panic. They are looking for ways to escape from the island. Zoe wants to escape too and get to the mainland to find her parents.

Box: Voc., p. 231

b) Now read the text below. You may not understand all the words, but don't worry. You can find an easier version of the story on pp. 130–131.

Floodland (adapted from the novel by Marcus Sedgwick)

2.13

Zoe ran. Harder than she had ever run in her life. She ran through °deserted streets, past °derelict buildings. Somewhere, not far behind, she could hear the gang coming after her. It felt as if her heart would °burst, but she didn't °slow down. She'd been planning to leave the island for a long time, but had been °putting it off. It was a big decision to leave the island in a °tiny rowing boat. Now she had no choice.

Box: Voc., p. 233

Zoe was a °loner. Most of the people left on Norwich °hung around together in groups, but she preferred to be on her own. It was safer that way, because you never knew °whom you could trust.
Someone had found out about the boat she'd been hiding. A boat was an escape route, a way to get away from Norwich, which got smaller every year, as the sea kept rising. Now a mob of about fifteen people was following her. There was only one way out: to get to her boat before they got to her. So she ran on.
"Get back here!" someone shouted angrily at her, though they couldn't see her.
It wasn't far to the little shed where she'd hidden *Lyca*, her boat. Just before she went round a corner, she heard more shouts from behind. They had seen her.
"There!"
"Come on!" shouted another voice. "Get her!"
Scared, she went round the corner, but her foot °slipped on the wet ground. She fell in the mud. She started to panic badly. She had dropped her bag as she fell, but there was no time to pick it up.
The sound of running feet came closer. Another two seconds and they would be round the corner. She got up and threw herself over a wall. She was in a graveyard. It went down a hill to where a small shed stood, near the water. Once it had °contained all the equipment for looking after the graveyard, but now it contained Zoe's boat.
"*Lyca*," Zoe panted as she opened the shed door, "please be here, *Lyca*."
It was all right. The boat was still there.

Pulling it across the grass, and then into the water, she looked behind her for the first time. The gang was °storming down the hill between the gravestones. Zoe moved faster. They were at the water now, and though one or two stopped, the rest came °splashing madly after her.

"Take me with you!"

"Come back! We won't hurt you. Just take us with you!"

Zoe could see their eyes, clearly. She saw fear. But she couldn't trust them. Since she'd lost her parents, she'd made it a rule not to trust anyone.

She looked at the crowd in the water again. If she went back, there'd be a fight over her boat, and she wouldn't have a chance of escaping. Slowly, she watched as the people °dragged themselves out of the water and back to the °shore. Natasha was there too. That hurt most of all. Natasha had been her only friend. Zoe used to see her when the °supply ships came, before they stopped coming. They used to have a little chat. Zoe suddenly remembered their conversation the last time they'd met. She had wanted to tell Natasha about her boat, and her plans to escape, but had decided not to. Maybe Natasha had guessed? It didn't matter now.

The crowd stood quietly, watching her as she rowed away.

Zoe didn't feel scared of them any more.

"Sorry," she said quietly. She began to cry, but she didn't stop rowing. Her uncut hair fell across her eyes, but she didn't stop to push it away. Her thin body rowed on until finally she had to °pause for °breath.

Feeling around in her pocket she took out her compass. It was the last thing she °owned that had °belonged to her parents. For that reason she had kept it in a pocket. If she hadn't, she'd have lost it when she dropped her bag.

She °pointed herself south-west, and rowed. She knew that the big bit of Britain was somewhere in that direction.

She was rowing away from all that she had ever known. It was a strange thing. Before now, she had never rowed a real boat.

Her dad had taught her.

"You'll need to know how to do this one day," he told her.

He'd taught her how to use the compass, as well as lots of stuff about survival. Just in case the time came when she was on her own. Box: Voc., p. 234

Sometimes, when they weren't busy, °they would sit in an old bath and pretend to row. It seemed like a game to Zoe at the time, but her dad made sure she was doing it right.

"Why don't you look where you're going?" she'd asked her dad.

"When you're rowing, you mean?" he said.

"Yes, why do you sit looking backwards?"

"It's the way you do it," he said. "You couldn't row as well facing forwards." Box: Voc., p. 232

It had always seemed strange to her.

Norwich was getting smaller and smaller. She was °heading into the unknown, without even looking where she was going.

She rowed and rowed, until her small supply of food had gone. She had put the compass on

the floor of the boat in front of her, and every few seconds she checked her direction. There was no sign of land now and she became more afraid. She looked at the compass all the time, it was her only chance now. Like °magic, its tiny hand kept pointing in the same direction. It knew where she was going, even if she didn't. She lost all °sense of time. The sun °beat down on her head, making her feel dizzy. She pushed the hair out of her eyes, but the sea wind blew it back across her face. She felt faint. She fell forward in the boat. In her head, she °replayed the °nightmare where she had lost her parents.

▸ KV 22 ▸ DFF 3.6 ▸ INKL pp. 52–54

2 Working with the text

a) O *The **characters:*** Make three true sentences about the characters in the text.

1 Zoe Black ...	A ... had already left the island.
2 Zoe's parents ...	B ... didn't have any parents.
3 Natasha ...	C ... was alone on the island without her parents.
	D ... wanted to hurt Zoe.
	E ... had been a kind of a friend to Zoe.

b) ***Headings:*** Match the seven correct headings to each paragraph (1–7) of the text.
Be careful – there are two headings more than you need.

A Zoe gets to her boat
B In the middle of the sea
C No compass
D Leaving the others behind
E Not far to the shed
F No choice – Zoe has to leave
G Using a compass
H Skills for survival
I No boat in the shed

Paragraphs:	1	2	3	4	5	6	7
Lines:	1–10	11–29	30–46	47–82	83–90	91–113	114–129
Headings:							

c) *The **plot:*** Complete these sentences with phrases from the text.

1 Zoe wanted to leave ... (lines 1–10).
2 She thought that it was better to be alone because ... (lines 11–29).
3 When Zoe went into the shed, she was happy because ... (lines 30–46).
4 We know that Zoe was sorry about leaving Natasha because ... (lines 47–82).
5 Zoe rowed south-west because ... (lines 83–90).
6 Zoe knew how to row the boat because ... (lines 91–113).
7 In the boat Zoe felt very scared because ... (lines 114–129).

d) *The **mood:*** Describe the mood of this story.
How does the story make you feel? Why?
– I think it's exciting / scary / sad / ... when ...

e) *The **narrator:*** Who tells this story?
- Is it a first-person narrator?
- Or is it a third-person narrator? More practice 6 p. 129

> ! A **first-person narrator** is a character in the story who tells us what happened to him or her and how he or she felt. (***I*** is used a lot.)
> A **third-person narrator** knows everything about one or sometimes about all the characters.
> (***He*** / ***she*** / ***it*** / ***they*** are used a lot.)

3 WRITING A message in a bottle

Imagine you're Zoe and you're in the little boat, in the middle of the sea. Write a message in a bottle to your parents. Tell them what has happened, how you feel and what your plans are. Write about 120 words.
Don't forget to write as a first-person narrator. More challenge 4 p. 126

▸ Workbook 11–14, p. 46 ▸ Text file 5, pp. 151–152

▸ KV 41 ▸ INKL p. 56

1 LISTENING Robots for the home

2.15

At the *Robotech* technology exhibition, we hear about three popular robots for the home.

a) Listen to the three presenters. Which of these robots (A–E) are they talking about?

A

B

C

D

E

b) Copy the table. Then listen again and take notes.

Robot	What can it do? (at least 3 things)	Who is it for?	Price

FIT FOR EXAMS

Taking notes while listening:
- Listen for **key words**. They're usually nouns, verbs or numbers.
- Don't write full sentences – just the key words.
- Use **symbols** and **short forms**:

= 'the same as'
≠ 'not the same as'
+ 'and'
etc. 'and so on'
e.g. 'for example'
!!! 'very important'
X 'not / no' ▸ *Skills file 6, p. 165*

2 SPEAKING A talk about gadgets and inventions

a) Pick one of these topics (1 or 2) for a short talk and think about the questions.

1 A gadget that I can't do without
- What is it?
- Why is it so important?
- What's special about it?
- When and where did you get it?
- How much did it cost?
- When do you use it?
- What would life be like without it?

2 A thing to make the world a better place
- What invention could make the world better?
- What would it look like?
- How would it work?
- How much would it cost?
- Why don't we have it now?
- Do you think it's realistic?
- When do you think we'll have it? More help p. 129

b) Make short notes for your talk.

c) Give your talk to the class (max. 2–3 minutes). Give each other feedback.

FIT FOR EXAMS

- **Structure** your talk well. You need a good introduction and summary.
- Show a **visual** – find a picture or do a drawing – and talk about it.

▸ *Skills files 9.1, p. 170; 11, pp. 179–180*

▸ *Workbook 15–16, p. 47*

3 WRITING How to complain effectively

a) Read both emails. Say briefly what each writer wants and why.

b) Do you think that both complaints are reasonable? Which email is more effective? Explain.

Dear Sir / Madam

I am writing to you because I am having problems with a fitness tracker that I bought from your shop two months ago.

1) It is very uncomfortable to wear. The idea of these trackers is to wear them all the time, but my skin gets irritated after a few hours, so I often have to take the device off.

2) The battery life is so poor that I have to recharge it every two hours. In addition, it takes a very long time to charge the battery, so that is more time when I cannot wear it.

3) The device is supposed to count my steps – but it is not accurate. I know because I counted them one day and it told me that I had done 1000 more steps than I really had.

Because of these problems I took the device back to your shop last week since I hoped that your staff would be able to solve the problem, but I was told that they could not help me. After that I sent two emails explaining the problem, but I have received no reply from you.

Under the circumstances I would like a full refund because this device does not work as it should. I attach a copy of the receipt. I look forward to hearing from you within 14 days.

Yours faithfully
Nazma Begum

I'm so fed up with this smart watch. It's really rubbish. In your adverts it said that the battery lasts for two days but that's a big lie. It doesn't even last for 8 hours. I bought it in that sale you had 3 weeks ago but I don't see why I should accept that it doesn't work well just because I got it a bit cheaper. I have the receipt. I asked the people in the shop but they were a bit vague. Oh, and another thing, the camera doesn't work very well. In the ads it says it's the best camera ever but it isn't as good as my old phone. I think you should give me my money back. You didn't reply to my last mail. Please reply to this one!

c) Analyse the first email. Describe briefly what the writer does in each paragraph and note down useful phrases. Example:

opening paragraph -> giving the general reason for the complaint (e.g. "I am writing to you because ...")

second paragraph -> adding more detailed reasons / problems (e.g. ...)

d) Rewrite the second email so that it is clearer and more effective. Make use of the structure and phrases from c).

More practice 7 p. 129

Fit for EXAMS

Complaints to businesses are usually made in **formal** letters or emails. Write politely and accurately.

▸ Skills file 10.3, p. 174

4 MEDIATION Passing on information

a) A drone advert Your friend Andrea has found an advert for a drone on a British website. But she can't understand it properly. Read the advert and answer her questions. Be careful: The advert doesn't provide everything Andrea wants to know.

Fly-Hi 100 Drone

The °latest °evolution in drone technology.
Train your flying skills with the Fly-Hi 100.
°Lightweight and easy to use.
The perfect drone for all experience levels.

- 0.3 megapixel camera with °live feed to the °remote control
- Light enough to fly indoors (500 °g)
- °Rubber feet for easy °landing
- Four °LEDs for night flights
- 30 minutes charging time

Don't forget to find out the rules for flying in your area. And always follow the rules.
This model is available from ***Chatwin Drones***.

Hi! Hab gerade eine Anzeige aus GB für eine Drohne gefunden (Link hier). Kannst du mir mit dem Englisch helfen? Was bedeutet das mit den 30 Minuten? Kann ich nur so lange damit fliegen? A. 17:23

You: …

Super, danke! Wie ist die Reichweite der Fernbedienung? Wie hoch und weit fliegt *Fly-Hi* denn überhaupt? 17:25

You: …

Sagen sie, ob ich damit Fotos machen kann? Hat das Gerät eine Beleuchtung? 17:27

You: …

Was soll das Ganze kosten, mit Versand nach Deutschland? 17:30

You: …

Steht sonst noch was Wichtiges in der Anzeige? 17:32

You: …

b) An email to the company
Write an email to *Chatwin Drones* and ask them for the information that you didn't find in the advert. Write in English, of course.

More practice 8 p.132 More challenge 5 p.132

FIT FOR EXAMS

When you mediate, think of **who** you're communicating with. If it's someone you know, use an **informal** style.
If it's a company, use a **formal** style.

▸ *Skills file 12, pp. 182–183*

▸ *Workbook 18–19, p. 50*

▸ *INKL p. 59*

5 VIEWING The Red Thunder

a) Watch the film up to 3:10. Then look at the stills below.
With a partner, complete the storyline for each scene.

1 Sarah meets Danny after school and ...

2 Sarah goes to her car, but ...

3 Sarah wants to borrow her mum's car, but ...

4 Sarah sees that ...

5 Sarah picks Danny up and ...

6 ...

b) What do you think will happen next? Make notes.
Walk around: Read your ideas to different partners. Listen to their ideas.
Then report to the class: Who do you think had the best ideas? What were they?

c) Now watch the rest of the film. Then talk in class: Were your predictions for the ending right? Do you think that it was a good ending? Why (not)?

d) Your response to the film: Discuss these questions:
- What did you find funny / sad / surprising in the film?
- What did you like or not like in the film?
- Did you notice the music in the film? If yes, in which scenes? How did it make you feel?
- Does the film remind you of any other films that you've seen? If yes, which ones?

More practice 9 p. 132 More challenge 6 p. 133

6 WRITING You and superheroes

You're going to write a text (100–180 words) about superheroes.
These questions can give you some ideas. Then plan and write your text.
- What usually happens in superhero films?
- How do superhero films usually end?
- If you were a superhero, what would your superhero powers be?
- Do you like superhero films?
- Compare and contrast this film with other superhero films that you have seen (e.g. the film *Walk or fly* in Unit 2).

▸ *Skills file 13, p. 184*

▸ KV 25 ▸ DFF 3.5 ▸ INKL pp. 60–63 ▸ INKL pp. 88–91

1 LANGUAGE Waterworld

Complete the blog with the correct form of the verbs in brackets.

All my life, science teachers … (1 tell) me that the planet is getting warmer and the sea is rising. But I … (2 not think) seriously about climate change. Then, last week I … (3 watch) a science fiction movie called *Waterworld*. It was °set in the future and it … (4 tell) the story of a terrible flood. Since then, I … (5 do) some research and I … (6 find out) that things are really serious.

> ! In paragraph one, use the ***simple past*** or ***present perfect***.
> ▸ Language file 5, p. 188

Experts believe that by 2060 more than a billion people in the world … (7 live) in cities near the coast. They also predict that °coastal cities – including London where I live – … (8 disappear) under water because of flooding. This means that in the future, more than a billion people in the world … (9 lose) their homes.

> ! In paragraph two, use the ***will*-future**.
> ▸ Language file 10, p. 190

So what can we do about it? Today governments … (10 spend) a lot of money on better flood systems, but I … (11 not think) this is the best solution. It … (12 sound) a bit crazy, but some people … (13 talk) about building cities on the water. This picture … (14 show) an interesting design by an °architect called Vincent Callebaut. He … (15 call) it the *Lilypad City*. … (16 it, not look) awesome? What a great idea!

> ! In paragraph three, use the ***simple present*** or ***present progressive***.
> ▸ Language files 1–2, pp. 185–186

2 LANGUAGE Rubbish island

Choose the correct form of the verbs (***active / passive***) to complete the article. // ● p. 133

Richart Sowa

°Nowadays plastic waste … (1 sees / is seen) as a big problem. In Mexico the artist Richart Sowa likes creating things from rubbish. Years ago he … (2 started / was started) collecting bags of empty plastic °jars and bottles. Then he … (3 used / was used) the rubbish to build an island on a lake, called *Joyxee Island*. More and more plastic bottles … (4 added / were added). Today his island … (5 makes / is made) of more than 150,000 °containers. Trees and bushes … (6 °planted / were planted) on the island to keep Richart's house cool. This is Richart's third island. His °previous two islands … (7 destroyed / were destroyed) by hurricanes.

▸ Language file 33, p. 205

▸ KV 25 ▸ INKL pp. 60–63 ▸ INKL pp. 88–91

3 WORDS The right word

a) Find a suitable English word for *Platz* in these sentences.

1 Wird es in Zukunft ausreichend *Platz* auf unserem Planeten geben?
2 Nach dem Sturm war nichts mehr an seinem *Platz*.
3 Der FC Liverpool ist auf *Platz* drei.
4 Bitte machen Sie *Platz* für den Krankenwagen.
5 Unsere Schule hat einen Tennis*platz* und einen Fußball*platz*.
6 Nehmen Sie bitte *Platz*.

Platz *Substantiv*
1 *(freier Raum)* room, space
2 *(Sitzplatz)* seat **~nehmen** to take a seat
3 *(Ort, Stelle)* place **an seinem ~** in its ~
4 *(Spielfeld)* field, beim Volleyball; Tennis court
5 **für jemanden/etwas ~ machen** make room for sb./sth.
6 **auf dem ersten/zweiten/... ~** in first/ second/... place

b) Use a dictionary to find suitable English words for *einfach* and *schwer* in these sentences.

EINFACH
1 Diese Zukunftsaufgabe ist für die Menschheit nicht *einfach*.
2 Eine *einfache* Fahrt nach Hannover, bitte.
3 Seine Idee ist *einfach* toll.

SCHWER
4 Was für eine *schwere* Tasche!
5 Die Aufgabe war sehr *schwer (schwierig)*.
6 Manchmal ist das Leben *schwer (nicht leicht)*.

c) Find a suitable German word for the underlined words in these sentences. You can use a dictionary.

MARK
1 Their dog is white with brown °marks.
2 I got °full marks in the maths test.
3 Take all the boxes that are marked with an X.

RUN
4 I can run a °marathon in less than 3 hours.
5 Hurry up, time is running out.
6 My friend runs an online business.

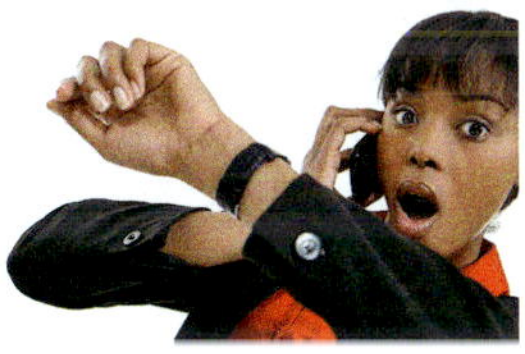

LOW
7 Food prices are low at the moment.
8 Everybody goes through °highs and lows.

d) Use a dictionary to complete the text.
In order to save our planet we have to change our ... (1 Lebensstil, drastisch). We need to act quickly to reduce ... (2 giftige Emissionen). Cars and trucks are a big problem, so we must use more ... (3 alternative Transportarten). And, as °pollution knows no ... (4 Grenzen), international ... (5 Zusammenarbeit) is ... (6 dringend notwendig).

More challenge 7 p. 134

▸ KV 25 ▸ DFF 3.1 ▸ INKL pp. 60–63 ▸ INKL pp. 88–91

4 WORDS Don't end it, °mend it!

Complete the text with the correct option (A, B, C or D).

People all over the world are organizing °repair cafes and repairing thousands of things every month. Have you ... (1) of this °initiative? Repair cafes are free and they are all about repairing things instead of throwing them ... (2). In a repair cafe °tools and materials are ... (3) to help you repair °electrical °appliances, bicycles, furniture, toys, etc. You'll also find expert volunteers, with all kinds of repair skills. Visitors bring ... (4) broken items. The °specialists help them to get started with their repairs. If you have nothing to repair, you can enjoy a cup of tea or coffee. Or you can help someone else ... (5) their repair job. For sustainable living, repairing things is ... (6) °reusing things. But most of all, repair cafes show how ... (7) fun and how easy repairing things can be.

A repair cafe

1	A ever gone	B ever heard	C ever listened	D ever seen
2	A in	B away	C across	D up
3	A sold	B selling	C provided	D provide
4	A their	B there	C her	D they're
5	A which	B where	C when	D with
6	A so important	B as important as	C most important	D important
7	A lots of	B lot	C many	D much

5 LISTENING My generation makes a difference

2.16

a) Hannah, a 16-year-old high school student in Melbourne, interviews three friends for her blog. They talk about young people making a difference. Which themes are discussed?

1 Own web campaigns
2 Dangers of social media
3 One meatless °weekday
4 Work and travel
5 Sustainable clothes
6 Personal worries
7 Car sharing

b) Listen again and complete the sentences with 1–6 words.

1 Elizabeth suggests giving up meat for one day a week because you can save ...
2 Naomi wants people to °donate their ...
3 Naomi is proud to be a member of a ...
4 Cooper thinks that things like music, movies and fashion are ...
5 Cooper is sure that teenagers can have a real °impact on ...
6 Hannah wants young people to share their worries and hopes with ...

c) Now you: Do you feel you can make a difference? What's important to you? Write a comment for Hannah's blog. Write about 80–100 words.

► DFF 3.3 ► DFF 3.8 ► INKL pp. 60–63 ► INKL pp. 88–91

6 MEDIATION An online chat with Eino

You are chatting with your Finnish friend, Eino. He has seen a selfie with the hashtag *#fixitselfie* and wants to know more. He has found the information below but he can't understand German. Answer Eino's chat questions.

What are the aims of the campaign?

How can I take part?

Why is the campaign important? (Give 3 reasons.)

Wegwerfen? Nein danke!

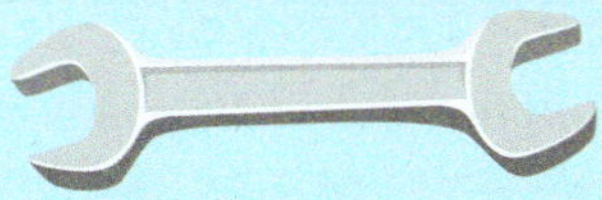

Die Europäische Nachhaltigkeitswoche steht vor der Tür. Auch du kannst mitmachen!

Reparieren ist zu unrecht out: Neue Dinge, die wir im Geschäft kaufen, sind oft nicht einfach zu reparieren. Sie werden hergestellt, um nur einige Jahre zu halten. Auch sind neue Produkte meist so billig, dass eine professionelle Reparatur oft nicht lohnt.

Das muss sich ändern! Reparieren soll sich wieder lohnen. Deshalb hat sich die Repair-Cafe-Stiftung zum Ziel gesetzt, Reparaturen zurück in unseren Alltag zu bringen und wertvolle Reparaturkenntnisse nicht zu verlieren. Warum ist das wichtig? Reparaturen helfen der Umwelt: Abfall wird reduziert, wertvolle Ressourcen und Energie werden eingespart, CO_2-Emissionen werden gesenkt.

So geht's: Zeig uns, was du repariert hast! Mach ein Foto von einem Gegenstand, den du im vergangenen Jahr repariert hast - oder hast reparieren lassen. Poste dieses Foto mit dem Hashtag *#fixitselfie* bis zum 08.06. auf sozialen Netzwerken. Attraktive Preise erwarten dich! Dein Foto hilft dabei, Menschen weltweit auf das Problem aufmerksam zu machen.

7 SPEAKING Is it better to recycle or buy new?

You're going to discuss if it's better to buy new things or to buy second-hand things and repair things. Read your role cards and prepare your arguments.
Try to think of your own ideas and examples to support your arguments.
Partner B: Go to p. 101.

Partner A:
You feel it's better to repair things or buy second-hand things.
Here are some of your arguments:

- cost (cheaper than new things)
- fun, creative
- more unusual and individual
- feel proud / good about yourself
- learn about how things work
- use less energy and reduce pollution

Goodbye and good luck

Wichtigen Wortschatz von diesen Seiten findest du im Vocabulary auf S. 238.

1 Making a graduation speech

When students graduate from high school in the US, it is common for one student to make a speech to say goodbye to classmates and celebrate their time together. The suggestions below come from a website giving advice on what to include in a graduation speech.

Things you could include in a graduation speech:
- thanks (e.g. to teachers, °fellow students, parents, coaches, ...)
- stories about classmates, teachers, trips, ...
- personal memories of time with the class
- what you have learned at this school
- where you and others will be in the future
- your advice to classmates
- a song, a poem, a joke, ...

2.17 **a)** Listen to Maya's speech. Which things on the list did she include?

2.17 **b)** Listen again and make notes about these questions.
1 What visuals do you think she included?
2 Which piece of advice do you like best?

c) How would you rate the speech? Explain your opinion. Refer to the advice below.

Simple rules for a successful speech
- **Keep it short.** Don't bore people.
- **Say nice things.** Don't °embarrass or be hurtful in your comments.
- **Make it personal.** Include everybody. Don't make it about you and your friends!
- **Include some °humour.** People love funny speeches.
- **Use short sentences.** They're easier to understand.
- **Repeat key words and phrases.**

d) **Discuss:** How is a speech different to a presentation?

2 NOW YOU A speech for your class

a) If you were preparing a speech like this for your class, what kind of things would you include? Discuss your ideas.
Then, working on your own, write a speech for your class, celebrating the end of Year 10. Try to follow the advice above.

b) Practise your speech, and then deliver it to your class or group. Ask for feedback.

3 LANGUAGE More on the passive

a) Complete the FOCUS box.

FOCUS

1 Here are some examples of ***passives*** from the speech.
- You will be °robbed!
- Your problems will not be solved in 30 minutes.
- I was sent this photo of you all.

a) Make these into ***active*** sentences. Begin with *Someone …* or *No one …*

b) Compare. What are the main differences between the ***passive*** and ***active*** sentences?

▸ *Language file 33, pp. 205–206*

2 In German you don't always use the ***passive*** in the same way as in English. How could you put the three ***passive*** sentences in **1** into German?

b) Complete the sentences. Use the ***simple past*** or ***past perfect*** (***active*** or ***passive*** forms).

1 When Maya first … (join) the class two years ago she … (welcome) by the other students.
2 They … (impress) her with their friendliness.
3 At the beginning of this year Maya … (elected) °class representative.
4 When she … (ask) to °give a graduation speech to the class, it made her nervous.
5 She … (prepare) by looking at examples of speeches that … (give) by other students.
6 She wanted a fun way to start her speech, so she … (show) an old photo of the class.
7 After Maya … (finished) her speech, everybody … (cheer) loudly.
8 Then another speech … (give) by the principal, Mr Connolly.
9 At the end Mr Connolly … (invite) to come to the front of the class again.
10 He … (give) a big card and a box of his favourite chocolates from all the students.

4 WORDS Useful °expressions

a) Translate the underlined phrases into German.
- You'°re expected to do so much homework in Year 10!
- You're supposed to be so serious.
- Here's an important lesson for life: Don't °have your nails done before rock climbing!
- Our teachers make us work hard, but we don't mind.
- On Fridays they let us eat fries.

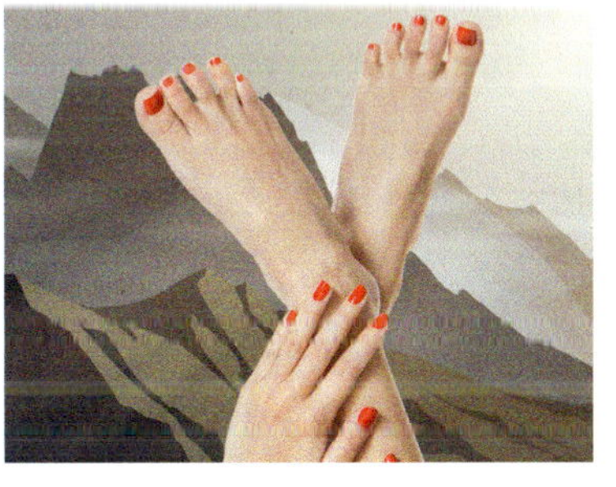

b) Complete the sentences for yourself.

1 At school we're expected to … because we're in year 10.
2 At home I'm supposed to … , but I usually don't.
3 I'm going to have my hair cut because …
4 My mum (dad / sister / brother / friend) makes me … , but I don't mind.
5 It's great when our teachers let us …

Students who are getting ready for their final exams (level B1, Mittlerer Schulabschluss) will find extra practice here. (For level A2/A2+, Hauptschulabschluss, go to pp. 92 ff.)

1 The environment and me

3.01

You will hear three short dialogues. You will hear them twice. Choose the correct picture – A, B or C – for each question.

1 What's the problem?

A

B

C

2 What's the right slogan?

A

B

C

3 Which shoes are they talking about?

A

B

C

2 The interview

3.02

You will hear a job interview. Read the eight statements below first, then listen to the interview. You will hear it twice. Are the statements true or false?

1 Daryl is still at school.
2 Daryl's dad does all the cooking at home.
3 Daryl has never worked in a restaurant before.
4 His favourite job is making salads.
5 He's good at working with other people.
6 The new job is a full-time job.
7 It's in a busy restaurant.
8 Daryl can start today.

▸ KV 26 ▸ KV 27 A–B ▸ KV 28 A–B

3 That's a nice car!

3.03

Three young people meet at a youth hostel in Germany – Stefan from Bielefeld, Taylor from Los Angeles and Julie from Liverpool. Taylor is showing the others some photos on her tablet. Listen and pick the right ending. There is only one possible answer per statement.

1 Taylor has had her car ...
- A for twenty years.
- B for fourteen years.
- C for at least three years.

2 With a hardship license in California ...
- A you can drive everywhere when you're 14.
- B you can only drive five miles.
- C you can only drive to school.

3 With a provisional licence in the UK ...
- A you can drive alone.
- B you have to drive with an adult.
- C you can't drive if you're 17.

4 With a provisional license in California ...
- A you must drive with someone over 21.
- B you can't take any passengers.
- C you can't drive between 11 p.m. and 5 a.m.

5 The way people get around in Germany is similar to the way they get around ...
- A in California.
- B in the UK.
- C in the US.

6 In the US most people ...
- A don't go to the shops.
- B go by bus to the shops.
- C drive to the shops.

4 Language change

3.04

Listen to the talk about how much the English language has changed. Then copy the table and complete the information below. You can listen to the talk twice.

1 Who was Shakespeare?	a famous writer
2 When did he live?	about ... years ago
3 Number of English speakers in 1600:	...
4 Number of native English speakers today:	...
5 Where native English speakers live today:	...
6 Modern words that Shakespeare wouldn't understand at all (two examples):	... ...
7 Words that Shakespeare used, but we use differently today (two examples):	... ...
8 Shakespeare probably wouldn't be against language change because (one reason):	...

5 Teens and their parents

3.05 Listen to these people talking about what teens and their parents fight about. You will hear the recording twice.
Who thinks what? Match the people (1–6) and the statements A–G.
Be careful – there is one more statement than you need.

A Most fights happen when I'm in a bad mood.

B My parents are always checking on me.

C I want to find a compromise, but my parents won't even discuss my ideas.

D The problem is that my parents try too hard to understand me.

E There's just no communication between me and my parents.

F There are no big issues between me and my parents.

G My parents treat me like a child.

1 Jess	2 Malik	3 Molly	4 Ethan	5 Kelly	6 Robbie

6 Just imagine – a refugee's journey

a) Part 1 Leaving home: First read the sentences 1–7. Then listen to part 1 and complete the sentences with a few words for each gap.
3.06

1. At the start of the story, the speaker's life seems ...
2. However, things change when one night soldiers take ...
3. When the teenager comes home from work, his mother is crying because ...
4. The teenager meets ...
5. The journey across the desert is extremely hard because the weather ...
6. The truck hits something on the road and ...
7. The journey across the sea is dangerous because ...

b) Part 2 In Europe: First read the tasks 1–6. Then listen to part 2 and answer the questions in one to five words.
3.07

1. When the teenager gets to Italy, his life is very hard. Give two reasons.
2. Who helps the teenager on his journey to Calais (two examples)?
3. How do people in the camp help? Name two things that they give the teenager.
4. What parts of his body does the teenager hurt when he's trying to get to England (3 answers)?
5. How long does the teenager spend in the refugee camp in France?
6. Why does the teenager think he was lucky in the end?

▸ *KV 29 A–B*

1 "I'm a European"

This text appeared on youthreporter, a website for young Europeans who are studying or working in other countries.

Europe. Here in Italy the word makes people think about the continent, and of course the economic crisis. People don't really think about a big community. Even I, an 18-year-old girl, have always felt Italian and not European. Well, this was true until last October when I had the chance to go to Berlin and spend three weeks learning German. This gave me the chance to cross physical and psychological boundaries.

At first I was a little unsure. For me Berlin was just the German capital, a cold city, a place where the German politicians complain about Italy's economic politics. And in the beginning I was worried about living with a host family, away from my friends.

But I was completely wrong. My journey turned into a wonderful experience. I discovered a modern and beautiful city full of young people from all over Europe. And I lost my prejudices about German people. Here in Italy people are warm and passionate, but I expected people from the north of Europe to be cold and detached. How wrong I was! My host family welcomed me, made me feel comfortable, showed me places where real Berlin people go, prepared my breakfast every morning, treated me like a daughter, helped me when I felt a little homesick because I was so far from my family.

I changed my opinion about German. I had thought that it was a rough-sounding language. Now I know it can be as romantic as the Eiffel Tower at night. This was the best experience ever as I met new people and I lost the narrow-minded way of thinking of my little town in the south of Italy. I learned to be a European.

a) In which paragraph (1–4) can you find the following information?

A The writer wasn't very enthusiastic about going to Berlin.
B Berlin is an international city.
C The writer thinks differently now about the German language.
D Why the writer went to Berlin.
E In the past, the writer's image of northern Europeans wasn't so positive.

b) Decide whether the following statements are true or false.
Give the line(s) in which you find the information.

1 The European identity is strong in Italy.
2 The writer is Italian.
3 She stayed in a Berlin hotel.
4 The writer enjoyed her time in Berlin.
5 She changed her opinion about German people.
6 She never missed home.
7 She feels differently about being European now.

2 The Bracelet by Ann Angel

1 Trevor never said hello when he came into my house. He just made himself comfortable on one of the kitchen stools. Today was no different, only when I sat down beside him, he pressed[1] warm metal into my palm[2] and closed my hand around it.

"Here," he said. Trevor was a guy of few words. I opened my palm to reveal[3] a silver charm bracelet. There was a silver heart locket at the centre. The bracelet was beautiful.

"Happy birthday," Trevor said. I looked from the bracelet to him, guessing what it might signify[4].

"It's your birthday, right?"

"Yeah, it's my birthday." I closed my hand around the bracelet, feeling its weight. The bracelet seemed like something you'd give a girl you thought you loved. Trevor and I had only been on two dates so far. His eyes searched my face to read my reaction.

"Thank you," I said, unsure what to think. I slid a fingernail under the heart locket and popped it open. Someone had put a piece of pink paper in each half of the heart. One side said "Worth Loving". The handwriting looked girlish, nothing like Trevor's handwriting. I looked again to see if my best friend Kat had written these words, but they were too nice for Kat's handwriting. The bracelet must have cost a lot.

2 Trevor cleared his throat[5] and said "Which birthday is it?"

"Sixteen. My family doesn't do parties," I explained before he could ask. "My mom usually makes a dinner for our birthdays. I think Kat's invited." He would already know Kat was coming. They shared about four classes and talked a lot. In fact, I had always thought those two would make a good couple and was surprised when Trevor asked me out. I looked at the bracelet. Had Trevor searched through the lockets to make sure his said "Worth Loving"? If he had gone to the trouble[6] of asking someone with nice handwriting to write the message for me, it meant something. I wasn't sure how I felt about him though.

"This bracelet is really pretty," I said. But I couldn't accept it. I didn't like Trevor enough to call him "Worth Loving".

"I gotta go to track practice or coach will kill me." He was off the stool, brushing a kiss on my cheek as he passed, and almost at the back door before he turned and added, "Maybe I'll come over later. After dinner."

He was gone before I had a chance to answer.

3 My mother came in with the twins – they were arguing. She put groceries down on the table and turned to Will and Josh. "Boys, I told you to knock it off[7] in the grocery store. And in the bakery. Now I'm telling you to knock it off in this house!"

---

[1]press [pres] *drücken* [2]palm [pɑːm] *Hand(fläche)* [3]reveal [rɪˈviːl] *zeigen, zum Vorschein bringen* [4]signify [ˈsɪɡnɪfaɪ] *bedeuten, signalisieren* [5]clear one's throat *sich räuspern* [6]go to the trouble *sich die Mühe machen* [7]knock it off *(infml)* *aufhören*

► KV 29 A–B

Josh punched[8] Will in the shoulder. "Yeah, jackass[9]".
"Josh and Will! Get Kelly's birthday cake out of the van!"
I warned, "That cake will be in pieces if you let one of them get it." I stood and put the bracelet on the table. "I'll get it."
"What's that?" Mom asked.
"A gift from Trevor."
She picked it up. "Are you and Trevor serious?"
"I didn't think so. But he's coming over later. He knows he's not invited for dinner."
I went upstairs. I wondered just what the value of this bracelet was.

4 Kat turned up later. As she lined her eyes she told me she was with Trevor when he stole the bracelet.
"The note was inside. It doesn't mean anything," she said. "The bracelets were near the door when we walked out of the store."
My stomach turned sour[10]. "So the bracelet is stolen?" I stared at the bracelet. "It means nothing."
I dropped the bracelet. Kat looked at it.
"Do you want the bracelet?" I asked.
"Of course not. He gave it to you," she answered.
"I don't really like it," I said.
Actually I didn't really like Kat all that much right now. And I didn't think I could stand[11] Trevor.
"Go ahead. Take the bracelet. It's yours," I told her.

---

[8]punch [pʌntʃ] *jn. boxen, mit den Fäusten schlagen* [9]jackass [ˈdʒækæs] *(AE, infml) Idiot* [10]my stomach turned sour [ˈsaʊə] *Mir wurde schlecht* [11]stand sb./sth. *jn./etwas aushalten, ertragen*

a) Match the correct heading (A – F) to each paragraph (1 – 4).
Be careful – there are two headings more than you need.

A **The family comes home**
B **Feeling disappointed**
C **A nice cake**
D **A birthday present**
E **The birthday party**
F **Boyfriend and girlfriend or not?**

b) Finish the sentences using words and phrases from the text.

1 When the writer looked at the present, she thought that the bracelet …
2 She didn't know Trevor very well because they …
3 When she opened the locket, the handwriting didn't look …
4 Trevor and Kat knew each other quite well because …
5 Trevor planned to come back after …
6 The two brothers were arguing everywhere, for example …
7 The bracelet was easy to steal from the store because …
8 In the end we know that the writer doesn't want the bracelet because she says, "…"

c) Find the information in the text. Give the line numbers.

1 The birthday present from Trevor surprised the writer. Give two reasons from the text.
2 The writer is an honest person. Prove this from the text.
3 Trevor doesn't know a lot about the writer. Find an example in the text to show this.
4 By the end of the story we know that the writer is disappointed. Give two reasons.

d) Answer the questions in complete sentences.

1 What do we learn about the narrator and her family?
2 What do we learn about Trevor's personality? (Name at least two things.)
3 Why doesn't the narrator like Kat in the end?

3 School in different places

1 Schooling on the move

Kelsie's family are fairground people[1]. So from about April to October the family is on the move around the UK. That makes going to school difficult. "We move every week or fortnight[2] to a new funfair. So I go to a school near our yard in the winter and in the summer I use 'distance learning' while we are travelling," explains Kelsie. "I get a work pack from school and I send my work in by email."

In fairground families, everyone helps out. "I do all sorts, I help with the machines – replacing light bulbs[3] and fixing things if they break. And I help out on our burger stand too." With these distractions[4] it isn't always easy to find the time to do school work. But Kelsie's parents make sure she keeps up with her school work. "I find that because my address says 'caravan site' some people expect I will be uninterested in my education. It's true that it's sometimes difficult for me to do my school work because of the way that I live. But I think I am actually more organized than most students, and I am very good at solving problems."

2 A day in the life of a homeschool student in Canada

We start school around 10 am. I get my planner, tablet, and computer and set to work. I don't work on all subjects every day. My mom lets me choose how to get my work done in the week. I just have to have it done by Sunday. My mom normally helps my brother and sister, but she is always available to answer any questions that I might have. If she can't figure something out[5], she looks it up on the internet. I work until lunchtime. I eat my lunch and then go back to work. I normally stop school around 2–3.

I think I'm lucky to be homeschooled. I didn't like 'normal school' – bells telling me when and where to go, wearing the same clothes as everyone else. I am very happy with the freedom that homeschooling gives me. I don't have to wait for others once I have understood a lesson. This allows me to spend time on things I enjoy, such as reading history books or being involved in extra-curricular activities.

3 Boat schools in Bangladesh

During the monsoon season in Bangladesh a third of the country floods as the continuous rainfall causes rivers to overflow. In some areas, roads are closed from July to October, when rivers rise as much as 12 feet. When the rain comes, thousands of schools have to close because of flooding and children's schooling is interrupted. Now an organization is bringing floating[6] schools to flood-prone[7] areas of the country. Their boats are outfitted with solar panels that power computers, lights and other equipment.

The floating schools collect children from their homes, teach them on board and return them at the end of the session. Then the school-boat moves on to the next village. Each boat has a classroom for 30 students and internet-linked computers and electronic resources.

[1]fairground people [ˈfeəgraʊnd] *Schausteller/innen* [2]fortnight [ˈfɔːtnaɪt] *zwei Wochen* [3]light bulb [bʌlb] *Glühbirne* [4]distraction [dɪˈstrækʃn] *Ablenkung* [5]figure sth. out *etwas herausbekommen* [6]float [fləʊt] *schwimmen* [7]...-prone [prəʊn] *...-anfällig*

a) Find the texts (1–3) that match the following descriptions:

A In this text you learn about a project to help students who can't go to school because of bad weather conditions.

B This text tells you about the personal experience of someone who never spends time in a regular school classroom.

C This text is about someone whose schooling is affected by the work that her family does.

b) Decide if these statements are true or false, then complete the sentences. You can quote from the text.

1 Kelsie has learned to be an independent learner.
This statement is (A) *true* (B) *false because the text says …*

2 Kelsie's family don't think that education is important.
This statement is (A) *true* (B) *false because the text says …*

3 The homeschool student works independently.
This statement is (A) *true* (B) *false because the text says …*

4 The Bangladeshi boat schools can create their own electricity.
This statement is (A) *true* (B) *false because the text says …*

c) Choose the correct solution.

1 In the summer months Kelsie doesn't
(A) find time for her school work.
(B) contact her teachers.
(C) go to school.
(D) stay interested in her school work.

2 The homeschool student
(A) misses being at a normal school.
(B) doesn't have time for extra-curricular activities.
(C) wishes there were more opportunities for sports.
(D) likes working at his own tempo.

3 All three types of schooling
(A) make use of the internet.
(B) are very common.
(C) use distance learning.
(D) are designed for kids who don't like normal school.

d) Scan text 1. Give two reasons why it's hard for fairground children to concentrate on their school work in the summer.

e) Scan text 2. Give two reasons why this student prefers homeschooling to normal school.

f) In text 3 the floating school boats are a combination of school bus and school house. Explain.

▸ KV 31 A–B

1 An interesting weekend

Du möchtest zum *Climate Change Challenge Weekend* nach Irland. Du hast den Flyer ausgedruckt und möchtest einige Mitschülerinnen und Mitschüler dafür begeistern mitzukommen. Beantworte ihre Fragen. Schreibe die Antworten in Stichpunkten auf.

a) Worum geht es?
b) Wo und wann findet das statt?
c) Welche Aktivitäten werden angeboten?
d) Wie ist die Verpflegung organisiert?
e) Wie ist die Unterbringung?
f) Was kostet sie?
g) Wie läuft die Anmeldung?
h) Wann ist Anmeldeschluss?

Trocaire

Working for a just world

CLIMATE CHANGE Challenge Weekend

Date: 1st – 3rd July
Location: Maynooth University, Ireland

Are you 15 – 17 years old?

Are you ready to act on climate change?

Do you want to:
- learn about the causes of climate change?
- experience the effects of climate change?
- become part of the fight for climate justice[1]?

What's involved?
Throughout the weekend you will examine the causes, effects and possible ways to tackle climate change. You will:
- take part in workshops.
- listen to guest speakers.
- do a climate change disaster simulation.
- watch documentary films.

We will also have a variety of entertainment in the evening to help participants, team leaders and staff unwind and relax.

Accommodation and catering details:
- All meals will be catered for, including special dietary requirements[2].
- Accommodation is provided in dormitories on the university campus.

To apply:
- Cost for the weekend: £25 / EUR 30
- For more information and application forms, please contact the Trocaire office.
- Closing date: 18th June

Your planet needs YOU!
Will you act?

[1]justice ['dʒʌstɪs] *Gerechtigkeit* [2]dietary requirements *(pl)* ['daɪətəri rɪ'kwaɪəmənts] *Ernährungsbedürfnisse*

▸ KV 31 A–B

2 Let's go in-line skating

Amira is new in Cologne. She has just come to Germany and has started to learn German, but she doesn't speak it very well yet. However, she speaks English well. Amira wants to go in-line skating, but she has never done it before. You have a friend, Luisa, who loves skating. But her English isn't very good. Help Amira to get the information that she needs.

Amira Skating looks fun, I'd love to try it. Can you ask Luisa if there's an in-line skating club here in Cologne?

You …

Luisa Ja, es gibt mehrere. Ich bin beim *Speed Team* – ein super Verein! Amira kann zum nächsten Treffen am Freitag mitkommen, wenn sie will.

You …

Amira That's great. Please tell Luisa that I'm a beginner. Ask her if I can learn to skate at the club.

You …

Luisa Ja, sicher. Ich kann es ihr beibringen. Ist ja leicht zu lernen. Amira hat wahrscheinlich keine Ausrüstung, oder?

You …

Amira No, I have nothing. What do I need – just the in-line skates?

You …

Luisa Ja, natürlich die Skates zuerst. Meine Schwester hat welche, Amira kann sie ausleihen. Die beiden haben etwa die gleiche Schuhgröße. Und dann braucht sie auch einen Helm und Gelenkschützer für Handgelenke, Knie und Ellenbogen – die sind besonders wichtig.

You …

Amira That's great, thanks. I'm really excited about trying. Where should we meet on Friday?

You …

Luisa Am Freitag ab 17 Uhr sind wir am Fühlinger See. Hier ist eine kleine Karte, mit einigen Hinweisen. Kannst du bitte Amira das Wichtigste erklären?

You *(For example: Where can you skate? How many kilometres? Is there any traffic there? Where do you begin? How can you get there? Do you have to be good at skating?)*

Amira I'm really looking forward to Friday. Please say a big thanks to Luisa.

You …

Skating am Fühlinger See

Wo: Fühlinger See, Köln-Seeberg
Länge: Länge: 8,5km (einmal um die Regattastrecke und wieder zurück)
Belag: feiner Asphalt
Hinweis: Die Strecke wird auch von Spaziergängern und Sportlern genutzt.
Start: Parkplatz P1 (Oranjehofstraße)
Schwierigkeit: für Anfänger geeignet
ÖPNV: Tram 12 bis Merkenich, dann Bus 121 bis Oranjehofstraße

1 Principals and principles[1] by Daniel Handler

In San Francisco the weather never gets hot, and when it does it lasts only three days. On the first day, the hot weather is a surprise, and everyone wanders around carrying their sweaters. On the second day, everyone enjoys the heat. And on the third day, the cold weather returns and it is just as surprising, and everyone wanders around shivering[2].

One of these three-day heat waves arrived when I was in seventh grade, and on the first day everyone was grumpy[3] because we had all dressed for fog and gloom[4] and now had to drag our sweaters all over school. We all agreed that the next day we'd dress for warm weather, but just as the day ended, the principal made an announcement over the loudspeaker. "Students at Herbert Hoover Middle School are not allowed to wear shorts," she said, in the tone of voice she always used – a tone of voice that sounded friendly but was actually unbearably wicked[5].

Everyone groaned – everyone but me. "She can't do that," I said, and reached into the back of my binder. On the first day of school, we'd all received a pamphlet: "Student Rights and Responsibilities." For some reason I'd saved it, and I read one of our rights out loud: "Students have the right to free dress." I convinced[6] everyone to wear shorts the next day in order to protest the wicked principal's unfair cancellation[7] of one of our rights.

The next day was wonderful because we were all dressed for the heat and nobody had to drag their sweaters around, but of course, I was sent to the principal's office – someone had ratted on[8] me. (To this day I suspect[9] Nancy Cutler, but I can't prove it.)
I said that free dress was one of our rights. She said that she was the principal and she was in charge[10]. I said that free dress was one of our rights. She kept pointing at me. I kept pointing at the pamphlet. The principal was one of those people who shouted at you until you cried, but I forced myself not to cry, biting my lip and blinking[11] very, very fast, until at last she gave up and I was allowed to return to my classmates, who applauded me. In celebration, we all wore shorts the next day, too, even though we knew the cold weather would return, and it did, and we were shivering and miserable.

In eighth grade we got a new version of the pamphlet. Instead of "Students have the right to free dress," it read "Students have the responsibility to dress appropriately." I threw it away.

If you stand up for your rights, you can count on the fact that the wicked people will find sneaky ways to change the rules. But you should stand up for your rights anyway, because there aren't enough sunny days in the world, and everyone should enjoy them.

[1]principle [ˈprɪnsəpl] *Prinzip* [2]shiver [ˈʃɪvə] *zittern* (vor Kälte) [3]grumpy *(infml)* [ˈɡrʌmpi] *mürrisch, brummig* [4]gloom [ɡluːm] *düstere Stimmung* [5]unbearably wicked [ʌnˈbeərəbli ˈwɪkɪd] *unerträglich bösartig* [6]convince [kənˈvɪns] *überzeugen* [7]cancellation [kænsəˈleɪʃn] *Aufhebung, Ungültigkeitserklärung* [8]rat on sb. *(infml) jn. verpfeifen, verraten* [9]suspect sb. [səˈspekt] *jn.verdächtigen* [10]be in charge *das Sagen / die Leitung haben* [11]blink [blɪŋk] *blinzeln*

▸ KV 32 A ▸ KV 32 B

- Read the tasks carefully.
- Write complete sentences.
- Make sure to write about all the aspects presented in each task.

a) Describe the narrator of this story. What do you learn about his or her life and personality? Give reasons for your opinion.

b) The narrator and the principal have different opinions about school clothes.
Explain the two opinions and say how they are different.

c) You have a choice here. Choose **one** of the following tasks.

1 *Students have the right to free dress.* (lines 16–17)

Comment on this statement from your point of view. Include the following aspects:
- Write about the **pros** and **cons** of rules about school clothes and uniforms.
- Give your personal opinion about free dress at school.
- Give examples from your experience at school.

or

2 *The next day I went to school wearing a new T-shirt. On the back it said "School is for idiots". That wasn't a good idea ...*

Continue in the way the story is told. Include the following aspects:
- the reactions of different people, e.g. other students, teachers and of course the principal,
- your opinion about this slogan,
- what happened in the end.

2 An email from the US

Here's part of an email from Alice, an American teenager.

Subject: What's next?

What's next?

This year I'm a Senior here at Norton High. So it's my last year at school. I'm both happy and sad about that – happy that I'm moving on to new things, sad that I'm leaving all my friends after so many years together. But life must go on. After the summer I'm going to go to a technical college in Santa Monica, California. What about you? When are you going to finish school? Are you going to study or are you going to do an apprenticeship[1]?

I want to learn to be a sound engineer. I'd love to work in the music industry some day – that'd be my dream. What kind of a job would you like to do later? Is it easy to find work in Germany? Or would you like to work abroad?

My friend's mom works at a recording studio here in LA and I've done some work experience there. It's a really cool job – you get to work with some great musicians and singers. Have you done any work experience? What was it like? ...

Write an email back to Alice and answer her questions. Write about 120–150 words.

[1] apprenticeship [əˈprentɪʃɪp] *Ausbildung, Lehre*

► KV 32 B

3 The story behind the picture

What is the story behind the picture? Imagine that this young woman is your friend. Write about the following aspects:

- Who is this young woman?
- Where is she?
- What is she doing?
- What has happened?
- How is she feeling?
- How did you help her?
- What will happen next?

Write about 150 words.

4 Creative writing

Choose one topic. Write a text of about 150–180 words. Count your words.

a) A blog entry:
Your family is planning to emigrate to South Africa. Write about how you feel about the move and leaving your home and friends.
What will you miss?
What are you looking forward to in your new home?
What will be exciting, fun, strange, difficult, different, etc.?
Write a blog entry about all this.

b) An article for an online travel magazine:
Think of a nice place that you've visited, or would like to visit. Describe it. Explain why you think it's so good. Give advice on the best time to go there, places to visit, activities, food, etc. Mention any interesting customs and traditions. Write a short article for an online travel magazine.

c) A diary entry:
A special day in my life
Think of a family celebration, a trip to a nice place, a great day with friends, an adventure, meeting someone special or any nice experience that you've had. Describe it. Say why it was so special. What were your feelings and thoughts?

Write a diary entry about this special day in your life.

d) A recommendation:
Think of a TV show, a film, a game or a book that you love. Think about these questions:
- Why do think it's so good?
- What do you like most about it?
- How often have you watched, played or read it? When?
- What do your friends or family think about it?
- Why would you recommend it? Is everything about it good?
- Do you have any criticisms?

Write a recommendation for a school magazine.

1 A great place to live

a) Describe the pictures. What can you see?

b) Talk about where you live and what it's like. Discuss the advantages and disadvantages.

c) If you could live anywhere in the world, where would that be?
Describe what it would be like. Give reasons for your answer.

2 Watch out!

a) What do you think the two people might say to each other? How are they feeling?

b) Talk about the dangers of cycling. How can cyclists stay safe on the roads?

c) Some people say there are too many cars on our roads. What do you think? Explain.

d) Would you like to learn to drive? Why (not)?

3 At a youth hostel

Situation: You've just checked into a youth hostel in the centre of Berlin. Pick one role card and read your role. Think about what you want to say, then speak to your partner.

Partner A

Your name is Julia/Alex. You're from Stuttgart and you're visiting Berlin for a week with your two friends. You've been in Berlin before, so you know the city quite well. You really like the zoo and also the Reichstag and you want to visit them again.
You see another traveller at the youth hostel reception, reading a travel guide in English.
You start a conversation.

> Find out some information about the other traveller.
> Suggest doing something together.

Partner B

Your name is Steven/Tanya. You're from Aberdeen in Scotland and you're visiting Berlin for the first time. You've just arrived and you don't know the city. You're here for three days. You don't speak much German and you're alone because your friend couldn't come.
You're at the reception and you're looking at your travel guide for some ideas, when someone speaks to you.

> Chat to the other person and ask him/her some questions.
> Ask for some tips for Berlin.

4 Congratulations!

Imagine that you and two friends have just won a competition. The prize – a one-week holiday together. You have five options. Discuss all of them, their advantages and disadvantages. Then decide together on one holiday.

Congratulations! You have won a week away!

Hiking in the Scottish Highlands

A beach holiday on the coast in Spain

A city visit – any city in Germany

A boat trip on the River Shannon, Ireland

A cycling tour of the Cotswold Hills in England

▸ KV 33 C ▸ KV 33 D

5 A conversation about part-time jobs

Talk about the jobs below. Ask your partner questions and react to your partner's opinions. You must keep the conversation going for at least 3 minutes.

- Would you like to do any of these jobs? Why (not)?
- What's good or bad about the jobs?
- Is there another kind of part-time job that you'd like to try? Give reasons.

6 Making plans for the weekend

Partner B: Go to p. 102. **Partner C:** Go to p. 101.

Partner A: You want to do something fun this weekend with your partners.

- First look at the cinema programme below. Choose one film that you would like to go to.
- Then talk to your partners. Tell your partners about the film. Listen to their suggestions.
- Finally agree together what you want to do.

LOST ZOMBIES

You probably think this is a horror film, but it isn't. There are a lot of zombies in it, but they aren't very scary. It's really a very funny comedy. You'll laugh a lot. The story is a bit silly, but the actors are very cool. A fun way to spend an evening.

Saturday at 6.30 pm and 9.00 pm

The heart of the sea

This is a very exciting action film. The story has been told before – a crew go out to catch a whale in terrible seas – but this film explores new worlds. The special effects are amazing, and the actors are very believable. Watch out for that whale – he will get you! Scary!

Friday at 4.00 pm, 6.00 pm and 8.30 pm

▸ KV 34 A–B ▸ INKL pp. 64–65

Students who are getting ready for their final exams (level A2/A2+, Hauptschulabschluss) will find extra practice here. (For level B1, Mittlerer Schulabschluss, go to pp. 76 ff.)

1 The interview

3.08

You will hear a job interview. You will hear it twice. Choose the correct picture for each question.

1 Which is Daryl's family?

A

B

C

2 Where does Daryl work?

A

Green Leaf Fruit and Veg

B

Captain's Point

C

Blue Bay *Fine Dining*

3 What does Daryl like making most?

A

B

C

4 What is Daryl's strength?

A

good with people

B

punctual

C

hard-working

5 Which job is Daryl applying for?

A

WANTED
Full-time waiters (37 hours)
Wednesday – Sunday
Apply: Cafola Cafe

B

Busy downtown restaurant looking for kitchen help.
Part-time only.
Apply with CV.

C

SUMMER JOB
Part-time chef wanted for small seaside cafe.
Must have experience.

▸ KV 34 A–B ▸ INKL pp. 64–65

2 That's a nice car!

3.09

Three young people are looking at photos together – Stefan from Bielefeld, Taylor from California, USA, and Julie from Liverpool, England.
Listen to their conversation about driving.
Decide whether sentences 1–7 are true or false.

1 Taylor has had her car for twenty years.
2 Taylor started driving when she was 14 years old.
3 With her first license Taylor could only drive to school.
4 In the UK you can get your first licence at the age of 16.
5 Most kids in California get a provisional license at the age of 16.
6 Stefan says that he'd like a car.
7 Taylor says that her friends in California drive everywhere.

3 Teens and their parents

3.10

Listen to these teenagers. They are talking about what they fight about with their parents.
You will hear the recording twice.
Choose the correct answer A, B or C.

1 Jess says that she fights with her parents because she isn't allowed to
- A stay out later than 10.30 pm.
- B go out with her friends.
- C stay at her friend's house.

2 Malik says that
- A his parents talk too much.
- B his parents always start a fight.
- C he and his parents don't talk

3 Molly says that at the moment she
- A is easy to live with.
- B isn't easy to live with.
- C is fun to live with.

4 Ethan says that his parents
- A don't care about him.
- B are always checking on him.
- C think he's very organized.

5 Kelly and her parents
- A often fight
- B never fight.
- C almost never fight.

6 Robbie had an argument with his parents because
- A they won't allow him to have a party.
- B he went to a party at his friend's house.
- C he wants to ask the whole school to his party.

EXAM FILE A2 READING

▸ KV 35 A–B ▸ INKL pp. 66–68

1 "I'm a European"

Complete the sentences below by choosing the best ending.

This text appeared on youthreporter, *a website for young Europeans who are studying or working in other countries.*

I'm an 18-year-old girl and I have always felt Italian and not European. Well, this was true until last October when I had the chance to go to Berlin and spend three weeks learning German. This changed my opinion.

At first I was a little unsure. For me Berlin was just the German capital, a cold city. And in the beginning I was worried about living with a host family, away from my friends.

But I was completely wrong. My journey turned into a wonderful experience.

I discovered a modern and beautiful city full of young people from all over Europe. And I lost my prejudices about German people. Here in Italy people are warm, and I expected people from the north of Europe to be cold. But I was wrong! My host family welcomed me, made me feel comfortable, showed me places where real Berlin people go, prepared my breakfast every morning, treated me like a daughter, helped me when I felt a little homesick because I was so far from my family.

I changed my opinion about the German language too. I had thought that it was an unattractive language. Now I know it can be very romantic. This was the best experience ever as I met new people and I lost the narrow-minded way of thinking of my little town in the south of Italy. I learned to be a European.

1 The writer is from ...
- A Italy.
- B Germany.
- C Berlin.

2 She went to Berlin ...
- A for a holiday.
- B to work.
- C to learn a language.

3 Before the writer went to Berlin ...
- A she was excited about it.
- B she wasn't very enthusiastic.
- C she didn't want to leave her family.

4 When she got to Germany ...
- A she was disappointed.
- B she was surprised.
- C she was uncomfortable.

5 The writer found that people in Berlin are ...
- A friendly.
- B cold.
- C romantic.

6 Now she feels differently about ...
- A the German climate.
- B the Italian language.
- C being European.

▸ KV 35 A–B ▸ INKL pp. 66–68

2 The Bracelet by Ann Angel

1 Trevor put something into my hand.
"Here," he said. Trevor didn't talk a lot.
I opened my hand and saw a silver bracelet with a silver heart locket at the centre. The bracelet was beautiful.
"Happy birthday," Trevor said. "It's your birthday, right?"
"Yeah, it's my birthday."
This bracelet seemed like something you'd give a girl you loved. Trevor and I had only been on two dates so far.
"Thank you," I said.
I opened the heart locket. Inside was a piece of pink paper with the words "Worth Loving". It wasn't like Trevor's handwriting. The bracelet must have cost a lot.

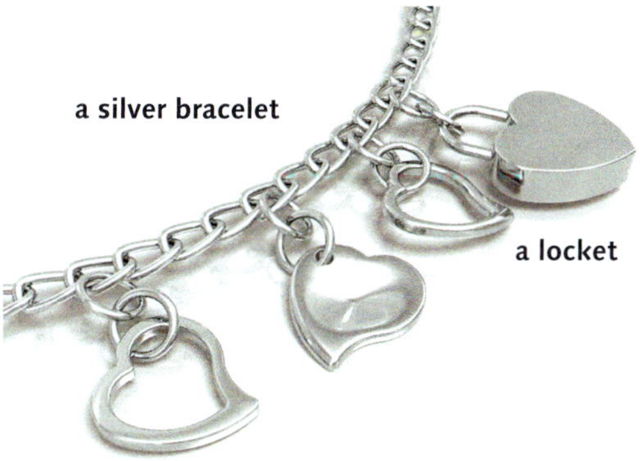

2 Trevor asked, "Which birthday is it?"
"Sixteen." Before he could ask I explained, "My family doesn't do parties. My mom usually makes a dinner for our birthdays."
I looked at the bracelet. Had Trevor searched through the lockets to find one that said "Worth Loving"? Did this mean something?
I wasn't sure how I felt about him.
"This bracelet is really pretty," I said. But I couldn't accept it. I didn't like Trevor enough to call him "Worth Loving".
"I gotta go to training." He was at the back door before he turned and added, "Maybe I'll come over later. After dinner."
He was gone before I had a chance to answer.

3 My mother came in with the twins – they were arguing. She put the groceries down and turned to Will and Josh. "Boys, I told you to stop fighting in the grocery store. And in the bakery. Now I'm telling you to stop in this house!"
Josh hit Will on the shoulder. "Yeah, jackass[1]."
I put the bracelet on the table.
"What's that?" Mom asked.
"A gift[2] from Trevor."
She picked it up. "Are you and Trevor serious?"
"I didn't think so. But he's coming over later. He knows he's not invited for dinner."

4 Kat came later. She told me that she was with Trevor when he stole the bracelet.
"The note was inside," she said. "The bracelets were near the door when we walked out of the store."
I felt ill. "So the bracelet is stolen?" I stared at the bracelet. "It means nothing."
I dropped the bracelet. Kat looked at it.
"Do you want the bracelet?" I asked.
"Of course not. He gave it to you," she answered.
"I don't really like it," I said. "Go ahead. Take the bracelet. It's yours," I told her.

---

[1]jackass ['dʒækæs] *(AE, infml) Idiot* [2]gift [gɪft] *Geschenk*

EXAM FILE A2 READING

▸ KV 35 A–B ▸ INKL pp. 66–68

a) Read the text *The Bracelet*. Then read the headings below. Choose the correct heading (A–E) for each paragraph (1–4). There is one more heading than you need.

Heading	Paragraph
A What does the message mean?	
B Feeling disappointed	
C The birthday party	
D A birthday present	
E The family comes home	

b) Complete the sentences about paragraphs 1 and 2 in about one to five words.

1 When the narrator opened her hand, she saw a silver ...
2 She didn't know Trevor very well because they had only been on ...
3 Inside the locket there were two words: ...
4 But Trevor didn't write these words because it wasn't like ...
5 The narrator can't invite Trevor to a party because her family ...
6 She told him that the bracelet was ...
7 Trevor couldn't stay because he had to ...
8 But he planned to ...

c) Match the sentence halves about the last two paragraphs.

1 When the family came home,
2 They were arguing everywhere,
3 When Mom saw the bracelet,
4 Kat told the story
5 When the narrator heard this,
6 The narrator offered Kat the bracelet,

A ... e.g. in the grocery store and the bakery.
B ... about stealing the bracelet.
C ... but she didn't want it.
D ... the twins were fighting.
E ... she asked what it was.
F ... she was shocked.

d) Are the statements true or false or not in the text?

1 Trevor was a chatty guy.
2 The narrator was surprised to get this present.
3 The bracelet looked expensive.
4 The narrator was in love with Trevor.
5 The narrator didn't invite Trevor to her birthday dinner.
6 The narrator never saw Trevor again.

e) Answer these questions in one to five words.

1 How do we know that Trevor didn't know a lot about the narrator?
2 How did Kat know that Trevor didn't buy the bracelet?
3 What do we learn about Trevor in this story?

▸ KV 36 ▸ INKL p. 69

1 An interesting weekend

Du möchtest zum *Climate Change Challenge Weekend* nach Irland. Du hast den Flyer ausgedruckt und möchtest einige Mitschülerinnen und Mitschüler dafür begeistern mitzukommen. Beantworte ihre Fragen. Schreibe die Antworten in Stichpunkten auf.

1 Die Veranstaltung findet an einer Uni statt? Stimmt das?
2 Was ist das Thema der Veranstaltung?
3 Wann genau findet sie statt?
4 Welche Aktivitäten werden angeboten?
5 Wo werden wir übernachten?
6 Wann ist Anmeldeschluss?
7 Was kostet die Teilnahme?

Trocaire | Working for a just world

CLIMATE CHANGE Challenge Weekend

Date: 1st – 3rd July
Location: Maynooth University, Ireland

Are you 15 – 17 years old?
Are you ready to act on climate change?

What's involved?
You will:
- take part in workshops.
- listen to guest speakers.
- watch documentary films.

Accommodation:
- All meals provided.
- Accommodation on the university campus.

To apply:
- Cost for the weekend: £25 / EUR 30
- Closing date: 18th June

Your planet needs YOU! Will you act?

2 Let's go in-line skating

Amira is new in Cologne. She can't speak much German, but her English is good. She's interested in this in-line skating track. Answer Amira's questions in English.

Where can you skate?
Is this track for in-line-skaters only?
How many kilometres can you skate there?
Where do you begin?
How can you get there?
Do you have to be good at skating?

Skating am Fühlinger See

Wo: Fühlinger See, Köln Seeberg
Länge: Länge: 8,5km (einmal um die Regattastrecke und wieder zurück)
Belag: feiner Asphalt
Hinweis: Die Strecke wird auch von Spaziergängern und Sportlern genutzt.
Start: Parkplatz P1 (Oranjehofstraße)
Schwierigkeit: für Anfänger geeignet
ÖPNV: Tram 12 bis Merkenich, dann Bus 121 bis Oranjehofstraße

▸ KV 37 ▸ INKL p. 70

1 An email from the US

Alice is your teenage friend in the US. Here's an email from her.
Read her email and write back to her. Answer all her questions. Think of a good beginning and ending for your email. Write 60–100 words in complete sentences.

Subject: What's next?

Hi

It was great to get your last email – thanks. This year is my last year at school. I'm happy that I'm moving on to new things, but sad that I'm leaving all my friends.
When are you going to leave school and how do you feel about that?

After the summer I'm going to go to a technical college in Santa Monica, California. I want to learn to be a sound engineer. **What's next for you? Are you looking for a job or an apprenticeship? Or are you going to go to a different school?**

My friend's mom works at a recording studio in LA and I've done some work experience there. It's a cool job – you work with some great musicians and singers. **Have you done any work experience? What was it like?**

I'd love to work in the music industry some day – that's my dream. **What kind of job would you like to do later?**
Write back soon. Bye for now.

Alice

2 Write about the picture

Write a text about the picture (about 60–80 words).
Write about the following aspects:
- Who is this teenager?
- Where is she?
- What is she doing?
- What has happened?
- How is she feeling now?
- What will happen next?

▸ KV 38 ▸ INKL pp. 71–73

1 Congratulations!

Imagine that you and your partner have just won a competition. The prize is a holiday – you can spend a week in one of the three places below.

a) Talk to your partner and tell him/her which holiday you would like best and why.

b) Decide together on one holiday.

Congratulations! You have won a week away!

The Scottish Highlands

Active holiday:
hiking • visit Highland Games • mountain biking • look for the Loch Ness monster • stay in a hostel • meet lots of people your age

A beach holiday on the coast in Spain

Relaxing holiday:
weather • activities on beach • beach volleyball • swimming pool • stay on campsite in tent

A city visit – any city in Germany

Sightseeing holiday:
visit tourist places • museums • famous places

Lots to do in the evening:
cinema • concerts • stay in city hostel

2 A conversation about part-time jobs

You and your partner are thinking about applying for a part-time job.

a) Talk to your partner about your ideas for a job.

b) Say what you think of your partner's ideas.

c) Decide which job you each want to apply for. (You can choose different jobs.)

what you're good at

inside / outside

with people / children / animals

working hours

working in a shop or restaurant, car wash, ...

babysitting, ...

walking dogs, garden work, ...

Unit 1

3 SPEAKING Holiday plans ► Unit 1, p. 23

Partner B:

a) You're planning your summer holidays. You've found this idea for a working holiday.
Read the ad and answer your partner's questions.

b) Then ask your partner about his / her idea. Ask questions like:
- What kind of holiday?
- Where?
- What kind of places?
- Ideas for a route?
- How long?
- Cost / Pay?
- Stay where?

c) Agree with your partner which of the two holidays you should go on and why.

Camping by the sea

We are looking for active young people to work on our campsite this summer.

Dates: July 1st to August 31st

Duties: Cleaning, helping with Kids Club, some office work.

You need to be able to speak English and another language (French or German).
You should have good communication skills.
Experience not necessary.

Pay: 7 euros per hour

°Minimum of 30 hours per week.

Accommodation: You will share a °mobile home with three other campsite workers.

Apply today: skyblue@work.fr

5d VIEWING Amar (all great achievements require time) ► Unit 1, p. 25

d) Partner B:

Describe your still to partner A and listen to him / her. Find out what's the same and what's different in your stills.
- What time of day is it?
- Why is Amar there?
- Do we see Amar in a close-up, a medium shot or a long shot? What effect does that have on the viewer?

● Think of a caption for your still.

Unit 2 **Stop! Check! Go!**

7 SPEAKING Typically German ▸ Unit 2, p. 51

Partner B: Listen to your partner. Which typically German things is he / she describing? Then describe these things to your partner without using the German word.

Vollkornbrot

Fahrradweg

Der grüne Pfeil

Unit 3 **Stop! Check! Go!**

7 SPEAKING Is it better to recycle or buy new? ▸ Unit 3, p. 73

Partner B: You think it's better to buy new things. Here are some of your arguments:

- cost (repairs take time; if they don't last long, you have to buy new in the end)
- repairing can be unsafe and risky
- shopping can be fun / easier / quicker
- old things are uncool
- supporting businesses and (perhaps) the °economy

Exam file

G Making plans for the weekend ▸ Exam file B1 SPEAKING, p. 91

Partner C: You want to do something fun this weekend with your partners.

- First look at the concert programme below. Choose one concert that you would like to go to.
- Then talk to your partners. Tell your partners about the concert. Listen to their suggestions.
- Finally agree together what you want to do and when.

Concert by new rock band *Little Blue Bikes*

They're only 18 and some of them are still at school, but they're going places. They write their own songs and do some covers. You won't be able to stand still. A lively evening is °guaranteed!

Saturday at 8 pm

Singer-songwriter Jessie Smith is back

Jessie wowed us last year with her fantastic voice and original songs. Now she's back again with new °material. Her music is very special. The lyrics are often very funny, especially when she raps. Not to be missed!

Friday at 9 pm

Exam file

6 Making plans for the weekend ▸ *Exam file B1, p. 91*

Partner B: You want to do something fun this weekend with your partners.

- First look at the sports centre programme. Choose one activity that you would like to do.
- Then talk to your partners. Tell your partners about the activity. Listen to their suggestions.
- Finally agree together what you want to do.

Fenway Sports Centre

Dodgeball: Come and play with us! You can just come along and join in. No experience needed. Beginners welcome. Mixed teams. Suitable for all ages. We guarantee you'll have a fun evening.

Tag rugby: Like rugby but with tags – so no bruises! Good fun for all ages – guys and girls. Beginners welcome – just turn up and join in. It's easy to learn. Great way to meet people and keep fit.

Saturday evening 7–9.00 pm

Friday evening 6–8.00 pm

English for jobs

3 NOW YOU Two role-plays – pick one ▸ *English for jobs, p. 156*

a) Partner B: You're a Danish programmer at *Unico Design* in Copenhagen, which is doing work for the software company *Intersoft* in Berlin. You have a quick question for Nina Pfeifer at *Inter_Soft* and you need her answer today. So you call her on the phone. You don't speak German.

b) Partner B: You're an online sales trainee at the Munich shoe company *Funshu*. You're travelling to the UK office in Manchester next week for a training seminar. While you're there, you'd like to meet with the sales manager and learn about their sales department. You call him directly. You only have time after 3 pm on Wednesday or Thursday.

English around the world

More practice 1 Your languages ▸ English around the world, p. 8

a) Discuss these questions with a partner:

- What languages do you speak?
- What's your first language?
- What's your second language?
- Do you think you'll need English in the future (when you leave school)?
- Where can English be useful?

b) Give a three-minute presentation about this to the class.

Unit 1

More help 3 Diversity and you ▸ Unit 1, p. 11

You can write about:

- the different cultures in your family / neighbourhood / ...
- the different languages you or your family can speak
- the festivals you and people from your neighbourhood celebrate
- the different cultures of some of your friends / classmates / ...
- how many different cultures there are in your class / school / town / ...
- things that you like about other cultures

More challenge 1 *Embrace diversity – embrace our differences* ▸ Unit 1, p. 11

This is a popular slogan in South Africa. It means that people should see diversity in a positive way.
Why do you think this is important in South Africa?
Why do you think it's important in Europe?
Write a short text about this. Swap your text with other students.
Explain your opinion and give examples.

More help 1 South Africa – then and now ▸ Unit 1, p. 12

Copy the diagram below. Make it as big as you like. Write each phrase from the box into part 1, 2 or 3.

allowed to have relationships with white people • better opportunities • can get good jobs • can go to white schools • drug problems • low-paid jobs • not allowed to go to white schools • poverty • segregated • unemployment • violence

Life for black people in South Africa

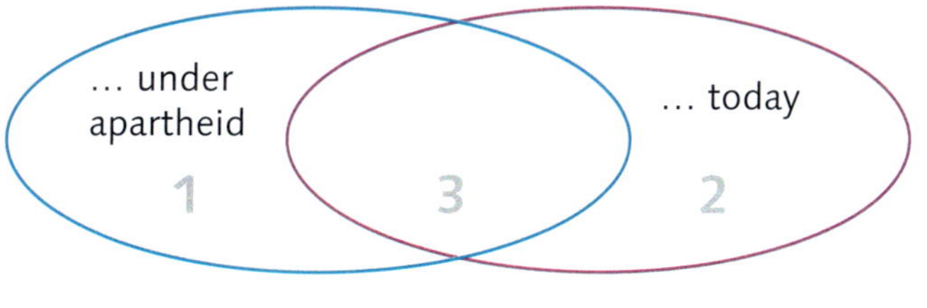

Unit 1

More practice 1 Questions on the article
▸ Unit 1, p. 13

1 What °features of apartheid does the article deal with? Describe at least three.
2 How have things changed for non-whites since the end of apartheid? Describe three things.
3 Not everything has got better since apartheid ended. Describe one thing that is worse.
4 What do you think life is like in suburbs and townships in South Africa today?

More challenge 2 A short talk about apartheid
▸ Unit 1, p. 13

a) Prepare notes for a short talk about apartheid. Use the texts on pages 10–13. Do some research on the internet too. Think about these questions:

- What was apartheid?
- Where and when did apartheid °exist?
- What was life like under apartheid?
- Why was it wrong?
- How and when did it end?
- Who fought against it?
- Are things better today? How?
- What still needs to change there?

b) Give your talk to the class. Invite questions.
▸ Skills files 5, p. 164; 9.1, p. 170

More help 1 A South African ad
▸ Unit 1, p. 14

Here are some ideas to help you to answer the questions about the ad.

1 Who do you think the ad is aimed at?

I think the ad is (°mainly / probably) aimed at	young / old people / families. South Africans / °foreign tourists. people who enjoy adventure.

2 What is its message? Try to finish one of these sentences about the ad.

I think the message of the ad is:	South Africa is a country for tourists who … You should go to South Africa if you love … South Africa is special because …

3 Is the ad effective? Think about the photos, the colours, and the words.

This ad	makes people want to … promises … doesn't show / mention …

4 How do you personally react to the ad?

- I liked / didn't like looking at … / reading … - I didn't understand … - I'd like to know more about …	- For me, the ad is / isn't effective because it makes / doesn't make me want to …

More help **2d** **YOUR TASK** **Where to go?** ▸ *Unit 1, p. 15*

Comment on the choices of the other students like this:

I agree with you. I think that it would be great to ...
I'm not so sure about that activity. Have you thought about ...?
I don't think it is fair to the sharks / ostriches / people in the townships / ...

More practice 2 **Talking about an ad** ▸ *Unit 1, p. 15*

Describe the advert on p. 14 and talk about the activities. Use your own words.

3 **A South African cartoon** ▸ *Unit 1, p. 17*

Complete the sentences with the correct form of the verbs in brackets.

1 In this cartoon a boy *is asking* (ask) a man for directions while his parents ... (wait) in their car.
2 They ... (be) probably from England because the boy ... (wear) a T-shirt with a British flag.
3 There ... (be) a sign for the Lion Park on the left and that's what the tourists ... (look for).
4 The boy ... (look) confused, and question marks show that he ... (not understand) what the man ... (say).
5 The cartoon is only funny if you ... (know) that some South African English words ... (be) different to British English.
6 The British boy ... (not know) that in South Africa when people ... (talk) about a robot, they ... (mean) a traffic light.

More help **4** **Describing a cartoon** ▸ *Unit 1, p. 17*

You have to write about the cartoon. Below are some useful phrases. ▸ *Skills file 11.2, p. 180*

1) Describe what you see in the cartoon. What is happening?	In the cartoon we can see ... / The elephant is sitting on ... / It's holding ... / It looks ...
2) What do you think the cartoon is about?	The cartoon is about people who go to Africa to °shoot ...
3) Explain what you think the artist wants to say.	I think the artist wants to say that these people are ... / (wild) animals are ... / ...
4) What do you think of the cartoon?	I think the cartoon is / isn't (very) funny. It is (very / quite / ...) effective because ... It makes me feel angry / cross / sad / ...

Returned (°adapted from the novel °*Scarred Lions* by Fanie Viljoen)

1.03

Trouble in the air

It was late in the afternoon. Friday. The streets were wet. The Underground was crowded. Everybody wanted to get home as soon as possible. It would rain again very soon.

I felt hunted …

There was trouble in the air. So I walked quicker – I felt hunted like an animal. I saw myself in a shop window. Black face, frightened eyes, the cut on my lip. And I felt like a stranger. Box: Voc., p. 214
How could this be? I had lived in London all my life. I lived here with my mum in a two-bedroomed council flat above the street. I went to school here. But somehow I was a stranger.
Buyisiwe. I thought about my name. A stranger's name.

Council flats in London

Why not James, Chris or Peter? Or even Jonathan? Why not any other name, like most of the boys in school? Buyisiwe. That is what they called me. A Zulu name that meant – 'returned'.

This is my home

Mum wasn't home yet. I switched on the TV on my way to the kitchen. In the kitchen I drank some milk. There was some pizza in the fridge. I heated it in the microwave and went back into the living room. I made myself comfortable on the couch. I thought about the fight I'd had at school with Jonathan.
"Zulu!" his voice was still in my ear. "What are you doing here, Zulu? Why don't you go live with your people?"
Your people! This is my home. I don't know any other place.

A difficult decision

Mum came in through the door.
"Don't just lie there, Buyi, come and help me. Why didn't you clean the flat?" she asked.
I looked at the untidy flat …
"I'm tired. It's Friday," I said.
There were tears in Mum's eyes.
"You don't make life any easier for me, you know, Buyi. You don't help me in the house. It's hard to keep food on the table, to keep a roof over our heads. I'm tired of it all! So I've made a decision."
"What decision?" I felt frightened again.
Something was different about mum.
"This is probably the most difficult decision I have ever made."
"Mum?" I now whispered.
"After what happened at school today, I know what I have to do."
"So you found out about it?"
"The school phoned me, Buyi." Her face was sad. "Mrs Fletcher told me about the fight. It wasn't your first fight … And now I know that the time has come."
Mum fell silent for a moment. Things were about to change, I knew it.
"You are fourteen now, Buyi. It's time for you to meet your father. I know he hasn't been here for you when you were growing up. But that will change now. He … he has agreed to look after you from now on."
"What?" I cried.

Mum nodded. “Buyi, you’re going to live with your father in South Africa.”

I couldn't sleep ...

Departure

I couldn’t sleep for days after my talk with Mum. Africa? Where is Africa? Why do I have to go to Africa? Just because I had a fight? Because I’m different?

Mum had planned everything. She got me a passport, got my father to pay for the ticket, packed my bags ... and one day we went to Heathrow Airport.

“I love you, Mum,” I said before I went to the departure hall. I don’t think I had ever said that before. We hugged. The time had come to leave.

2 Working with the text

Choose the correct words to complete the text.

Buyi lives in London with his mum, but he doesn’t ... (1 go to school / feel at home) there. This Friday was a very ... (2 wet / sunny) day. We learn that Buyi has problems ... (3 at school / at home). We find out that his mum has problems too – she seems very ... (4 stressed / bored). Now she has decided that Buyi’s dad should look after his ... (5 daughter / son). So the boy is going to ... (6 move to / leave) South Africa. Buyi is very ... (7 happy / worried) when he hears this news. He actually knows ... (8 a lot / nothing) about the country of his father.

3 Characterization

What do we learn about Buyi? Match the sentence parts.

1 Buyi is scared because ...	a) ... council flat in London.
2 He feels hunted ...	b) ... with other kids at school.
3 He has a cut ...	c) ... his dad.
4 His name is different ...	d) ... in Africa.
5 He lives in a ...	e) ... from the other kids’ names.
6 His mother is angry because Buyi ...	f) ... as he’s only fourteen years old.
7 He often has fights ...	g) ... doesn’t help at home.
8 He’s quite young ...	h) ... on his lip.
9 His dad lives ...	i) ... like an animal.
10 Buyi doesn’t know ...	j) ... there’s trouble in the air.

1 The story goes on

If you want to and find out about Buyi's first experiences in his new home, read on. You can use a dictionary.

Returned – part 2 (adapted from the novel *Scarred Lions* by Fanie Viljoen)

1.04

The land of my father

"°Ladies and gentlemen, we are getting ready to land at O R Tambo International Airport. Please °ensure that your °tray tables are °stowed, that all laptops and °electronic °devices are switched off and that your °seat belt is °fastened."

This was it. The moment I had been °dreading. °There was no °turning back now. Nervously I looked through the small window of the plane. The city of Johannesburg was below us – grey, with °splashes of green. Buildings as far as the eye could see, but it was different from London. There weren't many skyscrapers. As we °dropped lower I began to see more clearly: trees, houses, swimming pools. Lots of swimming pools. And cars. Thousands of them on the highways. Then suddenly the °scenery below us changed. Instead of large houses, there were smaller houses. Grey, with °silver roofs. Then again it changed to land with °tiny shacks – simple little houses that looked so poor.

As my feet touched the ground of Africa for the first time, I expected to feel something special – a feeling of coming home to the land of my father. But there was nothing. I knew that I didn't belong here either.

Disappointed

I walked into the arrivals hall where there was a sea of faces – people waiting for their loved ones, °tour operators waiting for the tourists, °chauffeurs waiting for business people. Who would be waiting for me?

"Your dad will °pick you up." That's what Mum said to me. I didn't really know what he looked like. I had seen his face on an old picture …

I looked at all the people. My heart was °thumping. My mouth was dry. What if he hadn't come? It was a scary thought. I'd be here all alone. Then I saw a sign. It had my name on it. Buyisiwe. The man carrying the sign looked around worriedly. But as soon as he saw me, he smiled. My dad had come for me. So this was him.

"Sawubona!" he said and held his hand out to me. "Hello!"

"Uh, hi," I said. My heart was still thumping. Meeting your father for the first time was a °mind-blowing experience.

"You're my dad." I don't know why I said that.

"No!" the man said. "I'm Lwazi. I work with your dad."

"So where is my dad then?"

"He had some work to do, so he asked me to come and pick you up."

Lwazi smiled again and °patted me on the shoulder.

I didn't like that at all. I expected my dad to come.

New friends?

Then a white boy and a black girl came running. They were about my age. Fourteen. They were smiling too. The boy shook my hand and put his arm around my shoulder.

"My name is Andre," he said excitedly.

The girl smiled °gently. Her dark brown eyes were kind as she introduced herself.

"And I'm Simoshile."

Lwazi took my trolley. Now I °felt more at ease.

"I'm sure you're tired, Buyisiwe. We have to °get going. There is still a long road °ahead."

I saw Simoshile stealing quick °glances in my direction. Was something wrong? I looked down to make sure my °fly was °done up. It was. I shook my head. It was probably nothing.

Andre talked a lot. He spoke English with a strange accent.

"I'm Afrikaans," he explained. "It is my home language. But I speak English °as well. And a little bit of isiZulu."

Three languages! How is that possible?

"That's nothing," said Simoshile. "I speak isiZulu and English. And a bit of Afrikaans, isiXhosa and siSwati."

She too had a strange accent, different from Andre.

"How many languages do you have in South Africa?" I asked.

"Eleven official languages," said Simoshile.

I only spoke English.

On the road

We were in the car – a 4x4 °off-road vehicle. I suddenly felt very tired – and afraid. Afraid of the °unknown. But I felt an excitement too.

We drove on the left side of the road, like we do in England. I saw '°townhouse °complexes'. Simoshile explained that people lived in apartments with big walls around them. She said that people here were °crazy about °security. They had security cameras, fences, walls, °security guards, security gates, security doors and alarms. Shocking!

°Minibus taxis °whizzed by us. They were crowded with lots of people in them. They didn't seem to °care about the rules of the road here. We were driving north. The scenery changed when we left the city and we drove through big open °spaces – grasslands. Then we drove past some poor shacks.

"It's a squatter camp," Simoshile explained. They were little °huts built with pieces of metal and wood. There was plastic over the windows. Some shacks didn't have windows. There were rocks on the roofs. It seemed terrible to me. How could people live like this?

Welcome to your new home

After a long time on the highway we turned onto a °dirt road. Now I knew why we needed an off-road vehicle.

"Do you see there?" Andre asked, pointing to some mountains in the °distance. "It's the Waterberg Mountain."

We came to a beautiful wooden gate. A security guard opened it. He knew Lwazi, Andre and Simoshile. He waved at us, smiling. "Ngiyabonga," Lwazi shouted. It probably meant 'thank you'.

We drove a bit further. There was a °buzz in the air. I didn't know what it was, but it seemed to come from the trees.

At last we arrived at some buildings with trees and gardens around them. It looked very nice.

"Welcome to your new home," Lwazi said.

"What is this place?" I asked.

"Don't you know?" he smiled. "It's a °game reserve."

"Do you like it?" Andre asked.

"Of course he does!" Simoshile said.

I nodded, trying to look brave, but I °was as scared as hell.

2 Imagine you're Buyi

You've just arrived in your new home in South Africa. Write a message to your mum.

You can tell her:

- about your journey
- what it was like when you arrived
- who met you at the airport
- your first impressions of South Africa and your new home
- what you have learned about South Africa already
- how you are feeling
- ...

Unit 1

More challenge 3 More on relative clauses ▸ Unit 1, p. 18

a) Complete the sentences below with a ***relative pronoun*** (*who*, *which*, *that*, *whose*). Sometimes more than one solution is possible. ▸ Language file 28, p. 201

1 Mandarin Chinese is the language ... has the largest number of native speakers.
2 But English is the language ... has the largest number of speakers worldwide.
3 This is because there are so many people ... use English as a second language.
4 Many people speak more than two languages fluently, ... is pretty amazing, in my opinion.
5 Someone ... speaks two languages is bilingual.
6 My friend, ... mum is French, speaks both English and French really well.
7 English is the language ... her family usually speaks together at home.
8 She speaks French to her mum's parents, ... don't speak English.

FOCUS

1 Sometimes the information in a relative clause is vital to the sentence.
Example: Monique is the girl whose mum is French.

The relative clause tells us which girl is meant. This is called a ***defining relative clause***.

2 A relative clause can also add extra information, which could be left out.
Example: My friend Monique, whose mum is French, speaks English at home.

Here the information about Monique's mum is extra. The sentence would make sense without it. (> My friend Monique speaks English at home.)

So the underlined clause is a ***non-defining relative clause***.
Note that commas are used here, but not in **1**. ▸ Language file 28, p. 201

b) Three of the relative clauses in a) are non-defining. Which ones are they?

c) Add information to these sentences. Use non-defining relative clauses.

1 My Irish friend David can't speak German. His father is Austrian.
My Irish friend David, whose ...
2 He often visits his Austrian grandmother. She lives in Graz.
He often visits ..., who ...
3 His °granny speaks English well. That's great.
His granny ..., which ...
4 But he can't speak to his young cousins. They can't speak English.
But he can't ..., who ...

More practice 3 Questions on the text ▸ Unit 1, p. 21

1 What was the weather like in London on this Friday?
2 We get the feeling that Buyi was in some kind of trouble. What tells us this?
3 Why do you think the story is called *Returned*?
4 What kind of relationship did Buyi have with his neighbours? Explain.
5 Buyi wasn't a °model son. Give some examples.
6 Buyi's mum wasn't happy about her decision to send Buyi to South Africa. How do we know this?
7 What kind of a relationship did Buyi have with his father? Why?
8 How did Buyi feel when he left his mum at the airport?

More help 3a Characterization ▸ Unit 1, p. 21

age	
home	London (line ...); two-bedroomed council flat (lines ... – ...); ...
personality	
appearance	black face (line ...); ...
feelings	scared (line ...); ...
relationships	

More challenge 4 Would you recommend this story? Why (not)? ▸ Unit 1, p. 21

Write a review of the story. Write about the main characters, the setting, the topic and the plot. Say what you like and what you don't like and give reasons. ▸ *Skills file 10.9, p. 178*

More practice 4 Good writing techniques (1) ▸ Unit 1, p. 21

> ! These techniques are also called °*stylistic devices*.

Good writers use different techniques to make their texts interesting. Here are three examples of techniques that you can find in *Returned* (on pp. 19 – 21).

a) °**Repetition:** Sometimes a writer repeats a phrase or a structure to °stress a point and make it stronger. For example in lines 3–6 of *Returned*:

There was trouble in the air. ... For days I could feel it – in the crowded trains in the London Underground, in the school classrooms, in the streets.

> ! You can talk about these questions in German, if you like.

1 Look at the lines above. What words are repeated? How many times? What point is the writer stressing?
2 Look at lines 19–26. What noun is repeated? How many times? What point is the writer stressing?
3 Now look at lines 57–60 and find the words that are repeated. What is the writer stressing?

b) °**Similes:** Sometimes a writer compares two different things by using 'like' or 'as'. This can create a strong image. For example in line 19 of *Returned*:

I felt like a stranger.

This is called a simile.

1 What point is the writer stressing (again)?
2 Look at lines 86–87 and find another simile. What image is the writer creating?

c) °**Metaphors:** Sometimes a writer compares two very different things, without using 'like' or 'as'. For example in lines 51–52 of *Returned*:

The cheese had turned a °dull yellow in a sea of olives, pineapple and some kind of meat.

1 What kind of image does this create for you? Is it negative or positive?
2 Look at line 90 and find another metaphor. Do you think this is a negative or positive image?

▸ *Skills file 8.5, p. 169*

Unit 1

More practice 5 An interview with Amar ▸ Unit 1, p. 25

In the film Amar doesn't tell us about his life. Instead we see what it's like.
Imagine you have the chance to interview Amar. Write a list of questions you would ask him.

More practice 6 Amar – a comment ▸ Unit 1, p. 25

Write a comment on the film.
- Describe the effect it had on you.
- What impressed you most about Amar's life? Explain.
- Why do you think the film won so many °awards around the world? ▸ Skills file 10.2, p. 174

More challenge 5 The film-maker's aims ▸ Unit 1, p. 25

Read the interview with the film-maker Andrew Hinton.
Prepare a short talk in German (one minute):
- Explain why he decided to make the film about Amar.
- Describe what the filming was like.
- Explain why he chose not to use music, dialogue or voice-over in the film.

Interview with film-maker Andrew Hinton *by Tahiat Mahboob*

How did you meet Amar, and what made you choose him as your film's subject?
I met Amar while visiting a school in Jamshedpur. I asked if there were kids who usually worked and went to classes. When I met Amar and he quietly explained what his day °consists of, six and a half days a week, 350 days a year, it really made me stop and think about how I use the time in my own life.

Your film is more than nine minutes long and °contains no dialogue. Why did you decide to tell the story in this way?
Amar doesn't say much. He has a quiet °determination which I think comes through in his °actions so I wanted his day to speak for itself, rather than trying to explain it with voice-over or dialogue. I tried music but it just didn't seem to work. I liked the °simplicity of the °natural sounds.

What were the challenges in getting such °intimate access to Amar's daily life? How did Amar and his family feel about being filmed?
I visited Amar's home with the school °headmaster, who explained that I wanted to film him for a day, and his mother and grandmother were a little °puzzled but quite happy.

You show a day in the life of Amar. Was it filmed in a day or did you have to spend some time for all of the pieces to fall into place?
It is very much filmed in one day. I'm a big fan of °*vérité* °film-making and so it felt important to be as honest in the °process as possible. No special effects, °retakes or °stunts in this film.

Unit 1 | Stop! Check! Go!

//● 1c Sharks ▸ Unit 1, p. 26

Complete the text. Use the ***simple present*** or the ***present progressive***.

1 Three sharks ... around a surfer, but he ... see them. (swim, not see)
2 People ... at the surfer because they ... to warn him. (wave, want)
3 A boy ... on his mobile phone and ... at the sharks. He is horrified because he ... that there will be an accident. (talk, point, think)
4 A girl ... up a white flag that ... a black shark on it. (put, have)
5 Swimmers ... out of the water because they ... the meaning of the flag. (run, know)
6 A man ... at the flag and it ... that he ... what it means. (look, seem, not understand)
7 Some surfers ... on the beach with their boards. They ... to go back into the water because they ... that sharks ... usually in the bay for long. (stand, wait, know, not stay)

▸ Language file 2, p. 186

More challenge 6 More false friends ▸ Unit 1, p. 27

a) Copy the table and add the missing words. Use a dictionary if necessary.

b) Make sentences for your partner. For examples, see 2a) on p. 27.

German	English
aktuell	
Art	
brav	
Chor	
Gymnasium	
Gift	
Platz nehmen	
sensibel	

English	German
°actual	
art	
brave	
°chorus	
°gymnasium	
°gift	
°take place	
°sensible	

Unit 2

More help 1 Digital citizens ▸ Unit 2, p. 33

These questions can help you to tell the story:

- Who is the story about?
- Where do you think they are?
- What are they doing?
- What happens next?
- What's their problem?
- How do they °solve it?
- How does the story end?

More practice 1 Talking about the film ▸ Unit 2, p. 33

Work in small groups. Pick three of these statements and talk about them. Do you agree or disagree? Give reasons and examples.

- This film is simple, but effective.
- It's strange that there's no talking in this film.
- We are all digital citizens now.
- The message of the film is: Young people can make a difference.
- Social media campaigns can be very good.

Then tell the class what you agreed on.

More challenge 1 UNICEF ▸ Unit 2, p. 33

This film was made by UNICEF.

a) Do some research. Find out what UNICEF is and what they do.

b) Tell the class what you have found out.

More challenge 2 A successful campaign ▸ Unit 2, p. 35

Prepare a short presentation about online campaigns for the class. Pick a) or b).

a) Find out about an online campaign that worked well. Describe how it worked.

b) Do you have ideas for an online campaign in your area? Describe what kind of campaign you think is necessary and how it could work.

More challenge 3 The last line ▸ Unit 2, p. 36

Read the last line of the poem again. Can you explain it – in German if you like? What does 'hypocrisy' mean? You can use a dictionary.

// 3a It's your future ▸ Unit 2, p. 37

1 Gary Turk says that when he was young he had no interest in ...

2 He says that politicians are old men in old ...

3 He thinks that we should stand up for ...

4 The people who fight the wars are the ...

5 We should be a part of ...

6 If we want to make a difference, we have to ...

More practice 2 Good writing techniques (2) ▸ Unit 2, p. 37

Poems sometimes have words that rhyme – they sound similar. You can hear the rhyme when you say the poem.

> ! These techniques are also called *stylistic devices*.

a) Say the first verse of the poem and pay special attention to the words that rhyme (here in red and blue).

b) Now say the second and third verses. Write down the words that rhyme. Use colours.

1.11 **c)** Listen to or watch the whole poem. Write down other words that rhyme. Compare.

d) Try to write your own poem. Read it to a partner. Together, improve your poems.

▸ *Skills file 8.5, p. 169*

IT'S YOUR FUTURE

When I was 18, politics was boring.

I didn't go and vote, I didn't pay attention,
I didn't really care at what age people got their pension.
That seemed ages away, I was just starting out,
I really had no interest in what politics was about.
(...)
So prove them all wrong, prove you have a voice,
Do the unexpected and accept you have a choice.
And vote, but first find out the truth,
Look at their policies and how it affects the youth.
(...)
You have a say, that needs to be respected,
People are dying for the right to have a leader that's elected.
So register to vote, be a part of democracy,
Doing nothing and complaining is outright hypocrisy.

Unit 2

More help **Step 1** ▸ Unit 2, p. 37

Here are some of the questions the Irish students asked in their survey.
You can choose from them, or make up your own questions:

Are you ...	☐ °male? ☐ female?
What age are you?	☐ 15 ☐ 16 ☐ 17 ☐ 18 ☐ 19
How often do you watch / read / listen to the news?	☐ daily ☐ 2 or 3 times a week ☐ never
Where do you get your news?	☐ mobile phone ☐ radio ☐ newspapers ☐ home computer ☐ tablet
Do you ever read newspapers?	☐ yes ☐ no
How interested in politics are you?	☐ very interested ☐ quite interested ☐ not interested
Do you think that young people should be interested in politics?	☐ yes, a lot ☐ a little ☐ no, not at all
Who do you discuss politics with?	☐ friends ☐ family ☐ classmates ☐ nobody
Do you think that politics is important for your daily life?	☐ yes ☐ no ☐ don't know
Have you ever spoken to a politician?	☐ yes ☐ no
Do you think that politicians really care about young people?	☐ yes ☐ no ☐ don't know
Do you trust politicians?	☐ yes ☐ no
If a politician came to your door, would you ...	☐ close the door? ☐ have a nice chat?
Can you imagine a °career in politics for yourself?	☐ yes ☐ no

More help **Step 4** ▸ Unit 2, p. 37

Tell the class about some of these things:

- How many students did you talk to?
- How many questions did you ask?
- What did you ask about?
- Are most students that you talked to interested or not interested in politics?
- What interesting / surprising / shocking results did you find?
- Can you give any advice to politicians?

Think of interesting ways to present the results of your survey (e.g. visuals like photos, tables, charts, etc.).

More help **Step 5** ▸ Unit 2, p. 37

Read the full report about the Irish survey.
You can use this text as a model or just pick out some useful words and phrases.

Report – a survey of Irish students

Introduction: What do young people think about politics and politicians?
We asked nearly 250 young people between the ages of 15 and 19. The results are surprising: While a lot of young people think that politics is important for their lives, not as many are interested in it.

The results: The survey found that 86% of the people we talked to do not trust politicians, while 61% would close the door if a politician came to their house. 73% believe that politicians don't really care about young people.
But most young people (67%) think that politics is important for their lives. And here's a surprising fact – most young people are interested in the news. 60% get their news on mobile phones. 48% watch the news on TV and only 16% read it in newspapers.

The conclusion: What does this mean?
Politicians should be more interested in young people. They should talk to young people more. They should listen to young people.

How interested in politics are you?

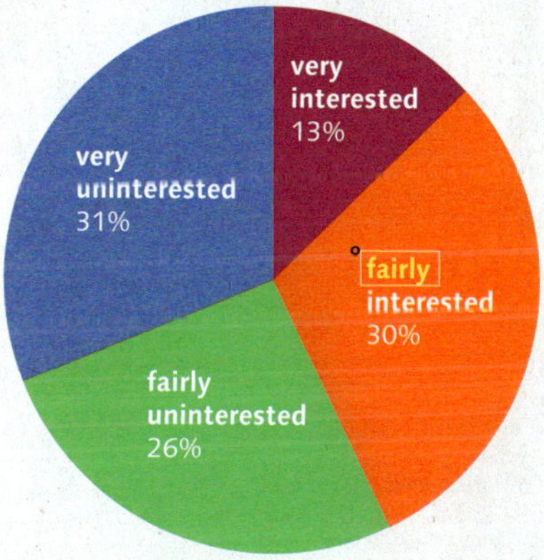

More practice 3 **One °good turn °deserves another** ▸ Unit 2, p. 39

Complete the story. Use the ***simple past***.

Dominique *wanted* (1 want) to take a taxi home after an evening out with friends. But when she … (2 look) in her °purse she … (3 cannot) find her bank card. A stranger … (4 see) that Dominique … (5 be) in trouble and he … (6 offer) her money. It … (7 be) a kind offer especially because the man … (8 not have) much money himself.

In fact he … (9 be) homeless and was living on the street. Dominique … (10 decide) to do something. She … (11 start) an online campaign to raise money and she even … (12 spend) a night on the city streets to find out what it … (13 feel) like. In the end she … (14 collect) over £40,000 for a local homeless charity.

More practice 6 **Your report** ▸ Unit 2, p. 40

Write a report like the ones in 5a) and b) (on p. 40) about any event you like.

Choose an event: a charity event, a play at school, a sports competition, a family event or an interesting news story.
→ **Plan** before you write. ▸ Skills file 10.1, p. 172
→ **Check** your text. Look especially at the past tenses. ▸ Language files 3–8, pp. 187–189

Unit 2

More practice 4 The Big Sleep Out

▸ Unit 2, p. 39

Complete the interview with the correct forms of the ***simple past***.

Reporter Yesterday fifteen Year 11 students from Green Lane School ... (1 take part) in a Big Sleep Out. I ... (2 speak) to their °spokesperson Katy about the experience.
So Katy, what ... (3 happen) in the Big Sleep Out?

Katy Basically on Friday night fifteen of us ... (4 sleep) outside the school.

Reporter ... (5 you, sleep) well?

Katy We ... (6 try) to sleep, but we ... (7 not sleep) very well.

Reporter ... (8 it, rain)? ... (9 you, get) wet?

Katy At the beginning of the night the weather ... (10 be) good. We ... (11 build) little houses out of °cardboard boxes. It ... (12 be) cold and we ... (13 not be) very comfortable. But it ... (14 be) OK. It ... (15 rain) a lot later though.

Reporter ... (16 the boxes, keep) you dry?

Katy No, they ... (17 not do)! We ... (18 get) very wet!

Reporter Why ... (19 you, organize) the Big Sleep Out?

Katy Well, we ... (20 have) a talk from a homeless charity and they ... (21 tell) us that they really ... (22 need) money. So we ... (23 think) this would be a good way to raise money for them.

Reporter ... (24 you, raise) much money?

Katy Yes, we ... (25 do). But we also ... (26 find out) what it's like to sleep outside in November. It ... (27 make) us think about the °conditions that homeless people live in.

More practice 5 A day to remember

▸ Unit 2, p. 39

Complete the text with the correct forms of the ***simple past***, the ***past progressive***, or the ***past perfect***.

It ... (1 rain) when the soccer team left school at 7 o'clock on Saturday. But soon the sun started to shine and it ... (2 not stop) all day. We were feeling excited by the time we ... (3 arrive) at the stadium at 11 o'clock. After we ... (4 look) around the changing rooms, we went out onto the °pitch. Wow! The stadium ... (5 be) huge.
We were out there on our own because the other team ... (6 not arrive) yet. We ... (7 get) a bit worried because at 11.45 they still hadn't °turned up. We ... (8 walk) back to the changing rooms when the other team came out at last. Wow, they ... (9 be) giants! We ... (10 feel) a bit scared of them, but then Mrs Brown came in and gave us a talk. After she ... (11 talk) to us for 15 minutes we felt great again.
We were ready for the match!
At °half-time things ... (12 not go) well. The other team ... (13 score*) two °goals, and we weren't feeling confident at all. So Mrs Brown ... (14 give) us another one of her talks. Basically, she told us that if we ... (15 work) harder, we could win. Well, she was right. By the end of the second half we ... (16 score) three goals. We had won the °championship! It truly was a day to remember!

*score a goal ['skɔː ə 'gəʊl] *ein Tor schießen*

//● 3 From the local news ► Unit 2, p. 39

Complete the reports. Use the ***simple past*** or the ***present perfect***.

a) There *was* (1 be) a big concert in the town centre last night, and John Young ... (2 come) into town to enjoy the music. He ... (3 start) the evening with a group of friends but he ... (4 not stay) with them. His parents are now worried because their son *hasn't come* (5 not come) home yet. They ... (6 speak) to all his friends, but nobody knows where he is.

b) Everybody ... (1 be) very surprised last Friday when the new sports shop in the high street ... (2 close) without warning. The shop workers are angry because all of them ... (3 lose) their jobs. They ... (4 organize) a protest, and it will take place on Tuesday outside the shop. So far they ... (5 not hear) anything from shop owners.

c) Many local students ... (1 do) their final school exams in April. They ... (2 wait) nervously since then for their results. At the local high school students ... (3 get) their results at 10 o'clock this morning. Some students are excited because they ... (4 do) well. But a few are quiet because they ... (5 not get) the results they were hoping for.

More help 4 Have you ever won something? What did you win? ► Unit 2, p. 39

Before you start: Prepare follow-up questions for each of the questions in the orange box – as many as you can. Make notes. Use these ideas or your own ideas.

Have you ever ...	Follow-up questions
- won something?	What did you win? ...
- had a part-time job?	What kind of job was it? ...
- taken part in a performance?	What kind of performance was it?
- raised money for charity?	How did you raise the money? How much money did you raise?
- lived somewhere different?	Where did you live? How long did you live there?

Unit 2

More challenge 4 REVISION Present perfect progressive

▸ Unit 2, p.39

FOCUS

You can use the ***present perfect progressive*** when an action started in the past but is still going on. It is often used with verbs like *live*, *work*, *study*.

Example: Some of the young refugees have been living in Australia for over a year.

▸ Language file 6, p. 188

Answer these questions about things you have been doing recently.

1 How long have you been learning English?
2 How long have you been going to the same school?
3 How long have you been living in the same place?
4 Do you or a friend play a sport? How long have you been playing that sport?
5 Do you or a friend play an instrument? How long have you been playing that instrument?
6 What are you doing right now? How long have you been doing it?

More practice 7 A newspaper report

▸ Unit 2, p. 43

Imagine that you are a journalist. Write a report (100–120 words) about the accident for your newspaper. Find a good title for the report – and use some headings too.

▸ Skills file 10.8, p. 178

More practice 8 Part 4: Vanessa's granny

▸ Unit 2, p. 44

2.04 Listen to part 4 of the conversation. When you hear the bell, try to mediate for Vanessa.

More practice 9 NOW YOU Talking to a tourist

▸ Unit 2, p. 44

Pick at least two topics and write short English texts explaining them to a foreign tourist.

- Feiertage, die Menschen in Deutschland feiern (z.B. den Tag der deutschen Einheit)
- typische Hobbys in Deutschland
- beliebte Fernsehserien in Deutschland
- Einschulung und erster Schultag in Deutschland
- mein deutsches Lieblingsessen

1.14

Face (adapted from the novel by Benjamin Zephaniah)

1 Walking around town

Martin, Mark, Matthew and Natalie walked down the street in silence. When they arrived at the top of Natalie's street, Mark and Matthew waited at the corner while Martin walked with her to her door. He had to make sure she got home safe.
The Gang of Three decided to go through an area that wasn't a nice place to live. They went through a building with no doors. There were needles everywhere on the floor.

2 Friends should stick together

As they walked through this area, they could hear the sound of a fast car. It was coming their way. In the dark they saw headlights. But they couldn't see the driver. The car stopped beside them. A shout came from the front passenger seat.

Box: Voc., p. 222

"Martin, man. It's me, Pete."
It was Peter Mosley. He used to go to Martin's school. But now he was in a gang, known for their crazy activities. The car was a red Ford. Martin didn't know the driver, who looked older.
Pete shouted, "Come on, let's go riding."
"Nah, we're going home," Martin answered.
"Come on, man. We'll just take you home."
"OK, just a lift home," Martin said as he opened the back door of the car.
Matthew was angry. "Are you really going? You're mad!" He walked away.
Martin and Mark got into the car.
"What kind of friends are you two? I thought friends should stick together," Matthew said as he turned and walked away.

3 Dangerous driving

Martin and Mark were excited. They had never been in a fast car like this before. They drove very fast. They went down one big road – the wrong way! When Martin saw this, he shouted, "Pete, let's go back, man! What's your friend's name?"
"My name's Apache," the driver said.
"How long have you had this car?" Martin asked.
Apache began to laugh. "Twenty minutes, man. I got this car twenty minutes ago."
"You stole it?" Martin asked.
Both Pete and Apache laughed. Martin and Mark looked at each other. They were scared.
"Just leave us here," Mark said.

4 The car chase

Pete shouted, "Cops behind us."
Apache drove faster. The police car stayed behind them.
Martin shouted angrily, "STOP!"
Apache wasn't listening.
The police put on their sirens and flashing lights. Apache and Pete seemed to love the excitement. They drove through a red traffic light.
"Let us out," Martin said. "STOP THE °BLOODY CAR!" he shouted.
Apache and Pete only looked at each other and laughed.

5 The crash

Box: Voc., p. 223

They crashed. The red Ford rolled over, throwing Pete out of the front window. The car landed on the other side of the road, upside down. There was a moment of silence.
The police came over. Apache climbed out of the front window and ran – into the arms of a police officer.
Mark climbed out of his side window and screamed, "Help. My friend is in there."
He tried to open Martin's door, but he couldn't.
"We'll deal with him," the officer said and put Mark in the back of a police car, next to Apache.
Then there was a loud explosion and there was fire in the car. Martin was quickly pulled out and put into an ambulance.
From the back of the police car Mark shouted, "That's my friend Martin. I want to go with him."
But nobody listened to him.

▸ KV 12 ▸ KV 15

6 No tears

Twenty-four hours later Martin's parents were sitting on chairs on each side of the bed. They were silent. A doctor came in and she looked at Martin.
"Hello Martin," she said. "You have had a very bad accident, you know. You have some burns on your face. But don't be too alarmed. Over time we can improve things. Have you any questions?"
Martin didn't reply. The doctor continued. "We are all here for you if you need us."
Martin could only say "Thank you" to the doctor. For the first time in his life he wanted to cry, but he didn't have any tears.

2 Understanding the text

What do we learn in the different parts?
Match the sentence parts.

1 In part 1 we get an idea of the area ...
2 In part 2 we learn that Matthew is ...
3 In part 3 Martin and Mark realize ...
4 In part 4 we learn that Pete and his friend ...
5 In part 5 we see the danger ...
6 In part 6 we learn that Martin's life ...

A that they have made a mistake.
B of 'joyriding'.
C where the teenagers live.
D has changed – probably forever.
E aren't afraid of the police.
F a strong character.

3 Working with the text

Finish the sentences with words and phrases from the text.

Part 1: This area of London isn't a nice place to live because in some buildings ...
Part 2: We know that this story happened at night because the teenagers couldn't see ...
Part 3: Martin and Mark changed their minds about being in the car. First they were ... but then they ...
Part 4: Apache and Pete were horrible. For example, when Martin and Mark wanted to stop ...
Part 5: Apache didn't care about the others. For example, when the car crashed ...
Part 6: When Martin learned that he had burns on his face, ...

4 WRITING A newspaper report

Imagine that you are a journalist. Write a report (80–100 words) about the accident for your newspaper. Find a good title for the report – and use some headings too. ▸ Skills file 10.8, p. 178

More help **4b** **READING** **#ILookLikeAnEngineer** ▸ *Unit 2, p. 46*

Complete this answer. Give line numbers where you can.

Perhaps Wenger's campaign can change stereotypes. For example in the text it says ... (lines ...)
It also says ... (lines ...)
On the other hand, maybe it can't. For example, the article also says ... (line ...)
Personally I think that ...

More challenge 5 **WRITING** **A comment** ▸ *Unit 2, p. 46*

Do you think that hashtag campaigns like Wenger's are a good idea? Why (not)?
Write a comment – at least 60 words. ▸ *Skills file 10.2, p. 174*

More challenge 6 **WRITING** **Two reviews** ▸ *Unit 2, p. 47*

a) Write a review of the film *Walk or fly*.
OR
b) Write a review of another film that you've seen recently.

- Write about things like the **location**, the **characters**, the **acting**, the **costumes**, the °**soundtrack**, etc.
- Does the video have a message? If yes, what is it?
- Did you enjoy it? Why (not)?
- Would you recommend it? ▸ *Skills file 10.9, p. 178*

Unit 2 Stop! Check! Go!

1 **LANGUAGE** **The European Parliament** ▸ *Unit 2, p. 48*

Look out for the signal words.

Complete this chat between Ralf, a German student on a class trip in Brussels, and Cathy, his Australian friend. Use the ***simple past*** or ***present perfect***. ▸ *Language file 5, p. 188*

Ralf: I'm in Brussels. My friends and I ... (1 just leave) the European Parliament. What an interesting place!

Cathy: Really? I ... (2 not visit) Brussels yet but I'd like to go there one day. I'm interested in European politics.

Ralf: I think politics is important. My class ... (3 do) a survey last year and we ... (4 find) that most young people didn't vote in the last European elections. I think that's terrible.

Cathy: Maybe people don't know about the advantages of the EU – like the euro. That makes it easier for people to travel, doesn't it? How long have you had the euro?

Ralf: In Germany we ... (5 get) the euro in 2002.

Cathy: Does the EU make a difference to your life in other ways?

Ralf: Yes, it does. For example, the EU Parliament ... (6 recently pass) a law to make mobile calls to other EU countries cheaper.

Cathy: So you think the EU is a good thing?

Ralf: I do. But this morning I ... (7 go) to a discussion about "Rules against misuse of trade secrets". I ... (8 never listen to) such a boring discussion!

Cathy: OK, so politics is important, but sometimes it isn't very interesting.

Unit 2 Stop! Check! Go!

More challenge 7 Fun in Detmold ▸ Unit 2, p. 51

Freja is a friend from Sweden. Help your family to have a conversation with Freja.

Vater Nächstes Wochenende können wir einige Dinge zusammen machen und Freja etwas von unserer schönen Gegend zeigen. Frag Freja, ob sie besondere Ideen hat, was sie sehen und tun mag.

1 You (to Freja) My parents would like to take you to see some of the interesting things in our area next weekend. Is there anything you would like to see?

Freja I read something about a monument called *Hermannsdenkmal*. I'd like to see that.

2 You (to your parents) ...

Vater Sag Freja, dass wir ihr gern das Hermannsdenkmal in Detmold zeigen würden. Das ist berühmt. Viele Touristen aus aller Welt kommen, um es sich anzusehen.

3 You (to Freja) ...

Mutter In Detmold gibt es am Wochenende einen tollen Flohmarkt. Frag mal, ob Freja Lust hat, den zu besuchen.

4 You (to Freja) ...

Freja Yes, that's a great idea. I love markets.

5 You (to your parents) ...

Vater Und wenn Freja möchte, werden wir dort auch etwas typisch Deutsches essen, nämlich eine Currywurst mit Pommes. Dort gibt es die beste weit und breit.

6 You (to Freja) ...

Mutter Oder man kann einen lippischen Pickert probieren. Das ist eine westfälische Spezialität, ein bisschen wie Pfannkuchen aus Mehl, geriebenen Kartoffeln, Milch, Eiern, Hefe und mit Rosinen. Lecker, aber sehr sättigend. Frag Freja, ob sie das probieren mag.

7 You (to Freja) ...

Freja Both meals sound great. I'd like to try both. Then I can tell my friends in Sweden about some typical German food and also a °speciality from Westphalia. And when I'm back in Sweden I can try making the Pickert for my family.

8 You (to your parents) ...

Unit 3

More practice 1 Working with words ▸ Unit 3, p. 54

a) Match the sentence endings (A–G) to explain the words (1–7) from pp. 54 and 55.

1	A driverless car ...	A	is usually found in a bedroom.
2	Contact lenses ...	B	is a gadget that flies on its own.
3	A pillow ...	C	are used by people who can't see very well.
4	An exoskeleton ...	D	is the colour you put on walls or °furniture, etc.
5	A scientist ...	E	is someone who works in science.
6	Paint ...	F	is a vehicle that drives itself.
7	A drone ...	G	is something that you can wear that gives you more strength.

b) Now use a dictionary (online, if you like) and explain these words from pp. 54 and 55 – in English or in German: *a parcel*; *a medicine*; *deliver*; *a firefighter*.

More practice 2 **Emma's diary** ▸ Unit 3, p. 57

Pick one of these times and write Emma's diary log entry. You can be imaginative. Say what you think and feel. Describe the scene. Example:

Monday morning: *When I opened my eyes, I felt great. I checked my ...*
Monday afternoon: *I got home from school at about 3.50 pm and I decided to ...*
Saturday afternoon: *It was a normal Saturday afternoon. I was in my favourite cafe with ...*
Saturday evening: *When I got home, I was a little tired, so I decided to watch ...*

More challenge 1 **The pros and cons of wearable technology** ▸ Unit 3, p. 57

What do you think of wearable technology? Write about the pros and cons. Give reasons and examples. Write about 120–160 words. Think about these questions:

- How many different devices can you name?
- Why do people like them so much?
- Are they cheap to buy?
- How useful and necessary are they?
- Are there any disadvantages or even dangers?

▸ Skills file 10.7, p. 177

More challenge 2 **Talk about a slide** ▸ Unit 3, p. 59

Choose one of these slides and prepare a short talk on the topic "Challenges for our environment". Then present it to the class.

Travelling ...

by train or by plane?

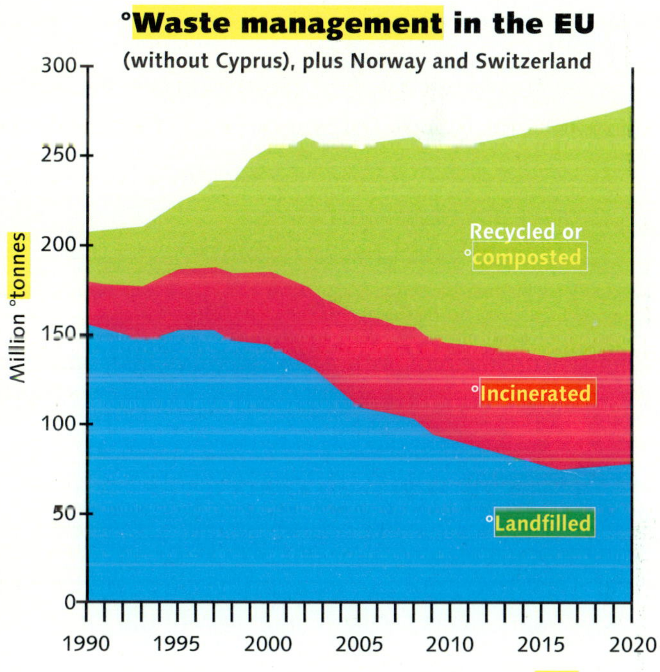

Source: *European Environment °Agency (2011)*

▸ KV 23

Unit 3

More practice 3 Good writing techniques (3)

▸ Unit 3, p. 59

a) °Contrast: In *Sorry*, the writer uses the technique of contrast. This means he puts two opposites together.

> These techniques are also called ***stylistic devices***.

1 Look at these lines from *Sorry*. Can you find the two opposites?

I'm guessing you probably know what is the Amazon desert, right?
Well believe it or not, it was once called the Amazon °rainforest.

What effect does this contrast have? Does this technique make you feel bored or interested?

2 Now look at these lines from *Sorry*. Can you find the two opposites here?

But most of all I want to say sorry about our °mindset,
Cause we had the nerve to call this °destruction – °progress.

What's the effect of using this contrast? How does it make you feel?

3 In these lines the contrast is very clear. What are the opposites?

And I'm sorry we didn't find another planet °in time to move to.
I am s...
You know what, °cut the °beat, I'm not sorry.
This future, I do not accept it ...

What is Prince Ea saying here? Does he surprise you? How?

▸ Skills file 8.5, p. 169

b) Other techniques (stylistic devices): Look at the lines below from *Sorry* (in 1 to 4). What writing techniques can you discover in them?

1 *Sorry, sorry we left you our mess of a planet.*
Sorry that we were too °caught up in our °doings to do something.
Sorry we listened to people who °made excuses to do nothing.

2 *We just didn't realize how special the earth was,*
Like a °marriage going wrong,
We didn't know what we had until it was gone.

3 *I'm sorry we used nature as a credit card ...*

4 *We are the root, we are the °foundation, this generation.*

> You don't have to understand all the words to discover the techniques. But you can use a dictionary.

> You can find a list of good writing techniques (***stylistic devices***) in ▸ Skills file 8.5, p. 169.

More challenge 4 Your view of the future

▸ Unit 3, p. 65

Pick a) or b) and write a short argumentative text.

▸ Skills file 10.7, p. 177

a) Does this story give us a pessimistic or an optimistic view of the future – or both? Give your opinion. What's your view of the future? Give reasons for your arguments.

b) *Rowing a boat is like life – you can't see what's ahead*. Do you agree or disagree with this statement? Give reasons for your answer.

//● 3 What do you think? ▸ Unit 3, p. 61

Complete the dialogue with suitable forms of the ***simple present*** or the ***will*-future**.

DrSpock I … (1 not think) humans … (2 ever, get) to Mars. What about you?
Spacecadet Well, I … (3 believe) that it … (4 happen) one day. Maybe it … (5 not happen) by 2030, but I … (6 be) sure that the scientists … (7 succeed) sometime in the future.
DrSpock Let's say they make it. How long … (8 it, take) to get there?
Spacecadet It's likely that the trip … (9 take) 8 months. It … (10 be) a long way!
DrSpock What … (11 you, think) life … (12 be) like on Mars?
Spacecadet It … (13 be) really difficult. The space pioneers … (14 not, be able) to go outside without special suits. They … (15 have to) wear them all the time as it's so cold. And there's the deadly radiation. If they … (16 stay) outside without a suit, they … (17 die).
DrSpock Where they … (18 they, live) then?
Spacecadet They … (19 have to) live under the ground at first. But I … (20 expect) that later they … (21 create) new habitats. I think it … (22 be) brilliant.
DrSpock Humans have made a big mess here on earth. I'm sure they … (23 make) the same mistakes if they … (24 go) somewhere else.
Spacecadet Maybe you … (25 be) right, but it's possible that we … (26 do) better next time!

▸ Language files 10–11, p. 190

More practice 4 Make predictions for your partner ▸ Unit 3, p. 61

a) Think: What do you think your partner's life will be like in ten years' time? Make predictions – as many as you can.
- Where do you think he / she will be?
- What job do you think he / she will have?
- Do you think he / she will have a car? What kind? (big / small / electric / …)
- Do you think he / she will be married or have a partner? Will he / she have children? How many?
- …

b) Pair: Listen to your partner's predictions and comment on them.
I think it's likely / unlikely that I will …
I'm sure that I will …
I don't think that I will …
I definitely will / won't …

c) Share: Tell the class one prediction that you hope will °come true and one that you hope won't come true – for yourself.

More practice 5 An evening with friends ▸ Unit 3, p. 61

Complete the sentences.
Use the ***will*-future** or the ***going to* future**.
If you're unsure, look at the box.

FOCUS

Remember: You usually use the ***will*-future** for predictions and the ***going to*-future** for plans.

In English you can also use the ***will*-future** when you make a quick decision or an offer.

Examples: *I'll take it!* (Ich nehme es!)
I'll come with you. (Ich komme mit!)
I'll help you! (Ich helfe dir!)

1 You meet your friends in town. They tell you about their plans for the afternoon. They say: "We ... (get) something to eat and then we ... (see) that new film in the cinema."
2 You don't think the film is very good. You say: "I don't think that I ... (like) that film."
3 One of your friends has read excellent reviews. He says: "The reviews say that people who like science fiction ... (love) it. You like science fiction, so I think you ... (enjoy) it."
4 Another friend tries to persuade you too. She says: "Please come. I'm sure we ... (have) a good time."
5 You decide to go to the cinema. You say: "OK, I ... (come) with you."
6 In the cafe one friend says: "I ... (visit) my grandmother later and she always gives me a big meal, so I ... (order) something small. What about you two?"
7 You look at the menu and decide quickly what you want. You say: "I ... (have) a hamburger and fries."
8 Your other friend isn't sure what to have. She says: "Do you think the curry ... (be) °vegetarian?
9 In the end you talk for too long and there's no time to eat anything. You say: "If we don't leave now, we ... (miss) the film!"

More challenge 3 **More ways of talking about the future** ▸ Unit 3, p.61

Read the text.

A grey day on Mars

Lucy woke up early. She looked out of the window of her °pod. "Another grey morning on Mars," she thought. The screen on her desk said: "Monday 1st February – 6.15 am."
"I'm not getting up yet," she thought. "Breakfast isn't until 7 today."
She thought back over her time on the Red Planet. She had °set off on her journey from earth over a year ago.
"In three week's time I'll be celebrating my birthday on Mars for the first time. We'll have been here for 6 months," she thought.
The alarm went off. "I'll get up now," she thought. "Breakfast starts in 10 minutes, and I'm not going to be late. We're having °pancakes today, my favourite."
Over breakfast the team discussed their plans for the day.
"I'm going outside today," Lucy °announced. "I'm going to check the °solar panels. Is anybody else coming?"
"I'll come with you," said Avril. "But while you're looking at the solar panels, I'll be checking the roof of the pod."
Lucy thought, "If there's a problem with the roof, it'll be serious." But she just nodded and smiled. "I'll see you in half an hour by the main door then. Will you have finished your breakfast by then?"
"Sure," said Avril. "I've already finished. I'll see you later."
"Great. See you later."

a) True or false? Find evidence in the text for your answers.
1 Lucy has to wait over an hour for breakfast.
2 Lucy's birthday is in March.
3 Lucy has been on Mars for less than 6 months.
4 Lucy is looking forward to breakfast.
5 She knows what's on the breakfast menu.
6 Lucy has already planned her work for the day.
7 Lucy and Avril are going to work together.
8 Lucy is worried about the roof.

b) The writer uses many different verb forms to talk about the future.
Look at the examples from the text in the box below.
Then find at least one more example of each form in the text on p. 128.

FOCUS

When talking about the timetable for the day, the writer uses the ***simple present***:
Example: Breakfast starts in 10 minutes.

When talking about something that's a fixed plan, the writer uses the ***present progressive***:
Example: We're having pancakes today.

When talking about something that will come to an end in the future, the writer uses the ***future perfect***:
Example: We'll have been here for 6 months in three weeks' time.

The writer also uses the ***progressive*** form of the **will-*future*** – also called the ***future progressive***.
Example: I'll be celebrating my birthday on Mars for the first time. ► *Language files 11–14, pp. 190–191*

More practice 6 Natasha's story or Zoe's story ► *Unit 3, p. 65*

Pick a) or b).

a) Tell the story in paragraph 4 (lines 47–82) from Zoe's point of view. Use the first-person narrator. Write about 60–80 words.

b) Tell the story in paragraph 4 (lines 47–82) from Natasha's point of view. Use the first-person narrator. Write about 60–80 words.

Then compare your text with someone who has written the other text.

More help 2a SPEAKING A talk about gadgets and inventions ► *Unit 3, p. 66*

Here are some ideas for gadgets and inventions that could make the world a better place:

- a homework robot
- smart highways (all vehicles are electric)
- virtual school from home
- medicine for all diseases
- silent cars
- an animal-human °translator
- underwater houses
- plastic bones
- space buses and hotels
- flying cars
- °rainmakers
- memory °pills
- virtual clothes
- °waterless washing machines
- cities in the sky

You can do some research and find some information about your idea:

- Does it already exist?
- Are scientists working on it?
- Is it realistic?
- Will it come soon?
- What are the advantages?
- Are there any disadvantages?
- Are there any dangers?

More practice 7 A terrible new phone ► *Unit 3, p. 67*

Your new mobile phone is terrible. It doesn't work as promised in the ad. Write a formal email to the online shop and complain about it. Write about 120 words. Say what's wrong with the phone (at least two things) and what you want the shop to do.

Floodland (adapted from the novel by Marcus Sedgwick)

2.14

Zoe ran. She could hear the gang coming after her. She had no choice – now she had to leave the island in her boat.

Most of the people left on Norwich stayed together in groups, but Zoe preferred to be on her own. It was safer that way because you never knew who you could trust. Now a mob of about fifteen people was following her. There was only one way out: to get to her boat before they got to her. So she ran on. "Get back here!" someone shouted angrily at her, though they couldn't see her. It wasn't far to the little shed where she'd hidden *Lyca*, her boat.

Scared, Zoe fell in the mud. She started to panic badly. She had dropped her bag as she fell, but there was no time to pick it up. She got up and threw herself over a wall. She was in a graveyard. It went down a hill to where a small shed stood, with Zoe's boat in it. "*Lyca*," Zoe panted as she opened the shed door, "please be here, *Lyca*." It was all right. The boat was still there.

Pulling it across the grass, and then into the water, she looked behind her. The gang was coming down the hill. Zoe moved faster. They were at the water now.
"Take me with you!"
"Come back! We won't hurt you. Just take us with you!"
Zoe could see their eyes, clearly. She saw fear. But she couldn't trust them. Since she'd lost her parents, she'd made it a rule not to trust anyone.
She looked at the crowd in the water. Natasha was there too. That hurt most of all. Natasha had been her only friend. They used to have a little chat. The crowd stood quietly, watching her as she rowed away.
"Sorry," she said quietly. She began to cry, but she didn't stop rowing.

She took her compass out of her pocket. She °pointed herself south-west, and rowed. She knew that a big bit of Britain was somewhere in that direction.

Before now, she had never rowed. Her dad had taught her in a bath.
"You'll need to know how to do this one day," he told her.
He'd taught her how to use the compass, as well as lots of stuff about survival. Just in case the time came when she was on her own.
"Why don't you look where you're going?" she had asked her dad.
"When you're rowing, you mean?" he said.
"Yes, why do you sit looking backwards?"
"It's the way you do it," he said. "You couldn't row as well facing forwards." Box: Voc., p. 232
It had always seemed strange to her.
Norwich was getting smaller and smaller. She was °heading into the unknown, without even looking where she was going.

She rowed and rowed. There was no sign of land now and she became more afraid. She looked at the compass all the time, it was her only chance now. The sun made her feel dizzy. She pushed the hair out of her eyes, but the sea wind blew it back across her face. She felt faint. She thought about the time when she had lost her parents.

2 Working with the text

a) The characters: Make three sentences about the characters in the text.

1 Zoe Black ...
2 Zoe's parents ...
3 Natasha ...

A had left the island on the last ship.
B didn't have any parents.
C was alone on the island without her parents.
D wanted to hurt Zoe.
E had been a kind of a friend to Zoe.

b) Headings: Pick the correct headings (A or B) for each paragraph of the text.

Paragraph (lines)	Heading A	Heading B
1 (lines 2–4)	Zoe leaves by boat	No choice – Zoe has to leave
2 (lines 5–15)	Not far to the shed	Zoe can't find the shed
3 (lines 16–24)	Zoe gets to her boat	Lost in a graveyard
4 (lines 25–42)	Zoe is sorry to leave	Leaving the others behind
5 (lines 43–46)	No compass	Using a compass
6 (lines 47–60)	Skills for survival	Zoe can't row
7 (lines 61–71)	Zoe feels great	In the middle of the sea

c) The plot: Complete these sentences with words or phrases from the text.

1 Zoe wanted to leave the island in a ... (lines 2–4).
2 She thought that it was better to be alone because it was ... (lines 5–14).
3 When Zoe went into the shed, she was happy because the boat ... (lines 16–24).
4 We know that Zoe was sorry about leaving Natasha because she had been ... (lines 25–42).
5 Zoe rowed south-west because she knew that a big part of Britain was ... (lines 43–46).
6 Zoe knew how to row the boat because her dad had ... (lines 47–59).
7 In the boat Zoe felt very scared because there was no sign of ... (lines 61–67).

3 WRITING A message in a bottle

You're Zoe and you're in the little boat, in the middle of the sea. Write a 'message in a bottle' from Zoe to your parents. Tell them what has happened, how you feel and what your plans are. More help p. 133

Unit 3

More practice 8 MEDIATION An email from the drone company ▸ Unit 3, p. 68

Read the email from the drone company. Find the information that Andrea needs and make notes for a phone call with her (in German).

Senden An alle Anhang Adressen Schriften Farben

Chatwin Drones - PUT THE FUN IN FLYING

Dear Sir/Madam,

Thank you for °getting in touch with Chatwin Drones. The Fly-Hi 100 drone is one of our most popular products. Here is some more information about it.
With a fully charged battery, the Fly-Hi 100 will fly for a maximum of nine minutes. It has a maximum speed of 1.5 metres per second. It's suitable for indoor and outdoor flying and it can fly to a °height of 100 metres and a °distance of 500 metres from the remote control. They are the °legal limits, so we recommend that you don't °exceed these limits. The drone weighs 412 g, including the battery. The battery is included when you buy the product. The °current price is £159. We offer free °delivery in the UK. If you are ordering from abroad, we recommend that you look up the normal °postal rates. But please °note, we do not deliver to the US.

Thank you for your interest in our products. Please don't °hesitate to get in touch if you need more information.

Eric Brown, Chatwin Drones Sales

More challenge 5 Rules for drones in Germany ▸ Unit 3, p. 68

Do some research on the internet. Find out about the rules for drones where you live.

- Do you need a °licence for a drone?
- How old do you have to be to buy a drone?
- How high can a drone fly?
- How far can it fly?
- Can it fly near airports?
- Can it fly in public places?
- Can you take photos or make films with a drone?

More practice 9 The characters ▸ Unit 3, p. 69

a) Pick one of the main characters in the film – Sarah, Danny or Dr Thun. Copy this table. Then watch the film again and make notes about your character. Discuss your notes with other students who have picked the same character.

Character	
Appearance	
Personality	
Interests	

b) What do we learn about the relationship between Sarah and her mother? Does the relationship change? Write a short comment.
Swap texts with other students and read their ideas.

c) Does your opinion of any of the characters change during the film? Answer this question with examples and give some reasons.

► KV 19

More challenge 6 A film still ► Unit 3, p.69

Describe the still in detail. ► Skills file 11.1, p.179

- Where does this scene take place?
- Describe the scene.
- How do the people look?
- What are their relationships?

°Examine the still.

- What is the camera shot (a long shot / a medium shot / a close-up?)
- What body language do we see? (Are the people friendly / aggressive /...?)
- What is its effect on the viewer? (How does it make him / her feel?)

Find a caption for the still and give reasons.

More help 3 WRITING A message in a bottle ► Unit 3, p.131

Use these questions to help you:

- Where are you now?
- How did you get there?
- How do you feel?
- What equipment do you have with you?
- What about food and drink?
- What's the weather like?
- What are your plans?
- What are you looking forward to?

Unit 3 Stop! Check! Go!

// 2 LANGUAGE Rubbish island ► Unit 3, p.70

Complete the article using the correct form of the verbs – ***passive*** or ***active***.

Richart Sowa

Nowadays plastic °waste ... (1 see) as a big problem. In Mexico the artist Richart Sowa likes creating things from rubbish. Years ago he ... (2 start) collecting bags of empty plastic jars and bottles. Then he ... (3 use) the rubbish to build an island on a lake, called *Joyxee Island*. More and more plastic bottles ... (4 add). Today his island ... (5 make) of more than 150,000 containers. Trees and bushes ... (6 plant) on the island to keep Richart's house cool. This is Richart's third island. His previous two islands ... (7 destroy) by hurricanes.

Unit 3 | Stop! Check! Go!

More challenge 7 Use your dictionary ▸ Unit 3, p. 71

a) Find suitable English words for the underlined words in these sentences.

ÜBERLEGEN

1 Beim Schwimmen ist sie mir überlegen.
2 Ich muss überlegen, ob ich nach Klasse 10 eine Ausbildung mache oder weiter zur Schule gehe.

BERECHNUNG

3 Ich hoffe, meine Berechnung des Preises ist richtig.
4 Er macht vieles aus purer Berechnung.

b) Try to guess the meaning of the underlined words, then check in a dictionary.

The world population has increased (1) greatly and this has brought many problems including the destruction (2) of complete ecosystems (3) and global warming. A reduction (4) in greenhouse gases (5) and the use of renewable (6) types of °energy – such as solar (7), wave and wind power – are now seen as essential (8).

Text file

More practice 1 The separation of powers in Germany ▸ Textfile 2, p. 140

Research the German equivalents[1] of the US branches and offices shown in the graphic on p. 140. Draw a diagram or find the missing information to complete the graphic below.

Talk about the separation of powers in the German system of government.

Legislative

Bundestag
elected for … (by all … who have the right to vote)

…
appointed by governments of the federal states

Exekutive

… *(Federal President)*
elected for … (by Bundesversammlung)

… *(Federal Chancellor)*
elected for … (by …), appointed by …

Bundesminister *(Cabinet)*
appointed by …

Judikative

Bundesverfassungsgericht
16 …, elected for 12 years (by Bundestag + Bundesrat), appointed by …

Bundesgerichte
(Other federal courts)

[1] equivalent [ɪˈkwɪvələnt] *Entsprechung, Gegenstück*

Wordbank: Discourse markers

▸ *More challenge 1, p. 31*

Discourse markers are words and phrases that organize language in discussions and written arguments, e.g. they show the structure of an argument or the speaker's attitude. They usually stand at the beginning of a sentence.

Opening a discussion
- What do you think about ...?
- Let's discuss ...
- How about ...?
- I'd like to suggest ...

Summing up and stating the result(s)
- To sum up our discussion, we think .../ agree that .../can't agree on ...
- Both/All of us agree that ...
- Everybody supports .../is for/against ...
- (We voted and) a majority is for/ against ...
- In any case, ...
- On the whole, ... / As a result, ...
- In short, ...
- It has become clear that ...

Asking for clarification
- Sorry, I didn't get that.
- Could you please give an example of ...?
- Are you saying that ...?
- Does that mean ...?
- In other words, ...?

Buying time
- Well, let me see ...
- I'm not an expert, of course, but I think/I guess/I'd say that ...
- Well, that's an interesting point.
- I see what you mean.

Changing the subject
- Oh, by the way, ...
- Another aspect of ... is ...
- Right, now let's discuss .../go on to ...

Giving your opinion
- In my opinion/view, ...
- If you ask me, ...
- I'd like to point out that ...
- Regarding ..., I think/suppose ...
- Apparently, ...

Agreeing
- I (definitely) agree (because) ...
- I think so too.
- (I think) you're right.
- It's true that ...
- That's a very good point.
- Yes, indeed.
- Certainly, ...

Disagreeing
- (I'm afraid) I don't agree.
- I'm not so sure about ...
- Yes/True, but don't forget ...
- (Sorry,) I think you're wrong / I don't think you're right.
- However, ...
- Although ..., ...
- In spite of this, ...
- On the contrary, ...
- Even so, ...
- ..., but nevertheless ...

Giving reasons/supporting your point
- To start/begin with, ...
- Firstly/Secondly, ...
- A good example for/against ... is ...
- Think of ..., for instance.
- What's more, ...
- On the one hand ..., but on the other hand ...
- Therefore, ...
- Since ..., ...
- No doubt ...
- As a consequence, ...

TF 1 PROJECT Around the world

1 Canada at a glance

a) Read this information from a travel guide about Canada. What did you already know?

b) If you were planning a trip to Canada, what else would you like to know? Together, note down at least five questions.

The beaver is a symbol of Canada

Niagara Falls, Ontario

The country

It's big! Damn big! In fact, it's the world's second largest country (after Russia). It's full of different landscapes – high mountains, huge glaciers[1], vast prairies[2], forests that go on forever, wild coasts ... Canada has it all! And Canada's climate is diverse too – from freezing winter temperatures (it can go to below 60 degrees Celsius in some places) to nice warm summer weather (top temperatures are around 25 degrees). About 90% of the population of Canada is squashed into the bottom part of the country, along the border[3] with the USA (where most of the cities are). And the rest of the country is almost empty – except for the wild animals, of course!

[1] glacier ['glæsiə] *Gletscher* [2] vast prairie [vɑːst 'preəri] *riesiges Grasland* [3] border ['bɔːdə] *Grenze*

▸ KV 39 ▸ KV 40 ▸ INKL pp. 74–79

The history

Canada's first inhabitants[4] probably came over a land bridge from Asia about 15,000 years ago and slowly moved south. Then, about 1000 years ago, the ancestors[5] of the modern Inuit people started to move down from Alaska. Around the same time the Vikings came, but they didn't stay. 500 years later, in 1497, the explorer[6] John Cabot arrived. He found cod here – a fish that Europeans liked to eat. Soon after that European fishermen started to arrive. In the 1530s the first French settlers came to Canada. They hunted beavers – for their fur[7] – and this became a huge business. So more and more Europeans came. In 1670 the English settled in the Hudson Bay area. There were many wars between the English and the French – until 1763, when France handed Canada over to Britain. In the 1850s gold was discovered in the west and lots of settlers moved there. Another important date is 1885, when the Canadian Pacific Railway was finished and many more people could travel west. In 1931 Canada became independent of Britain. However, even today the British Queen or King remains[8] the head of state[9].

Inuit family on a motorcycle at Inukjuaq

The newly married royal couple, Prince William and Catherine, on their visit to Canada in 2011

The people

For hundreds of years immigrants have been coming to Canada from all over the world – from Africa, Asia and Europe. Today Canada still has one of the highest rates of immigration in the world. As a result, Canada is a very multicultural country – and it's very accepting of[10] different cultures. Nearly every major Canadian city has a Chinatown, a Greektown, a Little Italy and a Little Punjab. Aboriginal Canadians (First Nations, Métis and Inuit) today make up about 4.3% of the population. Altogether there are about 200 different ethnic groups[11] in Canada and over 100 languages are spoken. The official languages are English and French. About 60% of the population speaks English as a first language and about 20% speaks French. One very important thing to remember is that Canadians are not Americans. If you ask Canadians what the differences are, you'll get lots of different answers: "Canadians are friendlier ... We're more polite and say 'sorry' a lot ... We're more tolerant ... We travel abroad more ... We like hockey more than football ... We don't carry guns ..." One thing is sure – Canadians get tired of being asked if they're American!

2 A talk about Canada

3.11

a) Listen to this talk. Does the talk answer any of your questions from 1b)?

b) Note down any other interesting facts that you learned about Canada from the talk.

c) Do some research to find the answers to any unanswered questions you have.

---

[4] inhabitant [ɪnˈhæbɪtənt] *Einwohner/in* [5] ancestor [ˈænsestə] *Vorfahr/in* [6] explorer [ɪkˈsplɔːrə] *Forschungsreisende/r* [7] fur [fɜː] *Fell, Pelz* [8] remain [rɪˈmeɪn] *(ver)bleiben* [9] head of state *Staatsoberhaupt* [10] be accepting of sb. *jm. annehmen, akzeptieren* [11] ethnic group [ˈeθnɪk] *Volksgruppe*

3 Your project

Pick a country where English is spoken (e.g. one of the countries in the pictures on pp. 138–139) and find some information about it. You can work alone, with a partner or in small groups. Think about the best way to present your information to the class.

Project steps

Step 1: Set your goals.
Decide what kind of information you want to find on the country you picked. For example, are you interested in:
- information for tourists,
- the history of the country,
- why English is spoken there,
- the lives of young people,
- ...?

Note down your questions.

Step 2: Get organized.
If you're working with a partner or partners, decide who will do what and how much time you have.
Decide how you want to present the information:
- on a poster,
- as a brochure,
- as a slide show with a voice-over,
- or even as a video.

Step 3: Do your research.
Use key words to do some internet research. Take notes about what you find out. Make sure that your information is correct – double-check. ▸ *Skills file 5, p. 164*

Step 4: Give your presentation.
All students should present their project to the class. Practise your presentation so that your performance is as smooth[12] as possible. ▸ *Skills files 4, p. 163; 9.1, p. 170*

You could ask some of these questions:
- What continent is this country in?
- What other countries is it near?
- What's the capital?
- What other big / famous cities are there?
- What's the landscape like?
- What can you find out about the history?
- What ethnic groups live there?
- Why is English spoken there?
- What can you find out about the people who live there?
- What about the wildlife, wild animals, etc.?
- What sights are there?
- What's this place famous for?
- What activities / sports can you do there?
- What famous singers and musicians come from there?
- ...

Colourful shop houses, Singapore

[12] smooth [smuːð] *glatt, reibungslos, problemlos*

The Gateway of India in Mumbai, India

Queenstown, New Zealand

Ocho Rios, Jamaica

Lagos, Nigeria

4 Feedback

Give some helpful feedback on the projects.

Be positive. Say the things that you liked.
Use phrases like this:

- The first / second / last part was really good.
- I liked the part where you ...
- It was very interesting to learn that ...
- Your visuals were good, especially ...

Give advice. Say what could be better.
Use phrases like this:

- Try not to talk so fast / slowly / quietly / ...
- Perhaps your visuals could be a bit clearer / ...
- Don't forget to smile / look at the audience / ...
- Maybe you read from your notes a little too much.

TF 2 USA: a balance of powers

"No country can be called free which is governed by an absolute power."

Thomas Paine (1737–1809), US founding[1] father

1 Power and the federal[2] government

a) Look at the quote above. What was Thomas Paine concerned about? What makes a country free?
Share your ideas. Then read the text.

When the US Constitution was written and signed in 1787, the authors or "founding fathers" wanted a system of government that didn't give any one person or group absolute power. So the Constitution divided[3] the federal government into three separate[4] branches: the legislative, the executive and the judicial branch.

Key terms
absolute ['æbsəluːt] *uneingeschränkt*
branch [brɑːntʃ] *Abteilung*
Constitution [kɒnstɪ'tjuːʃn] *Verfassung*
enforce [ɪn'fɔːs] *vollstrecken*
executive [ɪg'zekjətɪv] *ausführend*
justice ['dʒʌstɪs] / **judge** [dʒʌdʒ] *Richter/in*
judicial [dʒu'dɪʃl] *gerichtlich*
legislative ['ledʒɪslətɪv] *gesetzgebend*
representative [reprɪ'zentətɪv] *Abgeordnete/r*

A separation of powers

Legislative branch
makes the laws

The Capitol

Congress
consists of:
- **Senate**
  100 senators, two from each state; elected for six years (one third elected every two years)
- **House of Representatives**
  435 representatives, number from each state based on[5] population; elected for two years

Executive branch
enforces the laws

The White House

President
elected for four years

Vice[6] President
elected for four years

Cabinet
Secretaries[7]: heads of most important government departments[8]; appointed by the president

Judicial branch
interprets the laws

The Supreme Court

Supreme Court
nine justices; appointed by the president for life

Other federal courts

b) According to the text, why was a separation of powers important to the authors of the US Constitution?

c) Describe the three branches of government as shown in the graphic. The phrases in the box can help you.

Activate your English
The ... is made up of / represented by ...
The job / role of the ... is to ...
The ... is / are elected for ... years.
The ... is / are appointed by ...

More practice 1 | p. 134

[1]found [faʊnd] *gründen* (founding father = *Gründungsvater*) [2]federal ['fedərəl] *Bundes-* [3]divide [dɪ'vaɪd] *(auf)teilen* [4]separate ['seprət] *getrennt, separat* [5]based on ['beɪst ɒn] *auf der Grundlage von* [6]vice [vaɪs] *Vize-* [7]secretary *(AE)* ['sekrətri] *Minister/in* [8]department [dɪ'pɑːtmənt] *Ministerium, Amt*

2 Checks and balances

As part of the separation of powers, the founding fathers built a system of "checks and balances" into the Constitution that allows each branch of government to "check" the other branches. This system of control "balances" the power of the three branches. For example, Congress can make new laws, but the president must sign them before they can become official.

Key terms
act [ækt] *Gesetz*
appoint [əˈpɔɪnt] *ernennen*
declare [dɪˈkleə] *erklären*
check [tʃek] *zügeln, einschränken*
override [əʊvəˈraɪd] *aufheben*
propose [prəˈpəʊz] *vorschlagen*
veto [ˈviːtəʊ] *Einspruch erheben, Veto einlegen*

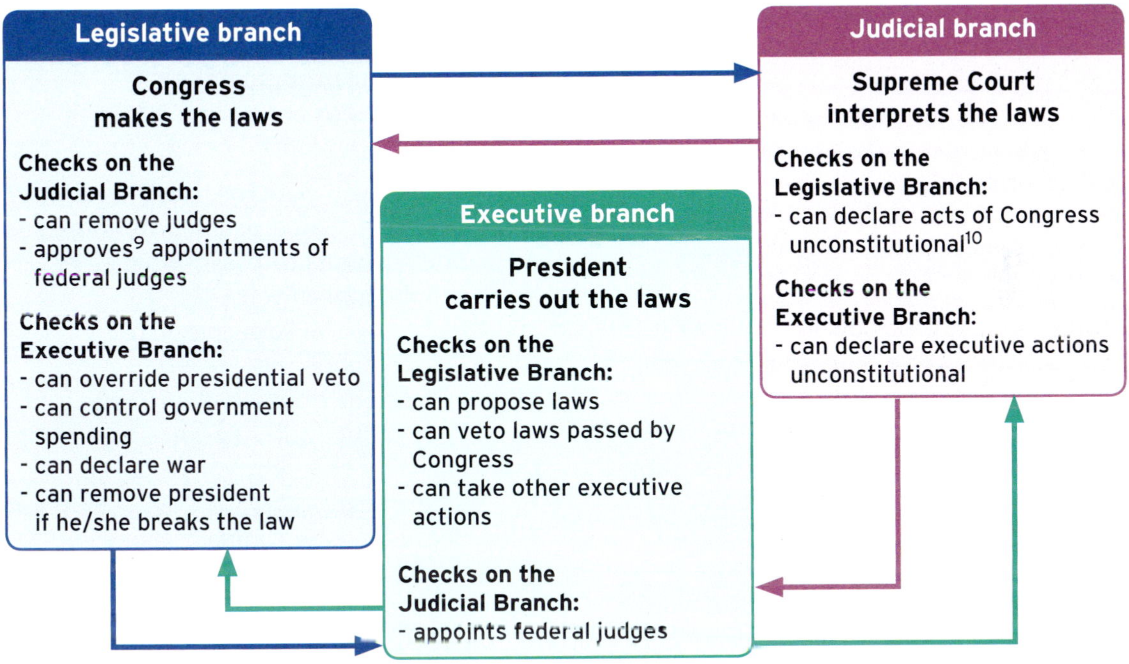

a) Complete these sentences to describe the checks and balances between the branches of government.

1 Congress can make a law, but *the president can veto the laws.*
2 The president can veto a law, but Congress ...
3 The president can take an executive action, but the Supreme Court ...
4 The Supreme Court interprets the laws, but the president ...
5 The president can appoint federal judges, but ...
6 Congress and the president can agree on a law, but ...

b) How do the role and the powers of the US president compare with those of the German chancellor and president? Do research and put your findings in a table. Present them in class.

US president	*German chancellor*	*German president*
Head[11] of government + Head of state	*Head of government*	*Head of state*
– runs the government *– represents the country*	*– runs the government*	*– mainly representative[12] functions*

[9] approve [əˈpruːv] *gutheißen, genehmigen* [10] unconstitutional [ʌnkɒnstɪˈtjuːʃənl] *verfassungswidrig* [11] head (of government/state) [hed] *Leiter/in, Vorsitzende/r (Staatsoberhaupt)* [12] representative [reprɪˈzentətɪv] *repräsentativ*

TF 3 The Question (adapted from a one-act play by Brent Hartinger)

1 Before reading

Before reading this play, think about this question: What are the main differences between a play and a story? ▸ Skills file 8.2–3, p. 168

A teenage boy's bedroom, with a bed, desk and a few old toys (ones with high teen appeal), lots of sports equipment, colognes and hair gel, along with a tie or two sticking out of a drawer. Two boys, Eric and Allen, enter. Both are eighteen. Allen is the trendier, better dressed of the two. Eric looks like an athlete. The boys have a natural, easy rapport with each other. They're right in the middle of an energetic conversation.

Allen *(impatiently)* So? Did you ask the question?

Eric What question?

Allen What do you mean what question? What other question is there? "Do you want to go to the prom[1]?"

Eric No, I didn't ask her if she wanted to go to the prom! I can't ask her! I don't even know her!

Allen Of course you know her. You just spent the last twelve years going to school with her.

Eric Yeah, and in all that time, I've probably spoken to her a grand total of six times. In five of those times, she didn't say anything back. Allen, I can't do this! What if she turns me down[2]?

Allen *(smiling)* I already told you, she won't turn you down! That's the beauty of this. I know for a fact she thinks you're cute, and that she wants to go to the prom with you. She just doesn't have the nerve to ask you.

Eric How do you know?

Allen I already told you! She told Jessica.

Eric Okay, okay. I'll ask her tomorrow.

Allen Call her tonight. Call her now. *(He turns for the door.)* I'll dial[3].

Eric *(stopping him)* Allen! What difference does it make when I ask her?

Allen Because if you don't do it tonight, you won't ever do it.

Eric And so what if I don't ever do it? I don't see what the big deal is.

Allen The big deal is that this is your senior prom! If you don't go to your senior prom, you'll regret[4] it. Maybe not now, maybe not tomorrow, but soon, and for the rest of your life.

Eric So I regret it.

Allen Just call her.

Eric Why do you want me to ask her so bad? Oh, I get it. You're ashamed of[5] me.

Allen Eric, I couldn't care less[6] what other people think of you.

Eric *(pouncing)* Ha! So people do think I'm strange!

Allen Eric, no one thinks you're strange. They should, but they don't.

Eric I just don't see why you're so determined[7] –

Allen Because I don't wanna be alone with Jessica all night long, okay?

Eric Then you ask Brittany to the prom.

Allen I don't wanna be alone with Brittany, either.

Eric Then who –?

Allen You, you idiot! I want to go to the prom with you. *(There is a pause.)*

Allen Wait. That didn't come out right. I mean I want you and Brittany to come to the prom with Jessica and me.

Eric *(turning away)* Oh.

Allen I want someone to talk to during dinner.

Eric Okay, okay. I'll call her.

Allen Now? *(He turns for the door.)*

Eric *(irritated)* Yes, now! You're obviously not going to stop bugging me[8] until I do.

Allen Wait!

Eric Now what?

Allen Let's practise first.

---

[1] prom [prɒm] *Schulabschlussball* [1] turn sb. down *jm. absagen, einen Korb geben* [3] dial ['daɪəl] *(Telefonnummer) wählen*
[4] regret [rɪ'gret] *bereuen* [5] be ashamed of [ə'ʃeɪmd] *sich schämen für* [6] I couldn't care less. *(infml) Es ist mir völlig egal.*
[7] determined [dɪ'tɜːmɪnd] *fest entschlossen* [8] bug sb. *(infml)* [bʌg] *jn. nerven*

Eric Oh no!

Allen Come on. Just do it. Okay, I'll pretend to be Brittany. You pretend to be you. You've just called me. *(He clears his throat; in a female voice.)* Hello? *(Eric stares at him with a smile.)*

Eric Is this really necessary?

Allen With anyone else, probably not. *("Brittany's" voice again)* Hello? Is anyone there?

Eric *(bored)* Hi, Brittany. I wanted to know if you wanted to go to the prom with me.

Allen *("Brittany's" voice)* Who is this? ... *(normal voice)* Come on! I'm just trying to get you to relax a little.

Eric *(very tense[9])* I'm relaxed, okay? I'm perfectly relaxed.

Allen I don't get it. Didn't you go to the prom before you met me? Last year? Or the year before?

Eric No *(quietly)*. I've never been to a dance, okay?

Allen What? Never?

Eric Never! Do I have to wear it on a sign around my neck? *(quietly)* I'm ... not sure I even know how to dance.

Allen *(smiling again)* Really?

Eric Allen!

Allen *(reassuringly[10])* Okay, okay. There's nothing to it. You just sort of ... *(he begins to sway[11])* Move to the music. That's the great thing about dancing – it's impossible to do it wrong. Do you have, like, a radio or something? Turn on some music.

Eric Yeah, sure. *(Eric turns the radio to some up-tempo song.)*

Allen Okay, just sort of ... go with the flow. *(Allen begins to dance. He's clearly practised for hours in front of a mirror, but he's actually pretty good.)*

Allen Now you try. *(Eric looks to see what Allen is doing, tries to mimic his moves.)*

Allen No, don't look at me. Just do whatever feels right. *(Eric tries again. He is embarrassingly awkward[12].)*

Allen You're too stiff. Try to loosen up[13].

Eric I thought you said it was impossible to do it wrong!

Allen I was wrong, okay? I'd never seen you dance. *(watching Eric)* That's better. *(They continue to dance. Eric is awkward.)*

Allen That's it! That's it. That's all you do. *(The song comes to an end. A slow song starts. There is an awkward pause.)*

Eric What if Brittany wants to ... slow dance?

Allen What?

Eric Slow dance. What if Brittany wants to slow dance?

Allen *(hesitantly[14])* Well ... it's sort of just the same thing, only you do it a lot slower, and you do it while holding onto someone else. *(They stare at each other for a second; the slow music continues to play.)*

Allen Oh, what the hell! *(Allen steps forward and takes Eric in his arms. They stay a foot apart.)*

Allen Okay, pretend I'm you and you be Brittany. I put my hands on your waist[15]. You put your hands on my shoulders.

Eric Like this?

Allen Close enough. Now we just sort of ... sway back and forth. I'll lead and you – Brittany – follow. *(They dance away.)*

Allen You know, there's not another guy on this planet that I'd do this with. *(They continue to dance. Eric is getting into it now – far better than before.)*

Allen Say, you're not bad. You're actually a lot better than Jessica.

Eric Come on.

Allen It's true! She dances like Frankenstein walks.

Eric Anyway ... *(An awkward silence. Then Allen speaks – less enthusiastically than before.)*

Allen Well ... I suppose we should call her now.

Eric *(quietly, head down)* Yeah, okay.

---

[9] tense [tens] *angespannt, verkrampft* [10] reassuring [riːəˈʃʊərɪŋ] *beruhigend* [11] sway (back and forth) [sweɪ] *(sich hin und her) wiegen* [12] awkward [ˈɔːkwəd] *unbeholfen* [13] loosen up [luːsn ˈʌp] *locker(er) werden, sich entspannen* [14] hesitant [ˈhezɪtənt] *zögerlich, zögernd* [15] waist [weɪst] *Taille*

(Allen starts for the door. Eric speaks, stopping him.)

Eric Well actually, there is one more thing.

Allen Yeah? *(There is another pause. Allen looks at Eric in confusion[16].)*

Eric Nothing. Never mind[17].

Allen No. Tell me.

Eric *(dismissively)* No, really. It's stupid.

Allen Come on.

Eric Well ... it's just that I ...

Allen Yeah?

Eric *(embarrassed, awkwardly)* Well, what if she wants me to ... kiss her good night?

Allen Huh?

Eric It's just that I've never actually kissed anybody before.

Allen *(quietly)* Oh.

Eric *(turning away)*
You probably think I'm an idiot asking all these stupid questions.

Allen No! No! There are no stupid questions. These aren't stupid questions. Not at all.

Eric So, um ... how do you do it?

Allen Well, there's nothing to it, really. You just sort of stand together, really close.

Eric Stand together close, okay.
(Eric and Allen step close together.)

Allen Don't pucker[18]. That's what everyone thinks at first, but it's not true.

Eric *(nodding)* Don't pucker. Okay, got it.
(They keep facing each other.)

Allen Then you just ... press your lips together.

Eric Press lips.

Allen And hold them there.

Eric Hold them there. How will I know when to stop?

Allen You just sort of ... know.

Eric Allen?

Allen Yeah?

Eric Do you ever think ...
(Suddenly, someone pounds on the door to Eric's bedroom. Both Eric and Allen start in alarm[13], then move to opposite sides of the room. The knock comes again. Eric turns to face the door.)

Eric What is it?
(A woman enters, Mrs. Sloan, Eric's mother. By interrupting, she has completely sucked the oxygen out of the room; even the light seems brighter now, and harsher.)

Mrs. Sloan Eric, your father needs to see you in the garage.

Eric Mom, I've kind of got company right now. Can you tell him I've got company?

Mrs. Sloan Oh, hello, Allen. I didn't know you were here.

Allen Hello, Mrs. Sloan.
(She notices the fact that they are on opposite sides of the room.)

Mrs. Sloan What are you boys doing?

Eric *(simultaneously with Allen)*
Reading comic books.

Allen *(simultaneously with Eric)* Playing a game!

Eric We're just hanging out! Tell dad I'll come down after Allen leaves.
(Mrs. Sloan lingers[20], staring at them suspiciously.)

Eric Anything else?

Mrs. Sloan No. No, I guess not. But we're having dinner in an hour.
Oh, and make your bed.

Eric *(quietly)* So I guess I should call Brittany now, huh?

Allen *(quietly)* Yeah, I guess you should.

Eric Okay, then. *(He starts for the door.)*

Allen Hey, maybe after the prom, we can drive up to the lake.

Eric With the girls?

Allen With 'em. Or without. Either way.
(They exit.) *(BLACKOUT)*
(END OF PLAY)

[16] in confusion [kən'fjuːʒn] *verwirrt* [17] Never mind. [maɪnd] *Egal.* [18] pucker ['pʌkə] *(die Lippen) kräuseln*
[19] start in alarm *vor Schreck zusammenzucken* [20] linger ['lɪŋgə] *verweilen, noch dableiben*

▸ KV 42 A–B ▸ KV 43

2 Setting

Read the play and make notes about these questions.

1 When do you think the play happens (in the present / the past)? Can you find any details that tell you this?

2 Where does the play take place? Describe how you think the stage would look.

> The **setting** of a story or play is where and when it happens.
> In a play you get information about the setting in the stage directions.

3 Plot

Pick the right ending to describe the plot. Find evidence for your answers in the text.

> The **plot** is what happens in a story or play and why it happens. Sometimes one action causes another.

1 In this play Allen wants Eric to ...
- A invite Jessica to the prom.
- B invite Brittany to the prom.
- C go to the prom alone.

2 But Eric has a problem because ...
- A he isn't interested in Brittany.
- B he hates proms.
- C he has no time.

3 We learn that Eric ...
- A doesn't know how to dance.
- B is a good dancer.
- C loves slow dancing.

4 We find out that ...
- A Eric wants to kiss Brittany.
- B Allen wants to kiss Jessica.
- C Eric is worried about kissing.

5 In the end we get the feeling that the boys ...
- A don't like each other.
- B are very good friends.
- C could be more than just friends.

4 Characterization

a) What do we learn about the two main characters? Make a table and write notes about: AGE, APPEARANCE, PERSONALITY, FEELINGS, SENSE OF HUMOUR, WORRIES.

> We learn about the **characters** of a play or story by looking at what they say and do, how they look, what they wear, and how they feel.
> In a play the stage directions – and the performance – are important too.

b) Write a characterization of one of the boys. Give examples and use quotes from the play.

▸ *Wordbank, p. 153*

5 Atmosphere

Finish these statements about the atmosphere with examples from the play

1 The atmosphere is light-hearted[21] when ... says ...
2 The atmosphere is a little tense when ...
3 The atmosphere changes when ...
4 In the end, the atmosphere is ...

> The **atmosphere** of a play or story is the feeling that the writer creates.
> It can be light-hearted or serious, positive or negative, tense or relaxed, etc. And of course the atmosphere can change.

6 Tell the story

Turn the play into a story – in not more than 180 words.
Use a first-person narrator (one of the boys) or a third-person narrator.

▸ *Skills file 8.2, p. 168*

[21] light-hearted *heiter, unbekümmert*

TF 4 Searching for a two-way street (a poem by Malorie Blackman)

1 While reading

Read this poem and answer the questions a) – f) on pp. 146–149.

SEARCHING FOR A TWO-WAY STREET

Before I was born,
Grown-ups[1] were passports
And driving licences
And bank accounts
And utility bills[2].

Communication was
Mobile phones
And cyber chats
And sign language
And face to face.

But people were
"Hello"
And hugs
And "Pleased to meet you"
And "How are you?"

Songs were
"Talk to me",
"See my side",
"Be with me",
"Love me."

And all those things
Were proof[3]
Of a person's identity.

All those things
Said
"I'm here,
I'm now,
I'm ready,
Willing[4]
And able
To communicate."

But that was
Before I was born.

Before I was born,
There weren't cameras
And scanners
And microchip readers
On every roof
On every street corner.

Before I was born,
School wasn't just a screen
And a virtual teacher.
Friends across the world
Had real faces,
Not faces chosen
In games or
From a menu.
We were more
Than just serial numbers[5]
And chips with everything.

Before I was born,
There was such a thing as
Secrecy[6]
Mystery
Privacy[7].
Before I was born.

Not any more.

a) What was life like before the speaker was born? Does the speaker think things were better then, or worse? Why? Give quotes from the poem.

[1] grown-up *Erwachsene/r* [2] utility bill [juː'tɪləti bɪl] *Betriebskostenabrechnung (Gas, Strom, Wasser)* [3] proof [pruːf] *Beweis(e), Nachweis(e)* [4] willing ['wɪlɪŋ] *bereit, gewillt* [5] serial number ['sɪəriəl nʌmbə] *Seriennummer* [6] secrecy ['siːkrəsi] *Geheimhaltung, Verschwiegenheit* [7] privacy ['prɪvəsi] *Privatsphäre*

When I was born,
A microchip was implanted[8]
At the base of my skull[9].
No microchip?
No state benefits[10],
No health care,
No travel,
No food aid[11],
No water deliveries,
No shelter[12],
No existence[13].
No microchip equals[14]
No anything.
Nothing.
No thing.
Not a thing.
So my Mum and Dad
Agreed,
When I was born,
To my microchip
Implant.
"We want our son
To survive in this world.
So yes to the chip."
Mum and Dad didn't like it,
They didn't want it,
But they had no choice.
And the government now knows
Where I am at all times.
Where any of us
Each of us
Are
At all times.
And we let them
Do that to us.

The government said,
"Law-abiding[15] citizens
Have nothing to fear[16]."

The government said,
"Those with nothing to hide
Have nothing to fear.
"The curtailment[17]
Of a personal freedom
Or two
Is a small price to pay
If we wish to have
Nothing to fear,"
The government said.

Those were the reasons
We gave up our mystery.

Better not to question.
Better not to know.
Better to accept.

And our information is fed
Back to computers.
State-of-the-art recording devices
That sit in silence
And capture[18] all movements
All meetings
All positions.

And Mum told me,
"Thirty years ago
This would've been
Inconceivable[19]."

And Dad said,
"Twenty years ago
This would've been
Unthinkable."

"Information shouldn't be
A one-way street," said Mum.
"Who watches the Watchmen[20]?"
Said Dad.

b) Since the speaker was born, life has changed. Describe how. Give some examples from the poem.
How does the speaker feel about these changes?

---

[8] implant [ɪm'plɑːnt] *implantieren, einpflanzen* [9] skull [skʌl] *Schädel* [10] state benefit ['steɪt benɪfɪt] *Sozialhilfe*
[11] food aid ['fuːd eɪd] *Nahrungsmittel(bei)hilfe* [12] shelter ['ʃeltə] *Unterkunft, Obdach* [13] existence [ɪg'zɪstəns] *Dasein*
[14] equal sth. ['iːkwəl] *einer Sache entsprechen* [15] law-abiding ['lɔː əbaɪdɪŋ] *gesetzestreu, die Gesetze befolgend*
[16] fear *(be)fürchten* [17] curtailment [kɜː'teɪlmənt] *Einschränkung (von Rechten)* [18] capture ['kæptʃə] *erfassen (Daten)*
[19] inconceivable [ɪnkən'siːvəbl] *unvorstellbar* [20] watchman, *pl* watchmen ['wɒtʃmən] *Wächter/in*

But they whisper the words
Behind closed doors.
It doesn't pay[21]
To stand and say
How you feel.
Not yesterday.
Not today.
Not tomorrow.
"Those days are over,"
Mum and Dad sigh.

There's a rumour[22]
Going round.
True or not?
Who can say?
But I think … true.
And this rumour?
The microchips in our heads
At the base of our brains
Relay[23] our thinking;
Maybe even control
Our thinking.

Just a rumour
But it's smoke …
So where's the fire?
Inside
Or outside
Our heads?

There's a rumour
Going round
That
Full thoughts[24]
Whole sentences
Can be tracked
Traced[25]
Monitored.
So I try
To think
In short
Sharp
Bursts[26].

My best friend
Denny told me
Staccato thoughts
Come across[27]
Like static
White noise[28].

No rhyme
No reason.
No sense
Nonsense[29].
True or not?
Who can say?

But now I think
In bursts
Like bullets[30]
Fired from a gun.
Proper[31] sentences
Could make me
… disappear.

Thoughts ought to be[32] private,
Information ought to be shared.
Communication should be
A two-way street.
An optional road to travel.
But a road we all
Can take
Nonetheless[33].

c) What do you think about the world the speaker lives in? Would you like to live in a world like that? Why (not)?

d) Do you think that the world in the poem is like our world?
- If yes, give some examples.
- If no, say why not.

[21] it doesn't pay *es zahlt sich nicht aus, es lohnt sich nicht* [22] rumour ['ruːmə] *Gerücht* [23] relay ['riːleɪ] *weitergeben, übermitteln* [24] thought *Gedanke* [25] trace sth. [treɪs] *etwas zurückverfolgen* [26] burst [bɜːst] *Explosion, Salve* [27] come across *herüberkommen, ankommen* [28] static white noise ['stætɪk] *weißes Rauschen, atmosphärische Störung* [29] nonsense ['nɒnsns] *Unsinn, dummes Zeug* [30] bullet ['bʊlɪt] *Kugel (aus Schusswaffe)* [31] proper ['prɒpə] *richtig, vollständig* [32] ought to be … [ɔːt] *sollte/n … sein* [33] nonetheless [nʌnðə'les] *trotzdem, nichtsdestoweniger*

"Those days
Are over,"
Mum and Dad murmur[34].
But I'm not prepared[35]
To believe that.
There has to be a way,
Some way,
To make my life
My own again.
Some way.

So I've started looking
For a means[36],
Some manner
To make my life
A two-way street.

And I will find it,
Because I'm not alone
In thinking
In bursts
Like bullets
Fired from a gun.
I'm not alone.
Because you are here
And I hope
You think the same.
Feel the same.

Our two-way street
We shall[37] find
We shall explore
We shall travel
Together.

e) In lines 199 – 229 of the poem, do you think that the speaker feels a little hopeful or only negative? Give reasons for your opinion.

ARTICLE 19
WE ALL HAVE THE RIGHT TO MAKE UP OUR OWN MINDS[38], TO THINK WHAT WE LIKE, TO SAY WHAT WE THINK AND TO SHARE OUR IDEAS WITH OTHER PEOPLE, WHEREVER THEY LIVE, THROUGH BOOKS, RADIO, TELEVISION AND IN OTHER WAYS.

f) Article 19 is from the Universal Declaration[39] of Human Rights. Do you think that the speaker agrees with it? Do you think this article is important? Why (not)?

2 Understanding the theme of the poem

Read the poem again. Then read these statements. Are they true or false? Quote the lines which give you the answers.

1 People weren't so friendly in the past. (Look at p. 146)
2 In the past, life was more personal. (p. 146)
3 In the modern world of the poem, you need a chip in your head to live. (p. 147)
4 In this new world, people are freer. (p. 147)
5 In this modern world, you can say what you think. (p. 148)
6 People say that the microchip controls what people think. (p. 148)
7 The computers can understand single words, but not full sentences. (p. 148)
8 The speaker asks us, the readers, to fight the microchip. (p. 149)
9 At the end of the poem, ARTICLE 19 says that we have the right to think for ourselves. (p. 149)

---

[34] murmur ['mɜːmə] *murmeln* [35] be prepared to do sth. *bereit sein, etwas zu tun* [36] means, *(pl) Mittel, Möglichkeit*
[37] we shall *wir werden (Futur)* [38] make up one's mind *sich entscheiden* [39] declaration [deklə'reɪʃn] *Erklärung*
(Universal Declaration of Human Rights = *Allgemeine Erklärung der Menschenrechte*)

3 More about the poem

a) Setting: When do you think this poem is set?
b) Point of view: What do we find out about the speaker?
c) Title: What do you think the title means? Look at lines 128–129 and 193–194 for help.
d) Rhyme: What can you say about rhyme in the poem?
e) Verses: What can you say about verses in the poem? ▸ *Skills file 8.4–5, pp. 168–169*

4 Stylistic devices ▸ *Skills file 8.5, p. 169*

a) Imagery:

1 What image does the poet want to create in lines 13–17?

But people were
"Hello"
And hugs
And "Pleased to meet you"
And "How are you?"

2 The poet uses some metaphors. Find examples in lines 1–22. Can you find other examples in the poem?

3 What is the effect of the images in the poem?

Imagery is when you use language to create a picture, an **image**, in the mind of the reader. The most common stylistic devices for creating images are similes and metaphors.

A simile is when a poet compares two things that are not really like each other using the words 'as' or 'like', e.g. in lines 184–187: "I think in bursts like bullets fired from a gun."

A metaphor compares two things without using the words 'as' or 'like', e.g. in lines 4–7: "Grown-ups were passports and driving licences and bank accounts". These words create a picture of normal life today.

b) Repetition:

1 Look at lines 1–58 on page 146 of the poem. Look for the phrase "Before I was born" How often can you find it? What point does the poet want to stress?

2 Now look at lines 60–75. What words are repeated? What point does the poet want to stress?

3 Can you find other examples of repetition in the poem? What is the writer stressing?

A writer sometimes **repeats** a word or phrase to show that it's very important – to stress a point.

E.g. "Before I was born" in lines 1–58.

c) Irony: Look at lines 110–112.

Better not to question.
Better not to know.
Better to accept.

Do you think that the poet really thinks this? If not, what does she really think?

Irony is when you say the opposite of what you really think.

E.g. "It's lovely weather" (when it's wet and cold outside).

▸ *Wordbank, p. 153*

5 Your response to the poem

How does the poem make you feel? Write a personal response and explain your feelings.

TF 5 Currents[1] (adapted from a short story by Hannah Voskuil)

1 First impressions

a) Read the first two lines of this short story. Before you read on, think about what you would like to know about this story and write your questions down. For example:
- Who? - Where? - Why? - What? - When?

b) Compare your questions. Then read on. Does the story answer all your questions?

> You should **read a short story slowly**. Read it more than once.
> While you read, **make notes** about the plot and the characters to help you to understand the story better.

Gary stood on the porch and looked at the ocean. His mother had switched off the light, but he didn't protest against the dark.

Before that, his mother, Josey, put her two shivering[2], twelve-year-old granddaughters to bed. "I want you both to go swimming first thing tomorrow. We can't have two seals[3] like you afraid of the water."

Before that, one of the girls held the hand of a wordless Filipino boy. They were watching the paramedics lift the boy's dead brother into an ambulance. At this time, the other girl got sick[4] over a toilet in the cabin[5].

Before that, the girl who would feel sick watched as the drowned boy's hand slid off[6] the stretcher. Nobody put the hand back on the stretcher, and it bounced[7] and dragged and bounced.

Before that, Gary saw the brown hair sink and resurface[8] as the body bobbed[9]. At first he thought it was seaweed[10].

Before that, thirty-five people struggled out of the water at the Coast Guard's command[11]. A lifeguard shouted over jet ski motors about the increasing[12] strength of the riptide[13].

Before that, the thirty-five people, including Gary and the two girls, formed a human chain and searched the waters for the body of a Filipino boy. The boy had gone under twenty minutes earlier and never came back up.

Before that, a lifeguard sprinted up the beach, shouting for volunteers. The two girls, resting lightly on their sandy bodyboards, stood up to help.

Before that, a Filipino boy pulled on the lifeguard's ankle[14] and gestured desperately[15] at the waves. "My brother," he said.

Before that, it was a simple summer day.

2 The narrator

a) Who tells this story – a first-person narrator or a third person narrator?

b) Does the narrator know more about one character in the story? If yes, who? And what do we learn?

> Remember: A **first-person narrator** is someone in the story. A **third person narrator** is outside the story and often knows more about one or more of the characters. ▸ *Skills file 8.2, p. 168*

▸ *Wordbank, p. 153*

[1] current ['kʌrənt] *Strömung* [2] shiver ['ʃɪvə] *zittern* [3] seal [siːl] *Robbe, Seehund* [4] get sick *sich übergeben (müssen)* [5] cabin ['kæbɪn] *Hütte* [6] slide off, slid, slid [slaɪd, slɪd] *heruntergleiten* [7] bounce [baʊns] *holpern* [8] resurface [riː'sɜːfɪs] *wieder auftauchen* [9] bob [bɒb] *sich auf und ab bewegen* [10] seaweed ['siːwiːd] *Seetang* [11] at sb.'s command *auf jds. Befehl* [12] increase [ɪn'kriːs] *zunehmen* [13] riptide [rɪp 'taɪd] *gefährliche Strömung* [14] ankle ['æŋkl] *Fußgelenk, Knöchel* [15] desperate ['despərət] *verzweifelt*

3 The plot

a) What exactly happens? Tell this story in simple sentences. Begin like this:

It's a summer day.
A Filipino boy speaks to …
The lifeguard runs …
Two girls …
…

The **plot of a short story** can be very complex because the writer doesn't have a lot of words to tell you everything.
So you need to **read between the lines**.
The plot doesn't just tell you the story, it also tells you **why** things happen.
The writer can create **tension**[16] in different ways, for example by telling the story in a special order. ▸ *Skills file 8.2, p. 168*

b) Now link some of the sentences in a) with some of the words below – to create a summary of the plot:
next / after that / because / but / although / however / while / when / …

c) Compare your summary with the original story. What are the main differences? ▸ *Skills file 10.4, p. 175*

4 More about the story

a) Setting: Where do you think the story is set? Why do you think that?

b) Characters: Make a character network for the story and show the relationships. You can start like this:

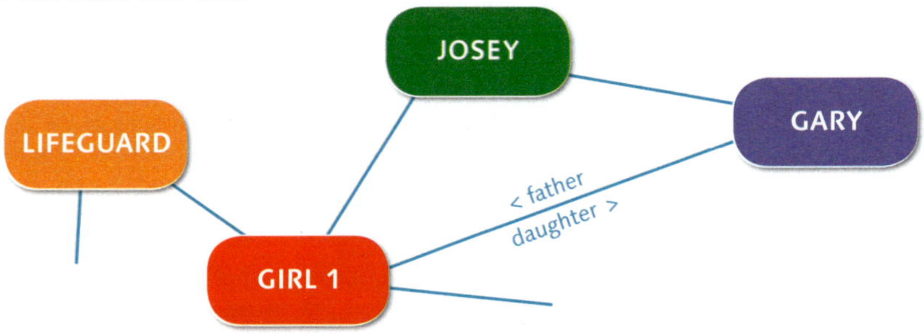

c) Imagery: What are the strongest images in the story for you?

d) Atmosphere: How does the story make you feel? What images does the writer use to create this feeling?

e) Style: How is this story different to other short stories that you have read? Is it effective?

5 Point of view

Write the story from the point of view of Gary or the lifeguard or one of the girls – in about 60 words.

[16] create tension ['tenʃn] *Spannung erzeugen*

WORDBANK Talking about texts

▸ Unit 1, pp. 21, 111 ▸ More challenge 1, p. 31 ▸ Unit 2, pp. 43, 115 ▸ More challenge 2, p. 53 ▸ Unit 3, pp. 65, 126 ▸ More challenge 3, p. 74 ▸ Text file 3, p. 145 ▸ Text file 4, p. 150 ▸ Text file 5, pp. 151–152 ▸ Skills file 8, pp. 168–169

Title, author, publication
- I'm going to talk about … *(title)* by … *(author)*.
- It was written in … *(year)* / (first) published in … *(year / for articles, interviews, etc. in … title of newspaper or magazine)*

Text type and genre
- … is a non-fictional / fictional (literary) text.

Non-fictional texts:
- The text deals with … / is about …
- … is a news story / a magazine article / a biography / an interview / a review / a speech / an advertisement / …
- It shows the author's opinion about … / attitude towards …, which is …
- The text doesn't give a personal opinion, but rather global / detailed information about …
- … *(title)* tries to convince us of … / to do …

Fictional (literary) texts:
- … *(title)* is a …:
  - narrative text (novel / short story …)
  - dramatic text (play / comedy / tragedy)
  - poetic text (poem / ballad / song …)

Setting, topic and plot
- The story / novel / play is set in 1980s Britain / …
- Its central topic is freedom / life in … / …
- It's about a young couple that's … Later they … and in the end …
- The poem describes … / reflects on …

Structure
- The article has a clear argumentative structure: introduction, arguments for and against …, conclusion.
- The novel is made up of two parts / ten chapters (covering ten years) / …
- The short story is told from the end to the beginning / starts abruptly / has a surprise ending / is open-ended / …
- The play consists of one act with only one scene / three acts / …
- The poem is made of … (regular) verses / stanzas with … lines (each).

Narrator / speaker
- The story is told by a first-person narrator, … *(name)*, who is a character in the story / by a third-person narrator, …, who is / isn't a character in the story.
- The narrator switches from one character's point of view to another's.
- The speaker of the poem describes … / feels … / shows us the world of …

Characters and characterization
- There is one main character in this short story, … *(name)*. He / She is described as … *(quotes)*.
- The other characters are not very developed / are stereotypes /
- We get to know a lot of characters and their relationships in this novel. First there's … His / Her best friend / competitor / worst enemy / is …, who …
- In this play, there are only two characters, … and … We learn a lot about them from the way they speak, e.g. … often says / asks / claims / defends … He's described as … in the stage directions: he often behaves like … / is secretly in love with … / …

Language and style
- The author uses the following **stylistic devices** to emphasize … / to make us feel … .
- The writer repeatedly **contrasts** … and … .
- **Repetitions** and **parallelisms** like … intensify the speaker's point.
- The writer uses **irony** to …
- The **style** of the article / story / poem / song may seem simple (short sentences, many repetitions, …), but there are strong **images** like …
- To speak of … as … is a very impressive **metaphor**.
- The artist compares … to … and also explains this **simile** later: … *(quotes)*
- The special sound of this poem is achieved by its regular / irregular **rhythm** and **rhyme** *(quotes)*. There are regular rhymes at the end of each line, e.g. … / There are no regular rhymes in this poem, but we often find **similar sounds** and intensifying repetitions like …

Mood and atmosphere
- The writer makes us feel angry about … / support …
- The overall effect of the language and imagery in this poem / story / chapter is a joyful / gloomy / threatening / … atmosphere.

Personal comments
- I think … is a well-written article / a thrilling novel / a beautiful / fine poem / …
- I especially liked …
- However, the part on … was quite boring / not convincing / not well written / …
- My favourite character is … because …

▸ KV 45

Esma Nitin, 21, and Max Keller, 19, are both trainees at the company SolarGo, a German producer of solar energy systems, in Leipzig. Esma works in the marketing department and Max works in the logistics centre.

Esma

Max

In the company

1 Small talk with visitors

Two Spanish trainees have arrived from the SolarGo office in Madrid. Esma is welcoming them.

Esma

3.12 **a)** Listen and correct these false statements.

1 Esma and Marta have never spoken before.
2 Marta and Luis took a taxi from the train station.
3 Luis met Max during his last visit to Leipzig.
4 Esma has to go because she has a lunch date.

3.12 **b)** Listen again and complete these phrases.

1 Nice to ...
2 Please ... me Esma.
3 Did you ... trip?
4 Let me ... around.
5 This is a lovely ...
6 ... is our logistics centre.
7 Please ... way.
8 Please ... seat.
9 Is this your ... to Leipzig?
10 It's great ... here.
11 I must ...
12 It was very ... you.

c) Copy the table and put the phrases in the right columns. Some fit in more than one column[1].

Greeting	Guiding a visitor	Small talk	Saying goodbye
...	...	...	...

2 NOW YOU Guided dialogue

Partner A:
You work for a German company.
– Begrüße B. Stell dich vor.
– Frage, wie die Reise war.
– Reagiere auf die Entschuldigung. Frage B nach der Unterkunft.
– Biete B an, ihm / ihr das Büro zu zeigen.
– Erkläre, dass das Gebäude ganz neu ist.
– Biete B etwas zu trinken an.

Partner B:
You arrive as a visitor.
– Reagiere, begrüße A und stelle dich vor.
– Beschreibe deine Reise. Entschuldige dich dafür, dass du spät kommst. Erkläre warum.
– Reagiere auf die Frage.
– Sage etwas Nettes über das Gebäude.
– Akzeptiere es. / Lehne es ab. Bedanke dich.

[1] column [ˈkɒləm] *Spalte*

► KV 45

3 Tell me about your job

a) Marta is interviewing Max to learn about what he does. Copy her job description form. Then listen to her interview with Max and fill in the form.

3.13

Compare your answers.

Job description

1. **Name:** MAX KELLER
2. **Job title:** ______
3. **Department:** ______
4. **Tasks:** ______
5. **Duration of traineeship[1]:** ______
6. **Further trainee tasks:** ______
7. **Full-time/Part-time:** ______
8. **Work hours:** ______

b) Luis wants to interview Esma, but he's not sure what to ask. Help him formulate a question for each of the points in the job description form above. Listen to Max's interview again if you need to.

c) Write down Luis's interview with Esma. Use the information about her that appeared months before in the company newsletter.

d) Practise the interview. Then swap roles

Who's new at SolarGo?

Name:
Esma Nitin

Department:
Marketing, main office in Leipzig

Job title:
Marketing assistant trainee

My job:
mostly helping write brochures, organize events and give presentations; also assisting the marketing director

My traineeship:
18 months; includes a six-month course and a final project

My work hours:
usually 9 am to 5.30 pm, Monday-Friday

[1] traineeship [treɪˈniːʃɪp] *Ausbildung(sverhältnis)*

 ▸ KV 46 ▸ DFF 4.3

Preparing for the trade fair[1]

1 Leaving a message

a) Esma is taking a phone call. Which phrase (A or B) are you more likely to hear?

	A		B
1	How can I help you?	OR	Why are you calling?
2	I want to talk to ...	OR	Could I speak to ..., please?
3	I'm sorry, but she's not at her desk right now.	OR	She's not here.
4	What do you want me to tell her?	OR	Would you like to leave a message?
5	Could you ask her to call me back ...?	OR	Tell her to call me.
6	Right. What was your name?	OR	Of course. Could you spell your last name for me, please?

3.14 **b)** Listen to the phone conversation and check your answers.

3.14 **c)** Listen again and write down how the caller and Esma begin and end their conversation. Compare notes. Then practise the conversation using different names and numbers.

2 Making appointments

3.15 **a)** Listen to Esma's three short phone conversations. In which conversation (A–C) do you hear the English phrases for these German ones?

1 Könnten Sie mir bitte sagen, worum es geht?
2 Ich möchte einen Telefontermin mit ihm vereinbaren.
3 Wann würde es Ihnen passen?
4 Aber nachmittags hat sie wieder Zeit.
5 Es tut mir Leid, da habe ich einen anderen Termin.
6 Das ginge gut bei mir.

3.15 **b)** Listen again. Write down the phrases from a) in English. Compare.

c) Ask your teacher for a printout of the three phone conversations. Practise speaking the different roles.

3 NOW YOU Two role-plays – pick one

a) **Partner B:** Go to p. 102.
Partner A: You're an office assistant at the Berlin software company *Inter_Soft*. Your boss, Nina Pfeifer, is in a meeting all afternoon. She has asked you to take a message if anyone calls for her. The phone rings. You begin the conversation – in German, of course.

b) **Partner B:** Go to p. 102.
Partner A: You're the British sales manager in the UK office of the German shoe company *Funshu*. You get a phone call from someone who wants to meet with you next week. You're free in the mornings and on Thursday afternoon.

[1] trade fair ['treɪd feə] *(Handels-)Messe, Fachmesse*

4 Ordering a product

Max is ordering equipment for the company's information stand at the trade fair.

a) Read his email to an Italian company. Find the German equivalents[1] for the underlined words.

Senden An alle Anhang Adressen Schriften Farben

An: office@aviva.it

Betreff: Product order

Dear Ms Canetti

Thank you for your reply and for your product catalogue.
With reference to our enquiry yesterday, we would like to place an order for the following items:

Catalogue No.	Description	Amount	Price/Item	Total
BN3402	Brochure shelves LUNGA	3	€78.00	€234.00

Payment will be by IBAN bank transfer to your account. Please confirm by email that you have received this order. Could you please also let us know when the delivery will be sent?

We look forward to receiving the goods soon.

Best regards
Max Keller

b) A SolarGo trainee is emailing Luc Didier at the French company *Spectra*. Rewrite her email in a formal style.
Use the email in a) as a model.

Hi Luc,
I wrote and asked about displays yesterday.
I want to order two of those big ones called "Astra". The ones that cost 270 euros.
The number in your catalogue is DF3420.
I'll pay you by IBAN.
Tell me if you get this order. And when are you going to send the displays?
Hopefully soon.
Bye, Anja (Weber)

! Writing a formal business email:
- Begin with *Dear Mr / Mrs / Ms* and the person's last name, or *Dear* and the person's full name, or *Dear Sir/Madam*.
- Close with *Regards / Best regards / Best wishes* and your full name.
- Use polite forms like *could, would, may,* etc. for questions and requests.
- Use formal words like *receive* instead of *get* and *enquiry* instead of *question*.
- Generally use *we* instead of *I*.

► Skills file 10.3, p. 174

[1] equivalent [ɪ'kwɪvələnt] *Entsprechung*

► KV 41

At the trade fair

1 Presenting a product

At the *Energy Expo* Esma is going to present one of the company's latest products. Her audience is mostly people who want to buy solar systems for their homes, so she decides to reduce her list of talking points today.

a) Agree on four points to drop from her list because they are less relevant.

SolarGo's EasySun system

1. Improved design
2. Easy to install
3. Invention of the solar cell (Solarzelle)
4. Fits every kind of roof
5. Produces more power than other systems
6. Saving money on electricity
7. More money-saving tips
8. Statistics on climate change
9. Helps protect the climate
10. SolarGo's 40-year success story

3.16 Now listen to the beginning of Esma's presentation. Did she drop the same points as you?

b) Esma uses two charts in her presentation. Look at charts A and B. Describe what each shows.
E.g.: The line diagram[1] shows the price of ... between ... The bar chart[2] shows how ...
Then briefly explain the changes or developments[3] that you see in the charts. ► *Skills file 11.3, p. 181*
E.g.: Between 19.. and 20.. the price went from ... to ...
Beginning in 20.., solar panel installations ...

3.17 **c)** Listen to Esma's presentation and compare your answers to the information she gives.

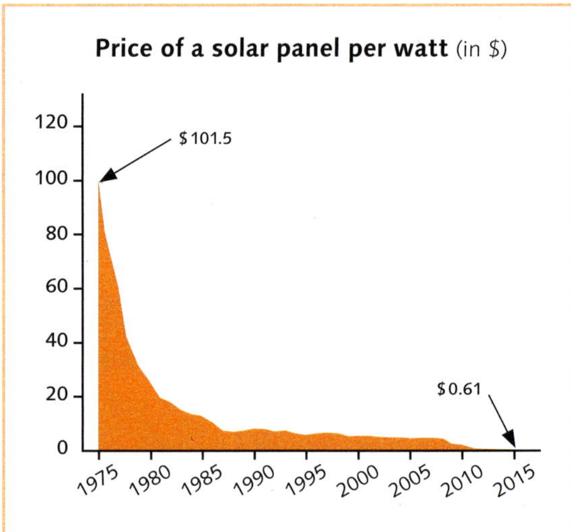

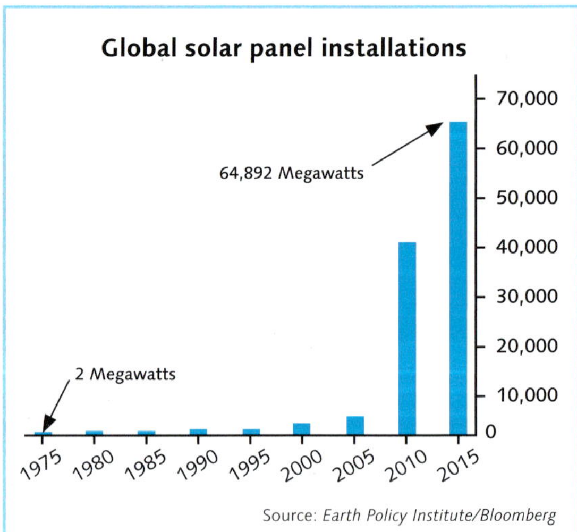

2 NOW YOU A presentation at a trade fair

Prepare a short presentation. You could talk about a product like a tablet or a mobile phone, or a service, a holiday destination, etc. Use suitable pictures, diagrams or charts if you can. Give feedback on your classmates' presentations. ► *Skills file 11.3, p. 181*

[1] line diagram *Liniendiagramm* [2] bar chart [bɑː] *Balkendiagramm* [3] development [dɪˈveləpmənt] *Entwicklung*

3 Explaining a brochure

Max is handing out brochures and answering visitors' questions at the SolarGo stand.
A Czech visitor wants to know about logistics if she orders the SolarGo system.
Max has only brochures in German left today.

a) Read the information.

Vorteile des SolarGo EasySun Systems

- **Schnell und effizient:** Lieferfristen: im Inland etwa 3 Tage / im europäischen Ausland etwa 7 Tage / weltweit 14-21 Tage
- **Komplettsystem:** Das *EasySun*-System enthält alle Komponenten, die Sie zur Errichtung und zum Betrieb Ihrer Solaranlage brauchen.

- **Dokumentation und perfekte Vorplanung:** Unsere leicht verständliche Übersicht listet alle Bauteile auf. Die Bauanleitung zeigt in klaren Schritten die Montage Ihrer Dachanlage. Das spart Zeit bei der Vorbereitung und bei der Installation.
- **Hilfe:** Unsere Service-Hotline garantiert schnelle Hilfe bei Bedarf.

- **Clevere Verpackung:** Mit unserer umweltfreundlichen und äußerst stabilen Verpackung kommt Ihre Lieferung sicher bei Ihnen an. Wir holen die leere Verpackung auf Wunsch wieder ab.
- **Maximale Absicherung:** Der Bausatz kommt mit einer kostenlosen Versicherung für zwei Jahre, die ab Installation gültig ist.

b) Answer the visitor's questions. ► *Skills file 13, pp. 182–183*

1 How long will the delivery take?
2 Do I have to order any parts separately?
3 How do I know if I've received all the parts?
4 What do I do if I have questions or problems?
5 It looks complicated. I bet it takes a long time to install.
6 I'm a bit worried that the panels won't arrive safely.
7 What happens if something breaks or doesn't work?

Useful words
Bausatz assembly kit
Verpackung packaging
Versicherung insurance

SKILLS FILE

Inhalt

STUDY AND LANGUAGE SKILLS — page

SF 1 Dealing with unknown words ____ 160
SF 2 Using a dictionary ____ 161
SF 3 Exam skills: How to do better in tests and exams ____ 162
SF 4 Doing project work ____ 163
SF 5 Doing research ____ 164

LISTENING AND READING SKILLS

SF 6 Listening ____ 165
SF 7 READING COURSE
- Skimming, Scanning ____ 166
- Finding the main point of a text ____ 166
- Reading for details ____ 166
- Reading between the lines ____ 167
- Marking up and note-taking ____ 167

SF 8 Reading literature ____ 168

SPEAKING AND WRITING SKILLS — page

SF 9 SPEAKING COURSE
- Giving a presentation ____ 170
- Successful conversations ____ 170
- Doing well in job interviews ____ 171
- Taking part in discussions ____ 172

SF 10 WRITING COURSE
- The steps of text writing ____ 172
- Writing a comment ____ 174
- Writing a letter/email of complaint ____ 174
- Summarizing texts ____ 175
- Writing a cover letter, a CV ____ 176
- A written discussion ____ 177
- Writing a report ____ 178
- Writing a book or film review ____ 178

SF 11 Talking about visuals (photos, cartoons, charts/diagrams) ____ 179
SF 12 MEDIATION COURSE ____ 182
SF 13 VIEWING SKILLS ____ 184

STUDY AND LANGUAGE SKILLS

SF 1 Dealing with unknown words ► Unit 1, p. 18 ► Unit 3, p. 62

Du kannst englische Texte verstehen, auch ohne alle Wörter zu kennen. Nicht immer ist Nachschlagen nötig.

- Schau genau auf Titel und (Zwischen-)Überschriften sowie den Zusammenhang (Kontext), in dem das unbekannte Wort steht.
- Achte auf Abbildungen und Bildunterschriften.
- Leider gibt es aber einige Wörter, die im Englischen und Deutschen ähnlich klingen oder aussehen, aber jeweils eine ganz andere Bedeutung haben. In der Übersicht rechts findest du einige Beispiele dieser so genannten ***false friends***.
- Viele Wörter sind im Deutschen und in anderen Sprachen dem Englischen ähnlich, z.B. *democracy, humour, loyal, religion, souvenir*.
- Unbekannte Wörter enthalten oft bekannte Teile:
  - in **Zusammensetzungen** (Komposita, *compounds*), z.B.:
    one-way street – (Einbahnstraße)
    baby car seat – (Kindersitz)
  - in **Ableitungen** mit Vor- und Nachsilben (*prefixes and suffixes*), z.B. *antisocial, disappear, multilingual, oversleep, reappear; washable, national, useful, childish, attractive, careless, percentage, performance, foundation, opener, racism, movement, happiness, leadership, pressure*
- Kennst du das Wort evtl. schon in einer anderen Wortart? So kann z.B. *dress* Nomen oder Verb sein. Was bedeutet *Students have the right to free dress?*

Some false friends

ENGLISH	GERMAN	GERMAN	ENGLISH
actual	tatsächlich	aktuell	**current**
brave	tapfer	brav	**well-behaved**
brief	kurz	Brief	**letter**
build	bauen	bilden	**make, form**
caution	Vorsicht	Kaution	**deposit**
chips	Pommes frites	Kartoffelchips	**crisps**
critic	Kritiker/in	Kritik	**criticism**
concern	Angelegenheit, Anliegen	Konzern	**corporate group**
eventually	schließlich	eventuell	**perhaps, possible**
failure	Versagen	Fehler	**mistake**
fast	schnell	fast	**almost**
guilty	schuldig	gültig	**valid**
handy	praktisch, handlich	Handy	**(mobile) phone**
kind	freundlich	Kind	**child**
map	Karte	Mappe	**folder**
mist	Nebel	Mist (Unsinn)	**rubbish**
note	Notiz	Note, Zensur	**mark**
personal	persönlich	Personal	**staff**
rent	Miete	Rente	**pension**
rock	Fels	Rock	**skirt**
sea	Meer, die See	der See	**lake**
sensible	vernünftig	sensibel	**sensitive**
serious	ernst	seriös	**respectable**
spend	ausgeben	spenden	**donate**
sympathetic	mitfühlend	sympathisch	**nice, friendly**
when	wann	wen	**who**
where	wo	wer	**who**
while	während	weil	**because**

SF 2 Using a dictionary ▸ Unit 3, p. 71

Wenn du ein Wort nicht erschließen kannst, helfen das *Dictionary* (*English-German* pp. 239 – 272) oder ein Wörterbuch für das Englische (entweder in Buchform oder im Internet).

1 Wörterbucheinträge sind immer alphabetisch

- *U* kommt vor *V*
- *value* kommt vor *vegetables*
- *vamping* kommt vor *vampire*

2 Zusammengesetzte Ausdrücke und *idioms*

Der Haupteintrag (z.B. ***ear***) steht farbig oder fett am Anfang. Daneben oder darunter findest du oft zusammengesetzte Wörter oder Redewendungen und Idiome, z.B. ***(be) all ears***.

3 Wortarten und Wortbedeutungen

- Oft ist das gleiche Wort ein Nomen (Substantiv), ein Adjektiv oder ein Verb, mit je unterschiedlichen Bedeutungen. Überlege zuerst, zu welcher **Wortart** das gesuchte Wort gehört und suche den passenden Eintrag. Diesen liest du dann genauer.
- Die Ziffern 1, 2 usw. bei einem Eintrag zeigen, dass ein Wort mehrere **Bedeutungen** hat. Lies immer alle Einträge bei der passenden Wortart und entscheide dann, welche Bedeutung in deinem Satz passt. Zusätzlich findest du Verweise auf den Gebrauch im *American* oder *British English* (*AE* bzw. *BE*).

  Welche Bedeutungen hat *fall* hier?

  The number of unemployed people has fallen since last fall.
  Is September a summer or a fall month?
  I fell asleep very fast yesterday because I was so tired.

- Besonders wenn du ein Wort in einem deutsch-englischen Wörterbuch suchst, achte genau darauf, welche Bedeutung in deinem englischen Satz passt.

4 Weitere Informationen im Wörterbuch

- Die Lautschrift zeigt dir, wie ein Wort ausgesprochen wird.
- Unregelmäßige Verbformen, Pluralformen, Steigerungsformen usw. stehen in Klammern hinter dem Haupteintrag.

5 Online-Wörterbücher

- Wenn du ein Online-Wörterbuch verwenden möchtest, erkundige dich vorher bei deiner Lehrperson, welche zu empfehlen sind.
- Achte auf dieselben Dinge wie bei gedruckten Wörterbüchern.
- Vorteil online: Du kannst dir meist die Aussprache per Audiodatei anhören.

---

usually ['juːʒuəli] meistens, normalerweise I

V

vacation [və'keɪʃn], [veɪ'keɪʃn] *(AE)* Ferien, Urlaub IV
vacuum cleaner ['vækjuəm kliːnə] Staubsauger V 3 (52)
vague [veɪg] vage, unbestimmt VI 3 (67)
vain [veɪn] eitel V 4 (79)
valley ['væli] Tal IV
value ['væljuː] Wert I **It's good value.** Es ist sein Geld wert. I
vamping ['væmpɪŋ] *spät in der Nacht noch aktiv sein* V 4 (88)

---

ear [ɪə] *Substantiv*
1 Ohr **2** Gehör **3** Ähre
IDM **(be) all ears** ganz Ohr sein
(be) up to one's ears in sth. bis zum Hals in etwas stecken
go in one ear and out the other *(umgs)* zum einen Ohr rein- und zum anderen rausgehen

---

fall [fɔːl] *Verb, Substantiv*
Verb **(fell, fallen)**
1 fallen, stürzen **The book fell off the table.** Das Buch fiel vom Tisch.
2 *(Zahlen)* fallen, sinken, zurückgehen **Their profits have fallen by 30%.** Ihr Gewinn ist um 30% zurückgegangen.
3 in einen Zustand geraten **fall asleep** einschlafen, **fall ill** krank werden, **fall in love (with)** sich verlieben (in)

Substantiv
1 Fall, Sturz
2 falls (Plural, bes. in Namen) (Wasser)fall **the Niagara Falls** die Niagarafälle
3 *(AE)* Herbst
4 *(Zahlen)* Rückgang

---

child [tʃaɪld] (***children*** ['tʃɪldrən])

SF 3 Exam skills: How to do better in tests and exams

▸ *Unit 1, p. 18* ▸ *Typical exam instructions, p. 280* ▸ *Exam file, pp. 76–99*

1 Learning from your mistakes

- Erkenne deine Fehler, damit du sie künftig vermeiden kannst.
- Wenn du eine Klassenarbeit oder einen Test korrigiert zurück bekommst, sieh dir die Vermerke deines Lehrers / deiner Lehrerin genau an. Sie zeigen dir, welche Arten von Fehlern du gemacht hast, z.B. SP – *spelling mistake*,

  WO – *word order*, G – *grammar mistake*,

  W – *(wrong) word(s)*, FF – *false friend*
- Lege dir eine **Fehlersammlung oder -kartei** an bzw. führe sie aus den vorangehenden Schuljahren fort. Möglich ist das in Papierform (Karteikärtchen / A5-Heft) oder in Dateiform. Diese Sammlung vervollständigst du nach jedem Test um deine korrigierten Fehler.
- Praktisch ist die Sammlung nach folgenden **Arten von Fehlern**:
  - Flüchtigkeitsfehler (häufig: SP): z.B. das Auslassen oder Vertauschen von Buchstaben / Wörtern / Satzzeichen
  - Vokabelfehler (häufig: W, SP, FF): Du verwechselst z.B. Wörter und Wendungen oder kannst sie nicht korrekt schreiben bzw. aussprechen; du benutzt falsche Präpositionen (z.B. ~~*in*~~ -> *on the internet*) oder *false* friends (z.B. ~~*actually*~~ -> *at the moment / currently*)
  - Grammatikfehler (häufig: G, W, WO, SP): Beispielsweise verwendest du falsche Verbformen (z.B. *she* ~~*do*~~ -> *does*; an article *sa~~yed~~* -> *saying*), benutzt die falsche Wortart (z.B. Adverb statt Adjektiv in *real~~ly~~ danger* -> *real*) oder du hast Probleme mit der Wortstellung in Sätzen.

Elephants in danger

Yetsreday read i an	‖ SP WO (G)
article in the internet	| W
sayed that elephants are	| G
in really danger.	| W (G)
According to the	| G
scientists it gives only	| W
352 271 elephants	| Komma!
actually in ...	‖ FF WO (G)

Was hilft?

- ✓ Konzentriere dich bei der Arbeit.
- ✓ Überprüfe alles gründlich vor der Abgabe (plane dafür genug Zeit ein).
- ✓ Lerne neue Wendungen statt nur Einzelwörter (z.B. *there is/are, on the internet, according to sb*).
- ✓ Höre, lies, sprich und schreibe neues Vokabular regelmäßig und gründlich.
- ✓ Vermeide *false friends* ▸ *SF 1*.
- ✓ Lerne neue Grammatik sorgfältig; schlage stets im *Language file* (pp. 185 – 209) oder in einer Englischgrammatik nach.
- ✓ Merke dir typische Wendungen als Muster.
- ✓ Wiederhole regelmäßig.
- ✓ Frage nach, wenn du etwas nicht verstehst.

2 Exam preparation

- Beginne zeitig mit der Prüfungsvorbereitung. Plane, welchen Stoff du in welchen Schritten und innerhalb welcher Zeit wiederholst. Hake Erledigtes ab.
- Lerne deine typischen Fehler zu vermeiden – mit Hilfe deiner Fehlerkartei.
- Informiere dich über typische Aufgaben. Stelle sicher, dass du sie richtig verstehst ▸ *Typical exam instructions, p. 280* und übe, z.B. mit dem ▸ *Exam file, pp. 76–99* und dem Workbook.

3 In the exam

- Schlafe dich vorher gut aus; sei pünktlich.
- Bleibe ruhig, optimistisch und konzentriert.
- Lies die Arbeitsanweisungen sehr genau – mehrmals! Oft hilft es, Wichtiges zu unterstreichen.
- Wenn du auswählen sollst, welche Aufgabe du bearbeitest, lies dir zuerst alle Angebote gründlich durch.
- Hake erledigte Aufgaben ab.
- Plane am Ende 5–10 Minuten ein, um alles noch einmal durchzulesen und zu korrigieren.

SF 4 Doing project work ▸ *Text file 1, pp. 136–139*

Ein Projekt ist meistens eine komplexe Aufgabe, die mehrere Stunden Arbeitszeit benötigt und in einer Gruppe bearbeitet wird. Ein mögliches Thema kann z.B. sein, dass ihr ein englischsprachiges Land vorstellen möchtet, das Produkt dazu z.B. eine mündliche Präsentation oder ein Poster.

1 Set your goals

Wählt euer Thema und entscheidet euch für ein Produkt. Schreibt auf, was euch an dem Thema interessiert und was ihr noch herausfinden möchtet.

> ! Das gewählte Produkt könnte sein: ein Poster, ein Vortrag, eine computergestützte Präsentation, eine Broschüre, eine Klassenzeitung, ...

2 Get organized

Macht euch einen Plan. Wer macht was bis wann? Verteilt die Aufgaben und legt einen Zeitplan fest, der regelmäßige Treffen beinhaltet. Denkt auch an eine inhaltliche Gliederung.

> ! Haltet die Ergebnisse in einem Protokoll fest, um bei späteren Missverständnissen nachschauen zu können.

3 Do your research

Benutzt unterschiedliche Medien für eure Recherche: Lexika, Fachbücher, Zeitschriften, Zeitungen, Karten und Atlanten. Ebenso sind schriftliche Anfragen und Interviews möglich. Bezieht auch das Internet in eure Recherchen mit ein. ▸ *SF 3* Skimmt das Material, um euch einen Überblick zu verschaffen. Macht euch Notizen in eigenen Worten und notiert die Quellen.

> ! Versucht Materialien zu finden, die das Thema von unterschiedlichen Gesichtspunkten aus beleuchten – beschränkt euch nicht auf eine Perspektive.

4 Organize your materials

Sobald ihr genug Material zusammenhabt, macht eine grobe Skizze, wie das fertige Produkt aussehen soll. Sortiert das Material und schreibt eure Texte.

> ! Gibt es spezielle Vorgaben von eurer Lehrerin / eurem Lehrer, die ihr berücksichtigen müsst?

5 Check your materials

Überprüft eure Texte und eure Abbildungen. Korrigiert eure Texte untereinander in der Gruppe. Ist alles logisch und übersichtlich aufgebaut? Dann ordnet eure Informationen und visuellen Hilfen sorgfältig an.

6 Give your presentation

Eine gute Präsentation gelingt euch, wenn ihr folgende Tipps beachtet:

- Übt eure Präsentation, wenn ihr etwas mündlich darstellt, und benutzt Karteikarten mit stichwortartigen Notizen.
- Sagt, worum es geht und fasst am Ende das Wesentliche kurz zusammen.
- Schaut die Zuhörenden an, lächelt und sprecht langsam und deutlich.
- Verweist auf die Abbildungen (Fotos, Illustrationen, Diagramme, ...). ▸ *SF 9.1; SF 11*

7 Give feedback

Als Gruppe könnt ihr nach einzelnen Abschnitten der Arbeit am Projekt sowie abschließend besprechen, was gut lief und was beim nächsten Mal verbessert werden sollte. Beginnt stets mit dem Positiven.
Verbindet dabei höfliche (!) Kritik immer mit guten Verbesserungsvorschlägen.

> ! **Include in your feeback on presentations**:
> - what was great
> - what the speaker could do better
> - what you didn't like
> - what you found interesting
> - what was missing

SF 5 Doing research ▸ Unit 1, p. 10; Text file 1, p. 138

1 Nutze unterschiedliche Quellen für deine Recherche

Bei der Informationssuche für ein Referat, eine Präsentation o.Ä. benutze mehrere unterschiedliche Quellen und Medien. Beachte auch die Hinweise zum Skimming und Scanning ▸ SF 7.1, 7.2.
Gleiche die gefundenen Informationen miteinander ab.

für alle Wissensgebiete

- Lexika (gedruckt und online, ggf. englischsprachig)
- Schulbücher und Begleitmaterialien

für aktuelle Informationen

- Zeitungen, Zeitschriften (gedruckt und online, ggf. englischsprachig)

für geographische und politische Informationen

- Karten und Atlanten (gedruckt und online)

2 Tipps zur Internetrecherche

So wird deine Internetrecherche leichter und bringt bessere Ergebnisse:

Wie suche ich, um weniger und bessere Ergebnisse (*hits*) zu bekommen?

- Überlege dir gute Stichwörter für dein Thema. Bereitest du z.B. eine Präsentation über *Nigeria* vor, wären der Landesname und *history, government, geography* ein Anfang. Weitere Ideen: *culture, ethnic groups, …*
- Gib die Stichwörter in eine Suchmaschine ein und setze die Einstellungen auf englischsprachige Websites.

Welche Websites sind zuverlässig?

- Offizielle und zuverlässige Websites im englischsprachigen Internet haben *domain names*, die auf *.gov* oder *.edu* enden.
- Weniger vertrauenswürdig sind Websites von Firmen (*.com*), persönliche Blogs, Fanseiten oder Websites von Interessengruppen. Auch hier kannst du Interessantes finden, solltest aber kritisch bei der Verwendung von Inhalten sein.

Wie verschaffe ich mir einen Überblick?

- Du kannst mit dem Skimming eines Artikels in einem online-Lexikon beginnen, z.B. der englischsprachigen Wikipedia (https://en.wikipedia.org).
- Häufig finden sich im Artikel bzw. am Ende weitere Links zum Thema.
- So findest du auch genauere Stichwörter für deine weitere Recherche.

Wie finde ich Websites wieder?

- Leg dir besonders interessante Websites in die Favoriten deines Webbrowsers. Strukturiere sie in eigenen Ordnern, die du innerhalb der Favoriten anlegen kannst.

Was kommt nach dem Suchen?

- Setz dir ein Zeitlimit für deine Recherche. Danach ordne dein Material. Prüfe, was evtl. fehlt und suche dann gezielt nur danach.

Was tun mit den gefundenen Informationen?

- Mach dir Notizen in weitgehend eigenen Worten ▸ SF 7.6. *Copy and paste*, also bloßes Zusammenkopieren, ist nicht sinnvoll.
- Zu jeder Notiz vermerke die Quelle (die Webadresse sowie das Zugriffsdatum).

Was tun mit unbekannten Wörtern und Wendungen?

- Unbekannter Wortschatz begegnet dir immer wieder in fremdsprachigen Texten. Für den ersten Überblick musst du nicht jedes Wort genau verstehen – erschließe die Bedeutung ▸ SF 1.
- Wichtige Wörter schlage im (Online-)Wörterbuch nach, v.a. wenn du sie selbst in deiner Präsentation verwenden willst. Vergiss die Aussprache nicht! Hör dir das neue Wort online an und übe es.

LISTENING AND READING SKILLS

SF 6 Listening

▸ *Unit 1, p. 22* ▸ *Unit 2, p. 45*
▸ *Unit 3, p. 66*

1 Vor dem Hören: bereite dich vor

- Lies sorgfältig die Aufgabenstellung. Die Aufgaben sagen oft, worum es in dem Text geht oder enthalten Schlüsselwörter.
- Stell dir die Situation oder die Geschichte vor: Worum wird es im Text gehen? Wer wird sprechen? Versuche vorauszuschauen.
- Überlege, was du selbst zum Thema schon weißt und welche englischen Begriffe vorkommen könnten.
- Wenn du dem Hörtext Abbildungen zuordnen sollst, schau sie dir vor dem Hören genau an.
- Konzentriere dich, denn du kannst den Text meist nur bis zu zweimal hören.

! Versuche zu erkennen, **was für eine Art Text** du hören wirst:

Nachrichten, Werbung, ein Gespräch, ein Interview, eine öffentliche Ansage oder eine *story*?

2 Beim Hören

- Beantworte schon beim ersten Hören möglichst viele Aufgaben (mach dir kurze Notizen, verwende Symbole und Abkürzungen).
- Die Informationen könnten in einer anderen Reihenfolge auftauchen.
- Im Hörtext können andere Wörter benutzt werden als in der Aufgabe, doch die Bedeutung ist ähnlich.
- Gib nicht auf, wenn du etwas nicht verstehst. Bleib ruhig und hör weiter zu. Vielleicht verstehst du beim zweiten Hören mehr.
- Achte auf Signalwörter, die dir das Verstehen erleichtern, z.B.:
  - Reihenfolge (*before, after, then, next, later, first, …*)
  - Gegensätze (*however, but, …*)
  - Gründe, Folgen (*because, so, …*)
  - Vergleiche (*larger/older than …, more, most, as … as*)
- Beachte auch, wie etwas gesagt wird: zum Beispiel verärgert oder besorgt, überrascht, freudig? Das kann ein Hinweis auf die Lösung sein.

! Höraufgaben können unterschiedliche **Arten des Zuhörens** von dir verlangen:

- **detailliertes Hören** Hier musst du genau zuhören, um wichtige Einzelheiten zu erfassen (z.B. bei einer Ansage am Bahnhof die Abfahrtszeit des Zuges).
- **globales Hören** Hier sollst du verstehen, worum es generell geht, z.B. den Hauptgedanken eines Textes erfassen. Du musst dafür nicht jedes einzelne Wort verstehen.
- **schlussfolgerndes Hören** Hier werden deine Vorüberlegungen und Vermutungen wichtig. Achte auf die Zusammenhänge. Wird etwas evtl. nur angedeutet, aber nicht vollständig ausgesprochen? Wie klingt die Stimme der Sprecher?

3 Nach dem Hören

- Vervollständige deine Notizen sofort.
- Konzentriere dich beim nächsten Hören auf eventuelle Lücken.
- Manchmal hilft auch Kombinieren (es ist in jedem Fall besser als gar nichts zu schreiben).

! **Tausche** dich mit Mitschülern und -schülerinnen **aus**. Haben sie gute **Tipps und Tricks**, z.B. für kurze Notizen und Symbole?

Ihr könnt, wenn das erlaubt ist, auch eure Notizen und Lösungen vergleichen.

SF 7 Reading course

1 Skimming ▸ *More challenge 1, p. 30* ▸ *Unit 2, p. 36*

Wofür? Mit dieser Technik verschaffst du dir einen **Überblick**, z.B. über eine Website oder eine Zeitungsseite.

Wie? Du musst nicht jede Einzelheit verstehen, also auch **nicht jedes Wort** lesen und verstehen. Achte vor allem auf Überschriften, Abbildungen und Bildunterschriften, hervorgehobene Wörter und den ersten Satz.

Beispiel: Du möchtest herausfinden, ob der Text „The dreams and reality of the *Born Frees*" auf S. 12 für eine Präsentation über Nelson Mandela geeignet ist.

Nein, denn zwar kommt sein Name einmal vor, aber das Hauptthema des Textes ist er nicht.

2 Scanning ▸ *Unit 1, pp. 10, 15, 21* ▸ *Unit 2, p. 43* ▸ *Unit 3, p. 56*

Wofür? Mit dieser Technik kannst du einen Text schnell nach **bestimmten Informationen** durchsuchen.

Wie? Du suchst nur bestimmte Informationen, die du über geeignete **Schlüsselwörter** findest. Lies nur dort genauer, wo sie stehen.

Beispiel: Du möchtest herausfinden, welches die beste Reisezeit für Südafrika ist. Überlege dir sinnvolle Schlüsselwörter und scanne dann den oder die geeignete(n) Text(e) auf S. 10–11. (Tipp: Dafür musst du zuerst skimmen, siehe ▸ *SF 7.1*.)

3 Finding the main point of a text ▸ *Unit 2, pp. 34, 50*

Wofür? Um herauszufinden, was die **Hauptaussage** eines Textes ist und wie sie sich aus seinen Hauptgedanken formt.

Wie? Für deinen **Überblick**, worum es in dem Text generell geht, benutzt du das Skimming (siehe ▸ *SF 7.1*).

Die **Hauptaussage** eines Textes findest du oft in seinem **ersten Absatz**, und dort oft im **ersten** oder **letzten Satz**.

Jeder **Absatz** eines Textes beinhaltet einen **Hauptgedanken**, der zur Hauptaussage beiträgt. Du findest den Hauptgedanken meist im **ersten** oder **letzten Satz** des Absatzes.

Beispiel: Du möchtest die Hauptaussage des Textes auf S. 34 formulieren. (Tipp: Beachte hier auch den Abschluss-Satz von Absatz 5.)

4 Reading for details ▸ *Unit 1, p. 16*

Wofür? Manchmal musst du in einem Text **jedes Detail** im Zusammenhang genau verstehen, z.B. bei Gedichten, Rezepten, Gebrauchsanweisungen und Aufgabenstellungen. In längeren Informationstexten oder Tabellen und Diagrammen ist es oft nur ein bestimmter Bereich, den du detailliert liest, weil du eine Information suchst. Welcher Bereich das ist, findest du mithilfe des Scanning heraus (siehe ▸ *SF 7.2*).

Wie? Lies **jedes Wort** und **jede Zahl** sehr **genau**. Achte auch auf Maßeinheiten. Benutze ein Wörterbuch für unbekannte Wörter.

Beispiel: Wie viele Ziffern musst du hier eingeben, damit der Safe schließt?
Wann sollst du den Safe offen hinterlassen?

OPERATING INSTRUCTIONS
You can operate this safe with your own 4-digit personal code.

TO LOCK: Close the door and enter your own 4-digit code.
Press # (LOCK). The safe will lock automatically and the word CLOSED will be displayed.

TO OPEN: Enter the 4-digit code that was used to lock the safe. It will unlock automatically and the word OPEN will be displayed.

IMPORTANT: Always leave the safe open at checkout.

5 Reading between the lines

▸ *Unit 1, p. 14*
▸ *Unit 2, p. 46*

Wofür? Wenn du Fragen zu einem Text beantworten sollst, ist es möglich, dass du die Antworten nicht eins zu eins im Text findest. Hier hilft es dir, **Schlussfolgerungen** aus dem Gelesenen zu ziehen. Wichtig ist diese Technik z.B. bei Kommentaren, Tagebuch- oder Blogeinträgen, Werbung und literarischen Texten.

Wie? Einfaches Schlussfolgern bedeutet, dass du Informationen aus **unterschiedlichen Textstellen** zusammenführst.

Beispiel: Sieh dir den Text auf S. 46 an und beantworte Frage 1 rechts.

Manchmal werden im Text **andere Wörter** benutzt als in der Aufgabe, doch die Bedeutung ist ähnlich oder gleich.

Beispiel: Beantworte anhand desselben Textes nun Frage 2 rechts.

Es gibt auch Fragen, auf die du im Text gar keine direkte Antwort findest. Und doch ist sie im Text enthalten, man könnte sagen, sie steht **„zwischen den Zeilen"**. Du musst sie schlussfolgern, also z.B. dein eigenes Wissen, aber auch begründete Vermutungen beim Lesen einbringen und kritische Fragen an den Text stellen.

Beispiel: Lies den Werbetext „An adventure around every corner" auf p. 14 und beantworte die Fragen 3–5 rechts.

(1) How do you know what I.A. Wenger thinks of the common stereotype of an engineer? *(lines 17–20; 28–30)*

(2) What prejudice against a young female software engineer did the negative comments show?
(lines 13–15; 23–25. Das Wort prejudice kommt im Text nicht vor. Erinnere dich an seine Bedeutung oder schlage es nach.)

(3) What image of the reader is created in the text?
(4) Why should somebody be filming the reader doing a bungee jump?
(5) Name three topics that aren't mentioned at all. Why do you think they aren't?

6 Marking up and note-taking

▸ *Unit 1, p. 12*

Wofür?
Du hast einen längeren Text mit vielen Fakten vor dir und sollst ihn später zusammenfassen oder inhaltliche Fragen beantworten. Wähle die für diese Aufgabe wichtigen Informationen aus und markiere sie.

Wie?
Du kannst die Stellen mit wichtigen Informationen z.B.:

- mit Textmarker hervorheben
- umkreisen
- unterstreichen

All das geht nur in elektronischen Texten oder auf Fotokopien bzw. Ausdrucken, aber nicht in geliehenen Büchern.

Wenn du dir zu den markierten Stellen **Notizen** machst (*note-taking*), kannst du diese später weiterverarbeiten, z.B. für eine Präsentation ▸ *SF 9.1*, einen Bericht oder eine Zusammenfassung ▸ *SF 9.3*.

! Schreibe nur Schlüsselwörter auf, nutze Ziffern (statt Zahlwörter: **7** statt **sieben**) und Symbole (**?**, **!**, **✓**, **≠**, **+**, **=**, **~**). Zum Beispiel:

screenagers:
- born into digital world (= world of screens)
- ~ 8 hrs daily screen time (multitasking)
- strong attraction + peer pressure
- ...

SF 8 Reading literature

▸ Unit 1, pp. 19–21 ▸ Unit 2, pp. 41–43 ▸ Unit 3, pp. 63–65
▸ Text files 3–5, pp. 142–152 ▸ Wordbank, p. 153

1 Differences between non-fictional and fictional (literary) texts

- **Sachtexte *(non-fictional texts)*** sind z.B. Texte in Zeitungen oder Online-Magazinen, Anzeigen, Kommentare, Reden, Gebrauchsanweisungen oder auch Sachbücher. Der Autor / Die Autorin schreibt über Themen der realen Welt mit dem Ziel, Lesende zu informieren oder auch zu überzeugen.
- **Literarische Texte *(fictional / literary texts)*** sind z.B. Romane, Kurzgeschichten oder Theaterstücke. Sie handeln von einer erdachten, nicht-realen Welt. Der Autor / Die Autorin entwickelt Figuren und stellt dar, was diese tun und fühlen sowie häufig auch, warum und mit welchen Folgen.

> ! Some **non-fictional text types**:
> (auto)biography, advert, article, comment, interview, news story, recipe, report, review, speech, travel guide

2 Narrative texts

- **Erzähltexte** sind z.B. Romane *(novels)* oder Kurzgeschichten *(short stories)* bestehen aus einem fortlaufenden Text, der manchmal in Abschnitte oder Kapitel unterteilt ist. Ein Erzähler (narrator) entwickelt um die Figuren *(characters)* einer Geschichte herum eine Handlung *(plot)*, die zu einer bestimmten Zeit und an einem bestimmten Schauplatz *(setting)* stattfindet.
- Die Charakterisierung *(characterization)* der Figuren kann direkt erfolgen (z.B. durch Adjective wie *shy*, *angry*). Oft erfolgt auch eine indirekte Charakterisierung darüber, was die Figuren sagen, denken oder fühlen.
- Durch bestimmte sprachlich-stilistische Mittel *(stylistic devices* ▸ *SF 8.5)* schafft der Erzähler eine bestimmte Atmosphäre *(mood / atmosphere)*, z.B. ruhig und friedlich oder spannungsvoll-bedrohlich.
- Die Ereignisse werden aus einer bestimmten Erzählperspektive *(point of* view) dargestellt. Dabei nimmt der Ich-Erzähler *(first-person narrator)* die Ich-Perspektive ein und ist Teil der Geschichte. Dagegen steht der Er-Erzähler *(third-person narrator)* eher außerhalb des Geschehens, kann aber auch sehr nahe bei einer Figur sein.

> ! **First-person narrator**: e.g. in ***Returned***, p. 19, lines 20 – 24:
> "How could this be? I had lived in London all my life. I lived here with my mum in a ..."
>
> **Third-person narrator**: e.g. in ***Face***, p. 41, lines 10 – 14:
> "The Gang of Three decided to cut through a housing estate. It used to be a nice place to live, but it wasn't any more. ..."
>
> E.g. in ***Floodland***, p. 63, lines 11 – 15:
> "Zoe was a loner. Most of the people left on Norwich hung around together ..., but she preferred to be on her own. It was safer that way ..."

3 Plays (Dramatic texts)

- **Dramen** werden von Darstellenden (Schauspielern / Sprechern) im Theater, in Filmen, Serien oder im Radio aufgeführt. Sie bestehen aus Dialogen *(dialogues)* und Monologen *(monologues)* in direkter Rede.
- Bühnenanweisungen *(stage directions)* geben meist Hinweise für die Darstellenden. Beim Lesen helfen sie dir dabei, die Aussagen der Figuren zusammen mit ihren dargestellten Handlungen zu verstehen oder auch dabei, dir den Schauplatz besser vorzustellen.

4 Poetry

- Gedichte *(poems)* werden in gebundener Sprache dargeboten, d.h. häufig in Versen *(verses / lines)* und Strophen *(stanzas)*, die auch ein wichtiges Gliederungselement sind.
- Anders als in der Alltagssprache findest du in Gedichten vielfältige stilistische Mittel wie Reim *(rhyme)*, Rhythmus *(rhythm)* und Wiederholung *(repetition)*. Die Sprechweise ist oft bildhaft, z.B. mit Hilfe von Vergleichen *(similes)* und Metaphern *(metaphors)*. ▸ *SF 8.5*

5 Stylistic devices (stilistische Mittel in literarischen Texten)

Begriff	Erläuterung	Beispiel
contrast *Kontrast*	Formulierung aus zwei gegensätzlichen, einander widersprechenden oder sich gegenseitig ausschließenden Begriffen	*call this destruction – progress* (from *Sorry*, p. 126) *an open secret; a controlled chaos* *in order to lead, you must walk behind*
imagery *Bildsprache*	Durch bildhafte Sprache sollen beim Lesenden Bilder erzeugt werden, um seine Sinne für das vertiefte Verstehen eines Textes anzuregen. Hierzu werden u.a. Vergleiche (*similes*) und Metaphern (*metaphors*) verwendet.	*So I've started looking* *For a means,* *Some manner* *To make my life* *A two-way street.* (from *Searching for a two-way-street*, p. 149, lines 209–213)
irony *Ironie*	Bedeutet, dass das Gegenteil von dem gesagt wird, was tatsächlich gemeint ist.	*Oh great! Now you have broken my new phone!*
metaphor *Metapher*	Metaphern sind eine Form des bildhaften Sprechens, bei der die Wörter in übertragener Bedeutung verwendet werden.	- *we must globally warm our hearts* - *change the climate of our souls* (from *Sorry*, p. 126)
parallelism *Parallelismus*	Eine bestimmte Struktur (Satzglieder oder Wörter) wird in mehreren aufeinander folgenden Satzteilen oder Sätzen beibehalten (paralleler Satzbau).	*Sorry, sorry we left you our mess of a planet.* *Sorry that we were too caught up in our doings to do something.* *Sorry we listened to people who made excuses to do nothing.* (from *Sorry*, p. 126)
repetition *Wiederholung*	Bezeichnet das mehrmalige Benennen des gleichen Wortes oder einer Wörterfolge in einem Text. Sie soll die Aussage verstärken oder bestimmte Sachverhalte betonen.	*Not yesterday. Not today. Not tomorrow.* (from *Searching for a two-way-street*, p. 148, lines 137–139)
rhyme *Reim*	Bezeichnet den Gleichklang zweier oder mehrerer Wörter vom letzten betonten Vokal an.	*So prove them all wrong, prove you have a voice,* *Do the unexpected and accept you have a choice* (from *It's your future*, p. 36, lines 7–8)
rhythm *Rhythmus*	Ist die Wiederholung bestimmter Gruppierungen von betonten und unbetonten Silben in einem Gedicht.	*I didn't go and vote, I didn't pay attention,* *I didn't really care at what age people got their pension.* (from *It's your future*, p. 36, lines 3–4)
simile *Vergleich*	Dient dem Vergleich von zwei Dingen, um die Aussage noch anschaulicher und deutlicher zu machen; ist meist an Wörtern wie *like* oder *as* erkennbar.	*But now I think* *In bursts* *Like bullets* *Fired from a gun.* (from *Searching for a two-way-street*, p. 148, lines 185–187)

SPEAKING AND WRITING SKILLS

SF 9 Speaking course

1 Giving a presentation

► *English around the world, p. 103* ► *Unit 2, p. 114* ► *Unit 3, p. 66*

Beachte diese Schritte, damit deine Präsentation erfolgreich wird.

► *Text files 1, p. 138; 6; p. 158*

a) PLANNING YOUR PRESENTATION

- **Recherchiere** dein Thema ► *SF 5* und fertige dir Notizen an (am besten gleich in Englisch ► *SF 7.6*).
- **Strukturiere** die Informationen, z.B. in einer Mindmap oder einer Gliederung (*outline*). Prüfe noch einmal, ob alle Informationen zum Thema passen.
- Wähle die **Form deiner Präsentation** aus: z.B. Vortrag, Folienpräsentation am Computer, Poster.
- Überlege, wie du dein Thema **anschaulich** und **interessant** gestaltest (Beispiele, und Visualisierungen, z.B. Abbildungen, Karten, Diagramme, evtl. Filmausschnitte). Überlege dir einen guten Einstieg.
- Bereite deine **Notizen** für die Präsentation (nur Stichwörter). Notiere kurze Erklärungen zu schwierigeren Begriffen, die deine Zuhörer/innen evtl. nicht verstehen.
- Bereite deine **Materialien** sorgfältig vor (Grafiken, Diagramme, Fotos usw.): Achte auf Lesbarkeit und Übersichtlichkeit.
- **Übe** deine Präsentation zu Hause und / oder mit Freunden. Achte auf die Zeit. Nummeriere deine Notizzettel bzw. Karteikärtchen. Überprüfe die technischen Hilfsmittel, die du verwenden willst (Laptop, Beamer usw.).

b) GIVING YOUR PRESENTATION

- **Schau** die Zuhörenden **an**. Warte, bis es ruhig ist. **Erkläre**, worüber du sprechen wirst und wie deine Präsentation aufgebaut ist.
- **Sprich langsam**, deutlich und möglichst **frei** (d.h. lies nicht nur ab).
- **Schau** die Zuhörenden **an**, **lächle**. Zeige, dass du deinen Vortrag gern hältst.
- Sprich in **kurzen**, **verständlichen Sätzen**. Vermeide zu viele unbekannte oder schwierige Wörter. Erkläre sie bei Bedarf.
- **Verweise** auf deine **Abbildungen** oder Fotos. Erkläre sie bei Bedarf.
- **Beende** deine Präsentation mit einer kurzen **Zusammenfassung** der wichtigsten Punkte, evtl. auch mit einer abschließenden Schlussfolgerung.
- **Bedanke** dich fürs Zuhören und frage, ob jemand **Fragen** hat oder sich äußern möchte.

2 Successful conversations

Unterhaltungen mit Menschen aus anderen Ländern gelingen gut, wenn du diese Hinweise beachtest. Sei höflich und aufgeschlossen! Verwende häufig *please*, *thank you* und *sorry*.

a) STARTING OFF

- **Eröffne** das Gespräch mit einer freundlichen Anrede oder Frage, möglichst mit etwas **Verbindendem**, z.B. über den Ort, die Situation usw. Mit jemandem, den du zum ersten Mal triffst, sprichst du etwas förmlicher als mit jemandem, den du schon kennst.
- Wenn es angebracht ist, stell dich vor.

USEFUL PHRASES
Excuse me, please.
Do you know ...? / Can I sit here?
Hello, how are you?
My name is ... Nice to meet you.

Hi there, are you from Sydney?
Hi, how is it going?
Hi, have you been here before?

b) KEEP THE CONVERSATION GOING

- Zeige dein **Interesse**, indem du Fragen stellst, z.B. auch Nachfragen.
- Antworte nicht nur mit wenigen Worten, das kann unfreundlich wirken.
- Erzähle auch etwas **von dir**, möglichst auf eine **positive** Art (vermeide es, zu jammern oder zu nörgeln).
- Wenn du etwas nicht verstehst, frage höflich nach.
- Wenn du etwas nicht sagen kannst, umschreibe das Wort.

USEFUL PHRASES
Fine, thanks. / Yeah, sure.
Yes, I am. / No, not really.

What about you? Do you like ...?/ I'm new here in ... / I really like these ... What do you think ...?

Could you say that again, please?
I don't know the English word. It's something that ... / like ...

c) A GOOD ENDING

- **Beende** das Gespräch so freundlich, wie du es begonnen hast.
- **Bedanke** dich, wenn du um Hilfe gebeten oder z.B. Tipps bekommen hast.
- **Verabschiede** dich höflich.

! Mache dir vor dem Gespräch möglichst klar, mit wem du sprichst. So wirst du z.B. mit Gleichaltrigen informeller umgehen als mit Älteren.

Denke auch an eventuelle kulturelle Unterschiede, z.B. beim Begrüßen und Verabschieden.

3 Doing well in job interviews

a) PREPARE YOURSELF

- **Bereite dich sorgfältig** auf das Vorstellungsgespräch **vor**. Übe deine **Gesprächsanteile**, z.B. vor einem Spiegel oder mit Freunden. Achte besonders auf eine freundliche, aber angemessen formelle **Körpersprache**.
- Wo liegen deine **Stärken** und **Schwächen**? Was sind deine besonderen **Interessen**?
- **Warum** bewirbst du dich um diese Tätigkeit?
- Welche **Arbeitserfahrungen** hast du?
- **Informiere dich vorab** über das Unternehmen bzw. den Betrieb und bereite auch einige **Fragen** an die Interviewer vor.

USEFUL PHRASES
Good morning, Ms / Mr ...
My name is ... and I'm really interested in this job because I like working with ...

I think this is a job I could do well because I already have some experience with ...
I'm quite good at ... / I'm not very good at ...

I'd like to know if I'll be working in a team or on my own.
Do I have to work at the weekends?

b) IN THE INTERVIEW

- Plane **genügend Zeit** für die Anfahrt und das Finden des genauen Interviewortes ein. Schalte dein **Smartphone stumm**, bevor du dort ankommst.
- **Begrüße** dein Gegenüber freundlich, stell dich noch einmal vor.
- Bleib **ruhig**, sei **freundlich** und **positiv**.
- Hör gut zu, sprich **deutlich** und nicht zu schnell. Sieh dein Gegenüber beim Gespräch an.
- Kontrolliere immer mal wieder deine **Köperhaltung**.
- Bleibe **ehrlich**, übertreibe nicht.
- Am Ende des Gesprächs **bedanke** dich und **verabschiede** dich freundlich.

4 Taking part in discussions

▸ Unit 1, pp. 13, 14 ▸ Unit 2, pp. 45, 52 ▸ Unit 3, pp. 54, 55
▸ Wordbank, p. 135

In einer (Klassen-)Diskussion tauschst du dich über Ideen und Meinungen aus. Dabei sollst du auf die Äußerungen deiner Gesprächspartner/innen eingehen und gleichzeitig deinen eigenen Standpunkt darstellen und begründen.

a) PREPARING A DISCUSSION

- Eine **inhaltliche Vorbereitung** auf das Thema der Diskussion ist sinnvoll, damit du nützliche **Wörter** und **Wendungen** parat hast. Notiere sie dir.
- Mache dich mit **unterschiedlichen Standpunkten** zum Thema vertraut und denke darüber nach, was deine Position ist.
- Notiere dir **Argumente**, die deinen bzw. andere Standpunkte unterstützen. (Beispielsweise in einem Rollenspiel kann deine Aufgabe sein, einen anderen Standpunkt als den eigenen zu vertreten.)
- Bereite deine **erste Äußerung**, mit der du in die Diskussion eintrittst, besonders gut vor.

STATING YOUR OPINION
In my opinion, / view, ...
Well, I'd say ...
(Personally,) I think / feel / believe ...
If you ask me, ...
First of all, ...
To start with, I'd like to point out that ...

b) HAVING THE DISCUSSION

- Wenn du die Diskussion **eröffnest**, beginne mit deinem vorbereiteten **Einstieg**.
- Häufiger wirst du dich auf deine **Vorredner/innen** beziehen. Du kannst ihrem Standpunkt **zustimmen** oder **nicht zustimmen** und dann deine vorbereitete Äußerung und passende **Argumente** vorbringen.
- In jedem Fall **höre** den Argumenten der anderen **genau zu** und beziehe dich in deiner Äußerung darauf.
- Bleibe stets **höflich** und lass andere ausreden.
- Manchmal wirst du **nachfragen** müssen, wenn dir etwas unklar oder unverständlich ist.

AGREEING
I quite agree. **(+)**
You're quite right. **(+)**
I think so too. **(+)**
You've got a (good) point there. **(+)**
That's true / right. / That's just it. **(++)**
I agree completely. **(++)**
I couldn't agree with you more. **(+++)**

DISAGREEING
I'm afraid I don't (quite) agree (there). **(-)**
I'm not so sure, really. **(-)**
Well, that's one way of looking at it, but ... **(-)**
It's not as simple as that (I'm afraid). **(-)**
I don't believe that at all. **(--)**
I don't agree with you at all. **(--)**
(Sorry,) I definitely disagree. **(--)**
(Sorry,) I think you're wrong. **(--)**

ASKING FOR CLARIFICATION
Sorry, I didn't get that. / Are you saying that ... ?
Does your last statement mean that ... ?
Could you please give an example of ... ?

SF 10 Writing course

1 The steps of text writing

a) PLANNING YOUR TEXT

- Über welches Thema willst / sollst du genau schreiben?
- Was für einen Text sollst du schreiben: z.B. eine E-Mail, das Ende einer Geschichte oder einen Sachtext (Beschreibung – *Describe ...*; Erläuterung – *Explain ...*; Erörterung – *Discuss ...*; Zusammenfassung – *Summarize ...*)?
- Sammle Ideen und / oder Argumente – z.B. in einem Mindmap oder in einer Liste.
- Recherchiere die für dein Thema notwendigen Informationen ▸ *SF 5*.
- Strukturiere dein Material: Schreibe deine geplante Gliederung (*outline*) auf.

Du brauchst
- eine Einleitung (*beginning / introduction*): Hier steht, worum es im Text insgesamt geht.
- einen Hauptteil (*middle / main body*): Dieser Teil ist in mehrere Absätze (*paragraphs*) gegliedert, die Details (Fakten, Beispiele usw.) und Argumente enthalten.
- einen Schluss (*ending / summary / conclusion*): Hier gibst du dem Text ein passendes, einprägsames Ende.

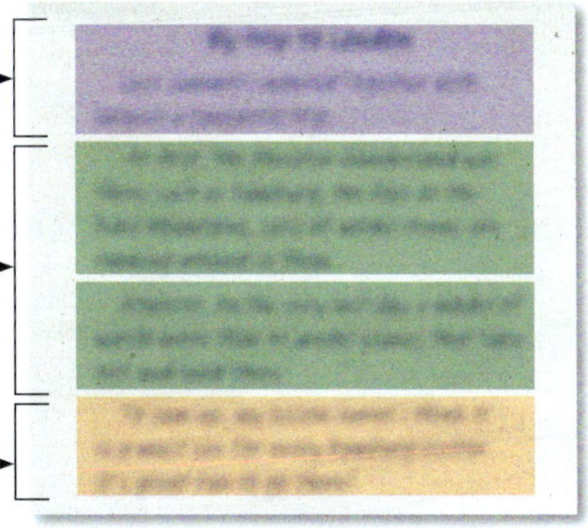

b) WRITING YOUR TEXT ▸ *Unit 3, p. 62*

- Nun schreibe den **ersten Textentwurf**. Halte dich an deine Gliederung.
- Beginne für jeden neuen Gedanken einen **neuen Absatz**.
- Jeder Absatz sollte mit einem **Einleitungssatz** (*topic sentence*) beginnen. Er drückt aus, worum es in diesem Absatz gehen wird.
- **Verbinde** deine Sätze mit passenden *linking* und *time phrases*.
- Verwende passende, **ausdrucksstarke** Wörter und Wendungen, z.B.:
  - **Adjektive** (zum näheren Beschreiben von Personen, Dingen, Orten usw.): *a peaceful voice*
  - **Adverbien** zum näheren Beschreiben von Handlungen, Vorgängen und Zuständen:
    It was raining heavily.
    oder zum Verstärken von Adjektiven: *an extremely sad story*; *He was deeply disappointed.*

USEFUL LINKING PHRASES

Konjunktionen (***conjunctions***):
but, and, because, so, on the one hand – on the other hand (einerseits – andererseits), ***although, however***
Demonstrativpronomen (***demonstrative pronouns***): *This is exactly …*. *That's the point.*
Relativsätze (***relative clauses***):
The platypus is an animal that I've never seen in real life.

USEFUL TIME PHRASES

Adverbiale Bestimmungen der Zeit (*time markers*): ***at first, next, finally*** (Reihenfolge)
for half an hour (Dauer), ***immediately, faster than …*** (Geschwindigkeit)
during our holiday, as he arrived, while … (zeitgleiches Geschehen)
two years ago, last spring (Zeitpunkt)

c) CHECKING AND REWRITING YOUR TEXT

- Wenn dein erster Textentwurf geschrieben ist, hast du viel geschafft, bist aber noch nicht fertig. Jetzt solltest du deinen Text **jemand anderem** zu lesen geben und um **Feedback** bitten.
- **Lies** selbst deinen Text **mehrmals** durch, je mit einem anderen Schwerpunkt:
  - Stimmt der **logische Aufbau**, die Struktur (Einleitung – Hauptteil – Schluss)? Sind die Absätze in sich logisch aufgebaut?
  - Sind die Sätze gut verbunden, liest sich der Text **flüssig** (*linking* and *time phrases*)?
  - Hast du deine **typischen Fehler vermieden**? (Gleiche mit deiner Fehlersammlung ab ▸ *SF 3.1*.)
  - Wenn du am Computer schreibst und ein **Rechtschreibprogramm** benutzt, wähle die richtige Sprache aus (z. B. *British/ American English*). Überprüfe jeden Korrekturvorschlag noch einmal in einem Wörterbuch. Achte dabei auf den Kontext ▸ *SF 2*.
  - Schau dir ein eventuelles **Feedback** genau an und überlege, was du davon übernehmen willst.
- Schreibe nun deinen Text in der **endgültigen Version**. Lass dir etwas Zeit, dann lies auch diese Version noch einmal kritisch durch und verbessere, wo das noch nötig ist.

Typische Fehlerquellen

- Groß- und Kleinschreibung
- Wörter die ähnlich klingen, aber unterschiedlich geschrieben werden: *your / you're; than – then; quiet – quite*
- unregelmäßige Pluralformen: *woman – women, child – children*
- Wörter mit „stummen" Buchstaben: *know, talk, listen*
- *word order* in Aussagen, Fragen ▸ *Language files 15, 16, pp. 192–193*
- unregelmäßige Verben und unregelmäßige Schreibungen: *try → tries, tried*
- Präpositionen: *on the internet, in the photo, go by bus, be good at …*
- Typische Wendungen, z. B.: „Was gibt's zum Abendbrot?" – *What's for dinner?* „Alles Gute!" – *All the best!*

2 Writing a comment ▸ Unit 2, p. 43 ▸ Unit 3, pp. 57, 62, 72

Auch beim Verfassen eines Kommentars bzw. einer Stellungnahme beachte die *Steps of text writing.* ▸ SF 10.1
In einem *comment* vermittelst du deine persönliche Meinung, begründest und argumentierst.

a) PLANNING YOUR COMMENT

- Lies die Aufgabe und den evtl. dazugehörigen Text genau. Notiere dir z.B. Stichwörter, fertige ein Mindmap an.
- Wenn du für oder gegen etwas Stellung nehmen sollst, sortiere deine Ideen schon in Pro und Contra-Argumente.

Denke bei der Gliederung (*outline*) an:
- ***beginning / introduction*** (Einleitung): Hier teilst du deinen Lesern mit, worauf du dich beziehst und was deine Meinung ist.
- ***middle / main body*** (Mittelteil): Hier begründest du deine Meinung mit (Pro-)Argumenten und Beispielen. Berücksichtige auch Gegenargumente (Contra).
- ***end / conclusion*** (Schluss): Hier ziehst du deine Schlussfolgerung aus den Argumenten des Mittelteils. Greife deine Meinung vom Anfang wieder auf.

smartphones in class?

PRO	CONTRA
- looking up words easily	- noisy - unconcentrated

USEFUL PHRASES FOR COMMENTS

- In my opinion, / experience, …
- I (definitely / really) think / don't think (that) …
- I agree / don't agree / disagree with …

- First of all, / first(ly), second(ly), …
- On the one hand – on the other hand / Additionally, …

- To sum up, …
- I'd like to finish by saying / underlining …

b) WRITING YOUR COMMENT

- Einige *useful phrases for comments* findest du rechts sowie in der ▸ *Wordbank, p. 135*.

c) CHECK AND CORRECT YOUR COMMENT

- Auch bei *comments* plane mindestens einen Textentwurf und eine gründliche Überarbeitung ein.

3 Writing a formal letter / an email of complaint ▸ Unit 3, p. 67

Für Beschwerdeschreiben (*letters / emails of complaint*) gelten die Regeln für formelle Briefe / E-Mails:
- klare Gliederung
- keine Kurzformen (*I'm* -> *I am* usw.)
- gründlicher Fehlercheck
- höflicher, aber bestimmter Stil

! Briefkopf mit Adressen und Datum

! Anlass der Beschwerde und Details: Beschreibe das Produkt und die Probleme bzw. Fehlfunktionen genau.

! Deine Vorschläge und höflichen Forderungen: möglichst mit Fristsetzung.

! Ein freundlicher Abschlusssatz und die Abschiedsformel mit deinem vollen Namen.

[your address]

[the company's address]

[the date]

Dear Sir / Madam

I recently bought … from your online shop. When I tried to use this product, I discovered that … does not work / does not last as long as promised / is faulty / is damaged / … Please find a copy of the receipt / credit card bill / … attached.

Since the return form and label were missing, I ask you to send them to me within seven days. I would like a full refund within 30 days of the date of this letter.

I look forward to your reply and hope this matter can be sorted out quickly.

Yours faithfully

[your first name and surname]

4 Summarizing texts ▸ *More challenge 2, p. 52* ▸ *Text file 2, p. 152*

Wenn du einen Text (mündlich oder schriftlich) zusammenfasst, gibst du die wichtigsten Informationen oder Ereignisse in kurzer Form wieder.

a) PLANNING YOUR SUMMARY

- Lies den Text: Für den ersten Überblick beginne mit dem Skimming und lies danach genauer, aber noch ohne etwas zu markieren oder dir Notizen zu machen.
- Bestimme die **Textsorte**, denn einen erzählenden Text fasst du etwas anders zusammen als einen Sachtext.
- Beim Finden der **wichtigen Informationen** helfen dir die ***fünf wh*-questions**. Markiere die wichtigsten Informationen im Text (auf einer Kopie) und fertige dann kurze Notizen an. Mit diesen schreibst du dann deine Zusammenfassung.

ERZÄHLENDE TEXTE (Geschichten, Romane, Romanauszüge usw.):	**SACHTEXTE** (Zeitungs- oder Magazinartikel usw.):
Thema, Ort, Zeit, grobe Handlungszüge	Thema, Fakten, Argumente (und ggf. wichtige Ereignisse)

WHO	**WHAT**
is the text about?	
WHAT happens	**WHAT** are the **main points** or **arguments**
in the text?	
WHERE / WHEN / WHY does it happen?	**WHERE / WHEN / WHY** is it important?

USEFUL PHRASES
- The text / story is about ...
- ... is a story about ...
- The article shows ... / deals with ...

b) WRITING YOUR SUMMARY

- ***beginning / introduction***: Hier nennst du das Thema, Titel und Autor/in des Originaltexts. Bei Zeitungsartikeln solltest du hier auch die Quelle nennen.
- Im **Hauptteil** fasst du die wichtigsten Fakten (eines Sachtexts) bzw. Handlungsschritte (eines erzählenden Textes) zusammen.
  - Fasse dich **kurz** (Der Umfang einer Zusammenfassung ist maximal **20%** des Originaltexts).
  - Fasse jeden Abschnitt in einem kurzen Satz zusammen.
  - Verwende deine eigenen Worte, schreibe den Text nicht ab.
  - Verwende keine direkte Rede.
  - Verzichte auf Einzelheiten und Beispiele.
  - Schreibe im ***simple present***, auch wenn der Originaltext eine oder mehrere andere Zeitformen verwendet.
  - Verbinde die Sätze und Textteile, so dass sich deine Zusammenfassung gut und flüssig liest. ▸ *p. 173*

c) CHECK AND CORRECT YOUR SUMMARY

- Auch bei *summaries* plane mindestens einen Textentwurf und eine gründliche Überarbeitung ein.
  - Enthält deine Zusammenfassung das Thema und die wesentlichen Fakten bzw. Handlungsschritte?
  - Hast du unwichtige Einzelheiten weggelassen?
  - Korrigiere Rechtschreib- und Grammatikfehler. ▸ *p. 173*
  - Ist dein Text logisch aufgebaut und gut zu verstehen?

Falls möglich, überprüft eure Zusammenfassungen im *partner check*.

5 Writing a cover letter (Bewerbungsschreiben)

Hinweis	Beispiel
Beginne mit *Dear Sir/Madam oder Dear Mrs/Mr/Ms ...*	Dear Sir/Madam
Sage, wie du auf die Stelle aufmerksam geworden bist, und dass du dich bewerben möchtest.	I read your online advertisement for an assistant in your hostel and I would like to apply for this job.
Nenne deine Arbeitserfahrungen und sage, warum du dich für die Stelle eignest.	I am a student and last year I had a Saturday job in a small hotel for five months. I helped with making beds and with the cleaning, and assisted at the reception desk, so I think that I would be very suitable for the job.
Verwende keine Kurzformen: *I'm => I am; it's => it is*	I am 16 years old and I speak English, German and Turkish. I am reliable and I enjoy working with people.
Diesen Satz kannst du immer verwenden.	My teachers say that I am a good team worker, and I have no problems working under pressure.
	I attach my CV and I look forward to hearing from you.
Schreibe am Ende *Yours faithfully* und deinen Namen.	Yours faithfully Samed Celik

6 Writing a CV (*curriculum vitae*, Lebenslauf)

Hinweis	Beispiel
	Samed Celik
Schreibe ganz oben deinen Namen, deine Adresse, Telefonnummer und Emailadresse.	Address: Grahnstr. 83a, 30165 Hannover Mobile: 0151 555 5010 Email: Samed.Celik@phone.de
Sage, wieso du dich für die Stelle interessierst und eignest.	**Personal statement** I am a confident student with good communication and telephone skills. I have some work experience, and I would like to learn new skills.
Nenne deine Stärken.	**Key skills** – Strong team member – Good computer skills – Friendly and polite – Turkish, German, good English
Sage, welche Schulen du besucht hast.	**Education** 2012 to now: Berg Gesamtschule, Hannover 2008 to 2012: Grundschule Sonnenstr., Hannover
Nenne Praktika, Ferienjobs oder andere Berufserfahrungen.	**Work experience** Hotel Adler: Cleaning, making beds, helping at the reception desk (part-time job)
Zähle deine wichtigsten Hobbys und Interessen auf – vor allem Teamsportarten oder ehrenamtliche Tätigkeiten.	**Interests** I am interested in computers and programming. I love playing basketball and I am in the school's basketball team.
Gib Referenzen an. Wer kann Positives über dich berichten?	**References** Sibylle Renz (English teacher), Berg Gesamtschule Christian Adler (manager), Hotel Adler

7 A written discussion ▸ Unit 1, p. 21 ▸ Unit 3 p. 59

Oft sollst du zu strittigen Fragen schriftlich Stellung nehmen und deine Sichtweise überzeugend darlegen. Zeige dabei, dass du dich gründlich mit dem Thema beschäftigt und die Pro-/ Contra-Argumente abgewogen hast.

a) PREPARING YOUR TEXT

- **Sammle** zuerst alle **Argumente** (z.B. in einem kurzen Brainstorming). Evtl. musst du vorher weiter recherchieren ▸ *SF 5*.
- Ordne deine Argumente gleich beim Sammeln in zwei Listen: ***pro*** und ***contra***.
- Schau dir die Argumentlisten an und bereite so die Gliederung *(outline)* deines Texts vor:
  - Was sind die **besten drei Argumente *contra*** und die **besten drei *pro***? Diese verwendest du, jeweils beginnend mit dem stärksten Argument.
  - **Nummeriere** die Argumente entsprechend dem Schema rechts.
- Notiere deine **Gliederung *(outline)*** gemäß dem Schema rechts.
  - Beginne mit den Argumenten, die **gegen *(contra)*** deine Sichtweise sprechen und stell **danach** die Argumente vor, die deine Meinung **unterstützen *(pro)***. (Auf diese Weise lassen sich die Contra-Argumente wirkungsvoller entkräften. Prinzipiell kannst du aber auch mit den Pro-Argumenten beginnen.)
  - Notiere jeweils **Beispiele** zu den Argumenten.
  - Überlege und notiere, in welche Richtung deine **Schlussfolgerung *(conclusion)*** gehen soll.

OUTLINE FOR A WRITTEN DISCUSSION

Topic: Can students do enough to save the planet?

1) Introduction: …
2) Arguments contra / against
   2.1) First argument: …
   2.2) Second argument: …
   2.3) Third argument: …
3) Arguments pro / for / supporting
   2.1) First argument: …
   2.2) Second argument: …
   2.3) Third argument: …
4) Conclusion: …

b) WRITING YOUR TEXT

- Nun formuliere mithilfe deiner *outline* die *written discussion* **ausführlich**.
- In der **Einleitung *(introduction)*** stellst du das Thema vor und beschreibst, worum es geht. Geh dabei von einem allgemein bekannten Problem oder einer persönlichen Erfahrung aus.
- Im **Hauptteil *(main body)*** präsentiere die Argumente *contra* und *pro*.
  - Nenne jeweils das Argument.
  - Erläutere es näher und begründe deine Meinung.
  - Unterstütze deine Meinung durch Fakten und Beispiele (aus deiner Recherche bzw. aus eigener Erfahrung).

  Formuliere logisch und flüssig, verbinde deine Argumente. ▸ *p. 173*
- Am Textende steht deine persönliche **Schlussfolgerung *(conclusion)***. Achtung: Hier keine neuen Argumente und auch keine Argument-Wiederholungen aus dem Hauptteil!

USEFUL PHRASES

… for your introduction:
A lot of people think …
You often hear people say that …,
… so the questions is: should … or not?

… for the main body of your text:
Firstly, …; Secondly, …;
Another argument for / against …
is …
For example, …
People think that because …
However, a lot of people feel …
On the one hand, …
On the other hand, we should not
forget …
So …; That is why …; Finally, …

… for your conclusion:
To sum up, I think / I would say …
After looking at all the arguments,
I think / I come to the conclusion
that …

c) CHECK AND CORRECT YOUR TEXT

- Auch bei *written discussions* plane mindestens einen Textentwurf und eine gründliche Überarbeitung ein. ▸ *p. 173*

8 Writing a report ▸ Unit 2, pp. 37, 120, 122

Auch beim Verfassen eines Berichts beachte *The steps of text writing*. ▸ SF 10.1
In einem *report* gibst du deinen Lesern kurze und sachliche Informationen.

a) PLANNING YOUR REPORT

Collect ideas
Notiere dir Stichwörter zu den fünf *wh*-Fragen und *how* in einer Mindmap oder Tabelle. Beispiel:

Footballers support refugees

Gelsenkirchen-Schalke, Germany – Yesterday Schalke's former professional Gerald Asamoah and Schalke's fans stood up for human rights and refugees.
Ghana born Asamoah started a campaign for refugees earlier this month. His campaign is called *#Stand up for human rights*! and was supported by thousands of fans who stood up holding posters with *#stehtauf* in their hands.
Asamoah started the campaign because he wanted to show that everybody could help. He said, "Everybody must show courage and they must hold up a sign that says, *Stand up*." The campaign is supported in many social networks by well-known footballers, e.g. Schalke's Benedikt Höwedes or Hamburg's Rene Adler.

Plan the structure of your report
Auch ein Bericht besteht aus *beginning*, *middle* und *end*.
Beginne mit den **wichtigsten Informationen**, um deinen Lesern eine schnelle Orientierung zu ermöglichen. **Weitere Informationen** kannst du ans Ende setzen. Informiere deine Leser kurz und knapp.

b) WRITING YOUR REPORT

Schreibe deinen Bericht auf und bilde Sinnabschnitte. Beachte: Wenn du über Vergangenes berichtest, musst du das *simple past* verwenden.

c) CHECK AND CORRECT YOUR REPORT

Plane auch bei einem *report* mindestens einen Textentwurf und eine gründliche Überarbeitung ein.

9 Writing a book or film review ▸ Unit 1, p. 111 ▸ Unit 2, p. 123

1 Worum geht es?

Nicht nur Fachleute wie Journalisten oder Kritiker schreiben Kritiken zu Filmen oder Büchern, sondern auch viele Nicht-Profis geben zunehmend ihre Meinung zu Büchern und Filmen, die sie gelesen oder gesehen haben, in Internetportalen wieder. Auch Mitschüler sind daran interessiert, wie dir ein Film oder ein Buch gefallen hat.

2 Wie schreibe ich eine Kritik?

Überlege dir vorab, ob du den Film / das Buch weiterempfehlen oder davon abraten möchtest. Dann baue deine Kritik wie folgt auf.

- **Einleitung** *(background information)*
  Nenne den Titel und das Genre (z. B. Komödie oder Thriller; Roman oder Sachbuch). Sag etwas über die wichtigsten Schauspieler bzw. Figuren und auch etwas zum Regisseur bzw. Autor. Du kannst wichtige zusätzliche Informationen zum Film oder Buch ergänzen (z.B. gewonnene Preise etc.)

USEFUL PHRASES
for writing a book or film review
... is a film / book by ...
It's a comedy / thriller / adventure film / documentary ...
The main actors / characters are ...

- **Hauptteil** (specific information)
  Gib eine kurze Zusammenfassung: Ort und Zeit der Handlung, Hauptpersonen und die wichtigsten Inhalte. Benutze dafür das ***simple present***. Schreibe über den Aufbau, den Handlungsverlauf (*plot*), den Schauplatz (*setting*), die Figuren (*characters*) und die Stimmung (*mood*).
  ▸ *Skills file 7.7, p. 168*
- **Bewertung und Empfehlung**
  (your opinion and recommendation)
  Schreib, wie dir der Film oder das Buch gefallen hat und sag, woran das lag. Fandest du Handlung spannend und interessant oder langweilig? Warum? Was war ansprechend und ungewöhnlich?

  Falls du einen Film kritisierst: Wie waren die Schauspieler, wie gefiel dir die Filmmusik? Kannst du Buch oder Film empfehlen oder nicht? Wem könnte der Film bzw. das Buch gefallen?

3 Check and correct your review

Plane auch bei einem *review* mindestens einen Textentwurf und eine gründliche Überarbeitung ein.

USEFUL PHRASES

The film / book is about ...
It's the story of ...
The action takes place in ...
The story begins when ...
Later ... In the end ...

I really enjoyed ...
I think it's one of the best films of the last few years because ...
Personally I think the story is exciting / weak / boring ...
The actors are just super / convincing ...
The special effects are amazing and the music is wonderful.
If you like action/romantic feelings/ to laugh, *(film title)* is the movie for you.
I can recommend / wouldn't read this book / watch this film because I'm (not) interested in ...
I think that this film / book will be popular with girls / boys / anybody who likes.

SF 11 Talking about visuals

1 Describing photos, pictures, filmstills ▸ *Unit 3, pp. 59, 133*

- Beginne **allgemein**: Welchen Ort, welche Gegenstände und welche Menschen siehst du? Was tun sie?
  In the photo we can see a little girl and a young man. They're sitting inside a big room, but not together.
- Beachte eine **Reihenfolge**: **Wen** oder **was** siehst du **wo** im Foto? Du kannst im Vorder- oder Hintergrund (*in the foreground / background*) beginnen. Benutze passende Ortsangaben (z.B. *in the middle of / at the top / ...*) und Präpositionen (z.B. *at / behind / between / in the background / in front of / near / next to / on ...*).
- Beschreibe **Personen** und **Handlungen**: z.B. ihr Aussehen, was sie gerade tun (dies im ***present progressive***):
  The girl is building something with dominoes. She looks happy.
- Formuliere **Vermutungen** über die **Personen** und ihre **Beziehung(en)** zueinander. Was fühlen oder denken sie (vermutlich) gerade?
  Was könnte als nächstes passieren?
  The man might be working. He looks busy. I think he is the girl's father. The girl is probably having fun and she's happy that her father is at home. Maybe they're going to have a video-call with grandma.

Beachte die "***non-progressive*** ***verbs***
▸ *Language file 2, p. 186*.

2 Talking about cartoons ▸ Unit 1, pp. 17, 105

- Cartoons (Karikaturen) sind humorvolle Zeichnungen mit oder ohne Text, die häufig ein aktuelles Thema kommentieren. Diese Schritte helfen dir beim Beschreiben und Verstehen eines Cartoons:

- ***(I) Describe what you see***

  Beschreibe die **Personen** / **Tiere** / **Dinge**: ihr **Aussehen** und ihre **Handlungen**. Beginne wieder allgemein und beschreibe in einer Reihenfolge mit Hilfe von Ortsangaben und Präpositionen.
  We see a protest situation, not with people, but with two penguins as angry protesters. Both birds are black and white. They seem to be alone in a polar landscape.
  The penguin on the left is holding a protest sign saying "White supremacy" and the one on the right is confronting him with a sign carrying the slogan "Black power!".

- ***(II) Name the topic / problem***

  Worum geht es deiner Meinung nach in diesem Cartoon?
  I think this cartoon is about racial problems and prejudices.

- ***(III) Explain the message***

  Was will der Cartoonist zum Ausdruck bringen / kritisieren / unterstützen? Was ist positiv, was negativ dargestellt?
  I think the cartoon criticizes racial prejudices. It is making fun of a serious human problem by employing animal protagonists.

- ***(IV) Evaluate the cartoon / Give your opinion***

  „Funktioniert" die Karikatur aus deiner Sicht, d.h. sind die eingesetzten Mittel (Figurenwahl, eventueller Text ...) effektiv? Hier kannst du auch Hintergrundwissen zum Thema des Cartoons einsetzen.
  Both penguins are shown as equally black and white and equally narrow-minded. The one on the left sees itself as only "white" and the one on the right as only "black". I think they have a lot in common and should stick together instead of fighting each other.
  The two slogans are historical, which makes this cartoon more serious. ...

supremacy [su:ˈpreməsi] – *Vorherrschaft*

USEFUL PHRASES
for talking about cartoons:

(I) At the top / bottom / in the middle / ... of the cartoon there is ...
The caption reads "..."

(II) This cartoon is about / shows / provides proof (for / against) ... / deals with ...

(III) The cartoon may be meant to ...
It's layout / use of colour ... / caption ... shows / criticizes / makes fun of ...

(IV) The cartoon addresses / doesn't address the problem / topic of ... very effectively ...
Using ... is very amusing / funny / ...
I especially like its irony seen against the complicated / tragic / ... background of ...

3 Talking about charts and diagrams ▸ Unit 1, p. 16

- Diagramme stellen statistische Vergleiche zwischen mindestens zwei Dingen dar. Dabei helfen sie komplexe Informationen zu veranschaulichen und leichter zu verstehen.
- Unterschiedliche **Formen von Diagrammen**:
  - Bar charts (Säulendiagramme) beschreiben in der Regel die Anzahl oder Größe von zwei oder mehr Dingen.
  - Pie charts (Kreis- / Tortendiagramme) geben einen Überblick über die prozentuale Verteilung.
  - Line graphs (Kurvendiagramme) stellen den Zusammenhang zwischen zwei oder mehr Variablen (Parameter) dar.
  - Charts (Tabellen) ermöglichen den Vergleich unterschiedlicher Daten anhand von Zahlen.
- So **beschreibst** du **Diagramme**:

  Um Diagramme zu beschreiben, ist es hilfreich, folgende Struktur zu nutzen.
  A: Einleitung
  What is the graph / chart about?
  The bar / pie chart / line graph is about … / deals with …
  The (horizontal) x-axis / (vertical) y-axis shows …
  The slices of the pie chart compare …
  Du solltest auch sagen, wo du das Diagramm gefunden hast.
  It is taken from …
  B: Beschreibung der dargestellten Informationen
  What does the graph / chart compare? What information does it give?
  … has the largest / smallest … is twice / three times … as big as …
  There are more than / almost twice as many … as there are …
  A majority / minority / … per cent of …
  Less than half / More than one third …
  The number … grows by … / sinks by … / does not change
  C: Schlussfolgerung
  What is the general conclusion?
  I was really surprised / shocked by …
  So / To sum up / All in all we can say …
- **Beachte** außerdem:

  Benutze das ***simple present***, wenn das Diagramm sich auf Fakten in der Gegenwart bezieht oder bei allgemeingültigen Aussagen:
  More than 55 per cent of German students under 10 have a smartphone.
  Benutze das ***simple past*** bei Fakten, die in der Vergangenheit liegen:
  73 per cent of the 10–12-year-olds had their own TV in 2012
  Benutze das **present perfect**, wenn du dich auf einen Zeitraum beziehst, der von der Vergangenheit bis heute reicht:
  The number of young people using social media has nearly doubled since 2011

What do 10 to 18-years-olds use their mobile for?

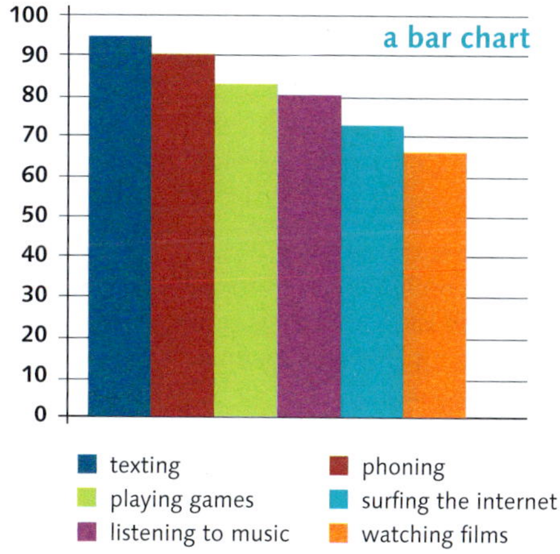

source: Bitkom

Use of social networks (10–18 yrs)

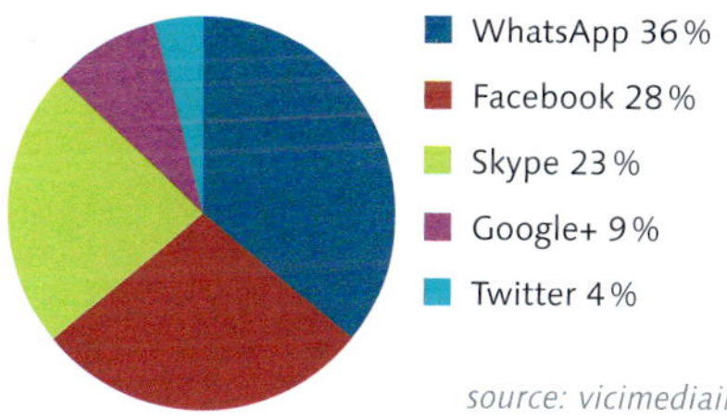

source: vicimediainc

a pie chart

Hours spent on media per day

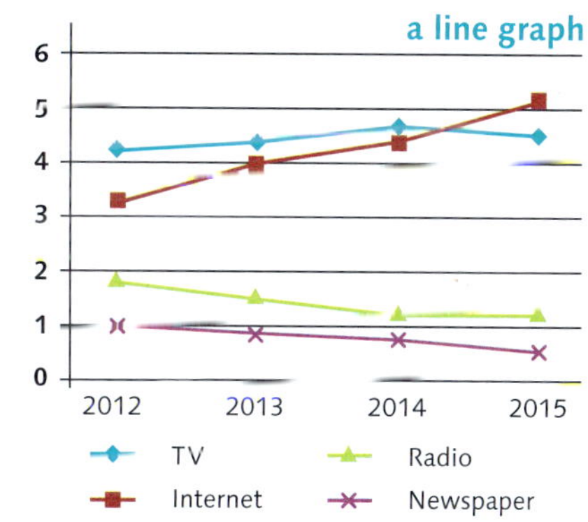

source: Bitkom

SF 12 MEDIATION COURSE ▸ Unit 1, p. 24 ▸ Unit 2, p. 44 ▸ Unit 3, p. 68

Mediation (auch: Sprachmittlung) bedeutet, zwischen Sprecher/innen unterschiedlicher Sprachen zu vermitteln und Informationen in der jeweiligen Sprache wiederzugeben.

1 Worum geht es?

- Du gibst englische Informationen mündlich **auf Deutsch** wieder, wie im Beispiel rechts.
- Oder du vermittelst deutsche Informationen **auf Englisch**, z.B. wenn bei dir an der Schule ein Austauschschüler zu Gast ist. Das kann mündlich geschehen (im Gespräch mit Anderen) oder auch schriftlich, wenn du dem Gastschüler z.B. eine Nachricht schreibst.
- Die unterschiedlichen Möglichkeiten von *mediation* (Deutsch ←→ Englisch, mündlich / schriftlich) fasst dieses Schema zusammen:

Freund: Können wir hier parken? Was sollen wir machen?

Du: Ja. Wir sollen einen Parkschein lösen und ihn sichtbar ins Auto legen.

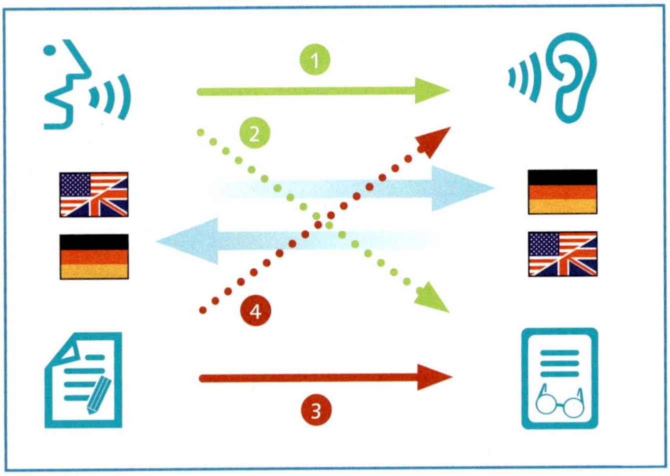

Beispiele:

1. Einem englischsprachigen Reisenden in Deutschland sagst du, was eben in der Bahnhofsdurchsage Wichtiges zu hören war.
2. Bei einem Telefonat mit einem englischen Jobanbieter machst du Notizen, die du einem Freund mailst.
3. Du mailst einer künftigen Gastschülerin die wichtigsten Inhalte eurer Schulordnung auf Englisch.
4. Du erklärst eine schriftliche Information mündlich in der anderen Sprache, vgl. das Beispiel im Foto oben.

2 Worauf musst du achten?

- *Mediation* ist keine Übersetzung. Gib also nur das **Wesentliche** sinngemäß wieder, lasse unwichtige Informationen weg.
- Verwende kurze und einfache Sätze.
- Wenn du **schriftliche Informationen** sprachmitteln sollst:
  - **Scanne** den Text gezielt nach den notwendigen Informationen. ▸ SF 7.2
  - Ist der Text länger und du brauchst viele Informationen daraus, **markiere** die wichtigsten Textstellen und mach dir ggf. **Notizen** in deinen eigenen Worten. ▸ SF 7.6
- Wenn du **mündliche Informationen** sprachmitteln sollst:
  - **Höre zielgerichtet** auf die notwendigen Informationen. ▸ SF 6
- Bei längeren Hörtexten und umfangreichen Informationen mach dir **kurze Notizen** während des Hörens. Überlege anschließend, wie du sie am besten in der anderen Sprache wiedergeben kannst.

! Wenn du schriftlich sprachmittelst, achte darauf, dass dein Text in der anderen Sprache nicht länger als ca. 40% des Originaltexts ist.

3 Paraphrasieren (Umschreiben unbekannter Wörter)

Manchmal fällt es schwer, Inhalte auf Englisch wiederzugeben, z.B. wenn dein Wortschatz nicht ausreicht oder dir manche Wörter im Stress nicht gleich einfallen. Dann nutze das Umschreiben *(paraphrasing)*. Die folgenden **Strategien** helfen dir.

- Umschreibe mit Wörtern, die eine ähnliche oder die **gleiche Bedeutung** haben (Synonyme) oder mit Vergleichen:
  It's the same as … / It's (very) similar to … / It works like …
- Umschreibe mit **gegensätzlichen** Wörtern (Antonymen):
  It's the opposite of …
  Seine Eltern leben getrennt. – *His parents don't live together.*
  Der See ist künstlich angelegt. – *The lake is not a natural one.*
- Umschreibe mit dem **Oberbegriff** statt der einzelnen Unterbegriffe (das hilft dir auch, dich kurz zu fassen):
  Wir müssen noch ein paar Tulpen und Osterglocken kaufen.
  – *We need (to buy) some flowers.*
  Oh nein, Fahrradventil und Schlauch sind kaputt!
  – *She's angry because she can't ride her bike.*
- Umschreibe mit **Unterbegriffen**, wenn du den Oberbegriff nicht kennst:
  Haben wir ausreichend Geschirr für die Party heute Abend?
  – *Are there enough plates and glasses, etc. for the party?*
- Umschreibe mit einer näheren Erläuterung, z.B. in **Relativsätzen**. ▸ *Language file 28, p. 201*
  It's somebody / a person who is known for …
  It's something that you use for …
  It's a place that … / where …
- Oft hilft das Prinzip ***Keep it simple***. Fällt dir eine einfache Erklärung des gesuchten Begriffs ein? Diese kannst du dann leicht auf Englisch formulieren, z.B.
  Selbstbedienung – *no waiter / waitress*
  Vollsperrung der A20 bis 24 Uhr
  – *The A20 motorway will be (completely) closed till midnight.*
  Schienenersatzverkehr
  – *There is no train, so we have to take the bus instead.*

4 Kulturelle und regionale Unterschiede

- Manche ‚typisch deutschen' Alltagsdinge oder Traditionen wird dein Gegenüber eventuell nicht kennen. Hierfür gibt es im Englischen meist gar keinen direkten Begriff. Du musst dann erklären, was du meinst. Typische Beispiele:
- **Rosenmontag** – *It's the most important day of carnival for people in the Rhine area. It's a holiday. People celebrate and wear costumes, and there are parades in the streets.*
- **Schultüte** – *It's a kind of special bag kids are given on their first day at school. There are sweets in it and little things you need at school, like pens and exercise books.*
- Natürlich wird es für dich auch Unbekanntes geben, wovon dein Gegenüber ganz selbstverständlich spricht. Dann frage höflich nach und bitte um eine Erklärung:
- *I'm sorry, I'm afraid I don't know this tradition / rule / habit / meal …*
  Could you please explain it?
  I've never done / eaten … this before. Could you help me, please?

SF 13 VIEWING SKILLS

▸ Unit 1, pp. 13, 25 ▸ Unit 2, pp. 32–33, 47 ▸ Unit 3, p. 59, 69

1 Vor dem Sehen: bereite dich vor

- Welche Art von Film wirst du sehen: a documentary, a movie, a commercial, a soap, the news, ...? Was weißt du bereits über die Art des Films?
- Lies sorgfältig die Aufgabenstellung. Worum könnte es gehen?
- Worauf musst du besonders achten? Was kann dir beim Verstehen helfen?
- Betrachte die Filmszenen im Buch vor dem Anschauen.

2 Beim Sehen

Häufig sollst du dich zum Schauplatz (*setting*), zu den Figuren (*characters*), zum Handlungsverlauf (*plot*) und zur Stimmung (*mood*) eines Filmausschnitts äußern. Nutze dieses Raster für Notizen:

a classroom in a British school, ... **setting**	four teenagers, a history teacher, ... **characters**
they talk about World War 1, ... **plot**	relaxed, sad, ... **mood**

Versuche beim ersten Sehen die wesentlichen Inhalte des Films zu erfassen. Beim zweiten Sehen kannst du dann auf Einzelheiten achten und deine Notizen ergänzen.

Kameraeinstellungen helfen dir, Inhalte und Gefühle besser zu verstehen.

- close-up
  Ein *close-up* ist eine Nahaufnahme eines Gesichts oder einer Gegenstandes. So kannst du z.B. am Gesichtsausdruck die Gefühle einer Person erkennen.
  What does Patrick look like in this close-up?
- long shot
  Ein *long shot* (auch: *wide shot*), die Totale, gibt dir einen Eindruck der gesamten Szene und des Schauplatzes.
  How many people are there? Where are they? Who are they?

Achte auf die Erzählstruktur des Filmes, z. B. *monologue*. Ein Monolog gibt dir die Möglichkeit, die Motive einer einzelnen Person besser zu verstehen.

Ein *flashback* (Rückblende) verändert die chronologische Reihenfolge. Dadurch kannst du Ereignisse besser verstehen oder erkennen, wieso jemand dieses oder jenes gemacht hat.
Why did the teenagers bully Patrick?
Filmtechniken werden eingesetzt, um z. B. Spannung, Lachen, Angst oder Freude auszulösen.
Weitere wichtige Aspekte beim Anschauen, auf die du achten kannst, um dein Verständnis zu schulen, wie Filme funktionieren: Farbe, Kameraführung, Kontraste, Licht, Perspektive, Schnitt, Ton, insbesondere die Filmmusik.

3 Nach dem Sehen

Vervollständige deine Notizen.
Dabei helfen dir die Redewendungen rechts.

USEFUL PHRASES
The film is about .... / It tells the story of ...
The close-ups of .... make it easier to understand ...
The wide shot of the classroom shows ...
The monologues helped me to understand ...
The flashbacks showed ...
There is no music in the film / The music is dramatic / sad / ... because...
I (don't) like the film because ...

Inhalt

TALKING ABOUT THE PRESENT — page

LF 1 The simple present — 185
LF 2 The present progressive — 186

TALKING ABOUT THE PAST

LF 3 The simple past — 187
LF 4 The past progressive — 187
LF 5 The present perfect — 188
LF 6 *The present perfect progressive — 188
LF 7 The past perfect — 189
LF 8 *The past perfect progressive — 189

TALKING ABOUT THE FUTURE

LF 9 The *going to*-future — 190
LF 10 The *will*-future — 190
LF 11 *The simple present: future meaning — 190
LF 12 *The present progressive: future meaning — 191
LF 13 *The future progressive — 191
LF 14 *The future perfect — 191

LF 15 Word order in statements — 192
LF 16 Word order in questions — 192
LF 17 Questions with passive and modals — 193

page

LF 18 *Questions with prepositions — 194
LF 19 The comparison of adjectives — 194
LF 20 Adverbs of manner — 195
LF 21 Adverbs of frequency — 195
LF 22 The comparison of adverbs — 195
LF 23 Indirect speech — 196
LF 24 Modal verbs and their substitutes — 198
LF 25 *If* ... (Conditional sentences type 1) — 199
LF 26 *If* ... (Conditional sentences type 2) — 200
LF 27 *If* ... (Conditional sentences type 3) — 200
LF 28 Relative clauses — 201
LF 29 Contact clauses — 202
LF 30 *Participle clauses instead of subordinate clauses — 202
LF 31 Reflexive pronouns — 203
LF 32 The *-ing*-form (the gerund) — 203
LF 33 The passive — 205
LF 34 Question tags — 206
LF 35 *The definite and indefinite article — 207
LF 36 *Countable and uncountable nouns — 208

Grammatical terms — 208

TALKING ABOUT THE PRESENT

LF 1 The simple present (Die einfache Form der Gegenwart) ▸ Unit 1, p. 17

Mit dem ***simple present*** drückst du aus, was **wiederholt** oder **nie** geschieht. Es steht häufig mit: *always, sometimes, often, never* oder Zeitangaben wie *every day, in the morning, at the weekend, on Monday.* Du benutzt das ***simple present*** auch, um **Gewohnheiten**, **Dauerzustände** oder **allgemein gültige Tatsachen** auszudrücken, z.B. *Mia likes football. Dublin lies on the coast. No means no.*

Bejahte und verneinte Aussagen

I/You/We/They He/She/It	like likes	sport.

I/You/We/They He/She/It	don't like doesn't like	sport.

Bei **bejahten Aussagen** fügst du bei *he/she/it* ein *-s* an das Verb.

! *he/she/it goes, watches, tries, hurries*

! Das Verb nach doesn't (hier: *like*) steht immer in der Grundform.
Das gilt auch für does in Fragen.

***Ja-/Nein*-Fragen und Kurzantworten**

Do you like Does he like	sport?	Yes, I do./No, I don't. Yes, he does./No, he doesn't.

Ja-/Nein-Fragen im ***simple present*** beginnst du mit *Do* oder *Does*.

Fragen mit Fragewort

Why do Ben's friends love football?

Wenn die Frage mit einem **Fragewort** anfängt, folgt direkt *do* bzw. *does*.

! Fragen mit **Fragewort** *Who* ▸ LF 16

LF 2 The present progressive (Die Verlaufsform der Gegenwart)

▸ Unit 1, p. 1

Mit dem ***present progressive*** sagst du, dass etwas **gerade jetzt** geschieht oder dass jemand **gerade etwas tut**. Das ***present progressive*** benutzt du auch, um Bilder zu beschreiben.
Häufige Zeitangaben in Sätzen im ***present progressive*** sind: *now, at the moment, just, still*.
Eine Verlaufsform gibt es im Deutschen nicht. Man sagt aber z.B.: „Ich bin gerade dabei, etwas zu tun."

Bejahte Aussagen

I'm / You're He's / She's They're	waiting.

Verneinte Aussagen

I'm not / You aren't He / She isn't They aren't	waiting.

Das ***present progressive*** bildest du mit einer Form von ***be*** + *verb* + ***-ing***.

! Beachte beim Schreiben:
write → writing *make → making*
plan → planning *stop → stopping*

Ja-/Nein-Fragen und Kurzantworten

Am I Are you Is he / she Are they	waiting?	Yes, I am. / No, I'm not. Yes, he / she is. / No, ... isn't. Yes, they are. /No, they aren't.

Ja-/Nein-Fragen beginnst du mit *Am / Are / Is*:
Is Mia going to football practice?
- Yes, she is. / No, she isn't. She's waiting for Li.

Fragen mit Fragewort

What's Mia doing today?

Ein **Fragewort** steht vor *am / are / is*:
Where are Mia and her friend going?

Present progressive or simple present?

Mia is playing football. (*present progressive*)
Mia spielt Fußball. (= gerade, jetzt im Moment)

Mia plays football. (*simple present*)
Mia spielt Fußball. (= regelmäßig, es ist ihr Sport)

Mia often plays football, but she isn't playing today because it's raining. ... oft ..., aber heute nicht, weil ... .

Für den Satz „Mia spielt Fußball." kannst du entweder das ***present progressive*** oder das ***simple present*** benutzen, je nachdem, was du ausdrücken möchtest:

present progressive:	***simple present:***
just, at the moment, now	*always, often, every day, on ...*

! Verben, die **Zustände** bezeichnen (z.B. *be, know, love, seem, want, weigh*), werden meist **nicht** in der ***progressive form*** verwendet, sondern **nur** in der ***simple form***. (Anders als Tätigkeits- und **Vorgangsverben** wie *go, read, rain*, die sowohl in der ***simple*** als **auch** in der ***progressive form*** auftreten.)
Merke dir folgende dieser **Zustandsverben** (sie werden auch ***"non-progressive" verbs*** genannt):
> für Regeln, Eigenschaften, Eigentum, Zugehörigkeit: *mean* („bedeuten"), *be, look* („aussehen"), *own, need, belong, include,* z.B.: *Practice means work. I need a day off. Li often looks* happy.*
> für Sinneswahrnehmungen, Meinungen, Wissen: *hear, see, seem, believe, (dis-)agree, suppose, understand, know,* z.B.: *He doesn't see well without his glasses. There seems to be a problem.*
> für Gefühle/Vorlieben: *like, love, prefer, hate, mind, want, wish,* z.B.: *Mia loves football. She wants to be really good at it.*

*Je nach Bedeutung und Aussageabsicht kann auch die ***progressive form*** möglich sein: *You look* („aussehen") *sad. What's wrong? - I'm looking for* („suchen") *my phone, but I can't find it. What do you think of* („denken von/über") *our new coach? - What are you thinking about?* („Worüber denkst du gerade nach?")

LF 3 The simple past (Die einfache Form der Vergangenheit) ▸ Unit 2, p. 39

Mit dem ***simple past*** sagst du, was **zu einer bestimmten Zeit** in der Vergangenheit geschah. Du verwendest es oft mit Zeitangaben wie *yesterday*, *last week*, *in July*, *two years ago*. Oft benutzt wird es für **Berichte** und beim **Erzählen von Geschichten**.

Bejahte Aussagen (regelmäßige Verben)

I/He/We/...	laughed a lot.

Bei **regelmäßigen** Verben bildest du das ***simple past*** durch Anhängen von -***ed*** an das Verb.

Bejahte Aussagen (unregelmäßige Verben)

I/He/We/...	bought a book.

Lerne die ***simple past***-Formen **unregelmäßiger** Verben. ▸ pp. 273–274

Verneinte Aussagen

I/He/We/...	didn't know all the people.

Wenn du sagen willst, was **nicht** geschah, setzt du *didn't* vor das Verb in der **Grundform**.

! Das Verb *be* (*was/were*) verneinst du **ohne** ~~*did*~~. *The comics weren't new.*

***Ja-/Nein*-Fragen und Kurzantworten**

Did you/she /...	like it?	Yes, I did./No, I didn't. Yes, she did./No, she didn't.

Ja-/Nein-Fragen im ***simple past*** beginnst du mit *Did*.

Fragen mit *be* (*was/were*) und Kurzantworten

Was I/he/she/it **Were** we/you/they	happy?	Yes, he was./No, he wasn't. Yes, we were./No, we weren't.

! *Ja-/Nein*-Fragen mit *Was/Were* bildest du **ohne** ~~*did*~~, ebenso die Kurzantworten.

Fragen mit Fragewort

What did Mia like best about the comic?

Did folgt direkt auf das **Fragewort**.

! Das Verb nach *did* (hier: *like*) steht immer in der Grundform. ▸ LF 15

LF 4 The past progressive (Die Verlaufsform der Vergangenheit)

Mit dem ***past progressive*** drückst du aus, dass eine Handlung in der Vergangenheit gerade im Gange war (zu einem Zeitpunkt oder als etwas anderes geschah).

Bejahte und verneinte Aussagen

I/He/She/It You/We/They	was/wasn't were/weren't	sleeping at 5pm.

Das ***past progressive*** bildest du mit ***was/were*** + *verb* + -***ing***. ▸ LF 2

***Ja-/Nein*-Fragen und Kurzantworten**

Was/Were ... taking ...?	Yes, I/he was./ No, they weren't.

Fragen mit Fragewort

What was Ben doing at 5 pm?

LF 5 The present perfect (Das *present perfect*) ▸ Unit 2, p. 39

Mia and Li are shopping. They've already been to six shops. "We haven't found a shirt for me yet, Mia." – "I know, but I'm hungry. I haven't eaten much today."

! Das ***present perfect*** wird **immer** mit *have/has* gebildet, auch wenn im Deutschen eine Form von „sein" steht.

Das ***present perfect*** drückt aus, dass etwas **irgendwann** geschehen ist. Der Zeitpunkt ist unwichtig. Es steht häufig mit: *just, already, always, ever, never, not … yet.*

Du bildest das ***present perfect*** mit ***have/has*** + 3. Form des Verbs (***past participle***).

! Beachte unregelmäßige Verben ▸ pp. 273–274.

Bejahte/verneinte Aussagen	
I/… 've/haven't He/… has/hasn't	bought …

Ja-/Nein-Fragen	
Have you/we … Has she/he …	bought …?

Fragen mit Fragewort
Why have Mia and Li gone to the new mall?

Kurzantworten
Yes, I/we … have. / No, I/we … haven't. Yes, she/… has. / No, she/… hasn't.

Present perfect with *since* and *for*

! Trotz Präsens im Deutschen benutzt du mit *since* und *for* das ***present perfect*** auf Englisch:
I've lived next door to Mia **since** my family came to the US. Mia has been my friend **for** six years. Ich bin Mias Nachbarin **seit** …

Das ***present perfect*** mit *since* oder *for* drückt aus, **seit wann / wie lange** etwas andauert.

Since nennt einen Anfangs**zeitpunkt**:
since 6 am, since 2018, since I was a baby, …

For umfasst einen **Zeitraum**: *for two months/ for years/for hours/for a long time.*

Present perfect or simple past?

! Das ***present perfect*** steht häufig in Sätzen mit Zeitangaben wie *just, already, often, always, never, ever, not … yet, before, since / for.*

- um zu sagen, dass etwas **irgendwann** geschehen ist, oft mit **Auswirkungen auf die Gegenwart**.
  Ben has **just** come back from LA.
- in Fragen mit *ever …?*
  Have you **ever** been to LA before, Ben?
- in Sätzen mit *since* und *for*
  His uncle has lived in LA **for** three years now.

! Das ***simple past*** muss stehen in Sätzen mit Zeitangaben wie *yesterday, last week, in July, two years ago, in 2016.*

- um zu sagen, dass etwas **zu einer bestimmten Zeit** geschehen ist, oft mit genauer Zeitangabe.
  In 2016 Ben's uncle started a cafe in LA.
- in Berichten und Erzählungen
  Ben wanted to help him. His uncle agreed.
- in Fragen mit ***When*** …?
  When did you leave for LA, Ben?

NEW LF 6 *The present perfect progressive ▸ Unit 2, p. 120

(Die Verlaufsform des *present perfect*)

Mit dem ***present perfect progressive*** sagst du, dass etwas **in der Vergangenheit** begonnen hat und **bis jetzt andauert** bzw. **gerade vorbei** ist. Es steht häufig mit Zeitangaben wie *since* … oder *for* …

Bejahte und verneinte Aussagen	
I/...'ve/haven't He/...'s/hasn't	been waiting long.

Du bildest das ***present perfect progressive*** mit ***have/has been*** + *verb* + ***-ing***.

Ja-/Nein-Fragen und Kurzantworten		
Have you/... Has he/...	been waiting long?	Yes, ... have/has. No, ... haven't/hasn't.

Fragen mit Fragewort
How long have you been waiting? Wie lange wartest du schon?

LF 7 The past perfect (Das *past perfect*)

When Li arrived at the party, Ben had already gone home. *(Erst ging Ben, dann kam Li.)*

Ben thought that Li had forgotten about the party.

! Das ***past perfect*** wird **immer** mit ***had*** gebildet, auch wenn im Deutschen „war" steht.

Mit dem ***past perfect*** (Plusquamperfekt oder **Vor**vergangenheit) drückst du aus, dass etwas noch **vor** etwas anderem in der Vergangenheit stattgefunden hatte.

Du bildest das ***past perfect*** mit ***had*** **+** 3. Form des Verbs (***past participle***).

▸ *pp. 273–274*

Bejahte und verneinte Aussagen		
I/... He/...	had/hadn't	forgotten ...

Ja-/Nein-Fragen und Kurzantworten		
Had I .../he ...	forgotten ...?	Yes, ... had. No, ... hadn't.

Simple past or past perfect?

Before Li left home, it had started to rain heavily.

Mit dem ***past perfect*** sagt du, was zeitlich vorangegangen war. Oft stehen dabei Zeitangaben wie *after, when, before, already*.

So Li took an umbrella with her, but she forgot her phone.

! Keine Vorvergangenheit (sondern ***simple past***), wenn etwas zur gleichen Zeit geschah.

NEW LF 8 *The past perfect progressive (Die Verlaufsform des *past perfect*)

Ben had been sleeping for ten hours when his phone rang.
(er hatte über einen langen Zeitraum geschlafen)

Mit dem ***past perfect progressive*** sagst du, dass etwas noch <u>**vor**</u> einem weiteren Ereignis **in der Vergangenheit** über **einen gewissen Zeitraum angedauert** hat.

Du bildest das ***past perfect progressive*** mit ***had been*** + *verb* + **-ing**.

Bejahte und verneinte Aussagen		
I/... He/...	had / hadn't been	... *ing*.

Ja-/Nein-Fragen und Kurzantworten		
Had I/.../he/...	been ...*ing*?	Yes, ... had. No, ... hadn't.

Fragen mit Fragewort
What had ... been you doing (when/before ...)?

TALKING ABOUT THE FUTURE

LF 9 The *going to*-future (Das Futur mit *going to*)

▸ Unit 3, p. 61

Mia's going to have a football match next Saturday.

Mia wird nächsten Samstag … haben.

Her brother Ben isn't going to come to the match.

Ihr Bruder hat nicht vor, es zu sehen.

What are we going to do on Sunday?

Was wollen wir am Sonntag machen?

Is the weather going to be fine?

Wird das Wetter gut?

! Stark umgangssprachlich hörst/liest du häufig *gonna*, z.B. *They're gonna watch the match*.

Wenn du ausdrücken möchtest, was jemand in der Zukunft **plant** oder **vorhat** sowie für **Vorhersagen** benutzt du das Futur mit ***going to***.

Es wird mit einer Form von *be* (*am*/*are*/*is*) gebildet, oft mit den Kurzformen:
'm*/*'re*/*'s* + *going to* + *verb

Verneinung:
Ben isn't going to be at Mia's match.
But she's not going to be angry with him.

Fragen und Kurzantworten:
Is it going to rain?
- (Look at the sky!) Yes, it is./No, it isn't.

LF 10 The *will*-future (Das Futur mit *will*)

▸ Unit 3, p. 61

Bejahte und verneinte Aussagen

I/You/He/She/It We/You/They	will like the concert. won't like all the songs.

***Ja-/Nein*-Fragen und Kurzantworten**

Will	I/you/ he /…	like all the songs?	Yes, … will. No, … won't.

Fragen mit Fragewort

Who will win the match tomorrow?
When will we get home?

! Englisch *I will* heißt im Deutschen „ich werde" und nicht „ich will".

Mit dem ***will-future*** kannst du über die Zukunft sprechen, z.B. über **Vermutungen** und **Vorhersagen** oder **spontane Entschlüsse**.
Es steht häufig mit Zeitangaben wie *tomorrow*, *(sometime) next week/year …*

Eine **Vermutung** beginnt oft mit *Maybe / I'm sure:*
I think I'll enjoy the concert. – I'm sure you will.

Bei **Vorhersagen** geht es oft um Dinge, die man nicht direkt beeinflussen kann:
It'll be winter soon.

Ein **spontaner Entschluss** ist oft ein Versprechen oder Angebot.
It's so hot! I'll buy you an ice cream.

Das ***will*-future** wird mit ***will* + verb** gebildet.

Die Kurzform von ***will*** heißt ***'ll***. Die Kurzform der **Verneinung *will not*** heißt ***won't***.

! Verwechsle nicht ***won't*** mit ***wouldn't***, der Verneinung von ***would*** *(würden)*. ▸ LF 26

NEW LF 11 *The simple present with future meaning

(Einfache Gegenwart mit Zukunftsbedeutung)

▸ Unit 3, pp. 128–129

A note at the door said 'Breakfast is at 7 tomorrow'.

… „Frühstück ist …".

Ben told his friends, 'My plane for LA leaves at 9.30 am.'

…: „Mein Flug(zeug) … geht um halb 10."

'My holiday job starts on Monday', said Li.

„Montag beginnt mein Ferienjob", …

Zukünftiges Geschehen drückst du mit dem ***simple present*** aus, wenn es durch einen **Fahrplan**, ein **Programm**, den **Kalender** o.ä. genau bestimmt ist.

Das ***simple present*** wird in solchen Fällen auch als ***'timetable future'*** bezeichnet und betrifft oft Verben wie *arrive*, *close*, *end*, *leave*, *open*, *start*, *stop*, *take place*.

NEW LF 12 *The present progressive with future meaning (Verlaufsform der Gegenwart mit Zukunftsbedeutung)

▸ *Unit 3, pp. 128–129*

When discussing plans for the day Lucy said, 'I'm going outside today.' (fest geplant)

Ben told a friend, 'We're all meeting again next Monday.' (fest verabredet)

Li is coming back from her uncle's tomorrow morning. (fest geplant)

Wenn etwas für die Zukunft **fest geplant** oder **verabredet** ist, verwendest du das ***present progressive***.

Das **Zukünftige** muss durch den **Zusammenhang** oder **Signalwörter** erkennbar sein, z.B. *next week*, *tomorrow* oder an zukünftigen Daten, z.B. *in 2031 / on Monday*, …

NEW LF 13 *The future progressive (Die Verlaufsform des *will-future*)

▸ *Unit 3, pp. 128–129*

Avril told Lucy, 'While you're looking at the panels, I'll be checking the roof.'
(Avril plant, währenddessen etwas anderes zu tun.)

Ben won't be practising all afternoon.
(… nicht den gesamten Nachmittag lang …)

Mit dem ***future progressive***, der Verlaufsform des ***will-future***, sagst du, dass etwas **in der Zukunft wie vermutet / geplant / gewohnt ablaufen** wird. Es steht häufig mit *next Monday/summer/…* , *tomorrow* oder zukünftigen Daten nach *in… / on …*

Du bildest das ***future progressive*** mit:
will /'ll + ***be*** + verb + ***-ing***.

Bejahte und verneinte Aussagen

I/… He/…	will / won't be	waiting for you.

***Ja-/Nein*-Fragen und Kurzantworten**

Will … be missing me?	Yes, … will. / No, … won't.

Fragen mit Fragewort

What will Li be doing while …?

NEW LF 14 *The future perfect (Die vollendete Form des *will-future*)

▸ *Unit 3, pp. 128–129*

Lucy asked Avril, 'Will you have finished breakfast by 7.30?' (… „Wirst du um … haben?“)

Ben will have repaired his bike when Li arrives.
(Er wird es geschafft haben, wenn sie kommt.)

Mia won't have written her graduation speech by next Friday. (Sie wird es bis … nicht geschafft haben.)

Mit dem ***future perfect*** drückst du aus, dass etwas zu einem **bestimmten Zeitpunkt in der Zukunft abgeschlossen** sein wird.

Das ***future perfect*** steht oft mit ***by*** *tomorrow / next year/…* oder einer Zeitbestimmung wie ***When*** *we get there, …*

Du bildest das ***future perfect*** mit:
will / 'll + ***have*** + ***past participle*** (3. Form)

▸ *pp. 273–274*

Bejahte und verneinte Aussagen

I/… He/…	will / won't have	done that by …

***Ja-/Nein*-Fragen und Kurzantworten**

Will	…	have done your homework by 8 pm?	Yes, … will. No, … won't.

Fragen mit Fragewort

What will you have achieved by your 20th birthday?

LF 15 Word order in statements
(Die Wortstellung in Aussagen)

Die Regel zur Wortstellung im englischen Satz ist **subject – verb – object**, kurz **S-V-(O)**.
Subjekt – Prädikat – (Objekt) (Ein Objekt gibt es nicht immer.)

! Anders als im Deutschen wird von **S-V-O nicht** abgewichen, z.B. bei Angaben des Orts, der Art und Weise *(In englischen Sätzen stellst du nicht um.)* bzw. Zeitangaben *(Gestern wusste ich das noch.)*

subject	verb	object	adverbial *(Adverbialbestimmung)*	
Mia	plays	football.		
She	can't play	an instrument.		
Ben and Mia	have bought	tickets.		
Ben and Mia	are interested in	music.		
They	didn't go		to concerts	last year.

Mia usually plays football. Ben sometimes phones Li.

Die **Adverbien der Häufigkeit** *usually, always, often, sometimes, never* stehen **zwischen Subjekt** und **Verb**.

Mia and Ben have already bought tickets.
They're just planning how to get to the concert.
Have you ever been to a concert?

Die **Adverbien der Zeit**, wie *already, ever, just, never* stehen **vor** dem ***present participle*** (-*ing*-Form) bzw. dem ***past participle*** (dritte Form) **des Verbs**.

Luckily Ben and Mia still got cheap tickets.
Ben und Mia bekamen glücklicherweise noch …

Die **Adverbien**, die sich auf den **gesamten Satz** beziehen, wie *perhaps/maybe, suddenly, finally, of course, at first* stehen meist am **Satzanfang**.

After the date with Li, Ben walked home happily.

Adverbien, die sich auf ein Verb bzw. eine Tätigkeit beziehen, stehen in der Regel **am Satzende**.

Ben had first met Li **at Mia's club two months ago**.

! Gibt es in einem Satz eine **Orts- und** eine **Zeitangabe**, gilt die **Regel „Ort vor Zeit".**

LF 16 Word order in questions (Die Wortstellung in Fragen)

Du erkennst einen Fragesatz daran, dass hier **vor** dem **Subjekt** eine gebeugte Form von *do, be, have* bzw. *will, can, may* steht.

Fragen mit *do/does* und *did*

Viele Fragen bildest du mit einer Form von *do*, einem Hilfsverb (*auxiliary*). Es „hilft" sozusagen dabei, dass die Wortstellung des zugrundeliegenden Aussagesatzes einfach erhalten bleiben kann. Vergleiche:

Aussagesatz (**S-V-O**)
Mia and Li play football.

→

Fragesatz (Hilfsverb-**S-V-O**)
Do Mia and Li play football? (*Ja-/Nein*-Frage)
When do Mia and Li play football? (Frage mit Fragewort)

Weitere Fragesätze:

question word	auxiliary *do(es)/did*	subject	(main) verb	
	Does	Ben	work	on Fridays?
	Did	he and Li	go	to the cinema?
What	does	Ben	watch	on TV?
Where	did	you	buy	that DVD?

Du beginnst die Frage mit (Fragewort +) *do/does/did*, dann folgen Subjekt und Hauptverb *(main verb)*.

! Keine **Umstellungen** von **Verb** und **Subjekt** wie im Deutschen:
Arbeitet Ben? → *Does Ben work?*

Fragen mit Formen von *be* und *have*

Wenn der Fragesatz eine Form von ***be*** oder ***have*** enthält, steht diese **vor** dem **Subjekt**.

question word	verb (forms of *be / have*)	subject	
	Is	Mia	Ben's sister?
	Are	Mia and Li	good friends?
	Have	you	been to school?
Where	were	you	last weekend?
What	are	Mia and Li	planning for Friday?

Ein **Fragesatz** mit *be* oder *have* wird gebildet, indem du die entsprechende Form, z.B. *is, was, were; have, has* **vor** das **Subjekt** stellst.

Fragewörter – *who, what, when, where, why, how, how long* – stehen am **Satzanfang**.

Subject and object questions (Fragen nach dem Subjekt oder dem Objekt)

Ben *likes Li.*

Who **likes** Li? – **Ben.**
Wer mag Li?

Who **does** **Ben** like? – Li.
Wen mag Ben?

The noise *disturbed Li.*
What **disturbed** Li? – **The noise.**
Was störte Li? – Der Lärm.
Li *shut the window.*
What **did** **Li** shut? – The window.
Was schloss Li? – Das Fenster.

Mit den Fragewörtern *who/what/which* kannst du nach dem Subjekt oder nach dem Objekt fragen.

! Beachte bei der Fragebildung die **S-V-(O)-Regel**.

Wenn das **Fragewort** nach dem **Subjekt** *(wer?/was?)* fragt, **folgt direkt das Vollverb** – **nie ~~do~~/~~does~~/~~did~~ als Hilfsverb**.

Wenn das **Fragewort** nach dem **Objekt** fragt *(wen?/wem?/was?)*, **folgt *do/does/did***.

! Das Hauptverb steht in der Grundform (Infinitiv).

LF 17 Questions with the passive and with modals

(Fragen im Passiv und mit Modalverben)

Fragen im Passiv

question word	form of *be*	subject	*past participle*	
	Is	Ben	called	*Benny* by his fans?
	Was	he	invited	to a party?
When	were	you	born,	Ben?
Why	isn't	your team	supported	by sponsors?

Da du das Passiv mit ***be + past participle*** bildest, beginnst du *Ja-/Nein*-Fragen mit der Form von ***be***, die hier Hilfsverb ist.

Bei Fragen mit **Fragewort** steht die Form von ***be*** **zwischen** Fragewort und Subjekt.

Fragen mit Modalverben

question word	*modal verb*	subject	(main) verb	
	Can	Ben	meet	Li on Friday?
	May	she	go	to a party then?
	Should	Li	ask	her parents?
When	will	Ben and Li	meet?	
What else	must	Ben	prepare	for the party?

Ja-/Nein-Fragen mit ***modals*** beginnen mit dem **Modalverb**.

Bei Fragen mit **Fragewort** steht das ***modal*** **zwischen** Fragewort und Subjekt.

NEW LF 18 *Questions with prepositions

(Fragen mit Fragewörtern und Präpositionen)

Ben waved goodbye to his team. Then he walked with Li to her house.

Ben and Li spent the afternoon with Li's family. They laughed at her mum's funny stories.

Now they are looking forward to next weekend. They're waiting for a visitor from Germany.

Who did Ben wave goodbye **to?**
Wem winkte Ben zum Abschied **zu**?

Who did he walk **with?**
Mit wem ging er spazieren?

Who did Ben and Li spend the afternoon **with?**
Mit wem verbrachten … den Nachmittag?

What did they laugh **at?**
Worüber haben sie gelacht/lachten sie?

What are they looking **forward to?**
Worauf freuen sie sich?

Who/What are they waiting **for?**
Auf wen/Worauf warten sie?

Präpositionen, z.B. *after, at, for, from, in, of, on, to* stehen **vor Nomen** oder **Pronomen**.

Es gibt auch viele typische **Wendungen** (Verb + Präposition), z.B. *look at, wait for, be afraid of, wave to, …* .

Wenn du **Fragen mit Präpositionen** bildest, stehen die **Fragewörter** *Who/What* **am Anfang**, die **Präpositionen** stehen häufig **am Ende der Frage**.

! Im Deutschen stehen die Präpositionen meist vor dem Fragewort, z.B.
*Mit **wem** spielst du gern?* → **Who** do you like to play **with**?

Häufig gibt es im Deutschen besondere Fragewörter, z.B.
***Womit** spielst du gern?* → **What** do you like to play **with**?

LF 19 The comparison of adjectives (Die Steigerung der Adjektive)

The comparison with *-er* /*-est* and *more*/*most*

Wenn du Personen oder Dinge vergleichst, benutzt du Steigerungsformen.
Mit der 1. Steigerungsform + ***than*** („als") vergleichst du zwei **unterschiedliche** Personen oder Dinge.

Ben thinks English is hard, but maths is harder than English. But today French seems to be the hardest of all.

Bei **kurzen** (einsilbigen) Adjektiven und bei Adjektiven mit der Endung ***-y*** hängst du für die Steigerung *-er* und *-est* an das Adjektiv:

cheap	*cheaper*	*(the) cheapest*

Li prefers a big bowl of ice cream – the biggest she can get.
But she doesn't have enough money for the most expensive one.

Bei **längeren** (zwei- oder dreisilbigen) Adjektiven stellst du ***more*** und ***most*** *vor* das Adjektiv:

expensive	*more expensive*	*(the) most expensive*

Chocolate looks good, it's better than vanilla. It's the best – and it's cheap too.

! Merke dir die **unregelmäßig** gesteigerten Adjektive, z.B.:

good	*better*	*(the) best*
much/many	*more*	*(the) most*

The comparison with *as … as*

Li doesn't think that ice cream is unhealthy.
It's as healthy as all the other things on the menu.

Mit dem Vergleich (***not***) ***as*** … ***as*** … kannst du ausdrücken, dass zwei Personen oder Dinge gleich (oder nicht gleich) sind.

LF 20 Adverbs of manner (Adverbien der Art und Weise)

Adjektive beschreiben **Nomen** näher. *Li was a happy girl after the basketball match.*

Adverbien der Art und Weise beschreiben **Verben** näher. *Li walked home happily.*

Adverbien der Art und Weise stehen nach dem Verb, oft am Satzende:

Li's morning was going terribly.
*(**Wie** lief der Morgen für Li? – Schrecklich.)*

She couldn't find her ticket and looked for it very carefully, but still couldn't find it.
She left the house angrily.

Then she ran to school fast.
She worked very hard in maths that day.
In the evening her team played well.

So Li walked home happily. She felt good in the end.

Du bildest ein Adverb der Art und Weise meist durch Anhängen von *-ly* an das Adjektiv.

! Merke dir **unregelmäßige** Adverbformen:

Adjektiv	**Adverb**
*Li is a **fast** runner.*	*Li ran **fast**.*
*She had a **hard** day at school.*	*She worked **hard** in class.*
*But she was **good** at sport.*	*She played **well**.*

! Nach Verben der Sinneswahrnehmung *feel, look, sound, taste, smell* folgt **kein** Adverb, sondern ein Adjektiv.

LF 21 Adverbs of frequency (Adverbien der Häufigkeit)

Diese drücken aus, wie häufig jemand etwas tut oder wie häufig etwas geschieht: *always, usually, often, sometimes, never*. (Zur Wortstellung in Sätzen ▸ *LF 15–16*)

Hi Li,
How's life back home? I sometimes wish you were here.
LA is always so exciting! I've never seen a place like this before.
I don't often check my emails as there's a lot of work to do in my uncle's cafe.
...

Adverbien der Häufigkeit stehen:

- nach ***be***:
  *LA **is** always exciting for tourists.*
- vor einem Vollverb:
  *I sometimes **wish** you were here.*
- bei zusammengesetzten Verbformen nach dem Hilfsverb (*don't, have, …*):
  *I **don't** often **check** my emails.*

LF 22 The comparison of adverbs (Die Steigerung der Adverbien)

Du kannst auch Adverbien steigern. Du bildest die zwei Steigerungsformen wie bei Adjektiven. ▸ *LF 19*

Ben spoke more slowly to help the new exchange student understand.
Of all the students, Ben was the most friendly to Moritz.
Everyone was fast, but Li was the fastest.

Adverbien, die auf *-**ly*** enden, steigerst du mit ***more/most***, z.B.

slowly — *more slowly* — *(the) most slowly*

Einsilbige Adverbien werden mit *-er/-est* gesteigert:

fast — *faster* — *(the) fastest*

The race went well, much better than Li had expected.

! Beachte:

well — *better* — *(the) best*

LF 23 Indirect speech (Indirekte Rede)

Direct speech **(Direkte Rede)**
Mia says, "I like my new friend Kai."
Mia sagt: „Ich mag meinen neuen Freund Kai."

Indirect speech **(Indirekte Rede)**
Mia says _ (that) she likes her new friend Kai.
Mia sagt, dass sie ihren neuen Freund Kai mag.

! Im Englischen steht vor der indirekten Rede **kein** Komma, und *that* („dass") wird oft weggelassen.

Mit der **direkten Rede** gibst du ***wörtlich*** wieder, was jemand sagt, schreibt oder denkt (bzw. gesagt/geschrieben/gedacht hat).

Mit der **indirekten Rede berichtest** du, was jemand sagt/schreibt/denkt. Einleitende Verben sind z.B.: *say, tell, add, answer, think, explain*.

! Achte bei der **indirekten Rede** darauf, dass sich Personen, Pronomen, Verbformen sowie Orts- und Zeitangaben ändern:
"I like my new friend." → … she likes her new friend.
"We are going to meet here again tonight." → (retold two days later) They were going to meet there again that night.

Indirect speech: backshift in statements (Indirekte Rede: *backshift* in Aussagen)

Mia said_ (that) she liked Kai.
Mia sagte, dass sie Kai mag/gut finden würde.

She told Kai her name was Mia and she hadn't been to that club before.
Sie sagte (zu) Kai, ihr Name sei/wäre Mia und sie wäre noch nie in diesem Club gewesen.

Mia: "I'm 16. I live in Braxton."
→ Kai to Dan: "Mia told me she's (*was*) 16. And she lives (*lived*) in Braxton."

Steht das einleitende Verb im ***simple past***, z.B. *said, told, added, answered, thought, explained*, verschiebt sich auch die Zeitform des Verbs der ursprünglichen Aussage meist ins ***simple past*** oder ins ***past perfect*** (letzteres häufiger in der Schriftsprache).
Dieses (Rück-)Verschieben in die Vergangenheit heißt auf Englisch ***backshift*** *(of tenses)*.
In der **Umgangssprache** wendet man den ***backshift*** *(of tenses)* bei immer noch gültigen (oder allgemeinen) Tatsachen **nicht immer** an.

Indirect speech: questions (Indirekte Rede: Fragen)

Dan asked Mia, "Where do you live?"
→ Dan asked Mia_ where she lived.
Dan fragte Mia, wo sie wohnt/wohne/wohnte.

He also asked, "How did you get here?"
→ He also wanted to know how she had got there.
Er wollte auch wissen, wie sie hergekommen war.

Mia asked, "How often are you at this club?"
→ Mia asked how often he was at that club.
… wie oft er … sei/wäre/sein würde.

Bei der Wiedergabe von **Fragen in indirekter Rede** musst du die **gleichen Regeln** wie bei Aussagen beachten:
- Personen, Pronomen, Verbformen sowie Orts- und Zeitangaben können sich ändern.
- Steht das **einleitende Verb** im ***simple past***, (rück)verschiebt sich auch hier die Zeitform des Verbs (***backshift***).

! Wie im Deutschen steht **am Ende** einer indirekten Frage **kein Fragezeichen**, sondern ein **Punkt**.

Fragewörter werden übernommen, jedoch entspricht die Wortstellung im Nebensatz jetzt Aussagesätzen, vgl. … *where ~~do/does/did~~ she lived.* -> ***subject*** – ***verb***: **S-V-(O)** ▸ LF 15

Dan asked Mia, "Do you like our music?"

→ Dan asked Mia_ if she liked their music.
Dan fragte Mia, **ob** sie die Musik seiner Band mochte.

Bei ***Ja-/Nein*-Fragen** wird (wie im Deutschen „ob") im Englischen ***if*** (oder *whether)* eingefügt. Auch hier gilt die **Wortstellung** von **Aussagesätzen**: **S-V-(O)**. ▸ LF 15

Indirect speech: commands, requests, advice
(Aufforderungen, Bitten, Ratschläge in indirekter Rede)

Ben told Dan, "Go and get us something to drink."
→ Ben told Dan **to** go and get them something to drink.
Ben forderte Dan auf, ihnen etwas zu trinken zu holen.

Aufforderungen, Befehle und **Ratschläge** werden in **indirekter Rede** meist eingeleitet mit: *tell/told sb.* ***to*** *(do sth.)*

And he added, "Don't hurry!"
→ And he told him **not to** hurry.
Und er fügte hinzu, dass er sich nicht zu beeilen brauche/bräuchte.

Bei **Verboten** und **Verneinungen** wird vor dem Infinitiv mit *to* das ***not*** eingeschoben: *tell/told sb.* ***not to*** *(do sth.)*
bzw. *ask/asked sb.* ***not to*** *(do sth.)*

Ben told Mia, "You shouldn't listen to Dan."
→ Ben told Mia not to listen to Dan.
Ben empfahl Mia, Dan nicht zuzuhören.

Ben said to Mia, "Please, don't trust that boy."
→ Ben asked Mia not to trust that boy.
Ben bat Mia, dem Jungen nicht zu trauen.

Bitten werden in **indirekter Rede** meist eingeleitet mit: *ask/asked sb.* ***to*** *(do sth.)*.

Dan asked her, "Can you give me your address, please?"
→ Dan asked her to give him her address.
Dan bat sie, ihm ihre Adresse zu geben.

Indirect speech: More on backshift (Indirekte Rede: Weiteres zum *backshift*)

Den ***backshift of tenses*** – das Rückverschieben in eine andere Zeitstufe in der Vergangenheit – kennst du von der Veränderung ***simple present*** zu **simple past**, wenn der **Einleitungssatz im *simple past*** steht, z.B.
Mia: "I like Dan." → *Later Mia told her best friend (that) she liked Dan.*

Mia: "Dan is a nice guy."
→ Mia told her friend Dan was a nice guy.

Mia: "We met at a music club."
→ Mia told her they had met at a music club.

Mia: "And I've never been there before."
→ Mia added she had never been there before.

She thought, "Next Saturday I'll meet him again."
→ She thought she would meet him again the following Saturday.

"And maybe I can learn more about their songs."
→ (And) Maybe she could learn more about their songs.

> **!**
> ***simple present*** *(is)* wird ***simple past*** *(was)*
>
> ***simple past*** *(met)* wird ***past perfect*** *(had met)*
>
> ***present perfect*** *(have been)* wird ebenfalls ***past perfect*** *(had been)*
>
> > ***will (future)*** *(will meet)* wird ***would*** *(would meet)*
>
> > ***can*** *(can learn)* wird ***could*** *(could learn)*

LF 24 Modal verbs and their substitutes

(Modalverben und ihre Ersatzformen)

Modal verbs (modale Hilfsverben) sind z.B. *can, must, should* und ihre Verneinungen. Du benutzt sie, um auszudrücken, was jemand **kann**, **darf**, **muss, soll** oder **nicht kann** usw.

Coach said, "You may leave earlier tonight." Great! Ben could go to the party and meet Li.
Der Trainer sagte: „Du darfst ...". Ben war ..., weil er ... konnte.

Modal verbs haben nur eine Form, z.B. *can*, *must* oder *may* für alle Personen, d.h. kein *-s* bei *he/she/it.*

He added that Ben shouldn't forget the match next week. "Well, should I stay then?", Ben thought.
... dass Ben ... nicht vergessen sollte. „Hhm, soll ich ...?"

Die **Verneinung** und die **Frage** werden **ohne** ~~do/does/did~~ gebildet.

"Can/May I borrow your black dress for the party, please?" Li asked her mum.
- "Yes, you can/may./No, you can't/may not."
„Darf ich ... - „Ja, du darfst./Nein, du darfst nicht."

Modal verbs stehen nur in Kurzantworten allein.

Li to Mia: "I'm sorry, I must go now. I have got to pick up mum's black dress from the dry-cleaner's. I'm allowed to wear it to the party!"
"I wasn't able to do it yesterday. I had to prepare the maths test today."

Modal verbs haben nur eine ***simple present***-Form. Weitere Zeitformen bildest du **mit anderen Verben** mit ähnlicher Bedeutung:

müssen:	*must*	→ ***have (got) to****
dürfen:	*can/may*	→ ***be allowed to***
können:	*can*	→ ***be able to***

Verneinte Aussagen

You mustn't play in the street.
! Du darfst nicht ...
You don't have/haven't got to play in a team.
You needn't play in a team.
Du musst/brauchst nicht ...

Verneinte Aussagen

You can't You aren't allowed to Du darfst nicht ...	play in the street. play in a team.

Verneinte Aussagen

The team can't The team isn't able to The team is unable to	win the game today.

***Ja-/Nein*-Fragen**

Can/May/Should/Must	I/he practise now?

Mit diesen Verben kannst du **alle Zeitformen** bilden, auch das *simple present*:

müssen

simple present: *must*; *have/has (got) to** (muss)
simple past: *had to* (musste)
future: *will have to* (wird ... müssen)
(**Have got to*: umgangssprachlicher; wird inhaltlich wie *have to* verwendet)

dürfen

simple present: *can/may*
oder *am/are/is allowed to* (darf)
simple past: *was/were allowed to* (durfte)
future: *will be allowed to* (wird ... dürfen)

können (fähig sein)

simple present: *can*; *am/are/is able to* (kann)
simple past: *could*; *was/were able to* (konnte)
future: *will be able to* (wird ... können)

Ja-/Nein-Fragen (Forts.)		
Do/Did I/you/they Does/Did he/she Have you/Has she	have to got to	practise hard?

Am/Are/Is … Was/Were … Will … be	allowed to …? able to …?

Kurzantworten	
Yes, you … can / may / should / must.	No, you can't / may not / shouldn't / don't have to.
Yes, you … do / did.	No, you don't / didn't.
Yes, you … are.	No, you aren't.
Yes, you … was.	No, you wasn't.
Yes, you … will.	No, you won't.

LF 25 *If* … (Conditional sentences type 1) (Bedingungssätze Typ 1)

Mit ***if***-Sätzen (Bedingungssätzen Typ 1) sagst du, was unter bestimmten Bedingungen geschieht oder geschehen wird: „**Was ist, wenn …**"

Nebensatz
If Mia's team plays well next time,
Hauptsatz
they'll win the summer contest.
Wenn Mias Team nächstes Mal gut spielt, werden sie den Sommer-Wettbewerb gewinnen.

Bedingungssätze bestehen aus zwei Teilsätzen:

Die **Bedingung** wird im ***if***-Satz (Nebensatz) genannt. Das Verb steht im ***simple present***:

If they ***play …,***

Die **Folge für die Zukunft** steht im **Hauptsatz**. Hier steht meist das ***will*-future**:

… they ***will …***

▸ *LF 10*

Their team will only finish in second place _ if they don't fight hard.
Ihr Team wird nur Zweiter sein, wenn sie nicht kämpfen.

= If they don't fight hard, their team will only finish in second place.
Wenn sie nicht kämpfen, wird ihr Team nur Zweiter sein.

Der ***if***-Teil kann am Anfang oder am Ende stehen.

! Anders als im Deutschen setzt man **kein Komma**, wenn der ***if***-Teil am **Ende** steht.

"I'll ask the coach for her advice when I see her."
wenn ich sie sehe.
(Es steht fest, dass Mia die Trainerin trifft. Dann fragt sie.)

"I'll ask the coach for her advice if I see her."
falls ich sie sehe. *(Es ist unsicher, ob sie sich treffen.)*

! Nicht verwechseln:
- ***when*** bedeutet „sobald wie", „dann, wenn"
- ***if*** bedeutet „wenn", „falls"

If you need advice, you **can/should** ask the coach.
Wenn ihr Rat braucht, könnt ihr /solltet ihr die Trainerin fragen.

Im **Hauptsatz** können auch stehen:
- *can, must, should* + Infinitiv

▸ *LF 24*

Please **phone** me if you want to talk to me.
Bitte ruft mich an, wenn ihr … wollt.

- oder eine Aufforderung bzw. Bitte (ein **Imperativ**).

LF 26 *If* … (Conditional sentences type 2) (Bedingungssätze Typ 2)

Mit Bedingungssätzen Typ 2 sagst du, was unter unwahrscheinlichen oder unsicheren Bedingungen geschehen würde: „**Was wäre, wenn …**"

Nebensatz
If Ben had enough money,
Hauptsatz
he'd travel everywhere.
Wenn Ben genug Geld hätte, würde er …

Hauptsatz
But Li wouldn't travel
Nebensatz
even if she won a trip around the world.
Aber Li würde nicht reisen, selbst/sogar wenn sie … gewinnen würde.

If you were on a world trip, you **could** forget about school.
Wenn du auf … wärst, könntest du … vergessen.

Da die **Bedingung** im ***if***-Satz unwahrscheinlich ist (hier: genug Geld), ist unsicher, ob die **Folge** im **Hauptsatz** (hier: das Reisen überall hin) Wirklichkeit wird.
Im Deutschen verwendet man hier oft ***würde/wäre/hätte***.

Auch ***if***-Sätze Typ 2 bestehen wie ***if***-Sätze Typ 1 aus zwei Teilsätzen: ▸ *LF 25*

Die (unwahrscheinliche) **Bedingung** steht im ***if***-Satz. Das Verb steht im ***simple past***, z.B. *had, won*.

Die (unsichere) **Folge** steht im **Hauptsatz**. Dort benutzt du *would* (Kurzform ***'d***) bzw. für die Verneinung *wouldn't* + Infinitiv.

! Auch bei Typ 2 kein Komma vor dem ***if***-Teil.
Im **Hauptsatz** kann auch *could* + Infinitiv stehen.

Forms of *would*

Bejahte und verneinte Aussagen

I/You/He/… We/…	'd/would/wouldn't	travel …

Ben would travel everywhere if he could, but Li wouldn't come with him.

***Ja-/Nein*-Fragen mit Kurzantworten**

Would I/he/we/…	travel …	Yes, … would. No, … wouldn't.

Would you go on a trip around the world if you had the chance? – Yes, you would.

Fragen mit Fragewort

Where/How/… would I/you/he/… …?

Where would you travel first – to the US or to South Africa?

LF 27 *If* … (Conditional sentences type 3) (Bedingungssätze Typ 3)

Mit Bedingungssätzen Typ 3 **stellst du dir vor**, was **in der Vergangenheit** unter bestimmten Bedingungen hätte geschehen können: „**Was wäre gewesen, wenn …**"

Nebensatz
If it had been warmer yesterday,
Hauptsatz
Li would have gone to the beach.
Wenn es gestern wärmer gewesen wäre, wäre Li zum Strand gegangen. *(Es war aber nicht wärmer, und Li war nicht am Strand.)*

Da die **Bedingung** im ***if***-Satz **nicht erfüllt** ist, können über die **Folge** im **Hauptsatz** nur Vermutungen angestellt werden.

Im Deutschen verwendet man oft ***wäre*** *gewesen/gegangen/… oder* ***hätte*** *gehabt/gegeben oder* auch ***würde*** gewesen sein/gehabt haben.

Hauptsatz
Li would have phoned Mia
Nebensatz
if she had had her new number.
Li hätte Mia (ja) angerufen, wenn sie deren neue Telefonnummer gehabt hätte. *(Aber sie kannte sie nicht oder hatte sie verlegt.)*

If Li had asked Mia's brother Ben, he could have helped her. ... hätte er ihr helfen können.

If she'd asked Ben, he'd have given her Mia's number. ... gefragt hätte, hätte er ihr ... gegeben.

Die (nicht erfüllte) **Bedingung** steht im ***if*-Satz**. Das Verb steht im ***past perfect*** z.B. *had been, had had, had helped.*

Die (vermutete) **Folge** steht im **Hauptsatz**. Dort benutzt du ***would/wouldn't*** + ***have past participle*** (3. Form).

! Auch hier steht kein Komma vor dem ***if***-Teil.

Im **Hauptsatz** kann auch ***could*** + ***have past participle*** stehen.

! Die **Kurzform** von ***would*** und von ***had*** ist ***'d***:

he'd (= he would) have given.
she'd (= she had) asked.

LF 28 Relative clauses (Relativsätze)

Someone who/that uses social media often has several profile pictures.

Li prefers pictures that/which are creative.

Mit Relativsätzen sagst du genauer, **wen** oder **was** du meinst. Sie werden eingeleitet mit den Relativpronomen

- ***who*** oder ***that*** für **Personen** und
- ***which*** oder ***that*** für **Dinge**.

! Relativsätze, die Personen oder Dinge näher bestimmen, stehen **ohne Komma** (anders als im Deutschen: Jemand, der ... / Bilder, die ...).

*Defining and non-defining relative clauses (Bestimmende und nicht bestimmende Relativsätze)

▸ *Unit 1, p. 110*

Im Englischen unterscheidet man **bestimmende** und **nicht bestimmende** Relativsätze.

Ben chose the photo _ that Li took.
(Ohne den Relativsatz *that Li took* wüsste man nicht, welches Foto gemeint ist.)

Bestimmende Relativsätze (***defining relative clauses***) sind **notwendig** dafür, dass man den Satz versteht und weiß, wer/was genau gemeint ist.

! ***Defining relative clauses*** stehen **ohne Komma**.

This photo, which was taken by Li, shows Ben on his bike. (Auch ohne den Relativsatz ist klar, was das Foto zeigt, also welches Foto genau gemeint ist.)

Li used a drone for the photo, which was really exciting. (Zusätzliche Bewertung, die sich auf den gesamten vorangehenden Satz bezieht.)

Mia, **who** is Ben's sister, doesn't like drones. Li, **whose** best friend Mia is, owns a drone, **which** she isn't allowed to use in Mia's garden.

Nicht bestimmende Relativsätze (***non-defining relative clauses***) geben **Zusatz**informationen, die man nicht unbedingt braucht, um zu wissen, von welcher Person/Sache die Rede ist. Man findet sie häufiger in geschriebenem Englisch.

! ***Non-defining relative clauses*** werden **mit Komma** abgetrennt.

! Es können nur die Relativprononomen ***who***, ***which*** und ***whose*** („dessen/deren") verwendet werden, nicht aber ~~***that***~~.

! In ***non-defining relative clauses*** darf das Relativpronomen nie weggelassen werden.

▸ *LF 29*

LF 29 Contact clauses (Relativsätze ohne Relativpronomen)

Objekt **Subjekt** des Relativsatzes

That's the girl ~~who~~ **I** chatted with yesterday.

Das ist das Mädchen, mit **dem** ich …

Objekt **Subjekt** des Relativsatzes

These are the pictures ~~that~~ **our friends** shared the most.

Das sind die Bilder, **die** unsere Freunde am häufigsten teilten.

Subjekt des Relativsatzes

That's the girl **who** chatted with me yesterday.

Das ist das Mädchen, **das** gestern … hat.

Subjekt des Relativsatzes

These are the pictures **that** were shared the most.

Das sind die Bilder, **die** am häufigsten … wurden.

Relativsätze **ohne** *who/that* heißen ***contact clauses***.
Wenn **nach** dem Relativpronomen (*who/that*) ein Pronomen oder Nomen folgt und vor dem Verb steht, darfst du *who/that* **weglassen**. (Denn hier ist das Relativpronomen **Objekt** des Relativsatzes und zum Verständnis nicht unbedingt notwendig.)

! Wenn das Relativpronomen (*who/that*) **direkt vor dem Verb** im Relativsatz steht, darfst du es **nicht** weglassen (weil es hier das **Subjekt** des Relativsatzes ist).

LF 30 Participle clauses instead of subordinate clauses
(Partizipialsätze anstelle von Nebensätzen)

(1) Walking down the street, Ben noticed a broken shop window.
(1a) **While** he was walking down the street, Ben noticed a broken shop window.
(1b) ***Während*** *er … entlang ging, bemerkte Ben …*

(2) Seeing two men near a van, he decided to watch them.
(2a) He saw two men near a van **and** decided to …
(2b) *Er sah zwei Männer nahe bei …* ***und*** *beschloss, …*

(3) Ben shouted loudly, expecting some sort of crime.
(3a) Ben shouted loudly **because** he expected … crime.
(3b) *Ben rief laut,* ***weil*** *er … Verbrechen erwartete.*

(4) Having noticed Ben, the men laughed, "It's OK. We're here to put in a new window."
(4a) **When** they had noticed Ben, the men laughed, "…
(4b) ***Als*** *sie Ben bemerkt hatten, lachten die Männer: „…*

(5) The men working at the window talked to Ben.
(5a) The men **who** were working … talked to Ben.
(5b) *Die Männer,* ***die*** *gerade …, sprachen mit Ben.*

Zur Verkürzung langer Sätze kann man **Partizipialsätze** verwenden. Sie enthalten Formen des Partizips:
- ***present participle***: ***verb*** + ***-ing***
- ***past participle***: ***verb*** + ***-ed*** (regelmäßige Verben; **!** unregelmäßige Verben ▸ *pp. 273–274*)

Im Englischen können Partizipialsätze anstelle eines (längeren) Nebensatzes stehen, vergleiche 1 und 1a. Im Deutschen braucht man aber immer den vollständigen Nebensatz (1b).

Partizipialsätze können u.a. **ersetzen**:
- **Nebensätze der Zeit** (oft bei Gleichzeitigkeit), die mit ***while***, ***when*** beginnen (1 ersetzt 1a).
- zwei **Hauptsätze**, die mit ***and*** verbunden wären (2 ersetzt 2a).
- **begründende Nebensätze**, die mit ***because***, ***as*** beginnen (3 ersetzt 3a).
- **Nebensätze**, die eine **Folge** ausdrücken (4 ersetzt 4a).
- **Relativsätze**, die beschreiben, was gerade vor sich geht (***present progressive***) oder ging (***past progressive***) (5 ersetzt 5a).

LF 31 Reflexive pronouns (Reflexivpronomen)

I ask myself how we can enjoy ourselves this evening.

Ich frage mich, wie wir uns heute Abend amüsieren können.

I think your little sister is old enough to look after herself.

Ich finde, deine …, auf sich selbst aufzupassen.

Reflexivpronomen (***myself***, ***yourself***, ***ourselves***, …) beziehen sich auf das Subjekt: (*I* – ***myself***, *you* – ***yourself***, *people* – ***themselves***):

Subjekt		Reflexivpronomen
I	*asked*	***myself*** *…*
We	*can enjoy*	***ourselves***.
Your sister	*can look after*	***herself***.

Reflexive pronouns

(I)	myself	(ich)	mir/mich
(you)	yourself	(du)	dir/dich
(he)	himself	(er)	sich
(she)	herself	(sie)	sich
(it)	itself	(er/sie/es)	sich

(we)	ourselves	(wir) uns
(you)	yourselves	(ihr) euch
(they)	themselves	(sie) sich

! Den Plural bildest du mit ***-selves***.

! Es gibt Verben, die im Deutschen reflexiv sind, im Englischen jedoch nicht. Das „sich, mich, mir, dir" usw. wird nicht übersetzt, z.B.:

Beispiele:

(to) feel	sich fühlen	*He doesn't feel well.*	Er fühlt sich nicht gut.
(to) hide	sich verstecken	*Let's hide!*	Verstecken wir uns!
(to) imagine	sich etwas vorstellen	*I can imagine that.*	Das kann ich mir vorstellen.
(to) look forward to sth.	sich auf etwas freuen	*I'm looking forward to it.*	Ich freue mich darauf.
(to) meet	sich treffen	*Let's meet at six!*	Treffen wir uns um sechs!
(to) remember	sich an etwas erinnern	*I don't remember.*	Ich erinnere mich nicht.
(to) wonder	sich fragen	*I wonder if …*	Ich frage mich, ob …
(to) worry	sich Sorgen machen	*Don't worry.*	Mach dir keine Sorgen.

LF 32 The *-ing*-form (the gerund) (Die *-ing*-Form bzw. das Gerundium)

Du kannst von vielen Verben eine ***-ing*-Form** bilden, etwa für die Verlaufsform (*present progressive*), z.B. *Li is driving to school in her own car today.* ▸ *LF 2*

Driving a car is cool.

(Das) **Autofahren** ist cool. / Ein Auto **zu fahren**, ist *cool*.

I love driving a car.

Ich liebe das **Autofahren**. / Ich liebe es, **Auto zu fahren**.

Als ***gerund*** bezeichnet man die *-ing*-Form, wenn sie als **Nomen** verwendet wird, hier z.B. als **Subjekt** oder **Objekt**:

Sport is cool. ◂▸ ***Driving*** *is cool.* **(Subjekt des Satzes)**

I love sport. ◂▸ *I love* ***driving***. **(Objekt des Satzes)**

Im Deutschen wird das ***gerund*** oft durch einen Infinitiv mit „zu" wiedergegeben.

I enjoy **helping** people. So I keep **working** with kids. I'd miss **teaching** them music.

Die ***-ing*-Form** (***gerund***) folgt oft auf bestimmte **Verben** als **Objekt,** z.B. *(dis-)like, enjoy, hate, keep, miss, start, finish, …*

I prefer **learning** languages. (or: *I prefer **to** learn languages.*)
I'll start **learning** German next term.
(or: *I'll start **to** learn German …*)

! Nach *like/love/hate/prefer/start/begin* kann auch ***to*** + **Infinitiv** *folgen:*
love/like to play *hate to learn* *begin/start to sing*

! Nach einigen Verben – z. B. *enjoy*, *finish*, *imagine*, *mind*, *miss*, *practise*, *suggest* – muss die ***-ing*-Form** (***gerund***) verwendet werden, nie ***to*** + **Infinitiv**.

I'm good at **playing** basketball. Our team is looking forward to **playing** against Boston City. We've always dreamed of **winning** against them.

Die *-ing*-**Form** (***gerund***) folgt nach **Präpositionen:** *at, about, after, for, in, of, to.*

! Es gibt einige **Wendungen**, denen das ***gerund*** **folgen muss**, z.B.:
- *dream of/about …ing*
- *(be) good/bad at …ing*
- *(be) interested in …ing*
- *get used to …ing*
- *look forward to …ing*

-ing-form (gerund) or *to*-infinitive? (Gerundium oder *to*-Infinitiv?)

Ben: I enjoy **chatting** with people.

Das ***gerund*** **(*-ing*-Form)** folgt meist nach bestimmten Verben als **Objekt**, z.B. *(dis-)like, enjoy, hate, start, …*

I want **to tell** them everything.

Nach **bestimmten Verben** darfst du **nur** den ***to*-Infinitiv** verwenden, z.B. *want to, would like to, need to, hope to …*

Li prefers **meeting** people. She prefers **to meet** them in real life.

Nach bestimmten Verben kannst du das ***gerund*** oder den ***to*-Infinitiv** verwenden. Die **Bedeutung** ändert sich **nicht**, z.B. bei *like, love, hate prefer, start, begin*.

"Stop **chatting** all day long."
Hör auf, … zu chatten.

At the door Ben stopped **to check** his emails. … blieb Ben stehen, um seine …

I'll never forget **skiing** for the first time.
Ich werde nie vergessen, wie ich …

Oh, I won't forget **to send** you the photos.
… werde nicht vergessen, dir die Fotos …

Mum remembers **buying** her first mobile.
… erinnert sich, dass/wie sie … hat.

Will dad remember **to give** me his headphones? … daran denken, dass er …?

! Unterschiedliche Bedeutungen hat die Verwendung von ***gerund*** oder ***to*-Infinitiv** nach diesen Verben:

stop + *gerund* ◄ mit etwas aufhören (… es zu tun)
stop + *to …* ◄ aufhören/anhalten, um etwas anders zu tun
forget + *gerund* ◄ vergessen, was man (früher mal) getan hat
forget + *to …* ◄ vergessen, was später (noch) zu tun ist
remember + *gerund* ◄ sich erinnern, was man mal getan hat
remember + *to …* ◄ daran denken, etwas (noch) zu tun

LF 33 The passive (Das Passiv)

Advertising companies make all sorts of ads.
Werbefirmen machen alle Arten von Werbung.

Special ads are made to target teens only.
... Werbung wird gemacht, nur um auf Teens abzuzielen.

"I'm often asked how much money is spent on ads."
Ich werde oft gefragt, ... ausgegeben wird.

Of course, ads aren't made for teens only.
Natürlich wird Werbung nicht nur ... produziert.

Yesterday a new tablet was presented on TV.
Gestern wurde ein neues Tablet ...präsentiert.

Years ago ads for cigarettes were shown everywhere.
Vor Jahren wurde noch Werbung ... überall gezeigt.

Slogans are often repeated in ads.
Man wiederholt oft Slogans in der Werbung.

The song in this ad was first sung **by** the *Beatles*.
Das Lied ... wurde zuerst von ... gesungen.

New tablet presented yesterday

Mit einem **Aktivsatz** sagst du, wer oder was etwas tut. Das Subjekt des Aktivsatzes führt die Handlung aus.

Ein **Passivsatz** drückt aus, mit wem oder was (= womit) **etwas geschieht**, oft ohne zu sagen, wer der/die „Verursachende" ist. (Subjekt ist im Passivsatz der, die bzw. das, womit etwas geschieht.)

Du bildest das Passiv mit einer **Form von *be*** und dem ***past participle*** (der **3. Form des Verbs**). ▸ *pp. 273–274*

simple present:	*am/are/is*	**+ *past participle*:**
	I'm	***asked*** *...*
how much money	*is*	***spent*** *on ...*
simple past:	*was/were*	**+ *past participle*:**
The street	*was*	***used*** *in ...*
The houses that	*were*	***shown*** *...*

! In vielen Passivsätzen wird ***be*** im Deutschen mit ***werden*** ausgedrückt (*werde, wird, wurdest, wurde, ...*).

! Im Deutschen gibt man englische Passivsätze häufig durch einen Aktivsatz mit „man" wieder:

! Zum Nennen des „Verursachers" verwendet man die Präposition ***by*** (*von/durch*).

In Überschriften und Schlagzeilen entfallen zudem meist die Artikel, die Form von *be* sowie Satzzeichen:
~~A~~ new tablet ~~was~~ presented yesterday~~.~~

*Other forms of the passive

▸ *More challenge 3, p. 75*

Das ***passive*** im ***simple present*** und ***simple past*** kennst du bereits. Passivsätze können auch in anderen Zeitformen, mit Modalverben oder im Infinitiv stehen. Das Passiv bildest du immer mit einer Form von ***be + past participle***.

present perfect	*All games have been sold.*
past perfect	*I took part in the game because I had been invited.*
going to-future	*The new game is going to be launched in a week.*
will*-future and *modal verbs	*The game will be sold all over the world. It **can** be downloaded from next week on. It **shouldn't** be played by kids.*
future perfect	*Millions of new games will have been invented by 2030.*
present progressive	*All sorts of games are being played today.*
past progressive	*The shop was closed. It was being prepared for a games event.*
passive infinitive	*This game is not to be played by children under 12 years.*

*The passive of verbs with two objects (Das Passiv von Verben mit zwei Objekten)

(active) Someone sent **her** a photo.

personal object — thing object

subject

(passive) **She** was sent a photo.
(**Ihr** wurde … geschickt.)

Manche Verben können **zwei Objekte** haben, z.B. *give / lend / offer / pay / promise / send / show / tell **somebody something***.
(**jemandem etwas** geben / leihen / anbieten / bezahlen / versprechen / schicken / zeigen / erzählen)

Englische Passivsätze mit diesen Verben beginnen meist mit der Person (die vom indirekten Objekt des Aktivsatzes zum Subjekt des Passivsatzes wird).

We were paid a lot of money for our new game.
(**Uns** wurde … bezahlt . / Wir bekamen … / Man zahlte uns …)

He will be given a prize for inventing this game.
(**Ihm** wird ein Preis für … gegeben werden. / Er wird einen Preis für … bekommen. / Man wird ihm einen Preis für … geben.)

Students are supposed to work hard.
(Von Studenten wird hartes Arbeiten erwartet. / Von Studenten wird erwartet, dass sie hart arbeiten. / … erwartet, hart zu arbeiten.)

What are we supposed to do?
(Was erwartet man von uns? / Was sollen wir tun?)

Deshalb heißt diese Form auch ***personal passive*** („persönliches Passiv"). Im Deutschen gibt es keine direkte Entsprechung dafür. Hier bleibt die Person Objekt des Passivsatzes (und steht im Dativ): **Ihr** wurde … geschickt. (Wem …?)

Man kann aber auch andere deutsche Formulierungen benutzen, z.B.: Man schickte ihr … / Sie erhielt …

Ähnlich wie das ***personal passive*** funktioniert auch die englische Wendung *be **supposed to** (do something)*, mit der man Erwartungen oder Verpflichtungen ausdrückt.

*The passive with prepositional verbs (Das Passiv von Verben mit Präpositionen)

(active) Everybody is talking **about** them.

verb form + **preposition** — object

(passive) **They** are being talked **about**.

subject — verb form + **preposition**

(Über sie wird geredet.)

Auch von vielen Verben, die fest mit einer Präposition verbunden sind (***prepositional verbs***), kann man das Passiv bilden, z.B.: *listen to / look at / look after / shout at / talk about / think of*.
Wie im Aktivsatz folgt auch im Passiv die Präposition direkt nach dem Verb.

LF 34 Question tags (Frageanhängsel)

Question tags werden im Englischen **in Gesprächen** oft verwendet. Diese Frageanhängsel an Aussagesätze benutzt man, um **Zustimmung** beim Gesprächspartner zu erreichen.
Sie werden aber auch verwendet als „echte" **Nachfrage**, wenn man unsicher ist.

Im Deutschen kennen wir „…, nicht wahr?" oder „…, nicht?" bzw. auch „ne?/ gell?/woll?/ja?/oder? /…?".

Look, **it's** a nice day today, **isn't** it? … nicht wahr?

You and I **can** go swimming, **can't** we? … oder?

And Ben **will** come too, **won't** he? … ja?

Im Englischen muss das Frageanhängsel aber jeweils unter **Rückbezug** auf das **(Modal-) Verb** und **die Person** des Aussagesatzes neu gebildet werden.

Wenn der **Aussagesatz bejaht** ist, wird das **Frageanhängsel verneint**.
Das Personalpronomen steht wie in einer Frage hinten.

The weather **wasn't** fine last week, **was** it?
But we **can't** expect too much, **can** we?

Wenn der **Aussagesatz verneint** ist, wird das **Frageanhängsel bejaht**.

The bus to the beach **leaves** at 4 pm, **doesn't** it?
You **didn't repair** your bike, **did** you?

Vollverben werden im Frageanhängsel durch *do/does* im ***simple present*** bzw. *did* im ***simple past*** ersetzt.

And you **don't want** to walk there, **do** you?
I'**m** your best friend, **aren't** I?

Das **verneinende *question tag*** für *I'm …* lautet ***aren't** I …?*.

NEW LF 35 *The definite and the indefinite article

(Der bestimmte und der unbestimmte Artikel)

Der bestimmte Artikel **the** entfällt, wenn ein Nomen ganz allgemein gebraucht wird.

Life here is sometimes hard.

Solche allgemein gebrauchten Nomen sind oft
- **abstrakte Begriffe** wie *life*, *history*, *nature*, *traffic*
- **Stoffbezeichnungen** wie *food*, *oil*, *water*, *air*
- **Nomen im Plural** wie *schools*, *students*, *people*

Wenn diese Nomen aber **näher bestimmt** sind, stehen sie **mit dem bestimmten Artikel *the***.

The film described the life of a singer.
The digital habits of the teens that you know …

! Der bestimmte Artikel steht im Englischen meist bei **Musikinstrumenten**:

play the piano, the guitar, the drums, …

Du benutzt den **unbestimmten Artikel a /an** im Englischen meist genauso wie im Deutschen.

Besonders zu beachten ist der unbestimmte Artikel aber

- **vor Berufsbezeichnungen** wie a teacher, …
  *I'm **a** **student**.* Ich bin Schüler/Schülerin.
- **in Wendungen** wie …
  *be in **a** hurry* es eilig haben
  *have/take **a** bath/shower* baden/duschen
  *have / take **a** look* mal sehen/schauen
- **im Sinne von „pro"** wie bei *a month, a kilo, …*
  *Our car does 70 miles **an** **hour**.* … pro Stunde.
- **vor vielen Krankheiten** wie *a cold, a headache, …*
  *I've got **a** **temperature**.* Ich habe Fieber.

Anders als im Deutschen gibt es **Zeitangaben** sowie viele **Ortsangaben** und viele **Wendungen**, in denen **im Englischen kein bestimmter Artikel** steht. Diese musst du wie Vokabeln lernen.

!		
Zeitangaben und Mahlzeiten:	*in May, on Monday, at night, at breakfast, after lunch*	im Mai, am Montag, in der Nacht, zum Frühstück, nach dem Essen
Straßen- und Eigennamen:	*along Main Street, on 14th Street*	entlang der …, in der …
Einrichtungen (allgemein):	*be at school, go to hospital*	in der Schule …, ins Krankenhaus …
Wendungen wie:	*on TV, at work, by bike/car/plane …*	im Fernsehen, bei der Arbeit, mit dem …

NEW LF 36 *Countable and uncountable nouns
(Zählbare und nicht zählbare Nomen)

countable nouns
a point — two points
a butterfly — these butterflies

uncountable nouns
advice • butter • damage • equipment • fruit • health • homework • information • meat • money • music • news • plastic • shopping • traffic • work

! Nicht zählbare Nomen haben **keinen Plural** und stehen **nie** mit ***a/an*** oder Zahlwörtern wie ***one/two/three/...*** .

Die meisten Nomen sind **zählbar**, du benutzt sie auch im **Plural**.

Von **nicht zählbaren** Nomen gibt es **keine Pluralform**, z.B. bei Dingen, die meist als **Masse** gesehen werden, wie *water, sugar, milk, wood, rice, bacon, furniture*, ... oder **abstrakten** Begriffen, wie *damage, love, peace*, ...

Mit Angaben wie *a piece of, a kilo of* kannst du die Menge oder Anzahl eines nicht zählbaren Nomens bestimmen, z.B.
two pieces of cake, ten kilos of meat, three litres / bottles of milk

Für „viel" verwendest du bei nicht zählbaren Nomen neben *a lot of* auch ***much***, z.B. *much homework, much fun, much money*
Bei zählbaren Nomen heißt es ***many***.

! Anders als im Deutschen sind einige Nomen **nicht zählbar**, d.h. sie haben **keinen Plural**, z.B. *damage, homework, information*.
I need some information about ... Ich brauche Informationen über ...
That's good news! Das ist eine gute Nachricht! / sind gute Nachrichten!

Grammatical terms (Grammatische Fachbegriffe)

active	['aktɪv]	Aktiv	*Li **went** to the party.*
adjective	['ædʒɪktɪv]	Adjektiv	*good, red, new, boring, ...*
adverb	['advɜːb]	Adverb	*today, there, outside, very, ...*
adverb of frequency	['friːkwənsi]	Häufigkeitsadverb	*always, often, never, ...*
adverb of manner	[ædvɜːb əv 'mænə]	Adverb der Art und Weise	*slowly, happily, well, ...*
article	['ɑːtɪkl]	Artikel	*the, a, an*
auxiliary	[ɔːg'zɪliəri]	Hilfsverb (zur Bildung von Fragesätzen, Zeitformen usw.)	***Did** Ben go to the party?*
backshift of tenses	['bakʃɪft]	Rückverschiebung der Zeitformen	*"I'**m** tired." She said she **was** tired.*
comparative	[kəm'pærətɪv]	Komparativ (1. Steigerungsform)	*older; more expensive*
comparison	[kəm'pærɪsn]	Steigerung	*old – older – oldest*
conditional sentence	[kən'dɪʃənl 'sentəns]	Bedingungssatz	*If we win, we'll go to London.*
contact clause	['kɒntækt klɔːz]	Relativsatz ohne Relativpronomen	*She's the girl **I love**.*
defining relative clause	[dɪ'faɪnɪŋ]	bestimmender Relativsatz	*I like teachers **who laugh a lot**.*
direct speech	[ˌdaɪrekt 'spiːtʃ]	direkte Rede	*"I love my dog."*
future	['fjuːtʃə]	Zukunft, Futur	
gerund	['dʒerənd]	Gerundium, *-ing*-Form	*I like **dancing**.*
***going to*-future**	['gəʊɪŋ tʊ fjuːtʃə]	Futur mit *going to*	***I'm going to stay** at home tonight.*
***if*-clause**	['if klɔːz]	*if*-Satz, Nebensatz mit *if*	***If we meet**, we'll talk.*
imperative	[ɪm'perətɪv]	Imperativ (Befehlsform)	***Open** your books. **Don't** talk.*
indirect speech	[ˌɪndərekt 'spiːtʃ]	indirekte Rede	*She said (that) **she loved her dog**.*
infinitive	[ɪn'fɪnətɪv]	Grundform des Verbs, Infinitiv	*go, open, see, read, ...*
***-ing*-form**		Gerundium, *-ing*-Form	*I like **dancing**.*
irregular verb	[ɪ'regjələ 'vɜːb]	unregelmäßiges Verb	*go – went – gone*
main clause	[ˌmeɪn 'klɔːz]	Hauptsatz	*If we meet, **we'll talk**.*
main verb	[meɪn vɜːb]	Hauptverb	*Did Ben **go** to the party?*

modal verb	[ˌməʊdl ˈvɜːb]	Modalverb, modales Hilfsverb	*can, must, should, may, …*
negative statement	[ˈnegətɪv]	verneinter Aussagesatz	*I don't like oranges.*
noun	[naʊn]	Nomen, Substantiv	*Ben, girl, man, time, name, …*
object	[ˈɒbdʒɪkt]	Objekt	*Ben has* ***an idea****.*
object question		Objektfrage, Frage nach dem Objekt	***Who did*** *Mrs Miller invite to tea?*
participle clause	[ˌpɑːtɪsɪpl ˈklɔːz]	Partizipialsatz	*Li shook her head,* ***laughing out loud****.* ***Warned by her dad****, she escaped.*
passive	[ˈpæsɪv]	Passiv	*Lots of films* ***are made*** *in LA.*
past participle	[pɑːst ˈpɑːtɪsɪpl]	Partizip Perfekt, 3. Form des Verbs	*happened, eaten, gone, …*
past perfect	[ˌpɑːst ˈpɜːfɪkt]	*past perfect* (Vorvergangenheit, Plusquamperfekt)	*I* ***had*** *already* ***gone*** *to bed when they arrived.*
past progressive	[pɑːst prəˈgresɪv]	Verlaufsform der Vergangenheit	*He* ***was playing*** *a drum.*
personal pronoun	[pɜːsənl ˈprəʊnaʊn]	Personalpronomen	*I, you, he, she, it, we, they, …*
plural	[ˈplʊərəl]	Plural, Mehrzahl	*sweets, carrots, sheep, …*
positive statement	[ˈpɒzətɪv]	bejahter Aussagesatz	*I like oranges.*
possessive determiner	[pəˌzesɪv dɪˈtɜːmɪnə]	Possessivbegleiter	*my, your, his, her, its, our, their*
possessive pronoun	[pəˌzesɪv ˈprəʊnaʊn]	Possessivpronomen	*mine, yours, his, hers, ours, theirs*
preposition	[prepəˈzɪʃn]	Präposition	*after, at, in, next to, under, with, …*
present participle	[ˌpreznt ˈpɑːtɪsɪpl]	Partizip Präsens	*checking, phoning, trying, planning, going, …*
present perfect	[preznt ˈpɜːfɪkt]	*present perfect*	*He* ***has drunk*** *your water.*
present perfect progressive		Verlaufsform des *present perfect*	*We****'ve been playing*** *for hours.*
present progressive	[preznt prəˈgresɪv]	Verlaufsform der Gegenwart	*They****'re having*** *lunch.*
pronoun	[ˈprəʊnaʊn]	Pronomen, Fürwort	
question	[ˈkwestʃən]	Frage(satz)	*What did you do yesterday?*
question tag	[ˈkwestʃn tag]	Frageanhängsel	*isn't he?, are you?, can't we?, …*
question word	[ˈkwestʃən wɜːd]	Fragewort	*what?, when?, where?, how?, …*
reflexive pronoun	[rɪˌfleksɪv ˈprəʊnaʊn]	Reflexivpronomen	*myself, yourself, himself, ourselves, …*
regular verb	[ˈregjələ ˈvɜːb]	regelmäßiges Verb	*help – helped – helped*
relative clause	[ˌrelətɪv klɔːz]	Relativsatz	*This is the dog* ***that bit me****.*
relative pronoun	[ˌrelətɪv ˈprəʊnaʊn]	Relativpronomen	*who, that, which, whose*
short answer	[ʃɔːt ˈɑːnsə]	Kurzantwort	*Yes, I am./No, I don't./…*
simple past	[sɪmpl ˈpɑːst]	einfache Form der Vergangenheit	*I* ***loved*** *the holidays.*
simple present	[sɪmpl ˈpreznt]	einfache Form der Gegenwart	*I always* ***go*** *to school by bike.*
singular	[ˈsɪŋgjələ]	Singular, Einzahl	
statement	[ˈsteɪtmənt]	Aussage(satz)	
subject	[ˈsʌbdʒɪkt]	Subjekt	***My dad*** *is working.*
subject question		Subjektfrage	***Who invited*** *Ben?*
subordinate clause (*also*: **sub-clause**)	[səˈbɔːdɪnət klɔːz] [ˈsʌbklɔːz]	Nebensatz	*I like cycling* ***because I like the sport****.*
substitute	[ˈsʌbstɪtjuːt]	Ersatzverb (anstelle v. Modalverb)	*be able to, be allowed to, have to*
superlative	[suˈpɜːlətɪv]	Superlativ	*cheapest, most expensive, …*
tense	[tens]	Zeitform des Verbs	
time word / time phrase	[ˈtaɪm wɜːd] [ˈtaɪm freɪz]	Zeitangabe	*yesterday, this morning, after school, before lunch*
verb	[vɜːb]	1. Verb 2. Prädikat	*go, help, look, see, …* ***Can*** *we* ***do*** *it alone? He****'s gone****.*
***will*-future**	[ˈwɪl fjuːtʃə]	Futur mit *will*	*I think our trip* ***will be*** *fun.*
***yes*/*no*-question**	[ˈjes ˈnəʊ kwestʃən]	Entscheidungsfrage	*Are you 15? Do you like films?*
word order		Wortstellung (im Satz)	

Das **Vocabulary** (S. 210–238) enthält alle neuen Wörter und Wendungen des Buches, die du lernen musst.
Sie stehen in der Reihenfolge, in der sie im Buch zum ersten Mal vorkommen.

Wenn du **nachschlagen** möchtest, was ein englisches Wort bedeutet oder wie man es ausspricht, dann solltest du das **Dictionary English – German** auf den Seiten 239–272 verwenden.

p. = page (Seite)
pp. = pages (Seiten)
sb. = somebody (jemand)
sth. = something (etwas)
pl = *plural* (Mehrzahl)
infml = *informal* (umgangssprachlich)
AE = *American English*
BE = *British English*

Unit 1: Embrace diversity

p. 10	**embrace** [ɪm'breɪs]	annehmen, mit offenen Armen begrüßen; (sich) umarmen	Are you ready to ~ new ideas? They said goodbye and **~d**.
	diversity [daɪ'vɜːsəti]	Vielfalt	Nomen: **diversity** – Adjektiv: **diverse** [daɪ'vɜːs] (vielfältig)
	multicultural [mʌlti'kʌltʃərəl]	multikulturell	There are people from many different cultures in the USA. It is a ~ society.
	rainbow ['reɪnbəʊ]	Regenbogen	a **rainbow** 
	colonize ['kɒlənaɪz]	kolonisieren	
	diamond ['daɪəmənd]	Diamant	! Betonung auf der 1. Silbe: **diamond** ['daɪəmənd]
	mix [mɪks]	Mischung	There will be a ~ of music at the festival.
	religion [rɪ'lɪdʒən]	Religion	Nomen: **religion** – Adjektiv: **religious** [rɪ'lɪdʒəs] (religiös) **religious building** = Sakralbau, Kirchengebäude
	colourful ['kʌləfl]	farbenfroh, bunt	
	wildlife ['waɪldlaɪf]	Tiere *(in freier Wildbahn)*, Tierwelt	You can find all kinds of ~ in Africa's national parks. The ~ of Africa is very different from the ~ in Europe.
	low [ləʊ]	niedrig, tief	**high ◄► low** **the high season** (die Hauptsaison) **the low season** (die Nebensaison)
	currency ['kʌrənsi]	Währung	Until 2001, Germany's ~ was the *Deutsche Mark*.
p. 11	**apartheid** [ə'pɑːtaɪt]	Apartheid *(früheres System der Trennung zwischen Weißen und Schwarzen in Südafrika)*	
	segregate ['segrɪgeɪt]	trennen *(nach Hautfarbe/Religion/Geschlecht)*	Verb: **segregate** – Nomen: **segregation**
	public ['pʌblɪk]	öffentlich	This is a ~ library. Everyone can borrow books here.
	system ['sɪstəm]	System	! Betonung auf der 1. Silbe: **system** ['sɪstəm]
	release sb. **from** sth. [rɪ'liːs]	jn. (aus etwas) freilassen, befreien	After 25 years, they were finally **~d from** prison.
	multilingual [mʌlti'lɪŋgwəl]	mehrsprachig	David speaks English and Spanish at home and German at school. He is ~.

Theme 1

p.12 **(back) then** [ðen]	damals	My grandma was born in 1952. Life was a lot slower **(back) ~**, she says. **!** **then** = **1.** dann, danach; **2.** damals
elect sb. **(to be)** sth. [ɪ'lekt]	jn. zu etwas wählen	**!** *English:* They **elected** him president. *German:* Sie **wählten** ihn **zum** Präsidenten.
memory (of) ['meməri]	Erinnerung (an)	My dad lived in Berlin twenty years ago. He says he has very nice **memories** of the city. **in memory of** = in Gedenken an
access ['ækses]	Zugang, Zutritt	
poverty ['pɒvəti]	Armut	Adjektiv: **poor** – Nomen: **poverty**
unemployment [ʌnɪm'plɔɪmənt]	Arbeitslosigkeit	**unemployment ◄► employment** (Arbeit, Anstellung)
suburb ['sʌbɜːb]	Vorstadt, Vorort	It's so noisy here in the town centre that we have decided to move to a **~**.
baker ['beɪkə]	Bäcker/in	a **baker** 
relationship [rɪ'leɪʃnʃɪp]	Beziehung	I can talk to my mum about everything. We have a really good **~**.
totally ['təʊtəli]	völlig, total	Adverb: **totally** (völlig, total) I feel **totally** free. Adjektiv: **total** (Gesamt-) the **total** number of pupils
date sb. [deɪt]	mit jm. gehen; sich (regelmäßig) mit jm. treffen; eine Beziehung mit jm. haben	Dad **~d** mum for years before they got married.
opportunity [ɒpə'tjuːnəti]	Gelegenheit, Möglichkeit, Chance	My brother thinks he'll have better job **opportunities** if he spends a year in Britain.

German „Möglichkeit"

• **opportunity** oder **chance** werden verwendet, wenn „Möglichkeit" im Sinne von **„Gelegenheit, Chance"** gemeint ist. (**opportunity** ist etwas förmlicher als **chance**.)	After school, I had the **chance/opportunity** to go to Australia for a year. Dad says he'll have a better **chance/opportunity** of getting a job if we move to Bristol.
• Wenn „Möglichkeit" im Sinne von **„Art und Weise"** gemeint ist, kann man **way** verwenden.	We'll have to swim – there's no other **way** to get/of getting to the island.
• Wenn man sagen will, dass etwas möglicherweise der Fall sein könnte – aber es ist nicht sicher, vielleicht sogar unwahrscheinlich –, dann verwendet man **possibility**.	Is there a **possibility** of seeing the Queen when we are in London? There is a **possibility** of snow in May, but it's very unlikely.

document ['dɒkjument]	dokumentieren	**!** **document** = **1.** dokumentieren ['dɒkjument] **2.** Dokument ['dɒkjumənt]

p. 13	**political** [pə'lɪtɪkl]	politisch	
	national holiday	Nationalfeiertag	France's **national ~** is 14th July. ! **holiday** = **1.** Urlaub; *(im Plural)* Ferien; **2.** Feiertag

Theme 2

p. 14	**in the wild** [waɪld]	in freier Wildbahn	
	in spite of [ɪn 'spaɪt əv]	trotz	**in ~ of** the bad weather = **although** the weather was bad
	unique [ju'ni:k]	einzigartig, einmalig	Everyone's eyes are **~**. (All eyes are different.) Gareth has a **~** collection of Beatles CDs.
	informative [ɪn'fɔ:mətɪv]	informativ, lehrreich	! Betonung auf der 2. Silbe: **informative** [ɪn'fɔ:mətɪv]
	conservation [kɒnsə'veɪʃn]	(Natur-)Schutz, Erhaltung, Bewahrung	I am interested in animal **~** because too many animals are dying out!
	step [step]	treten *(einen Schritt tun)*	Nomen: **step** (Schritt; Stufe) – Verb: **step**
	edge [edʒ]	Rand, Kante	He's going to **step** off the **edge** in a second.
	platform ['plætfɔ:m]	Plattform; Rampe	! **platform** = **1.** Bahnsteig, Gleis; **2.** Plattform; Rampe
	ostrich ['ɒstrɪtʃ]	Strauß *(Vogel)*	**Ostriches** are birds, but they can't fly.
	truly ['tru:li]	wahrhaft(ig), wirklich	Mr Clark was **~** surprised that we sang *Happy Birthday* to him at the beginning of class.
	weigh [weɪ]	wiegen	Which **~s** more: a kilo of apples or a kilo of paper?
	be aimed at sb. [eɪmd]	sich an jn. richten	Mum's comment that the living room needs to be tidied up **was ~ at** me!
	effective [ɪ'fektɪv]	effektiv, wirksam	Adjektiv: **effective** – Nomen: **effect** [ɪ'fekt] ! Betonung auf der 2. Silbe: **effective** [ɪ'fektɪv]
p. 15	**rather than** ['rɑ:ðə ðən]	anstelle von, (an)statt	She wants to stay at home **rather ~** go to the concert tonight. Olivia prefers to wear trousers **~ than** dresses.
	advance [əd'vɑ:ns]	Voraus-, Vorab-	an **~** warning/booking **in advance** = im Voraus
	reply [rɪ'plaɪ]	Antwort	= answer Nomen: **reply** – Verb: **reply** (antworten, erwidern)

preferable to sth. ['prefrəbl]	(einer Sache) vorzuziehen, besser als (etwas)	Verb: **prefer** – Adjektiv: **preferable** – Adverb: **preferably**

prefer – preferable – preferably

• **prefer (to)**	vorziehen; lieber mögen (als)	I **prefer** basketball **to** football. I**'d prefer to** stay at home today.
• **preferable (to)**	*(einer anderen Sache)* vorzuziehen; besser (als)	Is buying a house **preferable to** renting one? It's **preferable** to buy organic food rather than cheap food from the supermarket.
• **preferably**	vorzugsweise, am liebsten	We'd like to buy a house, **preferably** in the town centre.

insight (into) ['ɪnsaɪt]	Einblick (in), Verständnis (von)	The film gave me an ~ **into** life in Vietnam.
human ['hjuːmən]	Mensch; menschlich	! **human** = **1.** Mensch – animals and **humans** **2.** menschlich – It's only **human**. Für das deutsche „Mensch" wird oft auch **human being** verwendet: The earth is much older than **human beings**.
creature ['kriːtʃə]	Geschöpf, (Lebe-)Wesen	Last night I watched a scary movie about **~s** from Mars. ! Betonung auf der 1. Silbe: **creature** ['kriːtʃə]

Focus on language

.16	**instead of** [ɪn'sted əv]	anstatt, anstelle von	→ **instead of – instead** • I'd like pasta **instead of** chips, please. (= **anstelle von**) • I don't like chips. Can I have pasta **instead**? (= **stattdessen**)
	confused [kən'fjuːzd]	verwirrt	I was ~ when someone called traffic lights a "robot".
	in fact [ɪn 'fækt]	eigentlich, um genau zu sein	My homework wasn't hard. **In ~**, it only took me ten minutes.
	majority [mə'dʒɒrəti]	Mehrheit, Mehrzahl	There are 16 girls and 13 boys in my class. The girls are in the ~.
	century ['sentʃəri]	Jahrhundert	There are one hundred years in a ~.
	lingua franca [lɪŋgwə 'fræŋkə]	Lingua Franca (Verkehrssprache)	English is a ~ **franca** in many parts of the world.
.17	**permanent** ['pɜːmənənt]	permanent, (be)ständig	Is that a ~ tattoo?
	question mark ['kwestʃən mɑːk]	Fragezeichen	

Punctuation [pʌŋktʃu'eɪʃn] **(Zeichensetzung)**

.	**full stop** [fʊl 'stɒp]	Punkt	?	**question mark** ['kwestʃən mɑːk]	Fragezeichen
,	**comma** ['kɒmə]	Komma	!	**exclamation mark** [eksklə'meɪʃn mɑːk]	Ausrufezeichen
:	**colon** ['kəʊlən]	Doppelpunkt	-	**hyphen** ['haɪfn]	Bindestrich

.18	**typical (of)** ['tɪpɪkl]	typisch (für)	! *English:* What food is **typical of** your area? *German:* Welches Essen ist **typisch für** deine Gegend?

false friend [fɔːls ˈfrend]	„falscher Freund", Übersetzungsfalle	The English word "become" is a **false ~**: it looks like German "bekommen", but it means "werden".

Text

pp. 19–21 and pp. 106–107

take care of sb./sth. [teɪk ˈkeə]	sich um jn./etwas kümmern	I **take ~ of** my little brother when mum has to work late.
not (...) any more [eni ˈmɔː]	nicht mehr	This bag is very old. I do**n't** use it **any ~**.
return [rɪˈtɜːn]	zurückkehren, zurückkommen	I **~ed** to my hometown after 20 years. It had changed a lot.
crowded [ˈkraʊdɪd]	voller Menschen; überfüllt	**!** *English:* The city was very **crowded**. *German:* In der Stadt war es sehr voll. / Die Stadt war voller Menschen.
shop window [ʃɒp ˈwɪndəʊ]	Schaufenster	a **shop window** 
frightened [ˈfraɪtnd]	verängstigt	→ **frighten, frightened, frightening** • **it frightens me** = es macht mir Angst • **be frightened of** sth. = vor etwas Angst haben • **it's frightening** = es ist beängstigend
stranger [ˈstreɪndʒə]	Fremde(r)	
a two-bedroomed flat [ˈbedruːmd]	eine Wohnung mit zwei Schlafzimmern	
council flat [ˈkaʊnsl flæt]	Sozialwohnung	**council** = Rat, Gemeinderat, Stadtverwaltung
above [əˈbʌv]	oben; über, oberhalb (von)	They were standing on the roof. The cars looked very small from **~**. We live in a small flat **~** a bookshop. **above ◂▸ below**
somehow [ˈsʌmhaʊ]	irgendwie	**Somehow** I'll earn enough money for a new computer.
heat [hiːt]	erwärmen, erhitzen	Adjektiv: **hot** – Verb: **heat** – Nomen: **heat**
microwave [ˈmaɪkrəweɪv]	Mikrowelle	**heating** a meal in the **microwave** 
make oneself comfortable	es sich gemütlich machen	It was cold outside, so we **made ourselves ~** in front of the fireplace. 
people [ˈpiːpl]	Volk	**!** **people** = **1.** Menschen – A lot of **people** are afraid of dogs. **2.** Volk – the Zulu **people** (das Volk der Zulu) the native **peoples** of Africa (die Urvölker Afrikas)
decision [dɪˈsɪʒn]	Entscheidung	**make a decision** = eine Entscheidung fällen Verb: **decide** – Nomen: **decision**

silent ['saɪlənt]	still, ruhig; lautlos	**fall silent** = still werden, verstummen
be about to do sth.	im Begriff sein, etwas zu tun; kurz davor sein, etwas zu tun	I **was ~ to** leave the house when my phone rang.
from now on	von nun an, ab jetzt	**From ~ on**, I will make my bed every day. I promise.
passport ['pɑːspɔːt]	(Reise-)Pass	
hug [hʌg]	(sich) umarmen	I **~ged** my mum. = We **~ged**. Verb: **hug** – Nomen: **hug** (Umarmung)
characterization [kærəktəraɪ'zeɪʃn]	Charakterisierung	
characterize sth. ['kærəktəraɪz]	etwas charakterisieren, kennzeichnen; für etwas charakteristisch sein	Modern architecture **~s** this part of the city.
response [rɪ'spɒns]	Reaktion, Antwort	Nomen: **response** – Verb: **respond** [rɪ'spɒnd] (reagieren, antworten)

! Wenn du den Text auf den Seiten 19–21 gelesen hast, kannst du die folgenden neuen Wörter daraus zusätzlich lernen.

pp. 19–21

°**tunnel** ['tʌnl]	Tunnel	! Aussprache: **tunnel** ['tʌnl]
°**cover** ['kʌvə]	bedecken	Black and grey clouds **~ed** the sky. 
°**sudden** ['sʌdn]	plötzliche(r, s)	! • His **sudden** departure surprised us all. (Seine **plötzliche** Abreise …) • We were surprised when he **suddenly** left. (…, als er **plötzlich** aufbrach)
°**glimpse** [glɪmps]	kurzer Blick	**catch a glimpse of sth.** = einen Blick von/auf etwas erhaschen; etwas nur kurz zu sehen bekommen I was shocked when I caught a ~ of myself in the mirror.
°**echo** ['ekəʊ]	(wider)hallen	Verb: **echo** – Nomen: **echo,** *pl* **echoes**
°**hurry** ['hʌri]	sich beeilen; eilen	Verb: **hurry** – Nomen: **hurry** **be in a hurry** = es eilig haben, in Eile sein
°**every now and again**	ab und zu, von Zeit zu Zeit	= sometimes
°**certainly** ['sɜːtnli]	sicher(lich), gewiss	I can ~ understand that you do not want to take the train at 5 am, but it is 100 euros cheaper than the train at 7 am.
°**… and neither did I.** ['naɪðə]	… und ich auch nicht.	You didn't buy milk? Well, **~ did I**.
°**gulp** sth. **down** [gʌlp 'daʊn]	etwas hinunterschlingen, *(Getränk)* hinunterstürzen	She **~ed down** her drink and left the bar in a hurry.

°**straight** [streɪt]	direkt, gleich	We bought a takeaway pizza and ate it ~ from the box.
°**carton** [ˈkɑːtn]	(Papp-)Karton; Packung	! Betonung auf der 1. Silbe: **carton** [ˈkɑːtn]
°**leftover** pizza/cake/… [ˈleftəʊvə]	übrig gebliebene Pizza/ übrig gebliebener Kuchen/…	
°**turn yellow**	gelb werden	
°**olive** [ˈɒlɪv]	Olive	 **olives**  **pineapple**
°**pineapple** [ˈpaɪnæpl]	Ananas	
°**drift** [drɪft]	sich bewegen, driften; *(Gedanken)* wandern	The crowd **~ed** towards the stage when the concert started. When I read the story, my thoughts **~ed** to California and the beach.
°**sigh** [saɪ]	seufzen	 **rings** 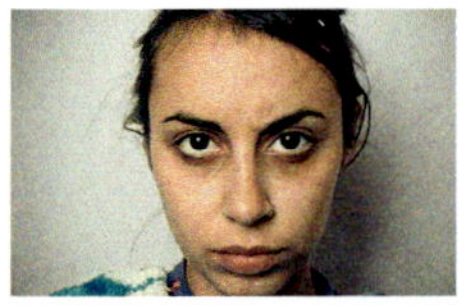 She has dark **rings** under her eyes.
°**ring** [rɪŋ]	Ring	
°**pale** [peɪl]	blass, bleich	
°**besides** [bɪˈsaɪdz]	außerdem	It's too late to go to the cinema. And ~, I've already seen the film.
°**dirty** [ˈdɜːti]	schmutzig	
°**dishes** *(pl)* [ˈdɪʃɪz]	Geschirr	**dirty dishes**
°**dustbin** [ˈdʌstbɪn]	Mülleimer	
°**struggle** [ˈstrʌgl]	kämpfen, sich abmühen	I am **struggling** to understand my French homework. I have so much trouble with the conditional!
°**fear** [fɪə]	Angst	I was afraid but didn't show my ~. ! **Angst haben (vor)** = **be afraid/scared/frightened (of)**
°**turn away**	sich abwenden, sich wegdrehen	He didn't say anything, he just **~ed away** and smiled.
°**stream** [striːm]	strömen	Tears were **~ing** down the little boy's face.
°**shake** [ʃeɪk], **shook** [ʃʊk], **shaken** [ˈʃeɪkən]	zittern; schütteln	His whole body was **~ing**.
°**financial** [faɪˈnænʃl]	finanziell	! Betonung auf der 2. Silbe: **financial** [faɪˈnænʃl]
°**difficulty** [ˈdɪfɪkəlti]	Schwierigkeit(en)	Adjektiv: **difficult** – Nomen: **difficulty**

°**talk** sth. **over (with** sb.**)**	etwas (mit jm.) besprechen	I need to **talk** something ~ with Mr Clark, then I'll come over to your house.
°**terror** [ˈterə]	(panische) Angst	
°**Where … anyway?** [ˈeniweɪ]	Wo … überhaupt?	Trecwn? How do you say that? And **where** exactly is this place, **anyway?** (*etwa:* Wo genau ist das denn überhaupt?)
°**… and off we went to …**	… ab ging's nach …	
°**bits** *(pl)* [bɪts] *(infml)*	Teile, Stückchen	I have seen **bits** on television … = Ich hab (mal) ein bisschen (was) im Fernsehen gesehen …
°**television** [ˈtelɪvɪʒn]	Fernsehen	
°**Do they even have streets?** [ˈiːvn]	Haben sie überhaupt Straßen?	
°**forever** [fərˈevə] (*BE auch:* **for ever**)	für immer, ewig (lange)	I hope they arrive soon. We can't wait ~.

Skills training

p.22 **giraffe** [dʒəˈrɑːf], *(pl)* **giraffe** *or* **giraffes**	Giraffe	two **giraffes** **!** Aussprache: **giraffe** [dʒəˈrɑːf] 
fill sth. **in** [fɪl ˈɪn]	etwas ausfüllen; etwas einsetzen	**! fill in** = **1.** ausfüllen – **fill in** a form **2.** einsetzen – **fill in** your name/the right word/the missing information
gap [ɡæp]	Lücke	The horses escaped through a ~ in the fence. Fill in the **~s** with the right verb from the box.
Wi-fi [ˈwaɪ faɪ]	WLAN	
check-in [ˈtʃek ɪn]	Check-in, Einchecken	
facilities *(pl)* [fəˈsɪlətiz]	Einrichtungen, Anlage(n), Geräte	The ~ at the first hotel were much better than the ones here!
thief [θiːf], *pl* **thieves** [θiːvz]	Dieb/in	 (Vor Dieben in diesem Bereich wird gewarnt!)
operate [ˈɒpəreɪt]	arbeiten, tätig sein	
unattended [ʌnəˈtendɪd]	unbeaufsichtigt	 (Unbeaufsichtigtes Gepäck wird sofort beseitigt.)
remove sth. [rɪˈmuːv]	etwas entfernen, beseitigen	
immediately [ɪˈmiːdiətli]	sofort	

	sth. **may** be destroyed [meɪ]	etwas wird möglicherweise vernichtet	I **may** go to Scotland next year, but I'm not sure yet. (Vielleicht fahre ich …)
p. 23	**wallet** ['wɒlɪt]	Brieftasche, Börse	
	be missing (from) ['mɪsɪŋ]	fehlen (bei/in)	When I arrived home, I noticed that my keys **were ~**. I couldn't open the door.
	ID [aɪ 'di:] **(= identification** [aɪdentɪfɪ'keɪʃn]**)**	Ausweis; Identifizierung, Legitimation	! *English:* Do you have any **ID**? *German:* Können Sie sich ausweisen?
	student card ['stju:dnt kɑ:d]	Schülerausweis; Studentenausweis	
	report sth. **(to)** [rɪ'pɔ:t]	etwas melden, anzeigen (bei) *(z.B. bei der Polizei)*	You should **~** this **to** the police. The car **was ~ed** stolen. (… wurde als gestohlen gemeldet.)
p. 24	**mediation** [mi:di'eɪʃn]	Vermittlung, Sprachmittlung	Nomen: **mediation** – Verb: **mediate** ['mi:dieɪt] (vermitteln)
	historical [hɪ'stɒrɪkl]	historisch, geschichtlich	There are a lot of ~ buildings in Paris.
	monument ['mɒnjumənt]	Monument, Denkmal	! Betonung auf der 1. Silbe: **monument** ['mɒnjumənt]
	provide [prə'vaɪd]	(an)bieten, zur Verfügung stellen	The hotel **~s** free Wi-fi.
	daily ['deɪli]	täglich	Two ~ meals are included in the price. (= Two meals per day …)
	minimum ['mɪnɪməm]	Minimum, Mindest-, minimal	Jake says he needs a ~ of £80 pocket money (= at least £80) per month.
	translate [træns'leɪt]	übersetzen	
p. 25	**some day** ['sʌm deɪ]	eines Tages	**Some ~** I will move to Japan.
	reaction (to) [ri'ækʃn]	Reaktion (auf)	Verb: **react (to)** – Nomen: **reaction (to)**
	stick [stɪk], **stuck, stuck** [stʌk]	(haften) bleiben	I can't get that song out of my head. It's **stuck** in my mind.
	mind [maɪnd]	Geist, Verstand; Gedanken	I will never forget the final scene of that film. It will always stick in my **~**. (= … wird mir immer im Gedächtnis bleiben)
	technique [tek'ni:k]	Methode, Technik	! Betonung auf der 2. Silbe: **technique** [tek'ni:k]
	voice-over ['vɔɪs əʊvə]	Off-Stimme; (Film-)Kommentar	
	close-up ['kləʊs ʌp]	Nahaufnahme *(Film)*	! • Adjektiv: **close (to)** [kləʊs] nah, dicht (bei, an) Many people don't like it if you stand too **~ to** them. • Verb: **close** [kləʊz] schließen
	medium shot ['mi:diəm ʃɒt]	Halbtotale *(Film)*	**medium** = mittel(groß); mittlere(r, s)
	shot [ʃɒt]	Aufnahme, Foto; *(Film)* Einstellung	! **shot** = **1.** Schuss; **2.** (Kamera-)Einstellung, Aufnahme *(Film)*
	long shot ['lɒŋ ʃɒt]	Totale *(Film)*	
	swap [swɒp]	tauschen	**swap places/roles with sb.** = mit jm. die Plätze/Rollen tauschen

Unit 2: Take a stand!

p.32	**take a stand (on/against sth.)**	Stellung beziehen (zu/gegen etwas)	I think it's important to **take a** strong **~ on/against** cyberbullying. (= to make it very clear that you are against cyberbullying) **stand** = Standpunkt, Haltung
p.33	**create** [kri'eɪt]	(er)schaffen, kreieren	Jonathan **~d** a special smoothie for his mum.

Theme 1

p.34	**activism** ['æktɪvɪzəm]	Aktivismus	**activist** ['æktɪvɪst] = Aktivist/in
	demonstration [demən'streɪʃn]	Demonstration	
	protest ['prəʊtest]	Protest(demonstration)	Verb: **protest** [prə'test] – Nomen: **protest** ['prəʊtest]
	these days	heutzutage	! Betonung auf **these**: **these days** ['ðiːz deɪz]
	airbrush ['eəbrʌʃ]	*(Foto)* retuschieren, nachbessern	That photo doesn't look like you at all. Did someone ~ it?
	petition [pə'tɪʃn]	Petition, Unterschriften-sammlung	
	signature ['sɪgnətʃə]	Unterschrift	Verb: **sign** [saɪn] – Nomen: **signature** ['sɪgnətʃə]
	power ['paʊə]	Macht, Kraft, Stärke	
	estimate ['estɪmeɪt]	schätzen	I ~ that we'll be at grandma's around 3 pm.
	get involved in sth. [ɪn'vɒlvd]	sich an etwas beteiligen, sich bei etwas engagieren	→ **get involved – be involved** • Lots of young people **get involved in** social projects. **(sich beteiligen/engagieren)** • **Are** you **involved in** this year's school play? **(beteiligt/engagiert sein)**
	meme [miːm]	Internet-Mem, Internetphänomen	= an idea, image, video, website, etc. which people get to know via the internet
	point sth. **out** [pɔɪnt 'aʊt]	auf etwas hinweisen, auf etwas aufmerksam machen	At the meeting Mr Jones **~ed out** that profits had gone down.
	via ['vaɪə]	über, durch, per	We flew to New York ~ Frankfurt.
	troll [trəʊl]	Troll, Kobold; *(in Online-Medien)* Provokateur/in	a troll 
	hurtful ['hɜːtfl]	verletzend	a ~ comment = a comment that hurts/that might hurt
	loads (of) [ləʊdz] *(infml)*	eine Menge	= lots (of)
p.35	**complete** [kəm'pliːt]	vollständig	Verb: **complete** (vervollständigen) Adjektiv: **complete** – Adverb: **completely**
	solve a problem [sɒlv]	ein Problem lösen	We had loads of problems at first, but in the end we **~d** them all.

Theme 2

p. 36	**care about** sth. [keə]	etwas wichtig nehmen	

care (about)

Do you care?	Kümmert dich das?/Interessiert dich das?
Does anybody care about our oceans?	Interessiert sich irgendjemand für unsere Ozeane?
I didn't care about money when I was younger.	Geld war mir egal/war mir nicht wichtig, ...
You should care about your health.	Deine Gesundheit sollte dir wichtig sein.
I don't eat meat. **I really care about** animals.	... Tiere liegen mir sehr am Herzen.
They are really rich. – **Who cares?**	... – Na und?/Wen interessiert das?

	chancellor ['tʃɑːnsələ]	(Bundes-)Kanzler/in	
	prime minister [praɪm 'mɪnɪstə]	Premierminister/in	The British **prime ~** lives at 10 Downing Street, London.
	politics ['pɒlətɪks]	Politik	! **politics** ist Singular, trotz des **-s** am Ende: **Politics is** very interesting for some people, and **it is** very boring for others.
	pay attention (to) [ə'tenʃn]	aufmerksam zuhören; achten (auf), aufpassen (auf)	• Could you all please **pay ~ to** what Ms Evans is going to tell you? • **attention** = Aufmerksamkeit Can I have everybody's **~** now, please? „Achtung, Achtung!" 
	pension ['penʃn]	Rente, Pension	! **False friends:** *English* **pension** = *German* **Rente** *English* **guest house** = *German* **Pension**
	ages *(pl)* ['eɪdʒɪz] *(infml)*	eine Ewigkeit	We had to wait for **~**. (= ewig lange) It took us **~** to find their house.
	what politics is about	worum es in der Politik geht	
	prove [pruːv]	beweisen; nachweisen	• I'm innocent! I didn't take the money. – Can you **~** it? • **prove sb. wrong** = beweisen, dass jemand Unrecht hat
	choice [tʃɔɪs]	(Aus-)Wahl	verb: **choose, chose, chosen** – noun: **choice**
	have a say (in sth.**)**	ein Mitspracherecht haben (in/bei etwas)	• I **had** no **~** in this decision. • **have one's say** = die/seine Meinung äußern What should change in our town? **Have your ~**!
	democracy [dɪ'mɒkrəsi]	Demokratie	! Betonung auf der 2. Silbe: **de<u>moc</u>racy** [dɪ'mɒkrəsi]
p. 37	**politician** [pɒlə'tɪʃn]	Politiker/in	

Focus on language

p.38	**robber** ['rɒbə]	Räuber/in	a **robber** 
	demand [dɪ'mɑ:nd]	fordern, verlangen	The workers **~ed** more money. Verb: **demand** – Nomen: **demand** (Forderung)
	praise [preɪz]	loben, rühmen	His teacher **~d** him for his hard work. Verb: **praise** – Nomen: **praise** (Lob)
	come across sth.	auf etwas stoßen, etwas *(zufällig)* finden	After two hours we **came ~** a beautiful village.
	refugee [refju'dʒi:]	Flüchtling	
	survival [sə'vaɪvl]	(das) Überleben	Nomen: **survival** – Verb: **survive** [sə'vaɪv] (überleben)
	remarkable [rɪ'mɑ:kəbl]	bemerkenswert	My grandfather died at the ~ age of 104.
	stage [steɪdʒ]	Bühne	
	news item ['nju:z aɪtəm]	Nachrichtenmeldung, Pressemeldung	**item** = Artikel, Gegenstand: I took my **~s** to the cash desk.
	performer [pə'fɔ:mə]	Künstler/in, Darsteller/in	

perform – performer – performance

- **perform** — aufführen; durchführen; auftreten *(Künstler/in)* — **Perform** the play/scene/dialogue for your class. The Beatles first **performed** in the USA in 1964.
- **performer** — Künstler/in — We walked along the Thames and watched the street **performers** on the Embankment.
- **performance** — Aufführung, Vorstellung; Auftritt — The Beatles' first **performance** in the USA was a huge success.

	interrupt [ɪntə'rʌpt]	unterbrechen	It's rude to ~ people when they're talking.
p.39	**be in progress** ['prəʊɡres]	im Gange sein	 
	take place [teɪk 'pleɪs]	stattfinden	Our next school trip will **take ~** in October. **! False friends:** *English* **take place** = *German* **stattfinden** *English* **take a seat** = *German* **Platz nehmen** *(sich hinsetzen)*
	raise money (for sth.**)** [reɪz]	Geld sammeln, auftreiben (für etwas)	My class **~d money** for a trip to England.
p.40	**wonderful** ['wʌndəfl]	wunderbar	

gingerbread ['dʒɪndʒəbred]	Honigkuchen, Pfefferkuchen	 a **gingerbread** man  a **gingerbread** house
delicious [dɪ'lɪʃəs]	köstlich, lecker	The pizza looked ~, but it didn't smell very nice.
comparison [kəm'pærɪsn]	Vergleich	Verb: **compare** – Nomen: **comparison** On this website you can make **~s** between different schools. **!** *English:* **make comparisons** *German:* **Vergleiche anstellen; vergleichen**
afterwards ['ɑːftəwədz]	hinterher, danach	We had fish and chips, and ~ we went for an ice cream.

Text

pp. 41–43 and pp. 121–122

forever (*BE auch:* **for ever**) [fər'evə]	für immer, ewig (lange)	I hope they arrive soon. We can't wait ~.
novel ['nɒvl]	Roman	
needle ['niːdl]	Nadel; Kanüle	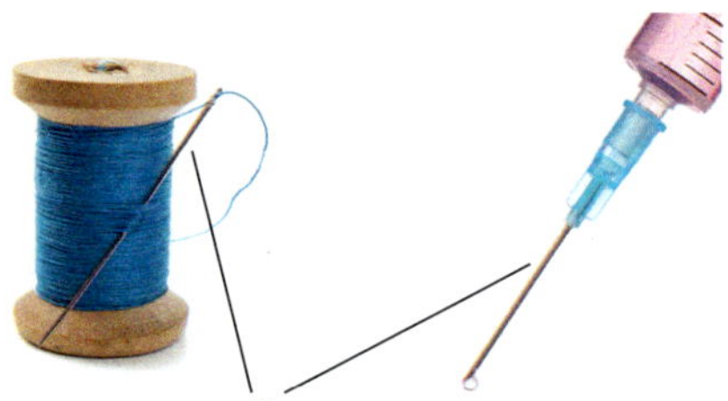 **needles**
come sb.'s **way**	auf jn. zukommen	Can you hear the train **coming our ~**?

way

1. Art und Weise	I like the **way** they dance in the video.	... die Art und Weise, wie sie ... tanzen
2. Weg	Excuse me, can you tell us the **way** to the station?	... den Weg zum Bahnhof ...
3. Richtung	Stop! You're going **the wrong way**. We have to go **this way**.	... in die falsche Richtung. ... hier entlang/in diese Richtung

headlight ['hedlaɪt]	Scheinwerfer(licht)	**headlights** 
lift [lɪft]	Mitfahrgelegenheit	Anyone going to Brighton next Saturday? I'm looking for a ~. **!** *English:* You don't have to walk. I can **give you a lift**. *German:* ... Ich kann **dich mitnehmen**.
mad [mæd]	wahnsinnig, verrückt	You want to go out in this weather? You must be ~.
chase [tʃeɪs]	Verfolgung, Verfolgungsjagd	Verb: **chase** – Nomen: **chase**
cop [kɒp] *(infml)*	Bulle *(Polizist/in)*	

put sth. **on**	etwas einschalten	
siren ['saɪrən]	Sirene	! Betonung und Aussprache: **siren** ['saɪrən]
flash [flæʃ]	blinken, leuchten	The police car's blue light was **~ing**. ! **flash one's headlights** = aufblenden, die Lichthupe betätigen  **flashing lights**  **flashlight** *(AE)* / **torch** *(BE)*
crash [kræʃ]	Unfall, Zusammenstoß	a car **crash** 
crash (into) [kræʃ]	zusammenstoßen (mit); einen Unfall haben	→ **crash (into)** • We/The car **crashed into** a van. • We/The car went off the road and **crashed into** a tree. • They **crashed**, and the driver had to be pulled out of the car. • The plane **crashed into** a block of flats.
explosion [ɪk'spləʊʒn]	Explosion	! Betonung auf der 2. Silbe: **explosion** [ɪk'spləʊʒn]
burn [bɜːn]	Verbrennung, Brandverletzung	Verb: **burn** – Nomen: **burn** **burns unit** *(in a hospital)* = Abteilung für Verbrennungen/Brandverletzungen
alarmed [ə'lɑːmd]	beunruhigt	The manager was ~ because profits had gone down.
over time	im Laufe der Zeit	**Over ~** I learned to love vegetarian food.
joyriding ['dʒɔɪraɪdɪŋ]	Joyriding *(eine Spritztour mit einem gestohlenen Auto machen)*	
change one's mind	es sich anders überlegen	Daniel had wanted to go out, but then he **~d his mind** and stayed home.

! Wenn du den Text auf den Seiten 41–43 gelesen hast, kannst du die folgenden neuen Wörter daraus zusätzlich lernen.

pp. 41–43

°**head somewhere** [hed]	in eine Richtung gehen/fahren	After school we all **~ed** home. He got up and **~ed** for the door.
°**walk** sb. **to** ...	jn. nach .../zu ... begleiten; jn. nach .../zu ... bringen *(zu Fuß)*	Jake always **~s** his girlfriend home/**to** the door.
°**cut through** sth. [kʌt]	etwas durchqueren; eine Abkürzung durch ... nehmen	

°**housing estate** ['haʊzɪŋ ɪsteɪt]	Wohnsiedlung	 a **housing estate**  **high-rise buildings**
°**high-rise building** [haɪ raɪz 'bɪldɪŋ]	Hochhaus	
°**screech** [skriːtʃ]	kreischen; *(Reifen, Bremsen)* quietschen	The car came to a stop with **~ing** tyres.
°**approach** [ə'prəʊtʃ]	sich nähern, näher kommen	As we **~ed** our house, we saw that the front door was open.
°**the headlights were on full beam** [biːm]	das Fernlicht war eingeschaltet	**beam** = (Licht-)Strahl
°**pull up**	anhalten, an den Straßenrand fahren	A taxi **~ed up** beside the man, and he got in.
°**persuade** [pə'sweɪd]	überreden, überzeugen	I didn't want to go to the party, but then Paul **~d** me that it would be fun.
°**furious** ['fjʊəriəs]	wütend	= very angry
°**be supposed to be/do** sth. [sə'pəʊzd]	etwas tun sollen / etwas sein sollen	We**'re** not **~ to** use our mobiles at school, but some of us do. I haven't heard their new CD yet, but it**'s ~ to** be really good.
°**speed** [spiːd], **sped, sped** [sped]	rasen, zu schnell fahren	Verb: **speed** – Nomen: **speed** (Geschwindigkeit)
°**speed hump** ['spiːd hʌmp]	Bodenschwelle, Bremsschwelle *(zur Verkehrsberuhigung)*	a **speed hump**  **hump** = Buckel, Hindernis
°**mate** [meɪt] *(infml)*	Freund/in, Kumpel	On Saturdays I always hang out with my **~s**.
°**scar** [skɑː]	Narbe	a **scar** 
°**put your foot down**	Gas geben *(Auto)*	
°**right behind him**	direkt hinter ihm	
°**junction** ['dʒʌŋkʃn]	(Straßen-)Kreuzung	a **junction** 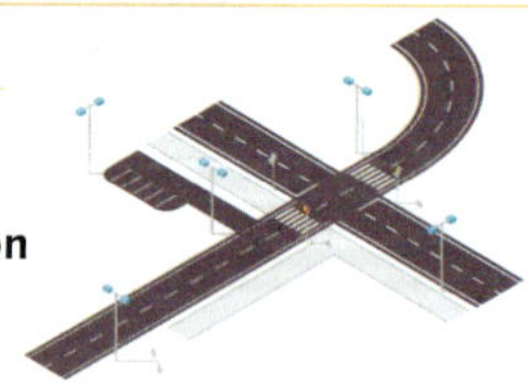
°**straight** [streɪt]	direkt, gleich	We bought a takeaway pizza and ate it **~** from the box.
°**damage** ['dæmɪdʒ]	(be)schädigen, schaden	Alcohol can **~** your health. The car was badly **~d**. (schwer beschädigt) Verb: **damage** – Nomen: **damage** (Schaden, Schäden)
°**unconscious** [ʌn'kɒnʃəs]	bewusstlos	

°**bloody** ['blʌdi]	blutig, voller Blut	Verb: **bleed, bled, bled** – Nomen: **blood** – Adjektiv: **bloody**
°**grab** [græb]	packen, greifen (nach)	I was late, so I **~bed** my school bag and ran to the bus stop.
°**paramedic** [pærə'medɪk]	Rettungssanitäter/in	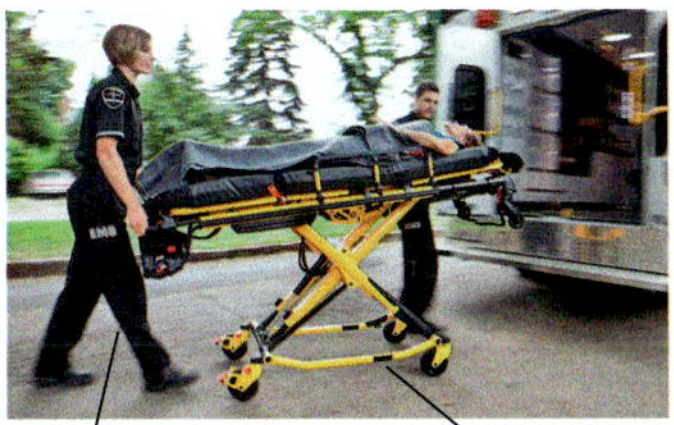 **paramedic** **stretcher**
°**stretcher** ['stretʃə]	Trage, (Trag-)Bahre	
°**rush** sb. **to …** [rʌʃ]	jn. auf dem schnellsten Weg nach …/zu … bringen	The driver was badly hurt, so the paramedics **~ed** him **to** the nearest hospital.
°**sleepless** ['sliːpləs]	schlaflos	We missed our plane and spent a ~ night at the airport.
°**love** [lʌv] *(infml)*	Liebling	
°**take it easy**	sich schonen	! **Take it easy.** *(infml)* = **1.** Reg dich nicht auf. / Bleib mal locker. **2.** Schone dich.
°**lie back**	sich zurücklehnen, sich entspannen	
°**nurse** [nɜːs]	(Kranken-)Pfleger/in	three **nurses** 
°**serious** ['sɪəriəs]	ernst(haft)	a **serious** accident/illness/problem/…
°**bruise** [bruːz]	Bluterguss, Prellung	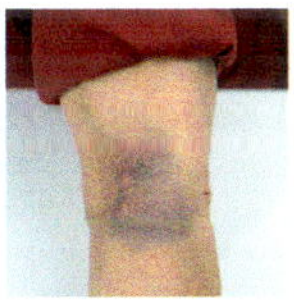 a **bruise**  **bones**
°**bone** [bəʊn]	Knochen	
°**counsellor** ['kaʊnsələ]	Berater/in; Betreuer/in	The high school ~ will help you if you have problems.

Skills training

p. 45 **revolution** [revə'luːʃn]	Revolution	! Betonung auf der 3. Silbe: **revolution** [revə'luːʃn]
wage ['weɪdʒ], *oft auch:* **wages** *(pl)*	Lohn, Gehalt	When dad was young, he had a ~ of £ 180 per week. These days, his **~s** are much higher.
conditions *(pl)* [kən'dɪʃnz]	Bedingungen, Verhältnisse	It's too cold and too noisy in this office. I can't work in these ~.
keep an eye on sb./sth.	jn./etwas im Auge behalten; ein (wachsames) Auge auf jn./etwas haben	**Keep an ~** on your little brother, please. I have to make a phone call.
sweatshop ['swetʃɒp]	Ausbeutungsbetrieb	

	factory ['fæktəri]	Fabrik	a **factory** 
	impossible [ɪm'pɒsəbl]	unmöglich	It's ~ to run a mile in two minutes. **possible ◄► impossible**
	inside out [ɪnsaɪd 'aʊt]	verkehrt herum, auf links *(Kleidung)*	You're wearing your T-shirt **inside ~**.
p. 46	**engineer** [endʒɪ'nɪə]	Ingenieur/in; Techniker/in	**software engineer** = Softwareentwickler/in
	billboard ['bɪlbɔːd] *(AE)*	Plakatwand, Werbeplakat	
	recruitment [rɪ'kruːtmənt]	Anwerbung, Einstellung *(von Personal)*	The ~ campaign for next year's teachers will start in February.
	quote [kwəʊt]	Zitat	Nomen: **quote** – Verb: **quote** (zitieren)
	put sth. **up**	etwas aufhängen *(Bild usw.)*	 They're **putting up** a picture.
	feature ['fiːtʃə]	vorkommen, mitwirken	She **was ~d** in the campaign. (Sie wurde in der Kampagne gezeigt/war Teil der Kampagne.)
	receive [rɪ'siːv]	erhalten, empfangen	a more formal word for **get** **receive a letter ◄► send a letter**
	encourage [ɪn'kʌrɪdʒ]	ermutigen, ermuntern	My parents **~d** me to apply for the job.
	male [meɪl]	männlich; männliche Person, männliches Tier	The police are looking for a 40-year-old ~. **male ◄► female**
	stereotype ['steriətaɪp]	Stereotyp, Klischee(vorstellung)	The film's main character doesn't seem real to me. It's just the ~ of a schoolgirl in love.
	people of colour	Nichtweiße, Menschen nichtweißer Hautfarbe	
	minority [maɪ'nɒrəti]	Minderheit	The boys in our class are in the ~. (= There are more girls than boys in our class.) **majority ◄► minority**
	engineering [endʒɪ'nɪərɪŋ]	Ingenieurwesen, Maschinenbau, Technik	
	career [kə'rɪə]	Karriere; (schulischer/beruflicher) Werdegang	"Should I have children first, or a ~ first?" she asked herself.
	gender ['dʒendə]	Geschlecht *(als soziales Merkmal)*	
	just about	so ziemlich, nahezu; (so) ungefähr	She knows **just ~** everything about cars. Oh no! My train is leaving … **just ~** now!
p. 47	**location** [ləʊ'keɪʃn]	Ort *(Standort; Einsatzort, Drehort)*	

storyline ['stɔːrilaɪn]	Handlung *(z.B. eines Films/ einer Geschichte)*	
script [skrɪpt]	Drehbuch	
rescue ['reskjuː]	retten	He fell into the river, but a dog **~d** him. Verb: **rescue** – Nomen: **rescue** (Rettung(sdienst))
identify [aɪ'dentɪfaɪ]	erkennen, identifizieren	Do you think you can ~ the boy who took your bike?

Unit 3: Future visions

pp. 54–55

vision ['vɪʒn]	Vision; Vorstellung	Is the driverless car just a ~ of the future? ! Betonung auf der 1. Silbe: **vision** ['vɪʒn]
exoskeleton ['eksəʊskelɪtn]	Exoskelett, Außenskelett	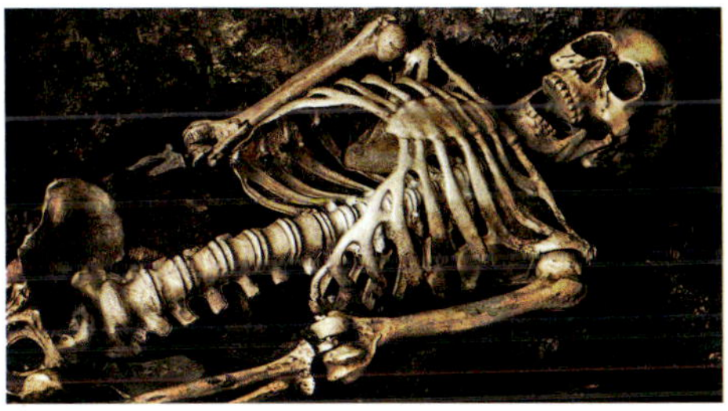 **skeleton** ['skelɪtn] = Skelett.
use [juːs]	Gebrauch, Verwendung	**make use of sth.** = Gebrauch machen von etwas, etwas nutzen My flat is very small, so I have to find clever ways to **make ~ of** the little space I have. ! Verb: **use** [juːz] – Nomen: **use** [juːs]
firefighter ['faɪəfaɪtə]	Feuerwehrmann/-frau	
deliver [dɪ'lɪvə]	(aus)liefern	Stay at home and be lazy! We ~ pizzas to your door.
drone [drəʊn]	Drohne	 a **drone**
parcel ['pɑːsl]	Paket, Päckchen	
medicine ['medsn]	Medizin; Arznei(mittel), Medikament	! Betonung auf der 1. Silbe: **medicine** ['medsn]
contact lens ['kɒntækt lenz]	Kontaktlinse	
power ['paʊə]	Energie, Strom	! **power** = **1.** Energie, Strom; **2.** Macht, Kraft, Stärke
pillow ['pɪləʊ]	Kopfkissen	
driverless ['draɪvələs]	fahrerlos, führerlos	= without a driver
scientist ['saɪəntɪst]	(Natur-)Wissenschaftler/in	

Theme 1

p.56 **watch** [wɒtʃ]	Armbanduhr	a **watch** 
touch [tʌtʃ]	berühren, anfassen	Don't ~ the plates. They're hot.
wearable ['weərəbl]	tragbar *(Kleidung)*	How many ~ electronic products do you own?
device [dɪ'vaɪs]	Gerät, Apparat	A watch is a ~ that tells you the time.
wireless ['waɪələs]	drahtlos, Funk-	

-less („-los")

driverless	fahrerlos, führerlos	**helpless**	hilflos	**meatless**	fleischlos
		homeless	obdachlos	**sleepless**	schlaflos
endless	endlos	**hopeless**	hoffnungslos	**wireless**	drahtlos

headphones *(pl)* ['hedfəʊnz]	*(ein)* Kopfhörer	**a pair of wireless headphones** 
carry ['kæri]	tragen; befördern, transportieren	She was **~ing** a heavy bag. It's a big ferry. It can ~ up to 120 cars. **!** *Nicht verwechseln:* • She's **carrying** two heavy bags. • She's **wearing** a red T-shirt. 
board [bɔːd]	Tafel *(im Klassenraum)*	
gym [dʒɪm]	Fitnessraum, Fitnessstudio	**! gym** = **1.** Sporthalle, Turnhalle; **2.** Fitnessraum, Fitnessstudio
data ['deɪtə]	Daten	**!** *English:* The **data shows** that … / The **data was** collected in … *German:* Die **Daten zeigen**, dass … / Die **Daten wurden** in … gesammelt.
exercise *(no pl)* ['eksəsaɪz]	Bewegung, *(körperliches)* Training	**! 1. exercise** *(no pl)* = Bewegung – My parents say I need more **exercise**. **2. exercise(s)** = Übung(en) – I couldn't do **exercises** 4 and 5.
p.57 **buzz** [bʌz]	summen	A lot of bees were **~ing** around the flowers.
finish sth. ['fɪnɪʃ]	etwas aufessen, austrinken; etwas aufbrauchen	**! finish** = **1.** (be)enden; **2.** aufessen, austrinken; aufbrauchen
groan [grəʊn]	stöhnen	He **~ed** when he read the message.
head-mounted display [hed maʊntɪd dɪ'spleɪ]	Datenhelm, Datenbrille, Videobrille	**display** = Bildschirm, Anzeige(gerät)

Theme 2

p. 58 **keep on**	weitermachen	**keep (on) doing sth.** ◄► **stop doing sth.**

keep, kept, kept

1. keep	Can I **keep** your pen or do you want it back? You should **keep** milk in a cool place. Put on some gloves to **keep** your hands warm. Be careful. **Keep away** from the fire. **Keep me posted**, please.	**behalten** **aufbewahren** **(warm/...) halten** **sich fernhalten von** **auf dem Laufenden halten**
2. keep sth. up	You're doing a good job. **Keep it up!**	**Mach weiter so!**
3. keep on	If you **keep on** like this, you'll get in trouble.	**weitermachen**
keep (on) doing sth.	We **kept (on) walking** till we got to a village. I tried to talk to him, but he **kept shouting** at me.	**etwas immer weiter/ immer wieder/ständig tun**

sustainable [sə'steɪnəbl]	nachhaltig, umweltverträglich; zukunftsfähig	To be ~, we have to plant as many trees as we cut down. **sustainable living** = nachhaltige Lebensweise
growth [grəʊθ]	Wachstum	Verb: **grow** – Nomen: **growth**
the Middle Ages *(pl)* [mɪdl 'eɪdʒɪz]	das Mittelalter	**!** *English:* The **Middle Ages are** sometimes called "The Dark Ages". *German:* Das **Mittelalter wird** manchmal „das Dunkle Zeitalter" genannt.
billion ['bɪliən]	Milliarde	= one thousand million (1,000,000,000)
7000 BC [biː 'siː]	7000 v. Chr.	
1000 AD [eɪ 'diː]	1000 n. Chr.	
p. 59 **graph** [græf], *BE auch:* [grɑːf]	Diagramm, Kurve	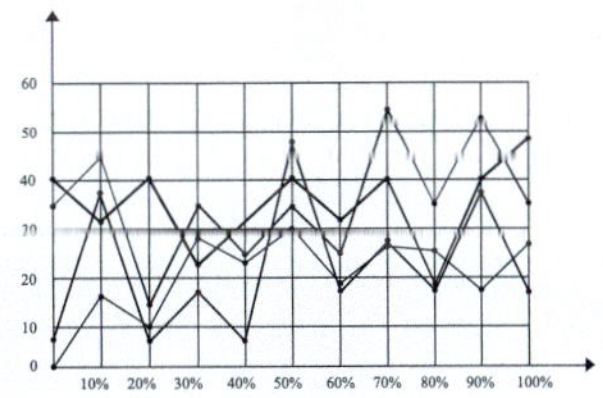 What do these **~s** tell us?
pessimistic [pesɪ'mɪstɪk]	pessimistisch	**!** Adjektiv: **pessimistic** – Nomen: **1. pessimist** ['pesɪmɪst] (Pessimist/in); **2. pessimism** ['pesɪmɪzəm] (Pessimismus)
optimistic [ɒptɪ'mɪstɪk]	optimistisch	**!** Adjektiv: **optimistic** – Nomen: **1. optimist** ['ɒptɪmɪst] (Optimist/in); **2. optimism** ['ɒptɪmɪzəm] (Optimismus)
in my/your/... view	meiner/deiner/... Ansicht nach	= in my/your/... opinion

Focus on language

p. 60 **frontier (with)** ['frʌntɪə]	Grenze (zu)	**new frontiers** = Neuland, neue Ufer
fascinate ['fæsɪneɪt]	faszinieren	I've always been **~d** by stories about other planets.
success [sək'ses]	Erfolg	Nomen: **success** – Adjektiv: **successful** – Verb: **succeed (in)** [sək'siːd] (Erfolg haben)

	Martian ['mɑːʃn]	Marsmensch	a person or creature from the planet **Mars** [mɑːz]
	planet ['plænɪt]	Planet	! Betonung auf der 1. Silbe: **planet** ['plænɪt]
	controversial [kɒntrə'vɜːʃl]	kontrovers, umstritten	His last book was **~**. Some people loved it but most hated it.
	prediction [prɪ'dɪkʃn]	Vorhersage, Voraussage	Nomen: **prediction** – Verb: **predict** [prɪ'dɪkt] (voraussagen, vorhersagen)
	by 8 pm / by next year / by 2030 / …	bis 20 Uhr / bis nächstes Jahr / bis (zum Jahr) 2030 / …	They should be here **~ 8 pm**. (= not later than 8 pm)
	difficulty ['dɪfɪkəlti]	Schwierigkeit(en)	I always have **difficulties** with Spanish verbs. Adjektiv: **difficult** – Nomen: **difficulty**
	pioneer [paɪə'nɪə]	Pionier/in	
	would-be ['wʊd biː]	künftige(r, s), angehende(r, s); Möchtegern-	What training do **~-be** space travellers need? I don't like those TV programmes with all the **~-be** pop stars. I think they're boring.
	sign up (for) [saɪn 'ʌp]	sich anmelden (für)	Dad has just **~ed up for** a cooking class.
	concentrate (on) ['kɒnsntreɪt]	sich konzentrieren (auf)	Verb: **concentrate** ['kɒnsntreɪt] – Nomen: **concentration** [kɒnsn'treɪʃn] (Konzentration) ! *English:* I can't **concentrate on** the test. *German:* Ich kann **mich** nicht **auf** den Test **konzentrieren**.
p. 61	**make it**	es schaffen, Erfolg haben	Will she **~ it** as a professional football player? I'd like to see you, but I won't **~ it** this evening.
	suit [suːt]	Anzug, Kostüm	 **suits** **a diving suit** **a spacesuit**
	lovely ['lʌvli]	sehr schön, wunderbar, herrlich	We had ~ weather last week. It was warm and sunny every day.
	choir ['kwaɪə]	Chor	a **choir** 
p. 62	**wishful thinking** [wɪʃfl 'θɪŋkɪŋ]	Wunschdenken	He thinks he'll be a famous rock star one day, but that's just **wishful ~**.
	destination [destɪ'neɪʃn]	Reiseziel, Fahrtziel	You will reach your ~ in seven hours.
	several ['sevrəl]	mehrere, einige	There are ~ good restaurants in our neighbourhood. (= more than a few)
	explore [ɪk'splɔː]	erforschen, erkunden	Do you think it's exciting to ~ other planets?

unfortunately [ʌnˈfɔːtʃənətli]	unglücklicherweise, leider	We were planning a barbecue, but ~ it rained. **fortunately** ◀▶ **unfortunately** (glücklicherweise ◀▶ unglücklicherweise)

Text

pp. 63–64 and pp. 130–131

global warming [gləʊbl ˈwɔːmɪŋ]	Erderwärmung	
cause sth. [kɔːz]	etwas bewirken, verursachen	The bad weather **~d** many problems. **!** *English:* The bad weather **caused** many trains **to be** late. (*nicht:* … ~~caused that~~ …) *German:* Das schlechte Wetter **bewirkte, dass** sich viele Züge **verspäteten**. / Das schlechte Wetter **verursachte die Verspätung** vieler Züge.
rise [raɪz], **rose** [rəʊz], **risen** [ˈrɪzən]	(an)steigen	Clouds of smoke **rose** from the building. Prices for food haven't **risen** much lately.
by accident	aus Versehen; zufällig	**! accident** = **1.** Unfall; **2.** Versehen; Zufall
little, less [les], **least** [liːst]	wenig	• **little** time ◀▶ **much** time **less** time ◀▶ **more** time **the least** time ◀▶ **the most** time • Travelling by train is **less** expensive than travelling by plane. Taking the bus is **the least** expensive.

(a) little — (a) few

(a) little steht mit **nicht zählbaren Nomen** wie **cheese, milk, money, time, traffic**.
few steht mit dem Plural von **zählbaren Nomen**.

! Beachte die Unterschiede zwischen **little** und **a little** und **few** und **a few**.	We had very **little money** (= *not much money*) when we were young.	**wenig/nicht viel** Geld
	Dad gave me **a little money** (= *some money*) and sent me to the shops.	**etwas/ein bisschen** Geld
	There were **few people** (= *not many people*) in the streets, so I felt a bit scared.	**wenige/nicht viele** Leute
	There were **a few people** (= *some people*) at the ticket office, but I didn't have to wait long.	**einige/ein paar** Leute

mainland [ˈmeɪnlænd]	Festland	**mainland** ◀▶ **island**
on my/your/her/… own [əʊn]	allein, selbstständig *(ohne Unterstützung)*	Ryan didn't want to dance, so Olivia danced **on her ~**. The cake looks great. Did you make it **on your ~**?
mob [mɒb]	Mob, Menschenmenge	A ~ of about 20 football fans was waiting on the platform.
shed [ʃed]	Schuppen *(Hütte, Lagerraum)*	a **garden shed** 

graveyard ['greɪvjɑːd]	Friedhof	an old **graveyard**  gravestones
pant [pænt]	keuchen, hecheln	You're **~ing** like a dog. You ran too fast.
fear (of) [fɪə]	Furcht, Angst (vor)	I was afraid, but didn't show my **~**. Brazil? Not with my **~ of** flying! ! **Angst haben (vor)** = **be afraid/scared/frightened (of)**
crowd [kraʊd]	(Menschen-)Menge	a **huge crowd** 
row [rəʊ]	rudern	 **rowing boat** ['rəʊɪŋ bəʊt] = Ruderboot
(just) in case … [keɪs]	(nur) für den Fall, dass …	Let's take an umbrella, **just in ~** it rains. **In (the) case** of fire, don't panic. (Im Falle von …)
bath [bɑːθ]	Bad; Badewanne	! *English:* **have a bath** *or* **take a bath** *German:* **baden, ein Bad nehmen** *(in der Badewanne)*
backwards ['bækwədz]	rückwärts; nach hinten	I'm learning to drive. I find it hard to drive **~**. And I often forget to look **~** in the mirror. **forward(s) ◄► backward(s)**
It's the way you do it.	So macht man das.	

German "man"

you **one**	**You** should wash **your** hands before every meal. **One** should wash **one's** hands before every meal. ! In der <u>Umgangssprache</u> wird meist **you** für das deutsche „man" verwendet, während **one** eher förmlich klingt.	▶ **Man (Jede/r)** sollte sich vor jeder Mahlzeit die Hände waschen.
they **people**	**They** say it always rains in England, but that's not true. **People** say it always rains in England, but that's not true.	▶ **Man** sagt (**Die Leute** sagen), dass es in England immer regnet, …
the passive	The boy **was taken** to hospital, but it was too late. Nothing **could be done**.	▶ **Man** brachte den Jungen ins Krankenhaus, … **Man** konnte nichts mehr tun.

facing forwards/ backwards ['feɪsɪŋ]	nach vorn/hinten schauend; mit dem Gesicht nach vorn/hinten	 He just stood there  a restaurant table
dizzy ['dɪzi]	schwindelig	All the noise and the lights made me feel **~**.
blow [bləʊ], **blew** [bluː], **blown** [bləʊn]	blasen, pusten; wehen *(Wind)*	I **blew** into the saxophone but couldn't get a sound. Please **~** out the candles when you leave. The wind was **~ing** all night.
faint [feɪnt]	schwindelig; schwach	Adjektiv: **faint** – Verb: **faint** (in Ohnmacht fallen)
p. 65 **narrator** [nəˈreɪtə]	Erzähler/in	**first-person narrator** = Ich-Erzähler/in
message in a bottle	Flaschenpost	
		! Wenn du den Text auf den Seiten 63–64 gelesen hast, kannst du die folgenden neuen Wörter daraus zusätzlich lernen.
pp. 63–64 °**deserted** [dɪˈzɜːtɪd]	menschenleer, wie ausgestorben	
°**derelict** ['derəlɪkt]	heruntergekommen, verfallen	 **derelict buildings**
°**burst** [bɜːst], **burst**, **burst**	bersten, platzen	
°**slow down** [sləʊ ˈdaʊn]	(sich) verlangsamen, langsamer werden	Don't drive so fast! There are children in the road – please **~ down**. 
°**put** sth. **off**	etwas verschieben, hinauszögern	Don't **~** it **off** till tomorrow. Do it now.

put		
put sth. in	Please **put in** (= fill in) your name and address.	einsetzen, eingeben
put sth. off	Do it now. Don't **put** it **off** till tomorrow.	verschieben, hinauszögern
put sth. on	It's cold outside. I'd **put on** a pullover. The driver **put on** the police car's siren.	**1.** anziehen; aufsetzen **2.** einschalten
put sth. up	Can you help me to **put up** this picture?	aufhängen

°**tiny** ['taɪni]	winzig	= very small **tiny** ◄► **huge**
°**loner** ['ləʊnə]	Einzelgänger/in	

°**hang around, hung, hung** *(infml)*	herumhängen	After school we often ~ **around** at the bus stop.
°... **whom** you could trust. [hu:m] *(fml)*	..., wem man trauen konnte.	
°**slip** [slɪp]	(aus)rutschen	He **~ped** on the wet grass and fell down.
°**contain** [kən'teɪn]	enthalten	I can't eat this chocolate. It **~s** nuts.
°**storm** [stɔ:m]	stürmen	The soldiers **~ed** down the hill and into the village.
°**splash** [splæʃ]	spritzen, platschen	Dogs love **~ing** through the water.
°**drag** [dræg]	zerren, (mit Mühe) ziehen, schleifen	I didn't feel great, but I **~ged** myself to work. (... ich schleppte mich zur Arbeit)
°**shore** [ʃɔ:]	Ufer *(eines Sees)*	 **shore**
°**supply** [sə'plaɪ]	Versorgung, Lieferung; Vorrat	We have no more **supplies**. We'll have to go shopping.
°**pause** [pɔ:z]	kurz innehalten, Pause machen	She **~d** a moment before she answered my question.
°**breath** [breθ]	Atem	**pause for breath** = kurz Pause machen, um Luft zu holen
°**own** [əʊn]	besitzen	I ~ this boat. = This is my boat. I'm the owner.
°**belong to** sb. [bɪ'lɒŋ]	jm. gehören; zu jm. gehören	This boat **~s to** me. = I own this boat.
°**they would sit ...**	sie saßen (früher) immer ...	

German "Früher ..." – <u>used to</u> + infinitive / <u>would</u> + infinitive

- Wenn man beschreiben will, was **früher** der Fall war, aber heute nicht mehr, dann kann man **used to ...** verwenden:

We **used to live** in Manchester.	Wir wohnten früher in Manchester.
Manchester United **used to be** my favourite team.	Früher war Manchester United meine Lieblingsmannschaft.
I **used to spend** a lot of money on sports magazines.	Ich habe früher immer viel Geld für Sportzeitschriften ausgegeben.

- Wenn es um <u>Handlungen</u> geht – also um Dinge, die man **früher immer gemacht** hat –, kann man auch **would ...** benutzen:

Grandpa **would visit** us every Sunday after church.	Opa besuchte uns jeden Sonntag nach der Kirche. / Opa pflegte uns jeden Sonntag ... zu besuchen.
We **would** often **go** for long walks in the woods.	Wir haben oft lange Spaziergänge im Wald gemacht.

°**magic** ['mædʒɪk]	Zauberei, Magie	! Betonung auf der 1. Silbe: **<u>magic</u>** ['mædʒɪk]
°**sense (of ...)** [sens]	Gefühl (von), (...-)Bewusstsein	His ~ **of** time is terrible. He's always late. **sense of time** = Zeitgefühl
°**beat down (on)** [bi:t], **beat, beaten** ['bi:tn] *(infml)*	runterknallen (auf) *(Sonne, Regen)*	The rain that was **~ing down on** the roof made a lot of noise.

	°**replay** sth. [riː'pleɪ]	etwas (vor dem inneren Auge) noch einmal Revue passieren lassen; sich etwas noch einmal vor Augen führen	She lay in bed and **~ed** her accident over and over again.
	°**nightmare** ['naɪtmeə]	Albtraum	= a very frightening dream or a very frightening experience After the attack I had terrible **~s** for months. Our flight was a ~. Everything went wrong!

Skills training

p.66	**robot** ['rəʊbɒt]	Roboter	
	exhibition [eksɪ'bɪʃn]	Messe; Ausstellung	This new device was presented at last year's technology ~. (Messe) I want to see the Chagall ~ at the museum. (Ausstellung)
	and so on	und so weiter	= etc.
	gadget ['gædʒɪt]	Gerät, Apparat, technischer Krimskrams	= a device, usually a small one, that does something useful
	do without sth.	ohne etwas auskommen	You can keep that pen. I can ~ **without** it. I have many more.
	drawing ['drɔːɪŋ]	Zeichnung	**do a drawing** = eine Zeichnung machen Nomen: **drawing** – Verb: **draw** [drɔː], **drew** [druː], **drawn** [drɔːn] (zeichnen)
p.67	**complaint** [kəm'pleɪnt]	Beschwerde	Verb: **complain** – Nomen: **complaint** **make a complaint (about sth.)** = eine Beschwerde vorbringen (über etwas), etwas beanstanden
	uncomfortable [ʌn'kʌmftəbl]	unbequem	**comfortable** ◄► **uncomfortable**
	take sth. **off** [teɪk 'ɒf]	etwas abnehmen, absetzen *(Brille, Hut)*, etwas ausziehen *(Kleidung)*	**put sth. on** ◄► **take sth. off**
	battery ['bætəri]	Batterie, Akku	**battery life** = Batterie-/Akku-Laufzeit
	poor [pɔː, pʊə]	schlecht, schwach, minderwertig	**!** **poor** = **1.** arm; **2.** schlecht, schwach, minderwertig
	in addition [ə'dɪʃn]	außerdem	This mobile is very expensive. **In** ~, it's made of plastic and will break easily.
	be supposed to be/do sth. [sə'pəʊzd]	etwas sein sollen / etwas tun sollen	We**'re** not ~ **to** use our mobiles at school, but some of us do. I haven't heard their new CD yet, but it**'s** ~ **to** be really good.
	count [kaʊnt]	zählen	I can ~ from 1 to 10 in Russian. Sure I'll help you. You can ~ on me!
	accurate ['ækjərət]	genau, präzise	= exact
	circumstances *(pl)* ['sɜːkəmstənsɪz]	Umstände	**under the circumstances** = unter diesen Umständen
	refund ['riːfʌnd]	Rückzahlung, (Kosten-)Erstattung	Nomen: **refund** ['riːfʌnd] – Verb: **refund** [rɪ'fʌnd] (erstatten, rückerstatten)

	attach (to) [ə'tætʃ]	anfügen; anhängen	Can you ~ the photos and mail them to me?
	receipt [rɪ'siːt]	(Kauf-)Beleg, Quittung, Kassenzettel	! **False friends:** *English* **receipt** [rɪ'siːt] = *German* **Beleg, Quittung, Kassenzettel** *English* **recipe** ['resəpi] = *German* **(Koch-)Rezept**
	within [wɪ'ðɪn]	innerhalb (von), in	We have to finish our project ~ two weeks.
	last (for) [lɑːst]	(an)halten, (an)dauern	! *German* **dauern**: **1.** *(Zeit benötigen)* **take** – It usually **takes** 15 minutes to get home, but this evening it **took (us)** an hour. **2.** *(andauern; halten)* **last** – A football match **lasts** 90 minutes. The battery **lasts for** 12 hours.
	vague [veɪg]	vage, unbestimmt	I have only a ~ idea about how a computer works.
	formal ['fɔːml]	formell, förmlich *(Kleidung)*	Your letter of application should be quite ~. It was just a party, so I didn't wear ~ clothes. **formal ◄► informal** [ɪn'fɔːml] (informell, locker)
p. 69	**thunder** ['θʌndə]	Donner	

MORE CHALLENGE 1

p. 30	°**poach** [pəʊtʃ]	wildern, unerlaubt jagen	= hunt illegally
	°**be at record level(s)** ['levl]	einen Höchststand / ein Rekordniveau erreicht haben	**level** = Niveau; Stufe
	°**consequence** ['kɒnsɪkwəns]	Konsequenz, Folge	I've been a bit lazy recently. The ~ was that I did badly in two exams. / **As a ~,** I did badly in two exams. **as a consequence** = als Folge, folglich ! Betonung auf der 1. Silbe: **consequence** ['kɒnsɪkwəns]
	°**certain** ['sɜːtn]	bestimmte(r, s), gewisse(r, s)	I don't want to give any names, but ~ people in our team are a bit difficult to work with.
	°**extinction** [ɪk'stɪŋkʃn]	Ausrottung, Aussterben	Nomen: **extinction** – Adjektiv: **extinct** [ɪk'stɪŋkt] (ausgestorben)
	°**anti-** ['ænti]	anti-, gegen-	
	°**moon** [muːn]	Mond	the **moon** 
	°**hunt** [hʌnt]	Jagd	**on the hunt** = auf der Jagd
	°**surround** [sə'raʊnd]	umgeben	An island is **~ed** by water on all sides.
	°**track** [træk]	(zurück-, nach)verfolgen, beobachten	! **track** = **1.** Pfad, (Feld-)Weg; **2.** (zurück-, nach)verfolgen, beobachten
	°**armed** [ɑːmd]	bewaffnet	**armed soldiers** 
	°**confront** sb. [kən'frʌnt]	jn. konfrontieren, jm. entgegentreten	! Betonung auf der 2. Silbe: **confront** [kən'frʌnt]

°**put** sth. *(+ Adverb)*	etwas *(auf eine bestimmte Art)* ausdrücken, formulieren	

put sth. politely/simply ...	**(etwas höflich/einfach/ ... ausdrücken)**
I don't understand. Can you **put it more simply**?	... Kannst du es einfacher ausdrücken?
To put it mildly, the service at the hotel was a disaster.	Gelinde gesagt, ...
The food was ... how shall I **put it**? ... a bit disappointing.	Das Essen war ... wie soll ich sagen? ...
As my brother put it, "You can't have everything."	Wie mein Bruder es ausdrückte, ...
I often find it difficult to **put my feelings into words**.	... meine Gefühle in Worten auszudrücken.

°**therefore** ['ðeəfɔː]	daher, deshalb	= a more formal word for "so" or "that's why"
°**at a time**	jeweils, ununterbrochen	**three weeks at a time** = drei Wochen am Stück
°**despite** [dɪ'spaɪt]	trotz	= in spite of

MORE CHALLENGE 2

p. 52 °**bicycle** ['baɪsɪkl]	Fahrrad	"Bike" is short for "**bicycle**".
°**shameful** ['ʃeɪmfl]	schändlich, beschämend	
°**well-heeled** [wel 'hiːld] *(infml)*	gut betucht, wohlhabend	A **~-heeled** area is one where lots of rich people live.
°**draw** sb.'s **attention to** sth. [ə'tenʃn]	js. Aufmerksamkeit auf etwas lenken	
°**instinctive** [ɪn'stɪŋktɪv]	instinktiv	! Betonung auf der 2. Silbe: **instinctive** [ɪn'stɪŋktɪv]
°**intervene (in)** [ɪntə'viːn]	eingreifen, einschreiten (in, bei); sich einmischen (in)	The kids are fighting again ... should we ~?
°**state** [steɪt]	Zustand	I was in a ~ of shock when I heard the news. ! **state** = **1.** Staat; **2.** Zustand
°**menacing** ['menəsɪŋ]	drohend, bedrohlich	If something or someone is ~, you're afraid of it/them.
°**curse** [kɜːs]	fluchen	He **~d** when he arrived on the platform and saw that his train had just left.
°**further** ['fɜːðə]	weiter; weitere	Stop there. Don't walk any ~. Do you have any ~ questions?
°**be about**	da sein, anwesend sein, sich aufhalten	There **weren't** many people ~ when the attack happened.
°**concerned (for/about)** [kən'sɜːnd]	besorgt (um)	A boy is missing from his home in Stoke-on-Trent. The police are **concerned for** his welfare.
°**welfare** ['welfeə]	Wohl, Wohlergehen	
°**motorcycle** ['məʊtəsaɪkl]	Motorrad	a **motorcycle** 
°**straight** [streɪt]	gerade	I like bends. **Straight** roads are boring when you're riding a motorcycle.

	°**If he were to …**	Wenn/Falls er …	→ • **If he were to win** the race, he would get a lot of money. (**Wenn/Falls er gewinnen sollte, …/ Sollte er gewinnen, …**) • **If it were to snow** tomorrow, we could go skiing. (**Wenn/Falls es schneien sollte, …/ Sollte es schneien, …**)
	°**retreat** [rɪ'triːt]	sich zurückziehen	I didn't want to get into a fight, so I **~ed**.
	°**inexplicable** [ɪnɪk'splɪkəbl]	unerklärlich	When something is ~, it cannot be explained.
	°**incident** ['ɪnsɪdənt]	Vorfall, Begebenheit	= something that happens
	°**pass** [pɑːs]	vorübergehen, vorbeigehen *(Zeit, Moment, Gelegenheit)*	When the first wave of shock has **~ed**, we'll be able to think clearly again. I wanted to tell her the truth, but the moment **~ed**, and then it was too late.
	°**account** [ə'kaʊnt]	Bericht, Beschreibung	Your ~ of the incident sounds very different from your friend's!
	°**that sort of thing** [sɔːt]	so etwas; dergleichen	What kind of music do you like? – Hip hop, rap, **that ~ of thing**.
	°**misgivings** *(pl)* [mɪs'gɪvɪŋz]	Bedenken	= bad feelings
p. 53	°**enrich** [ɪn'rɪtʃ]	bereichern, anreichern	= make sth. better, e.g. by adding things You can ~ this sauce by adding some cream.

MORE CHALLENGE 3

p. 74	°**fellow student** ['feləʊ]	Mitschüler/in	Our ~ **passengers** on the plane were very patient when our baby cried.
	°**embarrass** sb. [ɪm'bærəs]	jn. in Verlegenheit bringen	I hate it when my parents ~ me in front of my friends. It **~es** me when this happens. = I'm embarrassed by what happens.
	°**humour** ['hjuːmə]	Humor	! Betonung auf der 1. Silbe: **humour** ['hjuːmə] *English:* She has **a good sense of humour**. / She has **no sense of humour**. *German:* Sie hat **Humor**. / Sie hat **keinen (Sinn für) Humor**.
p. 75	°**rob** [rɒb]	ausrauben, berauben	A bank robber is someone who **~s** a bank. ! You **rob somebody/a bank/a supermarket**. (jn./etwas ausrauben, berauben) You **steal something from somebody**. (jm. etwas stehlen)
	°**class representative** [reprɪ'zentətɪv]	Klassensprecher/in	
	°**give a speech**	eine Rede halten	I'm always nervous when I have to ~ **a speech** or a presentation.
	°**expression** [ɪk'spreʃn]	Ausdruck	
	°**have** sth. **done (by** sb.**)**	etwas (von jm.) machen lassen	Your hair looks nice. Did you cut it yourself or did you ~ **it cut**? – I **had it cut by** Li.

Das **English – German dictionary** enthält den Wortschatz der Bände 1 bis 6 von *Lighthouse*. Wenn du wissen möchtest, was ein englisches Wort bedeutet, wie man es ausspricht oder wie es genau geschrieben wird, dann kannst du hier nachschlagen.

Im **Dictionary** werden folgende **Abkürzungen und Symbole** verwendet:

sb. = somebody · sth. = something · jn. = jemanden · jm. = jemandem
pl = *plural* (Mehrzahl) · *BE* = British English · *AE* = American English · *infml* = *informal* (umgangssprachlich)

° Mit diesem Kringel sind Wörter markiert, die nicht zum Lernwortschatz gehören.
Die **Fundstellenangaben** zeigen, wo ein Wort zum ersten Mal vorkommt.
Die Ziffern in Klammern bezeichnen Seitenzahlen:

I = *Lighthouse* Band 1 • II = *Lighthouse* Band 2 • III = *Lighthouse* Band 3 • IV = *Lighthouse* Band 4 • V = *Lighthouse* Band 5 • VI 1 (8) = *Lighthouse* Band 6, Unit 1, Seite 8

Tipps zur Arbeit mit einem Wörterbuch findest du im Skills file auf Seite 163.

A

a [ə] ein, eine I **£10 a week** 10 Pfund pro Woche II
able ['eɪbl]: **be able to do sth.** etwas tun können; fähig sein / in der Lage sein, etwas zu tun IV
Aboriginal [æbə'rɪdʒənl] Aborigine- *(die Ureinwohner/innen Australiens betreffend)* V
about [ə'baʊt]:
1. über I
2. ungefähr I
about me über mich I **be about to do sth.** im Begriff sein, etwas zu tun; kurz davor sein, etwas zu tun VI 1 (20) **I'm sorry about yesterday.** Es tut mir leid wegen gestern. II **The text is about ...** Der Text handelt von ... III **What about ...?** Wie wär's mit ...? I **What about you?** Und du? / Und was ist mit dir? I **what politics is about** worum es in der Politik geht VI 2 (36) **What's special about ...?** Was ist das Besondere an ...? III **Who is the text about?** Von wem handelt der Text? III **°be about** da sein, anwesend sein, sich aufhalten **°do sth. about it** etwas daran tun, etwas dagegen unternehmen
above [ə'bʌv] oben; über, oberhalb (von) VI 1 (19)
°abreast (of sb./sth.) [ə'brest] auf gleicher Höhe (mit jm./etwas)
°abroad [ə'brɔːd] im/ins Ausland
absolute ['æbsəluːt] absolute(r, s) IV
accent ['æksent] Akzent III
accept [ək'sept] akzeptieren, annehmen V
access ['ækses] Zugang, Zutritt VI 1 (12)
accident ['æksɪdənt]:
1. Unfall II
2. Versehen; Zufall VI 3 (63)
by accident aus Versehen; zufällig VI 3 (63)
accommodation [əkɒmə'deɪʃn] Unterkunft III
°accompany [ə'kʌmpəni] begleiten **accompanied by an adult** in Begleitung eines Erwachsenen
according to [ə'kɔːdɪŋ] laut, zufolge IV
account [ə'kaʊnt]:
1. Account, Konto V
°2. Bericht, Beschreibung
accurate ['ækjərət] genau, präzise VI 3 (67)
achievement [ə'tʃiːvmənt] Errungenschaft, Leistung V
across Dartmoor [ə'krɒs] über das Dartmoor II
act [ækt]:
1. handeln, sich verhalten; so tun, als ob V
2. Theater spielen; schauspielern II
°act out vorspielen, aufführen
action ['ækʃn]:
1. Aktion V
go into action einen Einsatz haben V
°2. Handlung, Tat
active ['æktɪv] aktiv II
activism ['æktɪvɪzəm] Aktivismus VI 2 (34)
activist ['æktɪvɪst] Aktivist/in VI 2 (34)
activity [æk'tɪvəti] Aktivität II
actor ['æktə] Schauspieler/in II
°actual ['æktʃuəl] tatsächliche(r, s), eigentliche(r, s)
actually ['æktʃuəli] eigentlich, tatsächlich V
AD [eɪ 'diː]: **1000 AD** 1000 n. Chr. VI 3 (58)
ad [æd] *(kurz für:* **advertisement***)* Anzeige, Inserat, Annonce V
°adapted from [ə'dæptɪd] (frei) nach
adapter [ə'dæptə] Adapter III
add (to) [æd] hinzufügen (zu) III
addicted (to) [ə'dɪktɪd] süchtig (nach), abhängig (von) V
addition [ə'dɪʃn]: **in addition** außerdem VI 3 (67)
address [ə'dres] Adresse, Anschrift I
°administration fee [ədmɪnɪ'streɪʃn fiː] Verwaltungsgebühr
admire [əd'maɪə] bewundern V
admission [əd'mɪʃn] Eintritt, Eintrittspreis IV
adopt [ə'dɒpt] adoptieren; *(Tier)* bei sich aufnehmen II
adult ['ædʌlt] Erwachsene(r) II
advance [əd'vɑːns] Voraus-, Vorab- VI 1 (15) **in advance** im Voraus VI 1 (15)
advantage [əd'vɑːntɪdʒ] Vorteil IV
adventure [əd'ventʃə] Abenteuer I
adventurous [əd'ventʃərəs] abenteuerlustig V
advert ['ædvɜːt] Anzeige, Werbung I
advertise (sth.) ['ædvətaɪz] Werbung machen (für etwas) V
advertisement [əd'vɜːtɪsmənt] Anzeige, Inserat, Annonce V
advertiser ['ædvətaɪzə] Werber/in, Werbetreibende(r) V
advertising ['ædvətaɪzɪŋ] Werbung, Reklame V
advice [əd'vaɪs] Rat(schlag), Ratschläge II **a piece of advice** ein Rat, ein Ratschlag IV
°affect [ə'fekt] beeinflussen, sich auswirken auf
afraid [ə'freɪd]: **be afraid (of)** Angst haben (vor) IV **I'm afraid** leider III
Africa ['æfrɪkə] Afrika I
after ['ɑːftə]:
1. nachdem IV
2. nach I
after dinner nach dem Abendessen/Abendbrot I **after that** danach IV **look after sb.** sich um jn. kümmern; auf jn. aufpassen I **run after sb.** hinter jm. herrennen IV
afternoon [ɑːftə'nuːn] Nachmittag I **in the afternoon** nachmittags, am Nachmittag I **on Friday afternoon** freitagnachmittags, am Freitagnachmittag I
afterwards ['ɑːftəwədz] hinterher, danach VI 2 (40)

again [ə'gen] wieder; noch einmal I °**every now and again** ab und zu, von Zeit zu Zeit
against [ə'genst] gegen III
age [eɪdʒ]:
1. Alter I
2. Zeitalter VI 3 (58)
ages *(pl, infml)* eine Ewigkeit VI 2 (36)
30 years of age 30 Jahre alt V
at the age of 16 mit 16; im Alter von 16 III
°**agency** ['eɪdʒənsi] Agentur, Organisation
aggressive [ə'gresɪv] aggressiv IV
ago [ə'gəʊ]: **two years ago** vor zwei Jahren III
agree [ə'griː]: **agree on sth.** in etwas übereinstimmen, sich einig sein bei etwas V **agree with sb./sth.** jm./etwas zustimmen; mit jm./etwas übereinstimmen II
agriculture ['ægrɪkʌltʃə] Landwirtschaft IV
ahead [ə'hed]: **Go ahead.** Nur zu. / Dann mal los. V
°**ahead (of sb./sth.)** vor, vorraus **There's still a long way ahead.** Es liegt noch ein weiter Weg vor uns.
aim [eɪm] Ziel III
aimed [eɪmd]: **be aimed at sb.** sich an jn. richten VI 1 (14)
air [eə] Luft II
airbrush ['eəbrʌʃ] (Foto) retuschieren, nachbessern VI 2 (34)
airport ['eəpɔːt] Flughafen III
°**alarm** [ə'lɑːm] Alarm; Alarmanlage
alarm clock [ə'lɑːm klɒk] Wecker I
alarmed [ə'lɑːmd] beunruhigt VI 2 (43)
alcohol ['ælkəhɒl] Alkohol IV
all [ɔːl]: **all (the)** alle I **all day** den ganzen Tag (lang) I **all over the world** auf der ganzen Welt IV **all right** gut; in Ordnung; OK IV **in all** insgesamt III **not ... at all** überhaupt nicht V
allergic (to) [ə'lɜːdʒɪk] allergisch (gegen) V
alligator ['ælɪgeɪtə] Alligator IV
allowed [ə'laʊd]: **be allowed to do sth.** etwas tun dürfen III
almost ['ɔːlməʊst] fast, nahezu, beinahe V
alone [ə'ləʊn] allein II **leave sb. alone** jn. in Ruhe lassen V
along the street [ə'lɒŋ] die Straße entlang II
alphabet ['ælfəbet] Alphabet I
already [ɔːl'redi] schon II
also ['ɔːlsəʊ] auch II
although [ɔːl'ðəʊ] obwohl V
always ['ɔːlweɪz] immer I
am [eɪ'em]: **9 am / 9 a.m.** 9 Uhr morgens/vormittags I
amazing [ə'meɪzɪŋ] erstaunlich III

ambulance ['æmbjələns] Krankenwagen II
American Indian [əmerɪkən 'ɪndiən] Indianer/in; indianisch IV
among [ə'mʌŋ] zwischen, unter *(mehreren Personen, Tieren, Dingen)* III
an [ən] ein, eine I
°**analyse** ['ænəlaɪz] analysieren, untersuchen
ancient ['eɪnʃənt] (ur)alt; antik IV
and [ænd], [ənd] und I **less and less** immer weniger III **more and more** immer mehr III
angry ['æŋgri] wütend II
animal ['ænɪml] Tier I
°**announce** [ə'naʊns] verkünden, bekanntgeben
announcement [ə'naʊnsmənt] Durchsage, Ansage; Bekanntgabe, Ankündigung IV
another [ə'nʌðə] ein anderer / eine andere / ein anderes; noch ein(e) II
answer ['ɑːnsə]:
1. Antwort I
2. antworten; beantworten II
answer the door aufmachen, zur/an die Tür gehen V **answer the phone** ans Telefon gehen V
anthem ['ænθəm]: **national anthem** Nationalhymne III
°**anti-** ['ænti] anti-, gegen
any ['eni]:
1. irgendein(e, r, s); jede(r) beliebige V
2. Any ideas? Irgendwelche Ideen? I
3. we don't have any ... wir haben kein/e ... II
not (...) any more nicht mehr VI 1 (19)
anybody ['enibɒdɪ]:
1. I didn't know anybody. Ich kannte niemanden. IV
2. *(in Fragen)* (irgend)jemand IV
anyone ['eniwʌn]:
1. I didn't know anyone. Ich kannte niemanden. IV
2. *(in Fragen)* (irgend)jemand IV
anything [els]:
1. Anything else? Sonst noch etwas? I **I can't do anything.** Ich kann nichts machen. II
2. *(in Fragen)* etwas, irgendetwas III
3. I'll do anything. Ich werde alles tun. III
anytime ['enitaɪm] jederzeit IV
°**anyway** ['eniweɪ]: **Where ... anyway?** Wo ... überhaupt?
anywhere ['eniweə]: **not (...) anywhere** nirgendwo; nirgendwohin III
apartheid [ə'pɑːtaɪt] Apartheid *(frühere System der Trennung zwischen Weißen und Schwarzen in Südafrika)* VI 1 (11)
apartment [ə'pɑːtmənt] Wohnung IV
appearance [ə'pɪərəns] Erscheinung(sbild), Aussehen V

apple ['æpl] Apfel I
°**appliance** [ə'plaɪəns] (Haushalts-)Gerät
application [æplɪ'keɪʃn] Bewerbung, Antrag V
application form [æplɪ'keɪʃn fɔːm] Bewerbungsformular, Antragsformular V
apply (for) [ə'plaɪ] sich bewerben (um) V
appointment [ə'pɔɪntmənt] Termin, Verabredung II
approach [ə'prəʊtʃ]:
1. Ansatz, Herangehensweise V
°**2.** sich nähern, näher kommen
appropriate [ə'prəʊpriət] angemessen, passend, geeignet IV
April ['eɪprəl] April I **April 1st joke** Aprilscherz IV
aquarium [ə'kweəriəm] Aquarium I
archery ['ɑːtʃəri] Bogenschießen II
°**architect** ['ɑːkɪtekt] Architekt/in
are [ɑː] bist; sind; seid I **Here you are.** Bitte schön. / Hier, bitte. I **How are you?** Wie geht's? / Wie geht es dir/euch? I **The mobiles are £10.** Die Handys kosten 10 Pfund. I
area ['eəriə] Gebiet, Gegend III
argue ['ɑːgjuː] argumentieren IV
argument ['ɑːgjumənt] Argument, Streit V
°**argumentative** [ɑːgju'mentətɪv] argumentativ
arm [ɑːm] Arm II
°**armed** [ɑːmd] bewaffnet
around [ə'raʊnd]:
1. um ... (herum) III
2. in ... umher, durch III
look around sich umsehen III **run around** umherrennen; herumlaufen II **See you around.** Bis dann. V
arrangement [ə'reɪndʒmənt] Vereinbarung II **make an arrangement** eine Vereinbarung treffen; etwas vereinbaren, etwas verabreden II
arrest sb. [ə'rest] jn. festnehmen, verhaften IV
arrival [ə'raɪvl] Ankunft III
arrive [ə'raɪv] ankommen II
art [ɑːt] Kunst I
article ['ɑːtɪkl] (Zeitungs-)Artikel III
artist ['ɑːtɪst] Künstler/in V
artistic [ɑː'tɪstɪk] künstlerisch; *auch:* künstlerisch begabt IV
as [æz], [əz]:
1. als, während IV
2. da, weil V
3. as a footballer/singer/... als Fußballer/in / Sänger/in / ... III
4. wie III
as much as $80 bis zu 80$; nicht weniger als 80$ IV **as much as you can** so viel, wie du kannst III **the same as ...** der-/die-/dasselbe wie ...; dieselben wie ... IV
as soon as [əz 'suːn əz] sobald, sowie III
Asian ['eɪʃn] Asiate/Asiatin; asiatisch IV

ask [ɑːsk] fragen I **ask for sth.** um etwas bitten II **ask questions** Fragen stellen I **ask sb. about sth.** sich bei jm. nach etwas erkundigen II **ask sb. the way** jn. nach dem Weg fragen II **ask sb. to do sth.** jn. bitten, etwas zu tun IV
asleep [ə'sliːp]: **be asleep** schlafen IV **fall asleep** einschlafen IV
assembly [ə'sembli] Schulversammlung, Morgenappell I
assistant [ə'sɪstənt] Helfer/in, Assistent/in V
astronaut ['æstrənɔːt] Astronaut/in V
at [æt], [ət]: **at (the age of) 16** mit 16; im Alter von 16 III **at 1 o'clock** um 1 Uhr / um 13 Uhr I **at a restaurant** in einem Restaurant I **at break** in der Pause *(zwischen Schulstunden)* II **at Ellie's house** bei Ellie daheim, bei Ellie zu Hause I **at first** zuerst, am Anfang II **at home** daheim, zu Hause I **at last** schließlich, endlich III **at least** mindestens, wenigstens II **at MARTINS** bei MARTINS I **at night** nachts, in der Nacht I **at school** in der Schule I **at the bottom (of)** unten, am unteren Ende (von) II **at the cinema** im Kino I **at the market** auf dem Markt I **at the moment** im Moment, gerade I **at the same time** zur selben Zeit, gleichzeitig V **at the top (of)** oben; am oberen Ende (von), an der Spitze (von) II **at the weekend** am Wochenende I **at this school** auf/an dieser Schule I **at work** bei der Arbeit, am Arbeitsplatz I
ate [eɪt], [et] *siehe* **eat**
attach (to) [ə'tætʃ] anfügen; anhängen *(an Brief, E-Mail)* VI 3 (67)
attack [ə'tæk]:
1. Angriff II
°2. angreifen
attention [ə'tenʃn] Aufmerksamkeit; Achtung! VI 2 (36) **pay attention (to)** aufmerksam zuhören; achten (auf), aufpassen (auf) VI 2 (36) °**draw sb.'s attention to sth.** js. Aufmerksamkeit auf etwas lenken
attic ['ætɪk] Dachboden IV
°**attitude** ['ætɪtjuːd] Einstellung, (Geistes-)Haltung
attraction [ə'trækʃn] Attraktion; Anziehungskraft V
audience ['ɔːdiəns] Publikum; Zuschauer/innen, Zuhörer/innen II
August ['ɔːgəst] August I
aunt [ɑːnt] Tante I
author ['ɔːθə] Autor/in IV
autumn ['ɔːtəm] Herbst II
available [ə'veɪləbl] erhältlich, verfügbar, *(Stelle)* frei IV **be available** zur Verfügung stehen, Zeit haben V
avatar ['ævətɑː] Avatar *(virtuelle Figur)* V
avenue ['ævənjuː] Allee, Prachtstraße *(in den USA oft Teil v. Straßennamen)* IV
average ['ævərɪdʒ] durchschnittlich; Durchschnitt V **on average** im Durchschnitt, durchschnittlich V
°**award** [ə'wɔːd] Preis *(Auszeichnung)*
away [ə'weɪ] weg, fort I **go away** verschwinden V
awesome ['ɔːsəm] *(AE, infml)* klasse, stark, großartig IV

B

back [bæk]:
1. zurück I
2. Rücken; Rückseite II
at the back hinten, im hinteren Teil IV
°**back cover** ['bæk kʌvə] Umschlagrückseite *(Buch)*
background ['bækgraʊnd] Hintergrund III
backstreet ['bækstriːt] *(kleinere)* Seitenstraße *(weitab von den Hauptstraßen)* V
backward(s) ['bækwədz] rückwärts; nach hinten VI 3 (64)
backyard [bæk'jɑːd] *(AE)* Garten *(hinter dem Haus)*, Hinterhof IV
bad [bæd] schlecht; schlimm I **... is bad news.** ... ist gefährlich. / ... ist (gar) nicht gut. V
badge [bædʒ] Anstecknadel, Button V
bag [bæg] Tasche, Beutel I
bagel ['beɪgl] Bagel IV
baked potato [beɪkt pə'teɪtəʊ] Ofenkartoffel *(in der Schale gebackene Kartoffel)* II
baker ['beɪkə] Bäcker/in VI 1 (12)
ball [bɔːl] Ball I **Pass the ball!** Spiel ab! III
ballroom dancing [bɔːlruːm 'dɑːnsɪŋ] Standardtanz II
ban [bæn]:
1. **ban (on)** Verbot (von) V
2. verbieten V
be banned verboten sein/werden IV
banana [bə'nɑːnə] Banane III
bank [bæŋk] Bank *(Geldinstitut)* II
barbecue ['bɑːbɪkjuː] Grillfest, Grillparty II
barn [bɑːn] Scheune, Stall I
basic ['beɪsɪk] einfach, elementar V
basically ['beɪsɪkli] im Prinzip, grundsätzlich V
basketball ['bɑːskɪtbɔːl] Basketball I
°**bastard** ['bɑːstəd] *(taboo)* Arschloch, Schwein
bat [bæt] Fledermaus III
bath [bɑːθ]:
1. Bad; Badewanne VI 3 (64)
have/take a bath baden, ein Bad nehmen *(in der Badewanne)* VI 3 (64)
2. **bath sb.** jn. baden VI 1 (24)
bathroom ['bɑːθruːm] Badezimmer, Bad I
battery ['bætəri] Batterie, Akku VI 3 (67)
battery life ['bætəri laɪf] Batterie-/Akku-Laufzeit VI 3 (67)
°**bay** [beɪ] Bucht
°**bazaar** [bə'zɑː] Basar
BC [biː 'siː]: **7000 BC** 7000 v. Chr. VI 3 (58)
be [biː], **was/were, been** sein I
beach [biːtʃ] Strand I **on the beach** am Strand I
°**beam** [biːm] (Licht-)Strahl **the headlights were on full beam** das Fernlicht war eingeschaltet
bear [beə] Bär I
beat [biːt]:
1. **beat, beat, beaten** schlagen, besiegen III
°**beat down (on)** *(infml)* runterknallen (auf) *(Sonne, Regen)*
°2. (Takt-)Schlag, Rhythmus
beaten ['biːtn] *siehe* **beat**
beautiful ['bjuːtɪfl] schön II
became [bɪ'keɪm] *siehe* **become**
because [bɪ'kɒz] weil I **That's because ...** Das liegt daran, dass ... IV
because of [bɪ'kɒz əv] wegen IV
become [bɪ'kʌm], **became, become** werden III
bed [bed] Bett I
bed and breakfast (B&B) [bed ən 'brekfəst] Frühstückspension; Zimmer mit Frühstück III
bedroom ['bedruːm] Schlafzimmer I
bedroomed ['bedruːmd]: **a two-bedroomed flat** eine Wohnung mit zwei Schlafzimmern VI 1 (19)
bee [biː] Biene III
been [biːn] *siehe* **be**
before [bɪ'fɔː]:
1. vor *(zeitlich)* I
before breakfast vor dem Frühstück I
2. bevor I
before you read bevor du liest I
3. vorher; zuvor II
I've never had a pasty before. Ich habe vorher noch nie / noch nie zuvor eine Pastete gegessen. II **the night before** die Nacht zuvor, die Nacht davor III
began [bɪ'gæn] *siehe* **begin**
begin [bɪ'gɪn], **began, begun** beginnen, anfangen III
beginning [bɪ'gɪnɪŋ] Anfang, Beginn III
begun [bɪ'gʌn] *siehe* **begin**
behave [bɪ'heɪv] sich verhalten, sich benehmen IV
behind [bɪ'haɪnd]:
1. hinter I
2. **leave sb./sth. behind** etwas/jn.

zurücklassen, etwas hinter sich lassen VI 3 (60)
believe [bɪ'liːv] glauben III
bell [bel] Glocke; Klingel III
belly button ['beli bʌtn] *(infml)* Bauchnabel IV
°**belong to sb.** [bɪ'lɒŋ] jm. gehören; zu jm. gehören
belongings *(pl)* [bɪ'lɒŋɪŋz] Sachen, Hab und Gut IV
below [bɪ'ləʊ] unten; unter, unterhalb (von) III
°**bench** [bentʃ] Bank *(zum Sitzen)*
bend [bend] Kurve III
beside [bɪ'saɪd] neben III
°**besides** [bɪ'saɪdz] außerdem
best [best] am besten II **Best wishes** Viele Grüße, … *(Briefschluss)* I **like sth. best** etwas am liebsten mögen II **my best friends** meine besten Freunde/Freundinnen I **the best of both worlds** das Beste von beidem I
best-known [best 'nəʊn] der/die/das bekannteste; am bekanntesten V
better ['betə] besser II **do better** besser abschneiden II
better-known [betə 'nəʊn] bekannter V
between [bɪ'twiːn] zwischen I
°**bicycle** ['baɪsɪkl] Fahrrad
big [bɪg]:
1. groß I
2. dick, schwer *(Person)* V
bike [baɪk] Fahrrad I **by bike** mit dem Rad I **go by bike** mit dem Rad fahren I **ride a bike** Rad fahren I
billboard ['bɪlbɔːd] *(AE)* Plakatwand, Werbeplakat VI 2 (46)
billion ['bɪliən] Milliarde VI 3 (58)
bin [bɪn]: **litter bin** Abfalleimer, Mülleimer II
bird [bɜːd] Vogel I
birthday ['bɜːθdeɪ] Geburtstag I **It's her birthday.** Sie hat Geburtstag. I **My birthday is on 5th May.** Ich habe am 5. Mai Geburtstag. I **on my birthday** an meinem Geburtstag I **When's your birthday?** Wann hast du Geburtstag? I
biscuit ['bɪskɪt] Keks, Plätzchen II
bit [bɪt] *siehe* **bite**
bit [bɪt]: **a bit** ein bisschen I °**bits** *(pl, infml)* Teile, Stückchen
bite [baɪt]:
1. Biss, (Insekten-)Stich V
2. **bite, bit, bitten** beißen II
bitten ['bɪtn] *siehe* **bite**
black [blæk] schwarz I
blame sb. (for) [bleɪm] jm. die Schuld geben (an); jm. Vorwürfe machen (wegen) III **Don't blame yourself.** Mach dir keine Vorwürfe. III
blazer ['bleɪzə] Blazer *(Jackett, oft Teil der Schuluniform)* I
bled [bled] *siehe* **bleed**
bleed [bliːd], **bled, bled** bluten V
blew [bluː] *siehe* **blow**
blind [blaɪnd] blind III
block of flats [blɒk] Wohnblock, Häuserblock III
blood [blʌd] Blut IV
°**bloody** ['blʌdi]:
1. blutig, voller Blut
2. *(taboo)* verdammt, Scheiß-
blouse [blaʊz] Bluse V
blow [bləʊ], **blew, blown** blasen, pusten; wehen *(Wind)* VI 3 (64)
blown [bləʊn] *siehe* **blow**
blue [bluː] blau I
blurb [blɜːb] Klappentext *(eines Buches)* V
blush [blʌʃ] erröten, rot werden III
BMX [biː em 'eks] BMX-Rad I
board [bɔːd] einsteigen, an Bord gehen IV
board [bɔːd] Tafel *(im Klassenraum)* VI 3 (56)
boardwalk ['bɔːdwɔːk] Steg, Uferpromenade *(aus Holz)* V
boat [bəʊt] Boot III
body ['bɒdi] Körper V
body painting ['bɒdi peɪntɪŋ] Körperbemalung V
boil [bɔɪl] kochen; zum Kochen bringen III
°**bomb** [bɒm]:
1. Bombe
2. einen Bombenanschlag verüben auf, bombardieren
°**bone** [bəʊn] Knochen
bonfire ['bɒnfaɪə] *(großes Freuden-)* Feuer II
book [bʊk]:
1. Buch I
2. buchen, reservieren III
boot [buːt] Stiefel II
booth [buːθ] Nische, (Sitz-)Ecke *(im Restaurant)* IV
bored [bɔːd] gelangweilt III
boring ['bɔːrɪŋ] langweilig I
born [bɔːn]: **be born** geboren werden/sein V **be born to sb.** als Kind von … geboren werden/sein VI 1 (12)
borrow ['bɒrəʊ] (aus)leihen, sich borgen I
bossy ['bɒsi] herrisch; rechthaberisch I
both [bəʊθ] beide III **the best of both worlds** das Beste von beidem I
bottle ['bɒtl] Flasche I
bottom ['bɒtəm] unteres Ende, Unterteil IV **at the bottom (of)** unten, am unteren Ende (von) II
bought [bɔːt] *siehe* **buy**
bowl [bəʊl] Schüssel III
bowling ['bəʊlɪŋ] Kegeln, Bowling II
box [bɒks] Kasten, Kiste, Kästchen I
box [bɒks] boxen III
boxer ['bɒksə] Boxer/in III
boxing ['bɒksɪŋ] Boxen III
boy [bɔɪ] Junge I
boycott ['bɔɪkɒt]:
1. Boykott IV
2. boykottieren IV
boyfriend ['bɔɪfrend] (fester) Freund I
°**bracket** ['brækɪt] Klammer
brain [breɪn] Gehirn V **brains** *(pl)* Verstand, Intelligenz, „Köpfchen" V
brave [breɪv] mutig III
bread [bred] Brot II
break [breɪk] Pause I **at break** in der Pause *(zwischen Schulstunden)* II
break [breɪk], **broke, broken** brechen; zerbrechen; kaputt gehen; kaputt machen IV **break down** eine Panne haben, kaputtgehen *(Auto)* V
breakfast ['brekfəst] Frühstück I **have breakfast** frühstücken I
°**breath** [breθ] Atem **pause for breath** kurz Pause machen, um Luft zu holen
°**breathtaking** ['breθteɪkɪŋ] atemberaubend
bridge [brɪdʒ] Brücke II
°**brief** [briːf] kurz (gefasst), knapp
brilliant ['brɪliənt] super, großartig III
bring [brɪŋ], **brought, brought** bringen, mitbringen I
Britain ['brɪtn] *(kurz für:* **Great Britain***)* Großbritannien II
British ['brɪtɪʃ] britisch I
°**Brittany** ['brɪtni] Bretagne
brochure ['brəʊʃə] Broschüre, Prospekt I
broke [brəʊk] *siehe* **break**
broken ['brəʊkən]:
1. zerbrochen, gebrochen; kaputt III
2. *siehe* **break**
°**Bronze Age** ['brɒnz eɪdʒ] Bronzezeit
brother ['brʌðə] Bruder I
brought [brɔːt] *siehe* **bring**
brown [braʊn] braun I
°**bruise** [bruːz] Bluterguss, Prellung
budget ['bʌdʒɪt]:
1. Budget, Haushalt V
2. haushalten *(sparsam sein)* V
budgie ['bʌdʒi] Wellensittich II
buffalo, *pl* **buffalo** *or* **buffaloes** ['bʌfələʊ] Büffel; Bison IV
build [bɪld], **built, built** bauen IV
building ['bɪldɪŋ] Gebäude III
built [bɪlt] *siehe* **build**
bully ['bʊli]:
1. Mobber/in, Tyrann/in V
2. tyrannisieren, mobben V
bump into sb. [bʌmp] mit jm. zusammenstoßen IV
bungee jump ['bʌndʒi dʒʌmp] Bungee-Sprung VI 1 (14)
burger ['bɜːgə] Hamburger II
burn [bɜːn]:
1. (ver)brennen V
2. Verbrennung, Brandverletzung VI 2 (43)
burns unit Abteilung für Verbrennungen/Brandverletzungen *(im Krankenhaus)* VI 2 (43)

°**burst** [bɜːst], **burst, burst** bersten, platzen
bus [bʌs] Bus I **by bus** mit dem Bus I **go by bus** mit dem Bus fahren I **on the bus** im Bus I
bus stop ['bʌs stɒp] Bushaltestelle II
bush [bʊʃ] Busch, Strauch III
business ['bɪznəs] Geschäft, Firma III
business studies ['bɪznəs stʌdiz] Wirtschaftskunde III
busy ['bɪzi]:
1. belebt; verkehrsreich III
2. **be busy** beschäftigt sein; viel zu tun haben I
The kitchen is too busy. In der Küche ist zu viel los. I
busybody ['bɪzibɒdi] Wichtigtuer/in V
but [bʌt], [bət] aber I
butter [bʌtə] Butter II
butterfly ['bʌtəflaɪ] Schmetterling V
buy [baɪ], **bought, bought** kaufen I
buzz [bʌz] summen VI 3 (57)
by [baɪ]: **by 8 pm/by next year/ by 2030/...** bis 20 Uhr/bis nächstes Jahr/ bis (zum Jahr) 2030/... VI 3 (60) **by accident** aus Versehen; zufällig VI 3 (63) **by bus/bike** mit dem Bus/ Rad I **by saying/asking** indem du sagst/fragst IV **by the way** übrigens V **come by** *(AE)* vorbeikommen, vorbeischauen *(besuchen)* IV **go by bus/bike/car** mit dem Bus/Rad/Auto fahren I **side by side** Seite an Seite IV **step by step** Schritt für Schritt V **written by** geschrieben von III
Bye. [baɪ] Tschüs. I
bystander ['baɪstændə] Zuschauer/in, *(unbeteiligte/r)* Beobachter/in V

C

cable ['keɪbl] Kabel, Drahtseil IV
cafe ['kæfeɪ] Café I
cafeteria [kæfə'tɪəriə] *(AE)* Kantine, Mensa IV
cage [keɪdʒ] Käfig I
cake [keɪk] Kuchen II
calculator ['kælkjuleɪtə] Taschenrechner I
calf, *pl* **calves** [kɑːf], [kɑːvz] Kalb IV
Californian [kælɪ'fɔːnɪən] kalifornisch IV
call [kɔːl] rufen, anrufen; nennen II
call sb. a racist name jn. mit einem rassistischen Wort beschimpfen V
call sb. names jn. beschimpfen V
be called genannt werden, heißen III
calm [kɑːm] ruhig, still III
calves [kɑːvz] *Mehrzahl von* **calf** IV
came [keɪm] *siehe* **come**
camel ['kæml] Kamel V
camera ['kæmərə] Kamera, Fotoapparat II
camp [kæmp]:
1. campen, zelten IV
2. Lager, Camp II
make camp sein Lager/Zelt aufschlagen V
camp fire ['kæmp faɪə] Lagerfeuer IV
campaign [kæm'peɪn] Kampagne V
campground ['kæmpgraʊnd] *(AE)* Campingplatz IV
campsite ['kæmpsaɪt] *(BE)* Campingplatz IV
can [kæn], [kən] können I **I can't ..., can I?** Ich kann doch nicht ..., nicht wahr? V **I can't do my homework.** Ich kann meine Hausaufgaben nicht machen. I
can [kæn] Dose V
°**cancel sth.** ['kænsl] etwas abbrechen; absagen, ausfallen lassen
candidate ['kændɪdət] Bewerber/in, Kandidat/in V
candle ['kændl] Kerze V
°**candlelit** ['kændllɪt] bei Kerzenschein
candy ['kændi] *(AE)* Süßigkeiten IV
canteen [kæn'tiːn] Kantine, (Schul-) Mensa I
°**canyon** ['kænjən] Cañon
cap [kæp] Mütze, Kappe III
capital ['kæpɪtl] Hauptstadt III
capital letter ['kæpɪtl] Großbuchstabe II
captain ['kæptɪn] Spielführer/in, Anführer/in; Kapitän/in V
caption ['kæpʃn] Bildunterschrift III
car [kɑː] Auto I **by car** mit dem Auto I **go by car** mit dem Auto fahren I
car park ['kɑː pɑːk] Parkplatz II
°**caramel** ['kærəmel] Karamell
card [kɑːd] Karte I
°**cardboard** ['kɑːdbɔːd] Pappe
care [keə]:
1. Versorgung, Betreuung V
take care of sb./sth. sich um jn./ etwas kümmern VI 1 (19)
2. Sorgfalt, Vorsicht V
with care vorsichtig, mit Bedacht V
3. **care about sth.** etwas wichtig nehmen VI 2 (36)
Do you care? Kümmert dich das? / Interessiert dich das? VI 2 (36) **I don't care.** Ich mach mir nichts draus. / Ist mir egal III **Who cares?** Wen interessiert das? / Was soll's? / Na und? IV
career [kə'rɪə] Karriere; (schulischer/ beruflicher) Werdegang VI 2 (46)
careful ['keəfl] vorsichtig II
carefully ['keəfəli]:
1. **drive carefully** vorsichtig fahren II
2. **listen carefully** aufmerksam/ genau zuhören II
carnival ['kɑːnɪvl] Karneval IV
carrot ['kærət] Karotte, Möhre, Mohrrübe II
carry ['kæri] tragen; befördern, transportieren VI 3 (56)
cart [kɑːt] Wagen, Karren IV
°**carton** ['kɑːtn] (Papp-)Karton; Packung
case [keɪs] Fall VI 3 (64) **(just) in case ...** (nur) für den Fall, dass ... VI 3 (64) **in (the) case of** im Falle von VI 3 (64)
cash desk ['kæʃ desk] Kasse V
casino [kə'siːnəʊ] (Spiel-)Kasino IV
castle ['kɑːsl] Burg, Schloss III
cat [kæt] Katze I
catch [kætʃ], **caught, caught** fangen, erwischen III **catch sth.** sich mit etwas anstecken; sich etwas einfangen *(Krankheit)* V
cattle *(pl)* ['kætl] Vieh, Rinder V
cattle station ['kætl steɪʃn] *(AustE)* Rinderfarm V
caught [kɔːt] *siehe* **catch** °**be caught up in sth.** von etwas gefangen sein, sich in etwas verheddern
cause sth. [kɔːz] etwas bewirken, verursachen VI 3 (63)
CCTV camera [siː siː tiː 'viː] Überwachungskamera III
CD [siː 'diː] CD I
CD player [siː 'diː pleɪə] CD-Spieler II
celebrate ['selɪbreɪt] feiern II
°**celebration** [selɪ'breɪʃn] Feier
celebrity [sə'lebrəti] Prominente/r, Promi V
cell phone ['sel fəʊn] *(AE)* Handy IV
Celsius (C) ['selsiəs] Celsius IV
cent [sent] Cent III
central ['sentrəl] zentral V **central Sydney** Sydney Stadtmitte V
centre ['sentə] Zentrum, Center I
century ['sentʃəri] Jahrhundert VI 1 (16)
cereals *(pl)* ['sɪəriəlz] Getreideflocken, Frühstücksflocken II
°**certain** ['sɜːtn] bestimmte(r,s), gewisse(r,s)
°**certainly** ['sɜːtnli] sicher(lich), gewiss
chain [tʃeɪn] Kette II
chair [tʃeə] Stuhl I
challenge ['tʃælɪndʒ] Herausforderung III
°**championship** ['tʃæmpiənʃɪp] Meisterschaft
chance [tʃɑːns] Gelegenheit, Möglichkeit, Chance IV
chancellor ['tʃɑːnsələ] (Bundes-)Kanzler/in VI 2 (36)
change [tʃeɪndʒ]:
1. (ver)ändern; sich (ver)ändern II
change one's mind es sich anders überlegen VI 2 (43)
2. wechseln IV
3. sich umziehen IV
4. Veränderung, Wechsel III
°5. Wechselgeld
channel ['tʃænl] Kanal II
chant [tʃɑːnt] Sprechgesang I
chaotic [keɪ'ɒtɪk] chaotisch IV
character ['kærəktə] Figur, Person *(in Roman, Film usw.)* III

characterization [kærəktəraɪ'zeɪʃn] Charakterisierung VI 1 (21)
characterize sth. ['kærəktəraɪz] etwas charakterisieren, kennzeichnen; für etwas charakteristisch sein VI 1 (21)
charge [tʃɑːdʒ] (auf)laden *(Batterie, Handy, …)* III
charity ['tʃærəti] Wohltätigkeit, wohltätige Zwecke; Wohlfahrtsorganisation III **charity shop** *Geschäft, das gespendete Waren für wohltätige Zwecke verkauft* II
chart [tʃɑːt] Diagramm, Tabelle IV
chase [tʃeɪs]:
1. **chase sb./sth.** jn./etwas jagen; hinter jm./etwas herrennen III
2. Verfolgung, Verfolgungsjagd VI 2 (42)
°**give chase** die Verfolgung aufnehmen
chat [tʃæt]:
1. Unterhaltung; Chat II
2. **chat (with)** chatten (mit); sich unterhalten (mit) II
chatty ['tʃæti] gesprächig; zum Plaudern aufgelegt III
cheap [tʃiːp] billig, preiswert II
check [tʃek]:
1. (über)prüfen, kontrollieren II **check sth. out** *(infml)* sich etwas anschauen, anhören; etwas ausprobieren IV **check the internet** im Internet nachschauen II
2. Kontrolle, Überprüfung IV
check-in ['tʃek ɪn] Check-in, Einchecken VI 1 (22)
cheek [tʃiːk] Wange IV
cheer [tʃɪə] jubeln, *(Sportler/innen)* anfeuern IV
cheerful ['tʃɪəfl] fröhlich, gut gelaunt V
cheese [tʃiːz] Käse III
°**cheetah** ['tʃiːtə] Gepard
chicken ['tʃɪkɪn] Huhn; (Brat-)Hähnchen I
child, *pl* **children** [tʃaɪld], [tʃɪldrən] Kind I
childcare ['tʃaɪldkeə] Kinderbetreuung V
chill [tʃɪl] *(infml)* relaxen, sich ausruhen II
chin [tʃɪn] Kinn V
chips *(pl)* [tʃɪps]:
1. *(BE)* Pommes frites I
2. *(AE)* Kartoffelchips IV
chocolate ['tʃɒklət] Schokolade II
chocolate bar [bɑː] Schokoriegel III
choice [tʃɔɪs] (Aus-)Wahl VI 2 (36)
choir ['kwaɪə] Chor VI 3 (61)
choose [tʃuːz], **chose, chosen** (sich) aussuchen, (aus)wählen IV
chore [tʃɔː] (Haus-)Arbeit, *(lästige)* Pflicht II **do chores** (Haus-)Arbeiten erledigen II
°**chorus** ['kɔːrəs] Refrain *(Lied)*
chose [tʃəʊz] *siehe* **choose**
chosen [tʃəʊzn] *siehe* **choose**

Christmas ['krɪsməs] Weihnachten II
church [tʃɜːtʃ] Kirche III
cigarette [sɪgə'ret] Zigarette V
cinema ['sɪnəmə] Kino I
circle ['sɜːkl] Kreis II
circumstances *(pl)* ['sɜːkəmstənsɪz] Umstände VI 3 (67) **under the circumstances** unter diesen Umständen VI 3 (67)
circus ['sɜːkəs] Zirkus II
citizen ['sɪtɪzn] Bürger/in V
city ['sɪti] (Groß-)Stadt I
civil rights *(pl)* [sɪvl 'raɪts] Bürgerrechte IV
class [klɑːs]:
1. (Schul-)Klasse I
2. Unterricht; Kurs II
class teacher ['klɑːs tiːtʃə] Klassenlehrer/in I
classmate ['klɑːsmeɪt] Mitschüler/in V
classroom ['klɑːsruːm] Klassenzimmer I
clean [kliːn]:
1. sauber IV
2. sauber machen, putzen I **clean sth. off** etwas abwaschen, abwischen, abputzen VI 2 (38) **clean sth. up** etwas aufräumen, sauber machen IV
cleaner ['kliːnə] Reinigungskraft V
clean-up ['kliːn ʌp] Reinemachen, Hausputz V
clear [klɪə] klar, deutlich, eindeutig III **speak clearly** deutlich sprechen II
clearing ['klɪərɪŋ] Lichtung V
clever ['klevə] schlau, klug II
cleverness ['klevənəs] Klugheit V
°**cliff** [klɪf] Klippe, Felsen
°**cliff walk** Klippenpfad
climate ['klaɪmət] Klima V
°**climate change** ['klaɪmət tʃeɪndʒ] Klimawandel
climb [klaɪm] klettern II
close [kləʊz]:
1. schließen, zumachen I
2. sich schließen III **close sth. down** etwas schließen, stilllegen *(Fabrik, Geschäft)* III
close (to) [kləʊs] nahe (bei, an) IV **(see sth.) close up** etwas aus der Nähe sehen VI 1 (15)
closed [kləʊzd]:
1. geschlossen IV
2. gesperrt *(Straße)* V
close-up ['kləʊs ʌp] Nahaufnahme *(Film)* VI 1 (25)
clothes *(pl)* [kləʊðz] Kleidung, Kleidungsstücke II
cloud [klaʊd] Wolke II
cloudy ['klaʊdi] wolkig II
club [klʌb] Klub I
coach [kəʊtʃ] Trainer/in II
coast [kəʊst] Küste IV **on the coast** an der Küste IV
°**coastal** ['kəʊstl] Küsten-
coat [kəʊt] Mantel III

cocoa ['kəʊkəʊ] Kakao II
coffee ['kɒfi] Kaffee I
cola ['kəʊlə] Cola II
cold [kəʊld]:
1. kalt II
2. Kälte; Erkältung II
collar ['kɒlə] Halsband II
collect [kə'lekt] sammeln II
college ['kɒlɪdʒ] höhere Schule, Fach(hoch)schule V
°**Cologne** [kə'ləʊn] Köln
colon ['kəʊlən] Doppelpunkt VI 1 (17)
colonize ['kɒlənaɪz] kolonisieren VI 1 (10)
colour ['kʌlə] Farbe I **people of colour** Nichtweiße, Menschen nichtweißer Hautfarbe VI 2 (46)
coloured ['kʌləd] farbig IV
colourful ['kʌləfl] farbenfroh, bunt VI 1 (10)
combat ['kɒmbæt] Kampf V
come [kʌm], **came, come** kommen I **come across sth.** auf etwas stoßen, etwas (zufällig) finden VI 2 (38) **come by** *(AE)* vorbeikommen, vorbeischauen *(besuchen)* IV **come home** nach Hause kommen I **come in** hereinkommen II **Come on, Luca!** Na los, Luca! / Komm, Luca! I **come up** auftauchen, herauskommen, aufkommen *(Frage)* V °**come true** wahr/Wirklichkeit werden
comedy ['kɒmədi] Comedyshow; Komödie II
comfortable ['kʌmftəbl] bequem II **be/feel comfortable (with)** sich wohlfühlen (bei/mit) V **make oneself comfortable** es sich gemütlich machen VI 1 (20)
comma ['kɒmə] Komma VI 1 (17)
command [kə'mɑːnd] Befehl V
comment (on) ['kɒment]:
1. Kommentar (zu) III
°2. **comment (on sth.)** (etwas) kommentieren
commercial [kə'mɜːʃl] kommerziell *(auf Gewinn ausgerichtet)* IV
common ['kɒmən] häufig; weit verbreitet IV
communicate (with sb.) [kə'mjuːnɪkeɪt] (mit jm.) kommunizieren; sich (mit jm.) verständigen IV
communication [kəmjuːnɪ'keɪʃn] Kommunikation, Verständigung V
community [kə'mjuːnəti] Gemeinschaft, Gemeinde IV
community service [kə'mjuːnəti sɜːvɪs] gemeinnützige Arbeit, Sozialdienst IV
company ['kʌmpəni] Firma, Gesellschaft IV
compare [kəm'peə] vergleichen IV **compare (with/to)** vergleichbar sein (mit), sich vergleichen lassen (mit) V
comparison [kəm'pærɪsn] Vergleich VI 2 (40) **make comparisons** Ver-

gleiche anstellen; vergleichen VI 2 (40)
compass ['kʌmpəs] Kompass II
competition [kɒmpə'tɪʃn] Wettbewerb III
complain [kəm'pleɪn] sich beschweren/beklagen III
complaint [kəm'pleɪnt] Beschwerde VI 3 (67) **make a complaint (about sth.)** eine Beschwerde vorbringen (über etwas), etwas beanstanden VI 3 (67)
complete [kəm'pli:t]:
1. vervollständigen VI 2 (35)
2. vollständig VI 2 (35)
complicated ['kɒmplɪkeɪtɪd] kompliziert V
°**compost** ['kɒmpɒst] kompostieren
concentrate (on) ['kɒnsntreɪt] sich konzentrieren (auf) VI 3 (60)
concentration [kɒnsn'treɪʃn] Konzentration VI 3 (60)
°**concerned (for/about)** [kən'sɜ:nd] besorgt (um)
concert ['kɒnsət] Konzert I
°**conclude** [kən'klu:d] schließen, schlussfolgern
conclusion [kən'klu:ʒn] Schluss(folgerung) V
conditions *(pl)* [kən'dɪʃnz] Bedingungen, Verhältnisse VI 2 (45)
confident ['kɒnfɪdənt] (selbst)sicher; zuversichtlich V
confirm [kən'fɜ:m] bestätigen III
°**confront sb.** [kən'frʌnt] jn. konfrontieren, jm. entgegentreten
confused [kən'fju:zd] verwirrt VI 1 (16)
connect [kə'nekt] verbinden IV
cons [kɒnz]: **the pros and cons** *(pl)* das Pro und Kontra; das Für und Wider V
°**consequence** ['kɒnsɪkwəns] Konsequenz, Folge
conservation [kɒnsə'veɪʃn] (Natur-) Schutz, Erhaltung, Bewahrung VI 1 (14)
°**consist of** [kən'sɪst] bestehen aus
contact ['kɒntækt]:
1. Kontakt III
2. Kontakt aufnehmen zu, sich melden bei V
contact lens ['kɒntækt lenz] Kontaktlinse VI 3 (54/55)
°**contain** [kən'teɪn] enthalten
°**container** [kən'teɪnə] Behälter, Gefäß
context ['kɒntekst] (Text-)Zusammenhang IV
continent ['kɒntɪnənt] Kontinent V
continue [kən'tɪnju:] weitergehen, weitermachen, (sich) fortsetzen V
contract ['kɒntrækt] Vertrag IV
°**contrast** ['kɒntrɑ:st] Gegensatz, Kontrast
°**contrast** [kən'trɑ:st] vergleichen, (einander) gegenüberstellen

control [kən'trəʊl]:
1. kontrollieren, beherrschen V
2. regulieren, bestimmen III
3. **control (of/over)** Kontrolle, Herrschaft, Macht (über) VI 3 (54/55)
controversial [kɒntrə'vɜ:ʃl] kontrovers, umstritten VI 3 (60)
conversation [kɒnvə'seɪʃn] Gespräch, Unterhaltung V
cook [kʊk]:
1. Koch, Köchin I
2. kochen, *(Essen)* zubereiten I
cooking ['kʊkɪŋ] *(das)* Kochen, Küche, Essen V
cool [ku:l]:
1. cool I
2. kühl II
3. **cool down** sich abkühlen; sich beruhigen V
cop [kɒp] *(infml)* Bulle *(Polizist/in)* VI 2 (42)
copy ['kɒpi] kopieren, abschreiben V
°**corn** [kɔ:n] *(BE)* Korn, Getreide; *(AE)* Mais
corner ['kɔ:nə] Ecke; (Mund-, Augen-) Winkel IV
correct [kə'rekt]:
1. korrekt, richtig IV
2. korrigieren, berichtigen II
cost [kɒst]:
1. **cost, cost, cost** kosten III
2. **costs** *(pl)* Kosten V
costume ['kɒstju:m] Kostüm, Verkleidung II
cottage ['kɒtɪdʒ] Häuschen, Hütte II
cotton ['kɒtn] Baumwolle IV
could [kʊd]:
1. **they could ...** sie konnten ... II
2. **you could ...** du könntest ... II
council ['kaʊnsl] Rat, Gemeinderat, Stadtverwaltung VI 1 (19)
council flat ['kaʊnsl flæt] Sozialwohnung VI 1 (19)
°**counsellor** ['kaʊnsələ] Berater/in; Betreuer/in
count [kaʊnt] zählen VI 3 (67)
country ['kʌntri] Land I **in the country** auf dem Land I
countryside ['kʌntrisaɪd] Landschaft, Umgebung, Natur III
couple ['kʌpl]: **a couple (of)** ein paar; ein Paar III
°**courage** ['kʌrɪdʒ] Mut **act of courage** mutiger Schritt
course [kɔ:s] Kurs, Lehrgang III
course [kɔ:s]: **of course** natürlich, selbstverständlich II
court [kɔ:t] Platz, Court *(Tennis, Basketball)* IV
cousin ['kʌzn] Cousin/e I
°**cover** ['kʌvə] bedecken
cover letter ['kʌvə letə] Anschreiben, Begleitschreiben, Motivationsschreiben V
cow [kaʊ] Kuh I

crab [kræb] Krebs *(Tier)* I
cracker ['krækə] (salziger) Keks IV
crash [kræʃ]:
1. Unfall, Zusammenstoß VI 2 (42)
2. **crash (into)** zusammenstoßen (mit); einen Unfall haben; abstürzen VI 2 (42)
crazy ['kreɪzi] verrückt III **go crazy** verrückt werden III
cream [kri:m] Sahne I
create [kri'eɪt] (er)schaffen, kreieren VI 2 (33)
creative [kri'eɪtɪv] kreativ V
creature ['kri:tʃə] Geschöpf, (Lebe-) Wesen VI 1 (15)
credit card ['kredɪt kɑ:d] Kreditkarte V
creep up (on sb.) [kri:p], **crept, crept** sich heranschleichen (an jn.) V
crept [krept] *siehe* **creep**
crew [kru:] Mannschaft, Team; Clique V
°**cricketer** ['krɪkɪtə] Kricketspieler/in
crime [kraɪm] Kriminalität; Verbrechen IV
crime series, *pl* **crime series** ['kraɪm sɪəri:z] Krimiserie II
crisps *(pl)* [krɪsps] Kartoffelchips II
critic ['krɪtɪk] Kritiker/in V
criticism ['krɪtɪsɪzəm] Kritik V
°**criticize** ['krɪtɪsaɪz] kritisieren
crocodile ['krɒkədaɪl] Krokodil I
cross [krɒs]:
1. überqueren II
2. Kreuz II
3. **be cross (with)** böse sein (auf), sauer sein (auf) II
crossroads, *pl* **crossroads** ['krɒsrəʊdz] (Straßen-)Kreuzung III
crowd [kraʊd] (Menschen-)Menge VI 3 (64)
crowded ['kraʊdɪd] voller Menschen; überfüllt VI 1 (19)
crown [kraʊn] Krone IV
cruise [kru:z]:
1. Kreuzfahrt IV
2. herumfahren *(mit dem Auto, ohne festes Ziel)* IV
°**crutches** *(pl)* ['krʌtʃɪz] Krücken
cry [kraɪ] weinen II
cucumber ['kju:kʌmbə] (Salat-)Gurke III
culture ['kʌltʃə] Kultur III
cup [kʌp]: **a cup (of)** eine Tasse ... I
curly ['kɜ:li] lockig V
currency ['kʌrənsi] Währung VI 1 (10)
°**current** [kʌrənt] aktuell, gegenwärtig
°**curry** ['kʌri] Curry(gericht), Curry-
°**curse** [kɜ:s] fluchen
curtain ['kɜ:tn] Vorhang, Gardine V
cushion ['kʊʃn] Kissen I
customer ['kʌstəmə] Kunde/Kundin III
cut [kʌt]:
1. Schnitt VI 1 (19)
2. **cut, cut, cut** schneiden II **cut the grass** Rasen mähen II °**cut sth.** etwas abbrechen, aufhören mit etwas °**cut through sth.** etwas

durchqueren; eine Abkürzung durch … nehmen

cute [kjuːt] niedlich, süß I

CV (= curriculum vitae) [siː 'viː], [kərɪkjələm 'viːtaɪ] Lebenslauf V

cyberbullying [saɪbə'bʊlɪŋ] Cybermobbing V

cycle ['saɪkl] Rad fahren, mit dem Rad fahren III **cycle tour** Radtour III

D

dad [dæd] Papa, Vati I

daily ['deɪli] täglich VI 1 (24)

damage ['dæmɪdʒ]:
1. *(no pl)* Schaden, Schäden V
°2. (be)schädigen, schaden

dance [dɑːns]:
1. tanzen I
2. Tanz III

dancer ['dɑːnsə] Tänzer/in III

danger ['deɪndʒə] Gefahr III

dangerous ['deɪndʒərəs] gefährlich I

dark [dɑːk]:
1. dunkel II
2. **(the) dark** (die) Dunkelheit VI 2 (41)

°**darkened** ['dɑːkənd] dunkel, verdunkelt, nicht angestrahlt *(z.B. Gebäude)*

darkness ['dɑːknəs] Dunkelheit, Finsternis IV

dart [dɑːt] (Wurf-)Pfeil II

dartboard ['dɑːtbɔːd] Dartscheibe II

data ['deɪtə] Daten VI 3 (56)

date [deɪt]:
1. Datum I
2. Verabredung, Date *(auch die Person, mit der man ausgeht)* IV
3. **date sb.** mit jm. gehen; sich (regelmäßig) mit jm. treffen; eine Beziehung mit jm. haben VI 1 (12)

daughter ['dɔːtə] Tochter III

day [deɪ] Tag I **get/have a day off** einen Tag frei bekommen/haben IV **I haven't eaten in days** ich habe tagelang nichts gegessen V **in the old days** früher II **one day** eines Tages, einmal IV **these days** heutzutage VI 2 (34)

°**day care** ['deɪ keə] Tagesbetreuung

°**day care centre** ['deɪ keə sentə] Tagesstätte

dead [ded] tot IV

deadly ['dedli] tödlich V

deal [diːl]: **a good deal** ein guter Deal, ein gutes Geschäft, ein gutes Angebot III **It's a deal!** Abgemacht! II **make a deal** ein Geschäft abschließen, vereinbaren II **no big deal** nichts Besonderes, kein Drama V

deal with sth. [diːl], **dealt, dealt** umgehen mit etwas, mit etwas fertigwerden, klarkommen V **deal with sb./sth.** sich um jn./etwas kümmern, sich mit jm./einer Sache befassen VI 2 (42)

dealt [delt] *siehe* **deal**

dear [dɪə]: **Dear …** Liebe/r … I **Dear Sir/Madam** Sehr geehrte Damen und Herren V **Oh dear.** Oje! II

debate [dɪ'beɪt] debattieren, diskutieren IV

December [dɪ'sembə] Dezember I

decide (to do sth.) [dɪ'saɪd] beschließen, (sich) entscheiden (etwas zu tun) IV

decision [dɪ'sɪʒn] Entscheidung VI 1 (20) **make a decision** eine Entscheidung fällen VI 1 (20)

deep [diːp] tief III

definitely ['defɪnətli] auf jeden Fall; ganz bestimmt III

degree [dɪ'griː] Grad II

delete [dɪ'liːt] löschen V

delicious [dɪ'lɪʃəs] köstlich, lecker VI 2 (40)

deliver [dɪ'lɪvə] (aus)liefern VI 3 (54/55) °**deliver a speech** eine Rede halten

°**delivery** [dɪ'lɪvəri] Lieferung

demand [dɪ'mɑːnd]:
1. fordern, verlangen VI 2 (38)
2. Forderung VI 2 (38)

democracy [dɪ'mɒkrəsi] Demokratie VI 2 (36)

°**demonstrate** ['demənstreɪt] zeigen, demonstrieren

demonstration [demən'streɪʃn] Demonstration VI 2 (34)

den [den] Versteck; Hobbyraum II

department [dɪ'pɑːtmənt] Abteilung III

department store [dɪ'pɑːtmənt stɔː] Kaufhaus III

departure [dɪ'pɑːtʃə] Abflug III

depressing [dɪ'presɪŋ] deprimierend V

°**derelict** ['derəlɪkt] heruntergekommen, verfallen

describe [dɪ'skraɪb] beschreiben I

°**description** [dɪ'skrɪpʃn] Beschreibung

desert ['dezət] Wüste IV

°**deserted** [dɪ'zɜːtɪd] menschenleer, wie ausgestorben

°**deserve** [dɪ'zɜːv] verdienen

design [dɪ'zaɪn] entwerfen, gestalten, entwickeln V

desk [desk] Schreibtisch I **front desk** Rezeption, Empfang *(z.B. Hotel)* V

°**desperate** ['despərət] verzweifelt

°**despite** [dɪ'spaɪt] trotz

dessert [dɪ'zɜːt] Nachtisch, Dessert II

destination [destɪ'neɪʃn] Reiseziel, Fahrtziel VI 3 (62)

destroy [dɪ'strɔɪ] zerstören IV

°**destruction** [dɪ'strʌkʃn] Zerstörung, Vernichtung

detail ['diːteɪl] Detail, Einzelheit IV

detailed ['diːteɪld] ausführlich, detailliert VI 3 (67)

detective [dɪ'tektɪv] Detektiv/in III

°**determination** [dɪtɜːmɪ'neɪʃn] Entschlossenheit

device [dɪ'vaɪs] Gerät, Apparat VI 3 (56) °**stylistic device** Stilmittel

°**diagram** ['daɪəgræm] Diagramm

dialogue ['daɪəlɒg] Dialog I

diamond ['daɪəmənd] Diamant VI 1 (10)

diary ['daɪəri] Tagebuch; Kalender I

dictionary ['dɪkʃənri] Wörterbuch, *(alphabetisches)* Wörterverzeichnis I

did [dɪd] *siehe* **do** **Did they go?** Sind sie gegangen? / Gingen sie? II **I didn't have a …** ich hatte kein/e … II

die [daɪ] sterben II

difference ['dɪfrəns] Unterschied I **make a difference** etwas bewirken, etwas ausmachen VI 1 (24)

different ['dɪfrənt] verschieden; anders I **different from** anders als III **in a different way** anders; auf andere Art und Weise III

difficult ['dɪfɪkəlt] schwierig, schwer I

difficulty ['dɪfɪkəlti] Schwierigkeit(en) VI 3 (60)

digital ['dɪdʒɪtl] digital V

diner ['daɪnə] *(AE) (kleines, preiswertes)* Restaurant IV

dinner ['dɪnə] Abendessen, Abendbrot I **have dinner** Abendbrot essen, zu Abend essen I

dinosaur ['daɪnəsɔː] Dinosaurier III

direct [də'rekt] direkt, unmittelbar V

direction [də'rekʃn] Richtung IV **directions** *(pl)* Wegbeschreibung(en) II

°**dirty** ['dɜːti] schmutzig

disability [dɪsə'bɪləti] Behinderung IV

disadvantage [dɪsəd'vɑːntɪdʒ] Nachteil IV

disagree (with sb.) [dɪsə'griː] anderer Meinung sein (als jemand); nicht übereinstimmen (mit jm.) III

disappear [dɪsə'pɪə] verschwinden IV

disappoint sb. [dɪsə'pɔɪnt] jn. enttäuschen IV

disappointed (with sb./sth.) [dɪsə'pɔɪntɪd] enttäuscht (von jm./etwas) II

disaster [dɪ'zɑːstə] Katastrophe, Desaster III

°**discourse marker** ['dɪskɔːs mɑːkə] Redemittel, Wendungen *(in Diskussionen und argumentativen Texten)*

discover [dɪ'skʌvə] entdecken; herausfinden III

discrimination (against) [dɪskrɪmɪ'neɪʃn] Diskriminierung (von) V

discuss sth. [dɪ'skʌs] über etwas diskutieren; etwas besprechen IV

discussion [dɪ'skʌʃn] Diskussion I

disease [dɪ'ziːz] Krankheit V

dish [dɪʃ] Gericht *(Speise)* III

°**dishes** *(pl)* ['dɪʃɪz] Geschirr

dishwasher ['dɪʃwɒʃə] Geschirrspülmaschine, Geschirrspüler II
dislikes ['dɪslaɪks]: **likes and dislikes** *(pl)* Vorlieben und Abneigungen IV
display [dɪ'spleɪ] Bildschirm, Anzeige(gerät) VI 3 (57)
head-mounted display Datenhelm, Datenbrille, Videobrille VI 3 (57)
°**distance** ['dɪstəns] Distanz, Entfernung **in the distance** in der Ferne
disturb [dɪ'stɜ:b] stören III
dive [daɪv]:
1. einen Kopfsprung machen I
2. tauchen II
3. Tauchgang VI 1 (14)
diver ['daɪvə] Taucher/in III
diverse [daɪ'vɜ:s] unterschiedlich, vielfältig VI 1 (10)
diversity [daɪ'vɜ:səti] Vielfalt VI 1 (10)
diving suit ['daɪvɪŋ su:t] Taucheranzug VI 3 (61)
dizzy ['dɪzi] schwindelig VI 3 (64)
do [du:], **did, done** machen, tun I **do a paper round** Zeitungen austragen II **do better** besser abschneiden II **do chores** (Haus-)Arbeiten erledigen II **do sport** Sport treiben I **Don't panic.** Keine Panik. / Immer mit der Ruhe. II **dos and don'ts** *(pl)* was man tun und lassen sollte V **I don't like blue.** Ich mag Blau nicht. / Ich mag kein Blau. I **it does have ...** es hat (ja/wohl) doch/tatsächlich... V **she doesn't have a ...** sie hat kein/keine/keinen ... I **What do you think?** Was meinst du? / Was denkst du? I
doctor ['dɒktə] Arzt/Ärztin, Doktor/in II
document ['dɒkjumənt] Dokument VI 1 (12)
document ['dɒkjument] dokumentieren VI 1 (12)
documentary [dɒkju'mentri] Dokumentarfilm II
dog [dɒg] Hund I
dogs' home [dɒgz 'həum] Hundeheim II
°**doing** ['du:ɪŋ] (das) Tun, Tat
dollar ($) ['dɒlə] Dollar III
°**donate** [dəʊ'neɪt] spenden
done [dʌn] *siehe* **do** **Well done.** Gut gemacht! I
donkey ['dɒŋki] Esel I
door [dɔ:] Tür I
dormitory ['dɔ:mətri] Schlafsaal III
°**dossier** ['dɒsieɪ] Mappe
dot [dɒt] Punkt, Pünktchen V
dot painting ['dɒt peɪntɪŋ] Punktmalerei; Punktgemälde V
°**doubt** [daʊt] Zweifel **there's no doubt (that)** zweifellos
down [daʊn] nach unten; hinunter, herunter I **down this hill** diesen Hügel hinunter I
downside ['daʊnsaɪd] Kehrseite, Nachteil III
downstairs [daʊn'steəz] unten; nach unten I
downtown [daʊn'taʊn] *(AE)* (im/ins) Stadtzentrum IV
°**drag** [dræg] zerren, (mit Mühe) ziehen, schleifen
drama ['drɑ:mə]:
1. Schauspiel, darstellende Kunst I
2. Drama IV
drank [dræŋk] *siehe* **drink**
draw [drɔ:], **drew, drawn** zeichnen VI 3 (66) °**draw sb.'s attention to sth.** js. Aufmerksamkeit auf etwas lenken
drawing ['drɔ:ɪŋ] Zeichnung VI 3 (66) **do a drawing** eine Zeichnung machen VI 3 (66)
drawn [drɔ:n] *siehe* **draw**
dream [dri:m]:
1. Traum I
2. **dream (about, of)** träumen (von) IV
dress [dres]:
1. Kleid II
2. Kleidung IV
3. sich anziehen, sich kleiden IV
get dressed sich anziehen IV
drew [dru:] *siehe* **draw**
°**drift** [drɪft] sich bewegen, driften, *(Gedanken)* wandern
drifter ['drɪftə]: **be a drifter** sich treiben lassen *(ziellos vor sich hinleben)* V
drink [drɪŋk]:
1. Getränk I
2. **drink, drank, drunk** trinken I
drive [draɪv], **drove, driven**:
1. *(mit dem Auto)* fahren II
drive carefully vorsichtig fahren II
2. (an)treiben III
driven ['drɪvn] *siehe* **drive**
driver ['draɪvə] Fahrer/in III
driverless ['draɪvələs] fahrerlos, führerlos VI 3 (54/55)
driver's license ['draɪvəs laɪsəns] *(AE)* Führerschein, Fahrerlaubnis IV
driving licence ['draɪvɪŋ laɪsəns] *(BE)* Führerschein, Fahrerlaubnis III
drone [drəʊn] Drohne VI 3 (54/55)
drop [drɒp] fallen; fallen lassen V
drove [drəʊv] *siehe* **drive**
drown [draʊn] ertrinken III
drug [drʌg] Droge IV
drums *(pl)* [drʌmz] Schlagzeug; Trommeln I
drunk [drʌŋk] *siehe* **drink** **be drunk** betrunken IV **get drunk** sich betrinken IV
dry [draɪ]:
1. trocknen III
2. trocken V
duck [dʌk] Ente I
dull [dʌl]:
1. langweilig, trist, öde IV
°2. *(Farben, Licht)* stumpf, trübe
dump [dʌmp] abladen *(Müll)* III
°**duration** [dju'reɪʃn] Dauer
during ['djʊərɪŋ] während IV
°**dustbin** ['dʌstbɪn] Mülleimer
duty ['dju:ti] Pflicht, Aufgabe; Dienst V **on duty** im Dienst V
DVD [di:vi:'di:] DVD I
DVD player [di:vi:'di: pleɪə] DVD-Spieler III
dynamic [daɪ'næmɪk] dynamisch V

E

each [i:tʃ] jede(r, s) (einzelne) II **each other** einander; sich (gegenseitig) IV
eagle ['i:gl] Adler IV
ear [ɪə] Ohr II
early ['ɜ:li] früh I
earn [ɜ:n] verdienen *(Geld)* V
earth [ɜ:θ] Erde II **on earth** auf der Erde II
earthquake ['ɜ:θkweɪk] Erdbeben III
east [i:st] Osten, nach Osten II
Easter ['i:stə] Ostern IV
eastern ['i:stən] östlich, Ost- IV
easy ['i:zi] einfach, leicht I **Take it easy!** *(infml) etwa:* Reg dich nicht auf. / Bleib mal locker. III °**take it easy** sich schonen
easy-going [i:zi 'gəʊɪŋ] gelassen, locker II
eat [i:t], **ate, eaten** essen; fressen I
eaten ['i:tn] *siehe* **eat**
°**echo** ['ekəʊ]:
1. (wider)hallen
2. *pl* **echoes** Echo
°**economy** [ɪ'kɒnəmi] (Volks-)Wirtschaft
edge [edʒ] Rand, Kante VI 1 (14)
editor ['edɪtə] Herausgeber/in; Redakteur/in IV **letter to the editor** Leserbrief IV
education [edʒu'keɪʃn] (Schul-)Bildung V
effect [ɪ'fekt] (Aus-)Wirkung, Einfluss, Effekt VI 1 (14)
effective [ɪ'fektɪv] effektiv, wirksam VI 1 (14)
e.g. [i: 'dʒi:] *(aus dem Lateinischen)* z.B. (zum Beispiel) II
egg [eg] Ei III
eight [eɪt] acht I
elect sb. (to be) sth. [ɪ'lekt] jn. zu etwas wählen VI 1 (12)
°**election** [ɪ'lekʃn] Wahl *(Abstimmung)*
electric [ɪ'lektrɪk] elektrisch, Elektro- IV
°**electrical** [ɪ'lektrɪkl] elektrisch, Elektro
°**electricity** [ɪlek'trɪsəti] Strom, Elektrizität
electronics [ɪlek'trɒnɪks] Elektronik II
elephant ['elɪfənt] Elefant I
elevator ['elɪveɪtə] *(AE)* Fahrstuhl, Aufzug, Lift IV
eleven [ɪ'levn] elf I

else [els]: **Anything else?** Sonst noch etwas? I **everybody else** alle anderen; jede/r andere II **something else** etwas anderes III **What else ...?** Was (sonst) noch ...? IV
email ['i:meɪl] **email sb.** jn. anmailen IV **email sth.** etwas mailen IV
°**embarrass sb.** [ɪm'bærəs] jn. in Verlegenheit bringen
embarrassed [ɪm'bærəst] verlegen II
embarrassing [ɪm'bærəsɪŋ] peinlich IV
embrace [ɪm'breɪs] annehmen, mit offenen Armen begrüßen; (sich) umarmen VI 1 (10)
emergency [i'mɜ:dʒənsi] Notfall II
emergency services *(pl)* [i'mɜ:dʒənsi sɜ:vɪsɪz] Rettungsdienste II
employee [ɪm'plɔɪi:] Arbeitnehmer/in, Angestellte(r) III
employment [ɪm'plɔɪmənt] Arbeit, Anstellung VI 1 (12)
empty ['empti]:
1. leeren II
2. leer III
enclose [ɪn'kləʊz] beifügen, beilegen *(einem Brief)* V
°**enclosed** [ɪn'kləʊzd] umschlossen; *(Straße)* lückenlos bebaut
encourage [ɪn'kʌrɪdʒ] ermutigen, ermuntern VI 2 (46)
end [end]:
1. enden, zu Ende gehen IV
2. Ende, Schluss I
in the end schließlich, zum Schluss II
ending ['endɪŋ] Endung; Ende *(eines Texts, einer Geschichte)* V **happy ending** Happy End II
endless ['endləs] endlos VI 3 (56)
enemy ['enəmi] Feind/in III
energetic [enə'dʒetɪk] energisch, energiereich V
°**energy** ['enədʒi] Energie
°**engage** [ɪn'geɪdʒ]: **it engages more than 172 countries** mehr als 172 Länder beteiligen sich daran / machen dabei mit
engine ['endʒɪn] Motor V
engineer [endʒɪ'nɪə] Ingenieur/in; Techniker/in VI 2 (46)
engineering [endʒɪ'nɪərɪŋ] Ingenieurwesen, Maschinenbau, Technik VI 2 (46)
England ['ɪŋglənd] England I
English ['ɪŋglɪʃ] Englisch; englisch I
enjoy [ɪn'dʒɔɪ] genießen II **Enjoy yourself/yourselves.** Viel Vergnügen! / Viel Spaß! III
enjoyable [ɪn'dʒɔɪəbl] angenehm, unterhaltsam IV
enough [ɪ'nʌf] genug II
°**enrich** [ɪn'rɪtʃ] bereichern, anreichern
enter ['entə] sich anmelden (für), teilnehmen (an) *(Wettbewerb)* V
enthusiast [ɪn'θju:ziæst] Enthusiast/in, Fan VI 3 (60)
enthusiastic [ɪnθju:zi'æstɪk] begeistert V
entry ['entri]:
1. Eintritt, Zutritt III
2. Eintrag *(in Wörterbuch/Tagebuch)* V
°**environment** [ɪn'vaɪrənmənt] Umwelt; Umfeld, Umgebung
episode ['epɪsəʊd] Episode; Folge III
equal ['i:kwəl] gleich(berechtigt) V
equipment [ɪ'kwɪpmənt] Ausrüstung III
eraser [ɪ'reɪzə] *(AE)* Radiergummi IV
escalator ['eskəleɪtə] Rolltreppe III
escape [ɪ'skeɪp]:
1. entkommen; fliehen IV
2. Flucht V
especially [ɪ'speʃəli] besonders; vor allem II
°**essential** [ɪ'senʃl] (absolut) notwendig, wesentlich
°**estate** [ɪ'steɪt]: **housing estate** Wohnsiedlung
estimate ['estɪmeɪt] schätzen VI 2 (34)
etc. [et'setərə] *(aus dem Lateinischen)* usw. (und so weiter) II
euro (€) ['jʊərəʊ] Euro III
Europe ['jʊərəp] Europa III
European [jʊərə'pi:ən] Europäer/in; europäisch IV
even ['i:vn] sogar, selbst III **not even** (noch) nicht einmal IV °**even though** auch wenn, obwohl *(betont)* °**Do they even have streets?** Haben sie überhaupt Straßen?
evening ['i:vnɪŋ] Abend I **in the evening** abends, am Abend I **on Friday evening** freitagabends, am Freitagabend I
event [ɪ'vent] Ereignis, Event IV **fund-raising event** Event zur Beschaffung von Geld/Spenden IV
ever ['evə] jemals, schon mal III **Have you ever ...?** Hast du schon mal ...? / Hast du jemals ...? III **Have you ever been to ...?** Bist du schon mal in ... gewesen? III **the most realistic game ever** das realistischste Spiel, das es je gegeben hat V
every ['evri] jede(r, s) I °**every now and again** ab und zu, von Zeit zu Zeit
everybody ['evribɒdi] jeder; alle I
everyone ['evriwʌn] jeder; alle II
everything ['evriθɪŋ] alles II
everywhere ['evriweə] überall II
°**evidence** ['evɪdəns] Nachweis(e), Beweis(e)
°**evolution** [i:və'lu:ʃn] Entwicklung
exact [ɪg'zækt] exakt, genau V
exam [ɪg'zæm] Prüfung V **final (school) exam** (Schul-)Abschlussprüfung V **take/do an exam** eine Prüfung machen V
°**examine** [ɪg'zæmɪn] untersuchen
example [ɪg'zɑ:mpl] Beispiel I **for example** zum Beispiel II
°**exceed** [ɪk'si:d] überschreiten
excellent ['eksələnt] ausgezeichnet, hervorragend IV
except (for) [ɪk'sept] außer, bis auf IV
exchange [ɪks'tʃeɪndʒ] (Schüler-)Austausch V
excited [ɪk'saɪtɪd] aufgeregt, gespannt I
excitement [ɪk'saɪtmənt] Aufregung, Begeisterung IV
exciting [ɪk'saɪtɪŋ] aufregend, spannend II
exclamation mark [eksklə'meɪʃn mɑ:k] Ausrufezeichen VI 1 (17)
°**excuse** [ɪk'skju:s]: **make excuses** sich herausreden, Ausflüchte machen
Excuse me, ... [ɪks'kju:z mi:] Entschuldigung, ... / Entschuldigen Sie, ... I
exercise ['eksəsaɪz]:
1. Übung, Aufgabe I
2. *(no pl)* Bewegung, *(körperliches)* Training VI 3 (56)
exercise book ['eksəsaɪz bʊk] Schulheft, Übungsheft I
exhibition [eksɪ'bɪʃn] Messe; Ausstellung VI 3 (66)
°**exist** [ɪg'zɪst] existieren
exoskeleton ['eksəʊskelɪtn] Exoskelett, Außenskelett VI 3 (54/55)
expect [ɪk'spekt] erwarten V
°**be expected to do sth.** etwas tun sollen/müssen; es wird erwartet, dass man etwas tut
expensive [ɪk'spensɪv] teuer I
experience [ɪk'spɪəriəns]:
1. erfahren, erleben IV
2. Erfahrung, Erlebnis III
in my experience nach meiner Erfahrung V
experiment [ɪk'sperɪmənt]:
1. Experiment, Versuch II
2. experimentieren III
expert ['ekspɜ:t] Experte, Expertin V
explain sth. (to sb.) [ɪk'spleɪn] (jm.) etwas erklären, (jm.) etwas erläutern IV
explore [ɪk'splɔ:] erforschen, erkunden VI 3 (62)
explosion [ɪk'spləʊʒn] Explosion VI 2 (42)
express [ɪk'spres] ausdrücken, zum Ausdruck bringen V
°**expression** [ɪk'spreʃn] Ausdruck
°**extinct** [ɪk'stɪŋkt] ausgestorben
°**extinction** [ɪk'stɪŋkʃn] Ausrottung, Aussterben
extra ['ekstrə] zusätzlich IV
extreme [ɪk'stri:m] extrem IV
extremely [ɪk'stri:mli] äußerst, höchst IV
eye [aɪ] Auge II **keep an eye on sb./sth.** jn./etwas im Auge behalten; ein

(wachsames) Auge haben auf jn./ etwas VI 2 (45)

F

face [feɪs]:
1. Gesicht I
2. **face sth.** vor etwas stehen; *(Problem)*; einer Sache ins Auge sehen, sich einer Sache stellen; einer Sache entgegentreten V
facing forwards/backwards nach vorn/hinten schauend;mit dem Gesicht nach vorn/hinten VI 3 (64)

facilities *(pl)* [fə'sɪlətiz] Einrichtungen, Anlage(n), Geräte VI 1 (22)
fact [fækt] Tatsache, Fakt IV **in fact** eigentlich, um genau zu sein VI 1 (16)
factory ['fæktəri] Fabrik VI 2 (45)
faint [feɪnt]:
1. in Ohnmacht fallen VI 3 (64)
2. schwindelig; schwach VI 3 (64)

°**fairly** ['feəli] ziemlich
°**fair-trade** [feə 'treɪd] Fairtrade-, aus fairem Handel
faithfully ['feɪθfəli]: **Yours faithfully** Mit freundlichen Grüßen *(Briefschluss)* V
fall [fɔːl] *(AE)* Herbst IV
fall [fɔːl], **fell, fallen** fallen; hinfallen I **fall asleep** einschlafen IV **fall down** hinfallen IV
fallen ['fɔːlən] *siehe* **fall**
false [fɔːls] falsch I
false friend [fɔːls 'frend] „falscher Freund", Übersetzungsfalle VI 1 (18)
family ['fæməli] Familie I
family name ['fæməli neɪm] Familienname, Nachname I
family tree ['fæməli triː] (Familien-) Stammbaum I
famous (for) ['feɪməs] berühmt (für, wegen) III
fancy ['fænsi] schick IV
fantastic [fæn'tæstɪk] fantastisch, wunderschön V
far [fɑː] weit (entfernt) II **as far as** bis *(räumlich)* V **so far** bis jetzt V
farm [fɑːm]:
1. Bauernhof, Farm I
2. Landwirtschaft betreiben V

farmer ['fɑːmə] Farmer; Bauer, Bäuerin III
farmyard ['fɑːmjɑːd] Hof *(eines Bauernhauses)* III
fascinate ['fæsɪneɪt] faszinieren VI 3 (60)
fashion ['fæʃn] Mode III
fast [fɑːst] schnell I
fast-food restaurant [fɑːst fuːd 'restrɒnt] Schnellimbiss V
father ['fɑːðə] Vater I
fault [fɔːlt] Fehler, Schuld V
favourite ['feɪvərɪt] Lieblings- I
fear (of) [fɪə] Furcht, Angst (vor) VI 3 (64)
feather ['feðə] Feder IV
feature ['fiːtʃə]:
1. vorkommen, mitwirken VI 2 (46) **be featured** gezeigt werden VI 2 (46)
°2. Merkmal, Eigenschaft
°3. (Dokumentar-)Bericht, Feature

February ['februəri] Februar I
fed [fed] *siehe* **feed**
fed up [fed 'ʌp]: **feel fed up** genervt sein, sauer sein; die Nase voll haben I
feed [fiːd]:
1. **feed, fed, fed** füttern I
°2. Feed *(Daten-Zufuhr; abonnierbare elektronische Nachricht im Internet)*

feel [fiːl], **felt, felt** sich fühlen; fühlen I **feel fed up** genervt sein, sauer sein; die Nase voll haben I **I don't feel like it.** Mir ist nicht danach. II **I'm not feeling well.** Ich fühle mich nicht gut. II
feeling ['fiːlɪŋ] Gefühl I
feet [fiːt] *Mehrzahl von* **foot** IV
fell [fel] *siehe* **fall**
°**fellow student** ['feləʊ] Mitschüler/in
felt [felt] *siehe* **feel**
female ['fiːmeɪl] weiblich III
fence [fens] Zaun III
ferry ['feri] Fähre I
festival ['festɪvl] Festival, Fest II
few [fjuː] wenige VI 3 (63) **a few** ein paar, einige II
°**fictional** ['fɪkʃənl] fiktiv, erfunden **non-fictional text** Sachtext
field [fiːld] Feld; Weide I **in the field** auf der Weide I
fight [faɪt]:
1. Kampf IV
2. **fight, fought, fought** kämpfen III (sich) streiten IV **fight sb.** jn. bekämpfen, gegen jn. kämpfen IV

fighter ['faɪtə] Kämpfer/in V
figure ['fɪgə] Zahl, Ziffer; Person *(Gestalt)*; Figur V
°**file** [faɪl] Datei; Ordner, Liste
fill [fɪl] füllen II **fill sth. in** etwas ausfüllen; etwas einsetzen VI 1 (22) **fill up** sich füllen IV
film [fɪlm] filmen III
film set ['fɪlm set] Filmset; Filmkulisse IV
film-maker ['fɪlm meɪkə] Filmemacher/in VI 1 (25)
°**film-making** ['fɪlm meɪkɪŋ] Filmgestaltung, Filmemachen
final ['faɪnl] letzte(r, s) V
finally ['faɪnəli] schließlich; abschließend III
°**financial** [faɪ'nænʃl] finanziell
find [faɪnd], **found, found** finden I **find out about sth.** sich über etwas informieren II **find sth. out** etwas herausfinden II
finder ['faɪndə] Finder/in V **Finders keepers, losers weepers.** Was man findet, darf man behalten. *(Redensart)* V
fine [faɪn] gut; in Ordnung I **I'm fine, thanks.** Danke, (es geht mir) gut. I
fine [faɪn]:
1. Geldstrafe III
2. **fine sb.** jn. zu einer Geldstrafe verurteilen IV

finger ['fɪŋgə] Finger III
fingernail ['fɪŋgəneɪl] Fingernagel V
finish ['fɪnɪʃ]:
1. beenden, zu Ende machen II
2. **finish sth.** etwas aufessen, austrinken; etwas aufbrauchen VI 3 (57)

fire ['faɪə]:
1. Feuer II
2. **fire sb.** jn. feuern, entlassen V **you'll get me fired** du schaffst es noch, dass ich entlassen werde V

fire escape ['faɪər ɪskeɪp] Feuertreppe, Notausgang V
fire escape ladder ['faɪər ɪskeɪp lædə] Feuerleiter V
fire station ['faɪə steɪʃn] Feuerwache I
firefighter ['faɪəfaɪtə] Feuerwehrmann/-frau VI 3 (54/55)
firework ['faɪəwɜːk] Feuerwerkskörper II **fireworks** *(pl)* Feuerwerk II
first [fɜːst]:
1. erste(r, s) I
2. zuerst, als Erstes I **at first** zuerst, am Anfang II

first-aid kit [fɜːst 'eɪd kɪt] Erste-Hilfe-Kasten II
Firstly, ... ['fɜːstli] Erstens ... III
first-person narrator [fɜːst pɜːsn nə'reɪtə] Ich-Erzähler/in VI 3 (65)
fish, *pl* **fish** [fɪʃ] Fisch I
fishing ['fɪʃɪŋ] Fischen, Angeln III
fist [fɪst] Faust II
fit [fɪt] fit II
fit in [fɪt 'ɪn] dazugehören; hineinpassen V
fitness ['fɪtnəs] Fitness V
fitting room ['fɪtɪŋ ruːm] Anprobe, Umkleide(kabine) V
five [faɪv] fünf I
fix sth. [fɪks] *(infml)* etwas in Ordnung bringen IV
flag [flæg] Flagge, Fahne II
flash [flæʃ] blinken, leuchten VI 2 (42) **flash one's headlights** aufblenden, die Lichthupe betätigen VI 2 (42)
°**flashback** ['flæʃbæk] Rückblende
flashing lights *(pl)* [flæʃɪŋ 'laɪts] Warnlicht, Blaulicht VI 2 (42)
flashlight ['flæʃlaɪt] *(AE)* Taschenlampe IV
flat [flæt]:
1. Wohnung I
2. flach, eben V

flew [fluː] *siehe* **fly**
flexible ['fleksəbl] flexibel V

flight [flaɪt]:
1. Flug III
°2. Flucht

flood [flʌd] überfluten, überschwemmen IV
floor [flɔː]:
1. Fußboden IV
2. Stock(werk) IV

flour ['flaʊə] Mehl III
flow [fləʊ] fließen IV
flower ['flaʊə] Blume; Blüte II
flown [fləʊn] *siehe* **fly**
flute [fluːt] Querflöte IV
fly [flaɪ], **flew, flown** fliegen III
focus (on) ['fəʊkəs] sich konzentrieren (auf) V
fog [fɒg] Nebel II
foggy ['fɒgi] neblig II
follow ['fɒləʊ] folgen; verfolgen III
follower ['fɒləʊə] Anhänger/in, Fan V
°**follow-up** ['fɒləʊ ʌp] Anschluss-, Folge-
food [fuːd] Essen; Lebensmittel; Futter I
fool [fuːl] Dummkopf, Narr/Närrin IV
foot, *pl* **feet** [fʊt], [fiːt] Fuß IV °**put your foot down** Gas geben *(Auto)*
football ['fʊtbɔːl] Fußball I
footballer ['fʊtbɔːlə] Fußballspieler/in III
for [fɔː], [fə] für I **for a few minutes** ein paar Minuten (lang) II **for example** zum Beispiel II **for lots of reasons** aus vielen Gründen III **for the last time** zum letzten Mal III **for two months** seit zwei Monaten III **What do you need money for?** Wofür brauchst du Geld? II **What's for homework?** Was haben wir als Hausaufgabe auf? I
force sb. to do sth. [fɔːs] jn. zwingen, etwas zu tun IV
forecast ['fɔːkɑːst] *(kurz für:* **weather forecast**) Wettervorhersage II
foreground ['fɔːgraʊnd] Vordergrund III
°**foreign** ['fɒrən] ausländisch, fremd
°**forest** ['fɒrɪst] Wald
forever (*BE auch:* **for ever)** [fər'evə] für immer, ewig (lange) VI 2 (41)
forget [fə'get], **forgot, forgotten** vergessen II **forget about sth.** etwas vergessen, nicht mehr an etwas denken II
forgot [fə'gɒt] *siehe* **forget**
forgotten [fə'gɒtn] *siehe* **forget**
form [fɔːm]:
1. Form I
2. Formular V

formal ['fɔːml] formell, feierlich *(Kleidung)* VI 3 (67)
fortunately ['fɔːtʃənətli] glücklicherweise VI 3 (62)
fortune ['fɔːtʃuːn] Vermögen IV **cost a fortune** ein Vermögen kosten IV
forward ['fɔːwəd] vorwärts, nach vorn II **look forward to doing sth.** sich darauf freuen, etwas zu tun IV **look forward to sth.** sich auf etwas freuen II
forwards ['fɔːwədz] nach vorne; vorwärts VI 3 (64)
fought [fɔːt] *siehe* **fight**
found [faʊnd] *siehe* **find**
°**foundation** [faʊn'deɪʃn] Fundament, Grundlage
four [fɔː] vier I
fox [fɒks] Fuchs II
freak [friːk] Freak; Fan II
free [friː]:
1. frei I
2. kostenlos II

freedom ['friːdəm] Freiheit IV
free-time activities [friː taɪm æk'tɪvətiz] Freizeitaktivitäten II
freezing ['friːzɪŋ] eisig, eiskalt II
French [frentʃ] Französisch; französisch I
French fries *(pl)* [frentʃ 'fraɪz] *(AE)* Pommes frites IV
fresh [freʃ] frisch II
Friday ['fraɪdeɪ], ['fraɪdi] Freitag I
fridge [frɪdʒ] Kühlschrank IV
fried [fraɪd] gebraten III
friend [frend] Freund/in I **be (good) friends with sb.** mit jm. (gut) befreundet sein V **make friends** Freunde finden II
friendliness ['frendlinəs] Freundlichkeit V
friendly ['frendli] freundlich I
friendship ['frendʃɪp] Freundschaft IV
fries [fraɪz]: **French fries** *(pl)* *(AE)* Pommes frites IV
frighten sb. ['fraɪtn] jm. Angst machen VI 1 (19)
frightened ['fraɪtnd] verängstigt VI 1 (19) **be frightened of sth.** Angst haben vor etwas VI 1 (19)
frightening ['fraɪtnɪŋ] beängstigend VI 1 (19)
from [frɒm], [frəm] aus; von I **from Monday to Friday** von Montag bis Freitag I **a text from mum** eine SMS von Mama I **I'm from Plymouth.** Ich bin aus Plymouth. / Ich komme aus Plymouth. I
front [frʌnt] Vorderseite; Fassade; Front IV **front wall** vordere Wand IV **at the front** vorn, im vorderen Teil IV **in front of** vor I
front desk [frʌnt 'desk] Rezeption, Empfang *(z.B. Hotel)* V
frontier (with) ['frʌntɪə] Grenze (zu) VI 3 (60) **new frontiers** Neuland, neue Ufer VI 3 (60)
fruit [fruːt] Obst I
fruit tea ['fruːt tiː] Früchtetee II
frustrate [frʌ'streɪt] frustrieren V
frustrating [frʌ'streɪtɪŋ] frustrierend V
fuel ['fjuːəl] Treibstoff, Kraftstoff V
full (of) [fʊl] voll (mit, von) III
full stop [fʊl 'stɒp] Punkt *(Satzzeichen)* VI 1 (17)
full-time job [fʊl taɪm 'dʒɒb] Ganztagsjob, Vollzeitjob IV
fun [fʌn] Spaß I **it's fun** es macht Spaß I
fun run ['fʌn rʌn] Volkslauf III
fund-raising event ['fʌndreɪzɪŋ ɪvent] Event zur Beschaffung von Geld/Spenden IV
funny ['fʌni] witzig, komisch II
°**furious** ['fjʊəriəs] wütend
°**furniture** ['fɜːnɪtʃə] Möbel(stücke)
furry ['fɜːri] flauschig; pelzig I
°**further** ['fɜːðə] weiter; weitere
future ['fjuːtʃə] Zukunft II
°**futurologist** [fjuːtʃə'rɒlədʒɪst] Zukunftsforscher/in

G

gadget ['gædʒɪt] Gerät, Apparat, technischer Krimskrams VI 3 (66)
game [geɪm] Spiel I
°**game reserve** ['geɪm rɪzɜːv] Wildschutzgebiet
gaming ['geɪmɪŋ] *(das)* Spielen am Computer V
gap [gæp] Lücke VI 1 (22)
garage ['gærɑːʒ]:
1. Garage I
2. (Auto-)Werkstatt II

garbage ['gɑːbɪdʒ] *(AE)* (Haus-)Müll, Abfall IV
garden ['gɑːdn] Garten I
gas [gæs] *(AE)* Benzin IV
gate [geɪt]:
1. Flugsteig III
2. Tor, Gatter III

gatecrash (a party) ['geɪtkræʃ] (bei einer Party) ungebeten erscheinen V
gatecrasher ['geɪtkræʃə] nicht eingeladene Person (die eine Party sprengt) V
gave [geɪv] *siehe* **give**
gear [gɪə] Ausrüstung II
gender ['dʒendə] Geschlecht *(als soziales Merkmal)* VI 2 (46)
general ['dʒenrəl] allgemein V
generation [dʒenə'reɪʃn] Generation V
geography [dʒi'ɒgrəfi] Geografie, Erdkunde I
German ['dʒɜːmən] Deutsch; deutsch I
Germany ['dʒɜːməni] Deutschland I
get [get], **got, got**:
1. bekommen I
2. holen, besorgen II
3. **get (to)** gelangen, (hin)kommen II
4. werden II

get around sich fortbewegen *(mobil sein)* IV **get dressed** sich anziehen IV **get drunk** sich betrinken IV **get lost** sich verirren, sich verlaufen IV **get married** heiraten IV **get off a plane/bus/train** aus einem Flugzeug/Bus/Zug aussteigen III **get on (well/badly) together** (gut/

schlecht) miteinander auskommen, zurechtkommen IV **get on a plane/bus/train** in ein Flugzeug/einen Bus/einen Zug einsteigen III **get out (of a car)** (aus einem Auto) aussteigen IV **get out (of)** herauskommen (aus) III **get ready (for)** sich fertig machen (für), sich vorbereiten (auf) I **get rid of sth.** etwas loswerden II **get sb. to do sth.** jn. dazu bringen, etwas zu tun VI 1 (21) **get started** anfangen III **get to do sth.** etwas tun können/dürfen; die Möglichkeit haben/bekommen, etwas zutun IV **get to know sb./each other** jn./sich kennenlernen IV **get up** aufstehen I **get used to sth.** sich an etwas gewöhnen IV **Do you get it?** *(infml)* Verstehst du? / Kapierst du? III

ghost [gəʊst] Gespenst, Geist III

giant ['dʒaɪənt] Riese/Riesin IV

°**gift** [gɪft] Geschenk

gingerbread ['dʒɪndʒəbred] Honigkuchen, Pfefferkuchen VI 2 (40)

giraffe, *pl* **giraffe** *or* **giraffes** [dʒə'rɑːf] Giraffe VI 1 (22)

girl [gɜːl] Mädchen I

girlfriend ['gɜːlfrend] (feste) Freundin I

gist [dʒɪst]: **the gist** *(no pl)* das Wesentliche; die Kernaussage(n) IV

give [gɪv], **gave, given** geben II **give a talk** einen Vortrag halten II **give up** aufgeben, aufhören IV °**give a speech** eine Rede halten

given ['gɪvn] *siehe* **give**

glamorous ['glæmərəs] glamourös V

glass (of) [glɑːs] Glas III

glasses *(pl)* ['glɑːsɪz] (eine) Brille II

°**glimpse** [glɪmps] kurzer Blick **catch a glimpse of sth.** einen Blick von/auf etwas erhaschen; etwas nur kurz zu sehen bekommen

global warming [gləʊbl 'wɔːmɪŋ] Erderwärmung VI 3 (63)

glove [glʌv] Handschuh II **a pair of gloves** ein Paar Handschuhe II

°**glucose** ['gluːkəʊs] Traubenzucker, Glukose

go [gəʊ], **went, gone** gehen; fahren I **Go ahead** Nur zu./Dann mal los. V **go away** verschwinden V **go by bus/bike/car/...** mit dem Bus/Rad/Auto/... fahren I **go crazy** verrückt werden III **go for a walk** einen Spaziergang machen, spazieren gehen II **Go for it, Luca!** Nichts wie ran, Luca! II **go home** nach Hause gehen I **go off** losgehen *(Wecker, Alarm, ...)* IV **go on** weiterreden, fortfahren; weitermachen III **go out** rausgehen, weggehen, ausgehen II **go shopping** einkaufen gehen I **go swimming** schwimmen gehen I **go to bed** ins Bett gehen I **go to school** zur Schule gehen I **Go to sleep!** Schlaf jetzt! I **go to work** zur Arbeit gehen I **go with** gehören zu, passen zu I **go wrong** schiefgehen III **How's it going?** Wie geht's? / Wie läuft's? I **I must go.** *(am Telefon)* Ich muss Schluss machen. I **I'm going to do some chores.** Ich werde ein paar Hausarbeiten erledigen. II **What's going on?** Was ist los? / Was gibt's? IV °**go off** ausgehen *(z.B. Licht)*

°**goal** [gəʊl] Tor *(Sport)*

goat [gəʊt] Ziege V

God [gɒd] Gott III

gold [gəʊld] Gold IV

gone [gɒn] *siehe* **go** **be gone** weg sein, nicht (mehr) da sein IV

good [gʊd] gut I **Good boy. / Good dog.** Braver Junge. / Braver Hund. II **Good luck.** Viel Glück. IV **Good morning.** Guten Morgen. I **be good at sth.** etwas gut können; gut in etwas sein II **be good with sth.** gut mit etwas umgehen können III **be no good at sth.** etwas nicht gut können; nicht gut in etwas sein III

Goodbye. [gʊd'baɪ] Auf Wiedersehen! I

good-looking [gʊd 'lʊkɪŋ] gut aussehend IV

got [gɒt] *siehe* **get**

government ['gʌvənmənt] Regierung; Regierungs- IV

gown [gaʊn] Robe IV

°**grab** [græb] packen, greifen (nach)

grade [greɪd] *(AE)* Klassenstufe, Jahrgang IV

graduation [grædʒu'eɪʃn] (Schul-, Universitäts-)Abschluss; Abschlussfeier IV

graffiti [grə'fiːti] Graffiti IV

°**gram (g)** [græm] Gramm

grammar ['græmə] Grammatik VI 1 (18)

grandad ['grændæd] Opa III

granddaughter ['grændɔːtə] Enkelin V

grandfather ['grænfɑːðə] Großvater I

grandma ['grænmɑː] Oma I

grandmother ['grænmʌðə] Großmutter I

grandpa ['grænpɑː] Opa I

grandparents *(pl)* ['grænpeərənts] Großeltern I

grandson ['grænsʌn] Enkel V

°**granny** ['græni] Oma

graph [græf], *BE auch:* [grɑːf] Diagramm, Kurve VI 3 (59)

grass [grɑːs] Gras; Rasen II **cut the grass** Rasen mähen II

°**grassland** ['grɑːslænd] Grasland; Steppe

gravestone ['greɪvstəʊn] Grabstein VI 3 (63)

graveyard ['greɪvjɑːd] Friedhof VI 3 (63)

°**gravity** ['grævəti] Schwerkraft

great [greɪt] großartig, prima I

Great Britain [greɪt 'brɪtn] Großbritannien II

green [griːn] grün I

greet [griːt] begrüßen V

grew [gruː] *siehe* **grow**

grey [greɪ] grau I

grin (at sb.) [grɪn] (jn. an)grinsen V

groan [grəʊn] stöhnen VI 3 (57)

groceries *(pl)* ['grəʊsəriz] Lebensmittel IV

grocery store ['grəʊsəri stɔː] Lebensmittelgeschäft IV

ground [graʊnd] (Erd-)Boden II

group [gruːp]:
1. Gruppe I
2. gruppieren IV

grow [grəʊ], **grew, grown**:
1. wachsen II
grow up aufwachsen; erwachsen werden IV
2. anbauen, anpflanzen IV
3. (allmählich) werden IV

grown [grəʊn] *siehe* **grow**

growth [grəʊθ] Wachstum VI 3 (58)

°**guarantee** [gærən'tiː] garantieren

°**guardian** ['gɑːdiən] Begleitperson

guess [ges]:
1. Vermutung IV
2. raten, erraten I
Guess what – ... Stell dir vor – ... III
I guess ... Ich nehme an, ... / Ich glaube, ... IV

guest [gest] Gast III

guest house ['gest haʊs] Pension *(Gästehaus)* VI 2 (36)

guide [gaɪd]:
1. Reiseführer *(Buch)* IV
2. Reiseleiter/in, Fremdenführer/in IV
3. Ratgeber, Einführung IV

guitar [gɪ'tɑː] Gitarre I

°**gulp sth. down** [gʌlp 'daʊn] etwas hinunterschlingen, (Getränk) hinunterstürzen

guy [gaɪ] *(infml)* Typ, Kerl II **guys** *(pl)* Leute *(als Anrede verwendet)* I

gym [dʒɪm]:
1. Sporthalle, Turnhalle III
2. Fitnessraum, Fitnessstudio VI 3 (56)

°**gymnasium** [dʒɪm'neɪziəm] Turnhalle, Sporthalle

gymnastics [dʒɪm'næstɪks] Gymnastik II

H

habit ['hæbɪt] (An-)Gewohnheit V

°**habitat** ['hæbɪtæt] Lebensraum

had [hæd] *siehe* **have**

hair [heə] Haar, Haare II

hairdresser ['heədresə] Friseur/in II **at the hairdresser's** beim Friseur II

hairdryer ['heədraɪə] Föhn, Haartrockner II

half [hɑːf]:
1. halbe(r, s) II
half an hour eine halbe Stunde II
2. **half**, *pl* **halves** Hälfte V

sixteen and a half sechzehneinhalb V
°**half-time** [hɑːf 'taɪm] Halbzeit(pause)
hall [hɔːl]:
1. Flur, Diele I
2. Halle II
hallway ['hɔːlweɪ] *(AE)* Korridor, Gang IV
hammer ['hæmə]:
1. Hammer V
2. hämmern V
hamster ['hæmstə] Hamster I
hand [hænd] Hand II **on the one hand** einerseits III **on the other hand** andererseits III **put up one's hand** sich melden; seine/die Hand heben V
handshake ['hændʃeɪk] Händedruck, Handschlag IV
°**handy** ['hændi] praktisch, nützlich
hang [hæŋ], **hung, hung** hängen IV
°**hang around** *(infml)* herumhängen
happen ['hæpən] geschehen, passieren I
happiness ['hæpinəs] Glück V
happy ['hæpi] glücklich, froh I
Happy birthday! Herzlichen Glückwunsch zum Geburtstag! I **happy ending** Happy End II
harbour ['hɑːbə] Hafen I
hard [hɑːd] schwer, schwierig; hart I
Hard luck! Pech (gehabt)! III **rain hard** stark regnen V **try hard** sich sehr bemühen, sich anstrengen IV
work hard hart arbeiten I
hard-working [hɑːd 'wɜːkɪŋ] fleißig III
has [hæz], [həz]: **he/she/it has ...** er/sie/es hat ... I
hat [hæt] Hut II
hate [heɪt] hassen, gar nicht mögen I
have [hæv], **had, had** haben I **Have a good day.** Ich wünsch dir einen schönen Tag. / Schönen Tag noch. I
have a party eine Party feiern I
have breakfast frühstücken I **have dinner** Abendbrot essen, zu Abend essen I **have lunch** (zu) Mittag essen I **have to do sth.** etwas tun müssen II **I have a sore leg.** Mein Bein tut weh. I **I'll have ...** Ich nehme ... *(beim Essen, im Restaurant)* II **Let's have a look.** Lass uns nachsehen. III °**have sth. done (by sb.)** etwas (von jm.) machen lassen
he [hiː] er I
head [hed]:
1. Kopf II
2. **head for sth.** auf etwas zugehen/zusteuern IV
°**head into sth.** sich in etwas hineinbegeben/-stürzen °**head somewhere** in eine Richtung gehen/fahren
headache ['hedeɪk] Kopfschmerzen II
heading ['hedɪŋ] Überschrift III
headlight ['hedlaɪt] Scheinwerfer(licht) VI 2 (41)
headline ['hedlaɪn] Schlagzeile IV
°**headmaster** [hed'mɑːstə] Schulleiter, Direktor
head-mounted display [hed maʊntɪd dɪ'spleɪ] Datenhelm, Datenbrille, Videobrille VI 3 (57)
headphones *(pl)* ['hedfəʊnz] *(ein)* Kopfhörer VI 3 (56)
health [helθ] Gesundheit V
health care ['helθ keə] Gesundheitsversorgung V
healthy ['helθi] gesund II
hear [hɪə], **heard, heard** hören I
heard [hɜːd] *siehe* **hear**
heart [hɑːt] Herz III
heat [hiːt]:
1. Hitze, Wärme V
2. erwärmen, erhitzen VI 1 (20)
heat stress ['hiːt stres] Hitzestress, Wärmebelastung des Körpers V
heavy ['hevi] schwer III
°**height** [haɪt] Höhe, Größe *(bei Menschen)*
held [held] *siehe* **hold**
helicopter ['helɪkɒptə] Helikopter, Hubschrauber IV
°**hell** [hel] Hölle **Where the hell is Africa?** *(infml)* Wo zum Teufel ist Afrika?
Hello. [hə'ləʊ] Hallo. / Guten Tag. I
helmet ['helmɪt] Helm I
help [help]:
1. Hilfe I
2. helfen I
Help yourselves. Bedient euch! / Greift zu! III
helper ['helpə] Helfer/in II
helpful ['helpfl] hilfsbereit; hilfreich, nützlich IV
helpless ['helpləs] hilflos VI 3 (56)
her [hɜː], [hə]:
1. sie; ihr I
2. **her dad** ihr Vater I
here [hɪə] hier; hierher I **Here you are.** Bitte schön. / Hier, bitte. I
near here hier in der Nähe II
hero, *pl* **heroes** ['hɪərəʊ] Held/in III
hers [hɜːz] ihre/r, ihrs *(zu „she")* V
herself [hɜː'self] sich III
°**hesitate** ['hezɪteɪt] zögern
Hi. [haɪ] Hallo. I **Say hi to everybody.** Grüß alle. I
hid [hɪd] *siehe* **hide**
hidden ['hɪdn] *siehe* **hide**
hide [haɪd], **hid, hidden** verstecken; sich verstecken I
high [haɪ] hoch III
high season [haɪ 'siːzn] Hauptsaison VI 1 (10)
high street ['haɪ striːt] Hauptstraße *(mit vielen Geschäften)* III
Highlands ['haɪləndz]: **the Highlands** *(pl)* das schottische Hochland III
highlight ['haɪlaɪt] Höhepunkt IV
°**high-rise building** [haɪ raɪz 'bɪldɪŋ] Hochhaus
°**highs and lows** *(pl)* [haɪz ən 'ləʊz] Höhen und Tiefen
highway ['haɪweɪ] Fernstraße *(in den USA; oft mit vier oder mehr Spuren)* IV
hike [haɪk] wandern IV
hiking ['haɪkɪŋ] Wandern IV
°**hilarious** [hɪ'leəriəs] urkomisch, unheimlich witzig
hill [hɪl] Hügel I
hilly ['hɪli] hügelig III
him [hɪm] ihn; ihm I
himself [hɪm'self] sich III
°**hippo,** *pl* **hippos** ['hɪpəʊ] Nilpferd
hire ['haɪə] mieten, leihen III
his [hɪz]:
1. sein/e I
2. seiner, seine, seins *(zu „he")* V
historical [hɪ'stɒrɪkl] historisch, geschichtlich VI 1 (24)
history ['hɪstri] Geschichte I
hit [hɪt], **hit, hit**:
1. schlagen; treffen IV
2. prallen/stoßen gegen/auf IV
hitchhiker ['hɪtʃhaɪkə] Anhalter/in, Tramper/in V
hi-tech [haɪ 'tek] High-Tech-, Hochleistungs- VI 3 (54/55)
hobby ['hɒbi] Hobby I
hockey ['hɒki] Hockey III
hold [həʊld], **held, held** halten IV
hole [həʊl] Loch III
hole punch ['həʊl pʌntʃ] Locher I
holiday(s) ['hɒlədeɪ]:
1. Ferien; Urlaub I
be/go on holiday in Urlaub sein/fahren III
2. **holiday** Feiertag VI 1 (13)
home [həʊm] Heim, Zuhause I **at home** daheim, zu Hause I **come/go home** nach Hause kommen/gehen I
dogs' home Hundeheim II
homeless ['həʊmləs] obdachlos IV
homesick ['həʊmsɪk]: **be/feel homesick** Heimweh haben II
hometown ['həʊmtaʊn] Heimatstadt IV
homework ['həʊmwɜːk] Hausaufgabe(n) I **I forgot my homework.** Ich habe meine Hausaufgaben vergessen. I **What's for homework?** Was haben wir als Hausaufgabe auf? I
honest ['ɒnɪst] ehrlich IV
hood [hʊd] Kapuze III
hood [hʊd] *(AE, infml) kurz für* **neighbo(u)rhood** IV
hoodie ['hʊdi] Kapuzenpullover, -jacke I
hoover ['huːvə] staubsaugen II
hope [həʊp]:
1. hoffen I
2. Hoffnung IV
hopeless ['həʊpləs] hoffnungslos VI 3 (56)

horrible ['hɒrəbl] scheußlich, ätzend, gemein V
°**horrified** ['hɒrɪfaɪd] entsetzt
horror ['hɒrə] Horror IV
horse [hɔːs] Pferd V
hospital ['hɒspɪtl] Krankenhaus I
°**host a party** [həʊst] eine Party veranstalten, feiern
hostel ['hɒstl] Herberge, Hostel III
hot [hɒt] heiß II
hot spot ['hɒt spɒt] Anziehungspunkt V **tourist hot spot** touristischer Anziehungspunkt V
hotel [həʊ'tel] Hotel III
hour ['aʊə] Stunde II **half an hour** eine halbe Stunde II **working hours** *(pl)* Arbeitszeit(en) V
house [haʊs] Haus I
°**housing estate** ['haʊzɪŋ ɪsteɪt] Wohnsiedlung
how? [haʊ] wie? I **How are you?** Wie geht's? / Wie geht es dir/euch? I **How many ...?** Wie viele ...? II **How much ...?** Wie viel ...? II **How much are ...?** Was (Wie viel) kosten ...? I **How much is ...?** Was (Wie viel) kostet ...? I **how to do sth.** wie man etwas tut / tun kann / tun soll III **How's it going?** Wie geht's? / Wie läuft's? I
however [haʊ'evə] allerdings; jedoch IV
hug [hʌg]:
1. (sich) umarmen VI 1 (21)
2. Umarmung VI 1 (21)
huge [hjuːdʒ] riesig III
human ['hjuːmən] Mensch; menschlich VI 1 (15)
human being [hjuːmən 'biːɪŋ] Mensch VI 1 (15)
°**humour** ['hjuːmə] Humor **sense of humour** (Sinn für) Humor
°**hump** [hʌmp] Buckel, Hindernis **speed hump** Bodenschwelle, Bremsschwelle *(zur Verkehrsberuhigung)*
hundred ['hʌndrəd]: **a hundred, one hundred** (ein)hundert I
hung [hʌŋ] *siehe* **hang**
hungry ['hʌŋgri]: **be hungry** hungrig sein, Hunger haben I
hunt [hʌnt]:
1. jagen IV
°2. Jagd
°**on the hunt** auf der Jagd
hurricane ['hʌrɪkən] Hurrikan, Orkan IV
hurry ['hʌri]:
1. **Hurry up.** Beeil dich. IV
°**hurry (home)** sich beeilen; (nach Hause) eilen
2. **be in a hurry** in Eile sein, es eilig haben III
hurt [hɜːt], **hurt, hurt** verletzen; wehtun II **be hurt** verletzt sein II **get hurt** sich verletzen II
hurtful ['hɜːtfl] verletzend VI 2 (34)
husband ['hʌzbənd] Ehemann IV
°**hyper-** ['haɪpə] Hyper-, Über-
hyphen ['haɪfn] Bindestrich, Trennstrich VI 1 (17)
°**hypocrisy** [hɪ'pɒkrəsi] Heuchelei, Scheinheiligkeit

I

I [aɪ] ich I **I'm ... (= I am)** ich bin ... I
ice [aɪs] Eis III
ice cream [aɪs 'kriːm] (Speise-)Eis II
ice hockey ['aɪs hɒki] Eishockey II
ice rink ['aɪs rɪŋk] Schlittschuhbahn, Eisbahn IV
ice skating ['aɪs skeɪtɪŋ] Schlittschuhlaufen II
ICT (Information and Communication technology) [aɪ siː 'tiː], [ɪnfəmeɪʃn ənd kəmjuːnɪ'keɪʃn teknɒlədʒi] Informations- und Kommunikationstechnologie I
ID (= identification) [aɪ 'diː], [aɪdentɪfɪ'keɪʃn] Ausweis; Identifizierung, Legitimation VI 1 (23)
idea [aɪ'dɪə] Idee I
ideal [aɪ'dɪəl] ideal III
identify [aɪ'dentɪfaɪ] erkennen, identifizieren VI 2 (47)
identity [aɪ'dentəti] Identität V
idiot ['ɪdiət] Idiot/in V
if [ɪf]:
1. wenn, falls II
2. ob II
ignorance ['ɪgnərəns] Ignoranz, Unwissenheit V
ignore [ɪg'nɔː] nicht beachten, ignorieren IV
ill [ɪl] krank II
illegal [ɪ'liːgl] illegal III
illness ['ɪlnəs] Krankheit V
image ['ɪmɪdʒ] Bild, Abbild; Vorstellung; Image IV
°**imagination** [ɪmædʒɪ'neɪʃn] Fantasie, Vorstellungskraft
imaginative [ɪ'mædʒɪnətɪv] einfallsreich, kreativ V
imagine sth. [ɪ'mædʒɪn] sich etwas vorstellen III
immediately [ɪ'miːdiətli] sofort VI 1 (22)
immigrant ['ɪmɪgrənt] Einwanderer/Einwanderin IV
immigration [ɪmɪ'greɪʃn] Einwanderung, Zuwanderung IV
°**impact** ['ɪmpækt] Einfluss, Auswirkung
impatient [ɪm'peɪʃnt] ungeduldig III
important [ɪm'pɔːtnt] wichtig I
impossible [ɪm'pɒsəbl] unmöglich VI 2 (45)
impressed [ɪm'prest] beeindruckt III
°**impression** [ɪm'preʃn] Eindruck
improve [ɪm'pruːv] verbessern IV
in [ɪn] in I **in a different way** anders; auf andere Art und Weise III **in all** insgesamt III **in England** in England I **in English** auf Englisch I **in front of** vor I **in my opinion** meiner Meinung nach III **in other words** mit anderen Worten V **in the 1990s** in den 90er-Jahren (des 20. Jahrhunderts) III **in the afternoon** nachmittags, am Nachmittag I **in the country** auf dem Land I **in the end** schließlich, zum Schluss II **in the evening** abends, am Abend I **in the field** auf dem Feld I **in the middle** in der Mitte I **in the morning** am Morgen, morgens I **in the old days** früher II **in the photo** auf dem Foto I **in the picture** auf dem Bild I **in town** in der Stadt I **I haven't eaten in days** ich habe tagelang nichts gegessen V **one in three** eine/r von drei(en) V
°**incident** ['ɪnsɪdənt] Vorfall, Begebenheit
°**incinerate** [ɪnsɪnə'reɪt] verbrennen
include [ɪn'kluːd] (mit) einschließen VI 1 (14)
included [ɪn'kluːdɪd] inbegriffen III
including [ɪn'kluːdɪŋ] einschließlich; darunter (auch) III
incredible [ɪn'kredəbl] unglaublich IV
independence [ɪndɪ'pendəns] Unabhängigkeit IV
independent [ɪndɪ'pendənt] unabhängig III
Indian ['ɪndiən]: **(American) Indian** Indianer/in; indianisch IV
indigenous (to) [ɪn'dɪdʒənəs] einheimisch (in) V **indigenous Australian** australische(r) Ureinwohner/in V **indigenous people** Einheimische, Ureinwohner/innen V
indirect [ɪndə'rekt] indirekt V
individual [ɪndɪ'vɪdʒuəl] Einzelne(r), Individuum; Person V
°**indoor** ['ɪndɔː] im Haus, drinnen stattfindend
indoors [ɪn'dɔːz] drinnen *(im Haus)* V
industry ['ɪndəstri] Industrie IV
°**inexplicable** [ɪnɪk'splɪkəbl] unerklärlich
influence ['ɪnfluəns]:
1. beeinflussen V
2. Einfluss V
inform sb. [ɪn'fɔːm] jn. informieren IV
informal [ɪn'fɔːml] informell, locker VI 3 (67)
information (about) [ɪnfə'meɪʃn] *(no pl)* Information(en) (über) III
informative [ɪn'fɔːmətɪv] informativ, lehrreich VI 1 (14)
ingredient [ɪn'griːdiənt] Zutat, Bestandteil V
°**initiative** [ɪ'nɪʃətɪv] Aktion, Initiative
inland [ɪn'lænd] landeinwärts, im Landesinneren/ins Landesinnere V
innocent ['ɪnəsnt] unschuldig IV
inside [ɪn'saɪd]:
1. drinnen; nach drinnen I
2. **inside sth.** in, innerhalb, im Innern von etwas IV

inside out [ɪnsaɪd 'aʊt] verkehrt herum, auf links *(Kleidung)* VI 2 (45)
insight (into) ['ɪnsaɪt] Einblick (in), Verständnis (von) VI 1 (15)
install [ɪn'stɔːl] installieren, einrichten III
instead [ɪn'sted] stattdessen, dafür III
instead of [ɪn'sted əv] anstatt, anstelle von VI 1 (16)
°**instinctive** [ɪn'stɪŋktɪv] instinktiv
°**instruction** [ɪn'strʌkʃn] Anweisung
instrument ['ɪnstrəmənt] Instrument I
interest ['ɪntrəst]:
1. Interesse V
°2. **interest sb.** jn. interessieren
interested ['ɪntrəstɪd]: **be interested in** sich interessieren für; interessiert sein an II
interesting ['ɪntrəstɪŋ] interessant I
international [ɪntə'næʃnəl] international III
interrupt [ɪntə'rʌpt] unterbrechen VI 2 (38)
°**intervene (in)** [ɪntə'viːn] eingreifen, einschreiten (in, bei); sich einmischen (in)
interview ['ɪntəvjuː]: **job interview** Vorstellungsgespräch V
°**intimate** ['ɪntɪmət] intim, eng, persönlich
intimidating [ɪn'tɪmɪdeɪtɪŋ] beängstigend, einschüchternd IV
into ['ɪntʊ] in (... hinein) I **into the living room** ins Wohnzimmer (hinein) I
introduce sb. to sb. [ɪntrə'djuːs] jm. jn. vorstellen, jn. mit jm. bekanntmachen V
introduction [ɪntrə'dʌkʃn] Einleitung, Einführung IV
invention [ɪn'venʃn] Erfindung V
invisible [ɪn'vɪzəbl] unsichtbar IV
invitation (to) [ɪnvɪ'teɪʃn] Einladung (zu, nach) I
invite (to) [ɪn'vaɪt] einladen (zu, nach) I
involved [ɪn'vɒlvd]: **involved in** beteiligt an, engagiert bei VI 2 (34) **get involved in sth.** sich an etwas beteiligen, sich bei etwas engagieren VI 2 (34)
iron ['aɪən]:
1. Bügeleisen V
2. bügeln V
°**Iron Age** ['aɪən eɪdʒ] Eisenzeit
irregular [ɪ'regjələ] unregelmäßig VI 2 (40)
irritate ['ɪrɪteɪt] (ver)ärgern, irritieren V
is [ɪz] *(er/sie/es)* ist I **..., isn't it?** ..., oder? / ..., nicht wahr? III **The calculator is £1.** Der Taschenrechner kostet 1 Pfund. I
island ['aɪlənd] Insel IV
issue ['ɪʃuː] (Streit-)Frage, Problem, Thema V
it [ɪt] er/sie/es I
item ['aɪtəm] Artikel, Gegenstand VI 2 (38) **news item** Nachrichtenmeldung, Pressemeldung VI 2 (38)
its [ɪts] sein/seine, ihr/ihre II
itself [ɪt'self] sich III

J

jacket ['dʒækɪt] Jacke, Jackett II
jam [dʒæm] Marmelade I
January ['dʒænjuəri] Januar I
°**jar** [dʒɑː] Glas *(z.B. für Marmelade)*, (Glas-/Plastik-)Gefäß
jealous (of) ['dʒeləs] eifersüchtig (auf), neidisch (auf) V
jeans *(pl)* [dʒiːnz] Jeans II
jelly ['dʒeli] *(AE)* Marmelade IV
job [dʒɒb] Job, (Arbeits-)Stelle I **on the job** bei der Arbeit IV
job advert ['dʒɒb ædvɜːt] Stellenanzeige V
job interview ['dʒɒb ɪntəvjuː] Vorstellungsgespräch V
join [dʒɔɪn]: **join a club** sich einem Klub anschließen; in einen Klub eintreten I °**join together** sich zusammenschließen
joke [dʒəʊk]:
1. Witz II
2. Witze machen, scherzen II
journalist ['dʒɜːnəlɪst] Journalist/in IV
journey ['dʒɜːni] Reise, Fahrt IV
joyriding ['dʒɔɪraɪdɪŋ] Joyriding *(eine Spritztour mit einem gestohlenen Auto machen)* VI 2 (43)
judo ['dʒuːdəʊ] Judo II
juice [dʒuːs] Saft I
July [dʒu'laɪ] Juli I
jump [dʒʌmp]:
1. springen III
2. zusammenzucken *(vor Schreck)* III
°**junction** ['dʒʌŋkʃn] (Straßen-)Kreuzung
June [dʒuːn] Juni I
junk food ['dʒʌŋk fuːd] ungesundes Essen II
just [dʒʌst]:
1. gerade (eben), soeben II
2. (einfach) nur, bloß III
3. einfach (so) IV
4. **just about** so ziemlich, nahezu; (so) ungefähr VI 2 (46)
just like Berry genau wie Berry II

K

keen [kiːn] (sehr) interessiert, begeistert V **be keen on sth./ on doing sth.** an etwas sehr interessiert sein, etwas unbedingt (tun) wollen V
keep [kiːp], **kept, kept**:
1. halten III
2. behalten III
3. aufbewahren IV
keep (on) doing sth. etwas immer weiter/immerwieder/ständig tun VI 3 (58) **keep an eye on sb./sth.** jn./etwas im Auge behalten, ein (wachsames) Auge haben auf jn./etwas VI 2 (45) **keep away from sb.** sich fernhalten von jm. IV **Keep it up.** Mach weiter so! II **Keep me posted.** Halt mich auf dem Laufenden. III **keep on** weitermachen VI 3 (58)
keeper ['kiːpə]: **Finders, keepers, losers, weepers.** Was man findet, darf man behalten. *(Redensart)* V
kept [kept] *siehe* **keep**
kettle ['ketl] (Wasser-)Kessel, Wasserkocher III
key [kiː] Schlüssel; Schlüssel- V
key skills *(pl)* ['kiː skɪlz] Schlüsselqualifikationen, Schlüsselkompetenzen V
kick [kɪk]:
1. treten, schießen III
kick *(infml)* (eine Gewohnheit/Handlungsweise) aufgeben, sich befreien von V
2. Tritt, Stoß, Kick V
kid [kɪd] Kind; Jugendliche(r) I
kidding ['kɪdɪŋ] *(infml)*: **Are you kidding?** Machst du Witze? / Willst du mich auf den Arm nehmen? IV
kill [kɪl] töten IV
killer ['kɪlə] Mörder/in V
°**kilogram, kilo** ['kɪləgræm], ['kiːləʊ] Kilo(gramm)
kilometre (km) ['kɪləmiːtə] Kilometer II °**kilometres per hour (kph)** Kilometer pro Stunde (km/h)
kind [kaɪnd] nett, freundlich II
kind (of) [kaɪnd] Art, Sorte II **kind of glamorous** irgendwie glamourös V **What kind of mistakes ...?** Was für Fehler ...? II
king [kɪŋ] König III
kingdom ['kɪŋdəm]: **the United Kingdom (the UK)** das Vereinigte Königreich III
kiss [kɪs]:
1. (sich) küssen V
2. Kuss V
kitchen ['kɪtʃɪn] Küche I
kitten ['kɪtn] Kätzchen, junge Katze II
knee [niː] Knie II
knew [njuː] *siehe* **know**
knife, *pl* **knives** [naɪf], [naɪvz] Messer III
knock (on) [nɒk] (an)klopfen (an) III
know [nəʊ], **knew, known** wissen; kennen I **get to know each other** sich kennenlernen IV **get to know sb.** jn. kennenlernen IV
known [nəʊn] *siehe* **know** **be well known** bekannt sein IV

L

lab [læb] Labor I
°**label** ['leɪbl] Etikett
ladder ['lædə] *(die)* Leiter V

lain [leɪn] *siehe* **lie**
lake [leɪk] (Binnen-)See II
lamp [læmp] Lampe I
land [lænd]:
1. landen III
2. Land, Grund und Boden IV

°**landfill** ['lændfɪl] deponieren, auf einer Mülldeponie ablagern
°**landing** ['lændɪŋ] Landung
°**landmark** ['lændmɑːk] Wahrzeichen, Sehenswürdigkeit
landowner ['lændəʊnə] Grundbesitzer/in IV
landscape ['lændskeɪp] Landschaft V
lane [leɪn] Gasse, Weg *(oft als Teil von Straßennamen)* II
language ['læŋgwɪdʒ] Sprache I
°**lantern** ['læntən] Laterne
large [lɑːdʒ] groß V
lasagne [lə'sænjə] Lasagne II
last [lɑːst] letzte(r, s) I **at last** schließlich, endlich III **for the last time** zum letzten Mal III
last (for) [lɑːst] (an)halten, (an)dauern VI 3 (67)
late [leɪt] spät I
lately ['leɪtli] in letzter Zeit V
later ['leɪtə] später I
°**latest** ['leɪtɪst]: **the latest ...** der/die/das neueste ...
laugh [lɑːf] lachen I **laugh at** lachen über, sich lustig machen über III
°**launch** [lɔːntʃ] starten, ins Leben rufen
law [lɔː] Gesetz IV
lay [leɪ] *siehe* **lie**
lazy ['leɪzi] faul I
lead [liːd] (Hunde-)Leine III
leader ['liːdə] Leiter/in, (An-)Führer/in II
lean [liːn] sich lehnen; sich beugen IV
learn [lɜːn] lernen I **learn a/your lesson** eine/deine Lektion lernen V
least [liːst] am wenigsten III **at least** mindestens, wenigstens II
leave [liːv], **left, left**:
1. abfahren; (weg)gehen II
2. verlassen III
3. zurücklassen II

leave a message eine Nachricht hinterlassen III **leave sb. alone** jn. in Ruhe lassen V **leave sb./sth. behind** etwas/jn. zurücklassen, etwas hinter sich lassen VI 3 (60) **leave school** von der Schule abgehen III
°**LED** [el iː 'diː] Leuchtdiode
left [left] links; nach links I **on the left** links, auf der linken Seite I
left [left] *siehe* **leave**
°**leftover pizza/cake/...** ['leftəʊvə] übrig gebliebene Pizza/ übrig gebliebener Kuchen/...
leg [leg] Bein I **I have a sore leg.** Mein Bein tut weh. I
°**legal** ['liːgl] legal, erlaubt
lend sb. sth. [lend], **lent, lent** jm. etwas leihen III
lent [lent] *siehe* **lend**
°**lentil** ['lentl] Linse *(Lebensmittel)*
°**leopard** ['lepəd] Leopard
less [les] weniger II **less and less** immer weniger III
lesson ['lesn] (Unterrichts-)Stunde I **learn a/your lesson** eine/deine Lektion lernen V **teach sb. a lesson** jm. eine Lektion erteilen V
let [let], **let, let** lassen IV **Let's have a look.** Lass uns nachsehen. III **Let's see.** Mal sehen. / Mal abwarten. III
letter ['letə]:
1. Brief I

letter to the editor Leserbrief IV
2. Buchstabe II

letter box ['letə bɒks] Briefkasten II
°**level** ['levl] Niveau; Stufe **be at record level(s)** einen Höchststand/ein Rekordniveau erreicht haben
liberty ['lɪbəti] Freiheit IV
library ['laɪbrəri] Bücherei, Bibliothek IV
°**licence** ['laɪsns] Lizenz, Erlaubnis
lie [laɪ]:
1. Lüge V

tell a lie/lies lügen V
2. **lie (to sb.)** (jn. an)lügen V

lie [laɪ], **lay, lain** liegen V °**lie back** sich zurücklehnen, sich entspannen
life, *pl* **lives** [laɪf], [laɪvz] (das) Leben I **way of life** Lebensweise V
lifeguard ['laɪfgɑːd] Rettungsschwimmer/in; Bademeister/in IV
lift [lɪft]:
1. Fahrstuhl, Aufzug, Lift IV
2. Mitfahrgelegenheit VI 2 (41)

give sb. a lift jn. (mit dem Auto) mitnehmen VI 2 (41)
light [laɪt] leicht IV
light [laɪt], **lit, lit** anzünden V **light a fire** (ein) Feuer machen V
lighthouse ['laɪthaʊs] Leuchtturm IV
lights *(pl)* [laɪts] Licht; Lampen III
°**lightweight** ['laɪtweɪt] leicht, Leicht-
like [laɪk] mögen, gernhaben I **like sth. best** etwas am liebsten mögen II **He doesn't like to be lonely.** Er mag es nicht, allein zu sein. I **I like watching TV.** Ich sehe gern fern. I **I'd (= I would) like to go home.** Ich würde gern nach Hause gehen. II **What would you like?** Was möchtest du? / Was hättest du gern? II **Would you like some tea/chips?** Möchtest du (etwas) Tee / (ein paar) Pommes frites? II
like [laɪk] wie I **like that** so, auf diese Weise IV **Like what?** Was (denn) zum Beispiel? III **I don't feel like it.** Mir ist nicht danach. II **What's it like?** Wie ist es? / Wie sieht es aus? I
likeable ['laɪkəbl] sympathisch, liebenswert IV
likely ['laɪkli] wahrscheinlich V **be likely to do sth.** wahrscheinlich etwas tun (werden) V
likes and dislikes *(pl)* [laɪks ən 'dɪslaɪks] Vorlieben und Abneigungen IV
°**limit** ['lɪmɪt] Grenze, Beschränkung
line [laɪn] Zeile; Linie IV
°**line sth.** [laɪn] etwas füttern, auskleiden, säumen
lingua franca [lɪŋgwə 'fræŋkə] Lingua Franca *(Verkehrssprache)* VI 1 (16)
lion ['laɪən] Löwe IV
lip [lɪp] Lippe V
lipstick ['lɪpstɪk] Lippenstift V
list [lɪst]:
1. Liste II
2. auflisten, aufzählen III

listen [lɪsn] zuhören I **listen carefully** aufmerksam/genau zuhören II **listen for sth.** auf etwas horchen, *(beim Zuhören)* auf etwas achten VI 3 (66) **listen to sb.** jm. zuhören I **listen to sth.** sich etwas anhören I
listener ['lɪsənə] Zuhörer/in III
lit [lɪt] *siehe* **light**
litre ['liːtə] Liter V
litter ['lɪtə] Abfall II
litter bin ['lɪtə bɪn] Abfalleimer, Mülleimer II
little ['lɪtl]:
1. klein I
2. wenig VI 3 (63)

a little money/time/... ein bisschen Geld/Zeit/... II
live [lɪv] leben; wohnen I
°**live** [laɪv] live
lives [laɪvz] *Mehrzahl von* **life** I
living ['lɪvɪŋ]: **(sustainable) living** (nachhaltige) Lebensweise VI 3 (58)
living room ['lɪvɪŋ ruːm] Wohnzimmer I
°**load** [ləʊd] (ver)laden
loads (of) [ləʊdz] *(infml)* eine Menge VI 2 (34)
lobby ['lɒbi] Eingangshalle IV
local ['ləʊkl] örtlich, Orts-, Lokal- III
location [ləʊ'keɪʃn] Ort *(Standort; Einsatzort, Drehort)* VI 2 (47)
locker ['lɒkə] Spind, Schließfach IV
lonely ['ləʊnli] einsam I
°**loner** ['ləʊnə] Einzelgänger/in
long [lɒŋ] lang II
long shot ['lɒŋ ʃɒt] Totale *(Film)* VI 1 (25)
look [lʊk]:
1. aussehen I
2. schauen, gucken I

Look, Adam. Sieh mal/Schau mal, Adam. I **look after** sich kümmern um; aufpassen auf I **look around** sich umsehen III **look at sth.** sich etwas anschauen I **look for sth.**

etwas suchen II **look forward to doing sth.** sich darauf freuen, etwas zu tun IV **look forward to sth.** sich auf etwas freuen II **look sth. up** etwas nachschlagen *(Wörter, Informationen)* IV **look up** aufschauen, hochsehen II **Let's have a look.** Lass uns nachsehen. III
°**lookout** ['lʊkaʊt] Aussicht
lose [lu:z], **lost, lost** verlieren II °**lose the police** *(infml)* die Polizei abhängen, abschütteln
loser ['lu:zə] Verlierer/in III **Finders, keepers, losers, weepers.** Was man findet, darf man behalten. *(Redensart)* V
lost [lɒst] *siehe* **lose** **get lost** sich verirren, sich verlaufen IV **I'm not lost.** Ich habe mich nicht verlaufen/verirrt. I
lot [lɒt]: **a lot (of); lots (of)** viel ..., viele ... I
loud [laʊd] laut III
love [lʌv]:
1. Liebe III
°**2.** Liebling
3. lieben, sehr mögen I
I'd (= I would) love to come. Ich komme sehr gern. / Ich würde sehr gern kommen. I **she loves going to ...** sie geht sehr gern zu/nach ...; sie liebt es, zu/nach ... zu gehen II
love life ['lʌv laɪf] Liebesleben III
loveable ['lʌvəbl] liebenswert IV
lovely ['lʌvli] sehr schön, wunderbar, herrlich VI 3 (61)
low [ləʊ] niedrig, tief VI 1 (10)
low season ['ləʊ si:zn] Nebensaison VI 1 (10)
°**lows** [ləʊz]: **highs and lows** *(pl)* Höhen und Tiefen
luck [lʌk]: **Good luck.** Viel Glück. IV **Hard luck!** Pech (gehabt)! III
luckily ['lʌkɪli] glücklicherweise; zum Glück III
lucky ['lʌki]: **you're lucky** du hast Glück I
lunch [lʌntʃ] Mittagessen I **have lunch** (zu) Mittag essen I
lunch box ['lʌntʃ bɒks] Brotdose II
lunchtime ['lʌntʃtaɪm] Mittagszeit II

M

machine [mə'ʃi:n] Maschine, Gerät III
mad [mæd] wahnsinnig, verrückt VI 2 (41)
madam ['mædəm] gnädige Frau V **Dear Sir/Madam** Sehr geehrte Damen und Herren V
made [meɪd] *siehe* **make** **be made of sth.** aus etwas (gemacht) sein IV
magazine [mægə'zi:n] Zeitschrift, Magazin II
°**magic** ['mædʒɪk] Zauberei, Magie
main [meɪn] Haupt- III
mainland ['meɪnlænd] Festland VI 3 (63)
°**mainly** ['meɪnli] hauptsächlich
majority [mə'dʒɒrəti] Mehrheit, Mehrzahl VI 1 (16)
make [meɪk], **made, made** machen, herstellen I **make a deal** ein Geschäft abschließen, vereinbaren II **make an arrangement** eine Vereinbarung treffen; etwas vereinbaren, etwas verabreden II **make friends** Freunde finden II **make it** es schaffen, Erfolg haben VI 3 (61) **make money** Geld verdienen III **make notes** (sich) Notizen machen *(zur Vorbereitung)* III **make sb. do sth.** jn. dazu bringen, etwas zu tun; jn. veranlassen, etwas zu tun IV **make sth. special** etwas zu etwas Besonderem machen III **make sure that ...** sicherstellen, dass ...; darauf achten, dass ...; dafür sorgen, dass ... V °**make sth. up** etwas erfinden, sich etwas ausdenken
make-up ['meɪkʌp] Make-up II
male [meɪl] männlich; männliche Person, männliches Tier VI 2 (46)
mall [mɔ:l] *(kurz für:)* **shopping mall** Einkaufszentrum III
°**mamba** ['mæmbə] Mamba *(Giftschlange)*
man, *pl* **men** [mæn], [men] Mann I
manage ['mænɪdʒ] verwalten, regeln V
management ['mænɪdʒmənt] Management, Leitung, (Geschäfts-)Führung V
manager ['mænɪdʒə] Manager/in; Geschäftsführer/in III
manners *(pl)* ['mænəz] Manieren IV
many ['meni] viele II **How many ...?** Wie viele ...? II
map [mæp] Stadtplan; Landkarte II
°**marathon** ['mærəθən] Marathon(lauf)
March [mɑ:tʃ] März I
mark [mɑ:k]:
1. kennzeichnen, markieren III
°**2.** Zeichnung, Fleck *(z.B. Tierfell)*
°**3.** (Schul-)Note, Zensur
°**full marks** *(pl)* die volle Punktzahl
market ['mɑ:kɪt] Markt I
°**marriage** ['mærɪdʒ] Hochzeit, Ehe
married (to) ['mærid] verheiratet (mit) II **get married** heiraten IV
Mars [mɑ:z] (der) Mars VI 3 (60)
Martian ['mɑ:ʃn] Marsmensch VI 3 (60)
mask [mɑ:sk] Maske II
match [mætʃ] Spiel; Wettkampf II
°**match** [mætʃ] passen (zu) **match with/to** zuordnen
°**mate** [meɪt] *(infml)* Freund/in, Kumpel
°**material** [mə'tɪəriəl] Material, Stoff
materials *(pl)* [mə'tɪəriəlz] Materialien, Hilfsmittel V
math [mæθ] *(AE)* Mathematik IV
maths [mæθs] *(BE)* Mathematik I
matter ['mætə]:
1. von Bedeutung sein, wichtig sein V
It doesn't matter. Es/Das ist egal. II
2. **What's the matter?** Was ist denn? / Was ist los? II
°**maximum, max.** ['mæksɪməm], [mæks] Höchst-, maximal, Maximum
May [meɪ] Mai I
may [meɪ]: **sth. may be destroyed** etwas wird möglicherweise vernichtet VI 1 (22)
maybe ['meɪbi] vielleicht I
°**mayor** [meə] Bürgermeister/in
me [mi:] mich; mir I **Me too.** Ich auch. I **It's me.** Ich bin es. I **Not me!** Ich nicht! I
meal [mi:l] Mahlzeit III
mean [mi:n]:
1. gemein, fies I
2. geizig II
mean [mi:n], **meant, meant**:
1. bedeuten III
2. meinen, sagen wollen III
meaning ['mi:nɪŋ] Bedeutung IV
meant [ment] *siehe* **mean**
meat [mi:t] Fleisch II
meatless ['mi:tləs] fleischlos VI 3 (56)
mechanic [mɪ'kænɪk] Mechaniker/in III
media *(pl)* ['mi:diə] Medien V **social media** soziale Medien/Dienste V
mediate ['mi:dieɪt] vermitteln *(erklären, inhaltlich wiedergeben)* VI 1 (24)
mediation [mi:di'eɪʃn] Vermittlung, Sprachmittlung VI 1 (24)
medicine ['medsn] Medizin; Arznei(mittel), Medikament VI 3 (54/55)
medium ['mi:diəm] mittel(groß); mittlere(r, s) VI 1 (25)
medium shot ['mi:diəm ʃɒt] Halbtotale *(Film)* VI 1 (25)
meet [mi:t], **met, met**:
1. sich treffen II
2. kennenlernen; treffen I
Nice to meet you! Freut mich, dich/euch kennenzulernen. I
meeting ['mi:tɪŋ] Treffen; Zusammenkunft; Besprechung IV
member ['membə] Mitglied IV
meme [mi:m] Internet-Mem, Internetphänomen VI 2 (34)
memorial (to sb./sth.) [mə'mɔ:riəl] Denkmal (für jn./etwas) IV
memory (of) ['meməri] Erinnerung (an) VI 1 (12) **in memory of** in Gedenken an VI 1 (12)
men [men] *Mehrzahl von* **man** I
°**menacing** ['menəsɪŋ] drohend, bedrohlich
°**mend** [mend] reparieren
menu ['menju:] Speisekarte IV
mess [mes] Durcheinander, Chaos IV
message ['mesɪdʒ]:
1. Botschaft III
2. Nachricht II
message in a bottle Flaschenpost VI 3 (65) **take a message** (jm.) etwas ausrichten III

messy ['mesi] unordentlich I
met [met] *siehe* **meet**
metal ['metl] Metall IV
°**metaphor** ['metəfə] Metapher *(Stilmittel, übertragene Bedeutung)*
metre ['mi:tə] Meter II
mice [maɪs] *Mehrzahl von* **mouse** III
microwave ['maɪkrəweɪv] Mikrowelle VI 1 (20)
middle ['mɪdl] Mitte I **in the middle** in der Mitte I **in the middle of nowhere** *etwa:* am Ende der Welt III
Middle Ages *(pl)* [mɪdl 'eɪdʒɪz]: Mittelalter VI 3 (58)
midnight ['mɪdnaɪt] Mitternacht III
might [maɪt]: **it might help** es hilft vielleicht; es könnte (vielleicht) helfen IV
migrant ['maɪgrənt] Zuwanderer, Zuwanderin III
mile [maɪl] Meile *(ca. 1,6 km)* II
milk [mɪlk] Milch II
milkshake ['mɪlkʃeɪk] Milchshake II
million ['mɪljən] Million III
mind [maɪnd]: **Do you mind?** Entschuldige mal! / Was fällt dir ein? IV
I don't mind ... Es macht mir nichts aus ... IV
mind [maɪnd] Geist, Verstand; Gedanken VI 1 (25) **change one's mind** es sich anders überlegen VI 2 (43)
°**mindset** ['maɪndset] Mentalität, Denkweise
mine [maɪn] meiner, meine, meins III
minimum ['mɪnɪməm] Minimum, Mindest-, minimal VI 1 (24)
minister ['mɪnɪstə] Minister/in VI 2 (36)
minority [maɪ'nɒrəti] Minderheit VI 2 (46)
minus ['maɪnəs] minus II
minute ['mɪnɪt] Minute II
mirror ['mɪrə] Spiegel I
°**misgivings** *(pl)* [mɪs'gɪvɪŋ] Bedenken
miss [mɪs]:
1. vermissen I
2. verpassen II
Miss Borowski [mɪs] Frau Borowski *(Anrede für unverheiratete Frauen)* I
missing ['mɪsɪŋ]: **be missing (from)** fehlen (bei/in) VI 1 (23)
°**mission** ['mɪʃn] Auftrag, Mission
mistake [mɪ'steɪk] Fehler II
°**misuse** [mɪs'ju:s] Missbrauch
mix [mɪks] Mischung VI 1 (10)
mob [mɒb] Mob, Menschenmenge VI 3 (63)
mobile ['məʊbaɪl]:
1. mobil V
2. *(kurz für:* **mobile phone***)* Mobiltelefon, Handy I
°**mobile home** [məʊbaɪl 'həʊm] (großer) Wohnwagen, Wohnmobil
mobile phone [məʊbaɪl 'fəʊn] *(kurz auch:* **mobile***)* Mobiltelefon, Handy I
model ['mɒdl] Fotomodell, Model V
°**a model son** ein Muster-Sohn, ein perfekter Sohn
moderator ['mɒdəreɪtə] Moderator/in *(z.B. bei Debatten)* V
modern ['mɒdn] modern V
mom [mɒm], [mɑ:m] *(AE)* Mama, Mutti IV
moment ['məʊmənt] Moment, Augenblick I **at the moment** im Moment, gerade I
Monday ['mʌndeɪ], ['mʌndi] Montag I
money ['mʌni] Geld I **make money** Geld verdienen III
monitor ['mɒnɪtə] Monitor, Bildschirm III
monkey ['mʌŋki] Affe I
month [mʌnθ] Monat I
monument ['mɒnjumənt] Monument, Denkmal VI 1 (24)
mood [mu:d] Stimmung, Laune IV
°**moon** [mu:n] Mond
more [mɔ:] mehr, weitere II **more and more** immer mehr III **more popular** beliebter II **more than** mehr als III
morning ['mɔ:nɪŋ] Morgen I **in the morning** morgens, am Morgen I **on Friday morning** freitagmorgens, am Freitagmorgen I
most [məʊst]: **the most boring ...** der/die/das langweiligste ... II **the most sports** die meisten Sportarten II
mostly ['məʊstli] hauptsächlich; meistens II
mother ['mʌðə] Mutter I
°**motorcycle** ['məʊtəsaɪkl] Motorrad
motto ['mɒtəʊ] Motto III
mountain ['maʊntən] Berg II
mounted ['maʊntɪd]: **head-mounted display** Datenhelm, Datenbrille, Videobrille VI 3 (57)
mouse, *pl* **mice** [maʊs], [maɪs] Maus III
mouth [maʊθ] Mund I
move [mu:v]:
1. (sich) bewegen III
2. **move (to)** umziehen (nach, in) II
movement ['mu:vmənt] Bewegung IV
movie ['mu:vi] Film IV
Mr Jahn ['mɪstə] Herr Jahn I
Mrs Schmidt ['mɪsɪz] Frau Schmidt *(Anrede für verheiratete Frauen)* I
Ms Lee [mɪz], [məz] Frau Lee *(allgemeine Anrede für Frauen)* I
much [mʌtʃ] viel II **as much as $80** bis zu 80$; nicht weniger als 80$ IV
How much ...? Wie viel ...? II **How much is ...? / How much are ...?** Was (Wie viel) kostet ...? / Was (Wie viel) kosten ...? I **miss/like/love sb. so much** jn. so sehr vermissen/mögen/lieben II **Thanks very much.** Danke sehr. / Danke vielmals. II
mud [mʌd] Schlamm, Matsch II
muddy ['mʌdi] schlammig, matschig III
muesli ['mju:zli] Müsli III
multicultural [mʌlti'kʌltʃərəl] multikulturell VI 1 (10)
multilingual [mʌlti'lɪŋgwəl] mehrsprachig VI 1 (11)
multitask [mʌlti'tɑ:sk] *mehrere Tätigkeiten gleichzeitig ausführen* V
mum [mʌm] Mama, Mutti I
museum [mju'zi:əm] Museum III
music ['mju:zɪk] Musik I
musician [mju'zɪʃn] Musiker/in I
must [mʌst]:
1. müssen I
mustn't do nicht tun dürfen II
I must go. *(am Telefon)* Ich muss Schluss machen. I
2. **... is a must.** *(infml)* ... ist ein Muss. IV
°**musty** ['mʌsti] muffig
my [maɪ] mein/e I
myself [maɪ'self] mich, mir (selbst) I
mystery ['mɪstri] Geheimnis II

N

nail [neɪl] Nagel V
nail polish ['neɪl pɒlɪʃ] Nagellack V
name [neɪm]:
1. benennen, nennen IV
2. Name I
call sb. a racist name jn. mit einem rassistischen Wort beschimpfen V
call sb. names jn. beschimpfen V
What's your name? Wie heißt du? I
narrator [nə'reɪtə] Erzähler/in VI 3 (65)
first-person narrator Ich-Erzähler/in VI 3 (65)
narrow ['nærəʊ] schmal, eng III
nation ['neɪʃn] Nation, Volk IV
national ['næʃnəl] national, National- III
national anthem [næʃnəl 'ænθəm] Nationalhymne III
national holiday [næʃnəl 'hɒlədeɪ] Nationalfeiertag VI 1 (13)
national park [næʃnəl 'pɑ:k] Nationalpark II
native ['neɪtɪv]: **Native American** amerikanische/r Ureinwohner/in IV
native animals/plants (ein)heimische Tiere/Pflanzen V
°**natural** ['nætʃrəl] natürlich
nature ['neɪtʃə] Natur IV
near [nɪə] in der Nähe von, nahe (bei) I
near here hier in der Nähe II
nearest ['nɪərɪst]: **the nearest ...** der/die/das nächstgelegene ... V
nearly ['nɪəli] fast, beinahe II
necessary ['nesəsəri] notwendig, nötig, erforderlich V
need [ni:d] brauchen, benötigen I
need to do sth. etwas tun müssen IV
needle ['ni:dl] Nadel; Kanüle VI 2 (41)
negative ['negətɪv] negativ II

negativity [negə'tɪvəti] negative Einstellung V
neighbour ['neɪbə] Nachbar/in II
neighbourhood ['neɪbəhʊd] Nachbarschaft, Viertel, Gegend II
neighbouring ['neɪbərɪŋ] benachbart, Nachbar- IV
°**neither** ['naɪðə]: **... and neither did I.** ... und ich auch nicht.
neon ['niːɒn] Neon; neonfarbig V
nervous ['nɜːvəs] nervös, aufgeregt I
net [net] *kurz für* Internet V
network ['netwɜːk]:
1. Netz; Wortnetz I
2. Netzwerk VI 3 (56)
never ['nevə] nie, niemals I **I've never had ...** ich habe (noch) nie ... gehabt II
new [njuː] neu I
New Year [njuː 'jɪə] Neujahr II
newcomer ['njuːkʌmə] Neuling IV
news [njuːz]:
1. Nachrichten I
2. Neuigkeiten II
... is bad news. ... ist gefährlich. / ... ist (gar) nicht gut. V
news item [njuːz 'aɪtəm] Nachrichtenmeldung, Pressemeldung VI 2 (38)
newsagent ['njuːzeɪdʒənt] Zeitungshändler/in II **the newsagent's** der Zeitungsladen II
newsletter ['njuːzletə] Mitteilungsblatt, Informationsblatt II
newspaper ['njuːzpeɪpə] *(oft auch kurz:* **paper***)* Zeitung III
next [nekst] nächste(r, s) I **Next ...** Als Nächstes ... II **next time** nächstes Mal II **the next day** am nächsten Tag III
next to ['nekst tə] neben I
nice [naɪs] nett, schön I **Nice to meet you!** Freut mich, dich/euch kennenzulernen. I
°**nick** [nɪk] *(infml)* klauen
nickname ['nɪkneɪm] Spitzname V
night [naɪt] Nacht I **at night** nachts, in der Nacht I
°**nightmare** ['naɪtmeə] Albtraum
nine [naɪn] neun I
nineties ['naɪntiːz]: **the 90s** die Neunzigerjahre II
no [nəʊ] nein I
no [nəʊ] kein, keine I **No way!** Auf keinen Fall! III
nobody ['nəʊbədi] niemand II
nod (to sb.) [nɒd] (jm. zu)nicken IV
noise [nɔɪz] Geräusch; Lärm I
noisy ['nɔɪzi] laut, voller Lärm I
°**non-** [nɒn] Nicht-
none [nʌn] keine(r, s) II
°**non-essential** [nɒn ɪ'senʃl] nicht lebensnotwendig, nicht unbedingt wichtig
°**non-fictional text** [nɒn fɪkʃənl 'tekst] Sachtext
normal ['nɔːml] normal, gewöhnlich I
north [nɔːθ] Norden; nach Norden II **north-east** Nordosten; nach Nordosten II **north-west** Nordwesten; nach Nordwesten II
northern ['nɔːðən] nördlich, Nord- IV
nose [nəʊz] Nase IV
nosey ['nəʊzi] *(auch:* **nosy***)* neugierig IV
not [nɒt] nicht I **not (...) anywhere** nirgendwo; nirgendwohin III **not ... yet** noch nicht II **not even** (noch) nicht einmal IV **Not me!** Ich nicht! I **I can't do anything.** Ich kann nichts machen. II **I'm not a boy.** Ich bin kein Junge. I **we don't have any ...** wir haben kein/e ... II
°**notably** ['nəʊtəbli] insbesondere, hauptsächlich
note [nəʊt]:
1. Notiz III
make notes (sich) Notizen machen *(zur Vorbereitung)* III **take notes** (sich) Notizen machen *(beim Lesen oder Zuhören)* III
°2. notieren; beachten
°**note sth. down** sich etwas aufschreiben, notieren
nothing ['nʌθɪŋ] (gar) nichts I
notice ['nəʊtɪs]:
1. (be)merken III
2. Notiz, Aushang, Anzeige III
novel ['nɒvl] Roman VI 2 (41)
November [nəʊ'vembə] November I
now [naʊ] nun, jetzt I **from now on** von nun an, ab jetzt VI 1 (20) **right now** jetzt gerade; im Augenblick III
°**every now and again** ab und zu, von Zeit zu Zeit
°**nowadays** ['naʊədeɪz] heutzutage
nowhere ['nəʊweə] nirgendwo; nirgendwohin III **in the middle of nowhere** *etwa:* am Ende der Welt III
number ['nʌmbə]:
1. Nummer I
2. Anzahl, Zahl III
°**nurse** [nɜːs] (Kranken-)Pfleger/in
nut [nʌt] Nuss I

O

o'clock [ə'klɒk]: **at 1 o'clock** um 1 Uhr / um 13 Uhr I
observer [əb'zɜːvə] Beobachter/in V
ocean ['əʊʃn] Ozean IV
October [ɒk'təʊbə] Oktober I
of [ɒv], [əv] von I **(just) the two of us** (nur) wir beide V **the best of both worlds** das Beste von beidem I **the last day of the holidays** der letzte Tag der Ferien I
of course [əv 'kɔːs] natürlich, selbstverständlich II
off [ɒf]:
1. **off the seats/the bridge/the bike/...** von den Sitzen/der Brücke/dem Rad/... (herunter) IV
2. **get/have a day off** einen Tag frei bekommen/haben IV
3. **go off** losgehen *(z.B.Alarm)* IV **start off (as)** anfangen (als) V °**... and off we went to ...** ... ab ging's nach ...
offer ['ɒfə] bieten, anbieten III
office ['ɒfɪs] Büro III
official [ə'fɪʃl] offiziell, amtlich IV
often ['ɒfn], ['ɒftən] oft I
Oh dear. [əʊ 'dɪə] Oje! II
OK [əʊ'keɪ] okay, gut, in Ordnung I **I'm OK, thanks.** Danke, (es geht mir) gut. I
old [əʊld] alt I **in the old days** früher II
old-fashioned [əʊld 'fæʃənd] altmodisch IV
°**olive** ['ɒlɪv] Olive
Olympic Games [əlɪmpɪk 'geɪmz] Olympische Spiele III
omelette ['ɒmlət] Omelette I
on [ɒn] auf I **on 5th May** am 5. Mai I **on earth** auf der Erde II **on Friday morning** freitagmorgens, am Freitagmorgen I **on Monday** am Montag I **on my birthday** an meinem Geburtstag I **on the beach** am Strand I **on the bus** im Bus I **on the job** bei der Arbeit IV **on the left** links, auf der linken Seite I **on the one hand** einerseits III **on the other hand** andererseits III **on the phone** am Telefon I **on the right** rechts, auf der rechten Seite I **on the Tube** in der (Londoner) U-Bahn III **on the way to ...** auf dem Weg zu/nach ... I **on time** pünktlich II **drive/run/go on** weiterfahren/-laufen/-gehen IV **go on** weiterreden, fortfahren; weitermachen III **straight on** geradeaus (weiter) II **What's going on?** Was ist los? / Was gibt's? IV
once [wʌns]:
1. einmal III
2. einst, *(früher)* einmal IV
one [wʌn]:
1. eins I
one day eines Tages, einmal IV **one way** einfache Fahrt IV
2. man VI 3 (64)
3. **the only one** der/die/das Einzige IV
two lollipops – a green one and a red one zwei Lutscher – ein grüner und ein roter IV
one-way ticket [wʌn 'weɪ tɪkɪt] einfache Fahrkarte IV
online [ɒn'laɪn] online, Online- V
only ['əʊnli]:
1. nur, bloß I
2. einzige(r,s) I
the only student der einzige Schüler / die einzige Schülerin I

3. the only one der/die/das Einzige IV
onto ['ɒntə], ['ɒntu] auf (... hinauf) V
open ['əʊpən]:
1. öffnen II
2. eröffnen IV
3. offen, geöffnet II
°**opening hours** *(pl)* ['əʊpənɪŋ aʊəz] Öffnungszeiten
operate ['ɒpəreɪt] arbeiten, tätig sein VI 1 (22)
opinion [ə'pɪnjən] Meinung III **in my opinion** meiner Meinung nach III
opportunity [ɒpə'tju:nəti] Gelegenheit, Möglichkeit, Chance VI 1 (12)
opposite ['ɒpəzɪt] Gegenteil II
optimism ['ɒptɪmɪzəm] Optimismus VI 3 (59)
optimist ['ɒptɪmɪst] Optimist/in VI 3 (59)
optimistic [ɒptɪ'mɪstɪk] optimistisch VI 3 (59)
option ['ɒpʃn] Option, (Wahl-)Möglichkeit IV
or [ɔ:] oder I
orange ['ɒrɪndʒ]:
1. orange(farben) I
2. Orange, Apfelsine II
orange juice ['ɒrɪndʒ dʒu:s] Orangensaft II
orca ['ɔ:kə] Orca, Schwertwal IV
order ['ɔ:də]:
1. bestellen IV
2. Bestellung IV
order ['ɔ:də] Reihenfolge III
order ['ɔ:də]: **in order to** um ... zu V
organic (vegetables) [ɔ:'gænɪk] Bio-(Gemüse) III
organize ['ɔ:gənaɪz] organisieren IV
original [ə'rɪdʒənl] Original-, ursprünglich; Original IV
ostrich ['ɒstrɪtʃ] Strauß *(Vogel)* VI 1 (14)
other ['ʌðə] andere(r, s) I **each other** einander; sich (gegenseitig) IV **in other words** mit anderen Worten V **the other day** neulich III
our ['aʊə] unser/e I
ours [ɑ:z], ['aʊəz] unsere/r, unseres V
ourselves [aʊə'selvz] wir/uns selbst III
out of ... ['aʊt əv] aus ... (heraus/hinaus) II
outdoor [aʊt'dɔ:] Freiluft-, Außen-, im Freien V **outdoor shop** Geschäft für Outdoor-Bekleidung und -Ausrüstung III
outdoors [aʊt'dɔ:z] im Freien, draußen V
°**outright** ['aʊtraɪt] völlige(r, s), totale(r, s)
outside [aʊt'saɪd]:
1. draußen; nach draußen I
2. außerhalb, vor III
over ['əʊvə]:
1. über III
over time im Laufe der Zeit VI 2 (43)
all over the world auf der ganzen Welt IV **walk/come over to sb.** zu jm. hinübergehen/-kommen IV
2. over 300 über 300, mehr als 300 III
3. be over vorbei sein, zu Ende sein I
over there [əʊvə 'ðeə] da drüben, dort drüben V
overspend [əʊvə'spend], **overspent, overspent (on sth.)** zu viel Geld ausgeben (für etwas) V
overspent [əʊvə'spent] *siehe* **overspend**
own [əʊn]:
1. on my/your/her/... own allein, selbstständig *(ohne Unterstützung)* VI 3 (63) **your own card/text** deine eigene Karte / dein eigener Text III
°**2.** besitzen
owner ['əʊnə] Eigentümer/in, Besitzer/in II
°**oxygen** ['ɒksɪdʒən] Sauerstoff

P

p [pi:]: **50p** 50 Pence I
pack [pæk] packen, einpacken II
packet (of) ['pækɪt] Packung, Päckchen, Schachtel III
page [peɪdʒ] Seite I **What page is it?** Auf welcher Seite sind wir? I
paid [peɪd] *siehe* **pay**
pain [peɪn]:
1. Schmerz(en) V
2. Don't be a pain. Nerv nicht. / Geh mir/uns nicht auf die Nerven. V **What a pain!** *etwa:* So ein Mist. / Es nervt! III
paint [peɪnt]:
1. lackieren, (be)malen, *(mit Farbe)* streichen V
2. Farbe, Lack VI 3 (64/65)
painter ['peɪntə] Maler/in V
painting ['peɪntɪŋ] Gemälde, *(gemaltes)* Bild; Malerei V **body painting** Körperbemalung V
pair [peə] Paar I
palace ['pæləs] Palast III
°**pale** [peɪl] blass, bleich
°**pancake** ['pænkeɪk] Pfannkuchen
panic ['pænɪk] in Panik geraten IV **Don't panic.** Keine Panik. / Immer mit der Ruhe. II
pant [pænt] keuchen, hecheln VI 3 (63)
pants *(pl)* [pænts] *(AE)* Hose IV
paper ['peɪpə]:
1. Papier I
2. Zeitung II
do a paper round Zeitungen austragen II
parade [pə'reɪd] Parade, Umzug IV
paradise ['pærədaɪs] Paradies IV
paragraph ['pærəgrɑ:f] Absatz *(im Text)* III
°**paramedic** [pærə'medɪk] Rettungssanitäter/in
°**paranoid** ['pærənɔɪd] paranoid, wahnsinnig
paraphrase ['pærəfreɪz] umschreiben, mit anderen Worten sagen V
parcel ['pɑ:sl] Paket, Päckchen VI 3 (54/55)
parents *(pl)* ['peərənts] Eltern I
park [pɑ:k] Park I
park [pɑ:k] parken III
°**parliament** ['pɑ:ləmənt] Parlament
part [pɑ:t] Teil II **take part in sth.** an etwas teilnehmen, bei etwas mitmachen III
°**particular** [pə'tɪkjələ] bestimmte(r, s), spezielle(r, s)
part-time job [pɑ:t taɪm 'dʒɒb] Halbtagsjob, Teilzeitjob IV
party ['pɑ:ti]: **have a party** eine Party feiern I
party-goer ['pɑ:ti gəʊə] Partygast V
pass [pɑ:s] Pass, Ausweis IV **visitor pass** Besucherausweis IV
pass [pɑ:s]:
1. pass sth./sb. an etwas/jm. vorbeigehen, vorbeifahren IV
°**sth. passes** etwas ist/geht vorbei *(Zeit, Moment, Gelegenheit)*
2. Pass the ball! Spiel ab! III
°**pass a law** ein Gesetz verabschieden
passenger ['pæsɪndʒə] Passagier/in, Fahrgast II
passenger seat ['pæsɪndʒə] Beifahrersitz VI 2 (41)
passive ['pæsɪv] Passiv IV
passport ['pɑ:spɔ:t] (Reise-)Pass VI 1 (21)
past [pɑ:st] Vergangenheit II
past the shop [pɑ:st] am Laden vorbei II
pasta ['pæstə] Pasta; Nudeln III
pasty ['pæsti] *Pastete mit Fleisch- und/ oder Gemüsefüllung* II
patient ['peɪʃnt] geduldig IV
°**patrol sth.** [pə'trəʊl] in/durch etwas patrouillieren
pattern ['pætn] Muster IV
°**pause** [pɔ:z] kurz innehalten, Pause machen **pause for breath** kurz Pause machen, um Luft zu holen
pavement ['peɪvmənt] *(BE)* Gehweg, Bürgersteig IV
pay [peɪ]:
1. Bezahlung, Lohn V
2. pay (for sth.), paid, paid (etwas) bezahlen III
it doesn't pay very well es wird nicht besonders gut bezahlt IV
PE (physical education) [pi: 'i:], [fɪzɪkl edʒu'keɪʃn] (Schul-)Sport I
°**peace** [pi:s] Frieden
peanut ['pi:nʌt] Erdnuss II
peanut butter ['pi:nʌt] Erdnussbutter II

peer [pɪə] Gleichaltrige/r, Ebenbürtige/r, jemand aus derselben sozialen Gruppe V
peer pressure ['pɪə preʃə] Gruppendruck, Gruppenzwang V
pen [pen] Kugelschreiber, Stift, Füller I
pence [pens] Pence I
pencil ['pensl] Bleistift I
pencil case ['pensl keɪs] Federmäppchen I
pencil sharpener ['pensl ʃɑ:pnə] Bleistiftanspitzer I
penfriend ['penfrend] Brieffreund/in II
°**penguin** ['peŋgwɪn] Pinguin
pension ['penʃn] Rente, Pension VI 2 (36)
people ['pi:pl]:
1. Leute, Menschen I
2. Volk VI 1 (20)
pepper ['pepə] Pfeffer V
per (day) [pɜ:], [pə] pro (Tag) III
per cent (%) [pə'sent] (*AE usually:* **per-cent**) Prozent IV
perfect ['pɜ:fɪkt] perfekt, ideal II
perform [pə'fɔ:m] aufführen; durchführen; auftreten *(Künstler/in)* VI 2 (38)
performance [pə'fɔ:məns] Vorstellung, Aufführung V
performer [pə'fɔ:mə] Künstler/in, Darsteller/in VI 2 (38)
perhaps [pə'hæps] vielleicht IV
permanent ['pɜ:mənənt] permanent, (be)ständig VI 1 (17)
person ['pɜ:sn] Person I
personal ['pɜ:sənl] persönlich V
personal computer [pɜ:sənl kəm'pju:tə] PC IV
personality [pɜ:sə'nælətɪ] Persönlichkeit; Charakter V
°**persuade** [pə'sweɪd] überreden, überzeugen
pessimism ['pesɪmɪzəm] Pessimismus VI 3 (59)
pessimist ['pesɪmɪst] Pessimist/in VI 3 (59)
pessimistic [pesɪ'mɪstɪk] pessimistisch VI 3 (59)
pet [pet] Haustier I
petition [pə'tɪʃn] Petition, Unterschriftensammlung VI 2 (34)
petrol ['petrəl] Benzin IV
petrol station ['petrəl steɪʃn] Tankstelle V
phone [fəʊn]:
1. anrufen I
phone for an ambulance einen Krankenwagen rufen V
2. Telefon I
answer the phone ans Telefon gehen V **on the phone** am Telefon I
phone call ['fəʊn kɔ:l] *(oft auch kurz:* **call***)* (Telefon-)Anruf II
phone number ['fəʊn nʌmbə] Telefonnummer I
photo ['fəʊtəʊ] Foto I **in the photo** auf dem Foto I **take photos** fotografieren, Fotos machen II
photographer [fə'tɒgrəfə] Fotograf/in IV
phrase [freɪz] Ausdruck, (Rede-)Wendung I
piano [pi'ænəʊ] Klavier, Piano I **play the piano** Klavier spielen I
pick [pɪk]:
1. (aus)wählen, aussuchen II
°**pick sth. out** etwas auswählen, heraussuchen
2. **pick sth. up** etwas aufheben *(vom Boden)*, etwas hochheben II
pick up kaufen, *(aus einem Geschäft)* mitbringen V **pick sb. up** jn. abholen III
pickpocket ['pɪkpɒkɪt] Taschendieb/in III
picnic ['pɪknɪk] Picknick I
picture ['pɪktʃə] Bild I **in the picture** auf dem Bild I
°**picture-perfect** [pɪktʃə 'pɜ:fɪkt] bildschön, Traum-, Bilderbuch-
piece [pi:s]: **a piece of ...** ein Stück ... IV **a piece of advice** ein Rat, ein Ratschlag IV
piercing ['pɪəsɪŋ] Piercing II
°**piezoelectric** [pi:zəʊɪ'lektrɪk] piezoelektrisch *(aus Verformung Strom gewinnend)*
pig [pɪg] Schwein I
°**pill** [pɪl] Pille
pillow ['pɪləʊ] Kopfkissen VI 3 (54/55)
°**pineapple** ['paɪnæpl] Ananas
pink [pɪŋk] pink, rosa I
pioneer [paɪə'nɪə] Pionier/in VI 3 (60)
°**piss sb. off** [pɪs 'ɒf] *(taboo)* jn. verärgern
°**pitch** [pɪtʃ] Platz, (Spiel-)Feld
pizza ['pi:tsə] Pizza II
place [pleɪs]:
1. Ort, Platz, Stelle I
swap places with sb. mit jm. die Plätze tauschen VI 1 (25)
2. **take place** stattfinden VI 2 (39)
plan [plæn]:
1. planen I
2. Plan II
plane [pleɪn] Flugzeug III
planet ['plænɪt] Planet VI 3 (60)
plant [plɑ:nt]:
1. Pflanze IV
°2. pflanzen
plastic ['plæstɪk] Plastik, Kunststoff II
plastic bag ['plæstɪk bæg] Plastiktüte II
plate (of) [pleɪt] Teller III
platform ['plætfɔ:m]:
1. Bahnsteig, Gleis II
2. Plattform; Rampe VI 1 (14)
play [pleɪ]:
1. spielen I
play the piano Klavier spielen I
2. Theaterstück II
player ['pleɪə] Spieler/in III
playground ['pleɪgraʊnd] Spielplatz IV
please [pli:z] bitte I
pleased [pli:zd] froh, erfreut, zufrieden V **Pleased to meet you.** Freut mich Sie kennenzulernen. V
plot [plɒt] Handlung(sverlauf) *(z.B. Film/Geschichte)* V
Plus, ... [plʌs] Und außerdem ... IV
pm [pi:'em]: **5 pm/5 p.m.** 5 Uhr nachmittags/abends; 17 Uhr I
°**poach** [pəʊtʃ] wildern, unerlaubt jagen
°**poacher** ['pəʊtʃə] Wilderer/Wilderin, Wilddieb/in
pocket ['pɒkɪt] Tasche *(Manteltasche, Hosentasche, etc.)* II
pocket money ['pɒkɪt mʌni] Taschengeld II
°**pod** [pɒd] Behälter, Kapsel
poem ['pəʊɪm] Gedicht I
°**poet** ['pəʊɪt] Dichter/in
point [pɔɪnt]:
1. Argument V
good point gutes Argument V
make a point ein Argument vortragen V **make your point** sagen, wie du darüber denkst V
2. Punkt III
point of view Standpunkt III **1.6 million (one point six million)** 1,6 Millionen (eins Komma sechs Millionen) IV
point (to sb./sth.) [pɔɪnt] (auf jn./etwas) zeigen, deuten II **point sth. out** auf etwas hinweisen, aufmerksam machen VI 2 (34) °**she pointed herself south-west** sie richtete ihren Kompass auf Südwest aus
police *(pl)* [pə'li:s] Polizei II
police officer [pə'li:s ɒfɪsə] Polizist/in III
police station [pə'li:s steɪʃn] Polizeiwache, -revier IV
policy ['pɒləsi] Politik, Richtlinie(n), Bestimmung(en) III
polite [pə'laɪt] höflich IV
political [pə'lɪtɪkl] politisch VI 1 (13)
politician [pɒlə'tɪʃn] Politiker/in VI 2 (37)
politics ['pɒlətɪks] Politik VI 2 (36)
°**pollution** [pə'lu:ʃn] (Umwelt-)Verschmutzung
pond [pɒnd] Teich I
pony ['pəʊni] Pony I **ride a pony** auf einem Pony reiten I
ponytail ['pəʊniteɪl] Pferdeschwanz *(Frisur)* V
poor [pɔ:], [pʊə]:
1. arm II
poor Ellie (die) arme Ellie II
2. schlecht, schwach, minderwertig VI 3 (67)
popular ['pɒpjələ] beliebt, populär II

population [pɒpju'leɪʃn] Bevölkerung, Einwohner(zahl) IV

porch [pɔːtʃ] *(AE)* Veranda IV

port [pɔːt] Hafen; Hafenstadt III

portrait ['pɔːtreɪt] Porträt V

position [pə'zɪʃn] Position, Stelle, Platz IV

positive ['pɒzətɪv] positiv II

possibility [pɒsə'bɪləti] Möglichkeit VI 1 (12)

possible ['pɒsəbl] möglich III

post [pəʊst] posten *(im Internet veröffentlichen)* V

post office ['pəʊst ɒfɪs] Postamt II

°**postal** ['pəʊstl] Post-

postcard ['pəʊstkɑːd] Postkarte II

posted ['pəʊstɪd]: **Keep me posted.** Halt mich auf dem Laufenden. III

poster ['pəʊstə] Poster I

postman/-woman ['pəʊstmən, -wʊmən] Briefträger/in III

potato, *pl* **potatoes** [pə'teɪtəʊ] Kartoffel II

pound (£) [paʊnd] Pfund *(britische Währung)* I

poverty ['pɒvəti] Armut VI 1 (12)

power ['paʊə]:
1. Macht, Kraft, Stärke VI 2 (34)
2. Energie, Strom VI 3 (54/55)

practice ['præktɪs]:
1. *(AE)* üben; trainieren IV
2. Übung; Training IV

practise ['præktɪs] *(BE)* üben; trainieren IV

praise [preɪz]:
1. Lob VI 2 (38)
2. loben, rühmen VI 2 (38)

°**precise** [prɪ'saɪs] genau, präzise

predict [prɪ'dɪkt] voraussagen, vorhersagen VI 3 (60)

prediction [prɪ'dɪkʃn] Vorhersage, Voraussage VI 3 (60)

prefer sth. (to sth.) [prɪ'fɜː] etwas *(einer anderen Sache)* vorziehen II **I'd (= I would) prefer …** ich würde … vorziehen; ich würde lieber … III **prefer to do sth.** etwas lieber tun III

preferable to sth. ['prefrəbl] (einer Sache) vorzuziehen, besser als (etwas) VI 1 (15)

preferably ['prefrəbli] vorzugsweise, am liebsten VI 1 (15)

prejudice ['predʒudɪs] Vorurteil, Voreingenommenheit V

°**premises** *(pl)* ['premɪsɪz] (Betriebs-) Gelände

prepare [prɪ'peə] vorbereiten; sich vorbereiten III **prepare for sth.** sich auf etwas vorbereiten III

preposition [prepə'zɪʃn] Präposition IV

present ['preznt]:
1. Gegenwart II
2. gegenwärtig V

present ['preznt] Geschenk I

present sth. (to sb.) [prɪ'zent] (jm.) etwas präsentieren, (jm.) etwas vorstellen III

presentation [prezn'teɪʃn] Referat, Präsentation V **give a presentation** ein Referat halten V

°**presenter** [prɪ'zentə] Moderator/in

°**presidency** ['prezɪdənsi] Präsidentschaft

president ['prezɪdənt] Präsident/in III

pressure ['preʃə] Druck V

pretend (to be sth.) [prɪ'tend] so tun, als ob (man etwas wäre) V

pretty ['prɪti] hübsch IV

°**previous** ['priːviəs] vorherige/r/s, vorige/r/s,

price [praɪs] (Kauf-)Preis I

pride [praɪd] Stolz III **pride (in sth.)** Stolz (auf etwas) IV

prime minister [praɪm 'mɪnɪstə] Premierminister/in VI 2 (36)

prince [prɪns] Prinz III

princess [prɪn'ses] Prinzessin III

principal ['prɪnsəpl] Rektor/in, Schulleiter/in I

prison ['prɪzn] Gefängnis IV **put sb. in prison** jn. ins Gefängnis sperren V

prize [praɪz] Preis, Gewinn III

probable ['prɒbəbl] wahrscheinlich VI 3 (61)

probably ['prɒbəbli] wahrscheinlich III

problem ['prɒbləm] Problem I

°**process** ['prəʊses] Verfahren, Ablauf, Prozess

product ['prɒdʌkt] Produkt V

professional [prə'feʃənl] professionell, Profi- IV

profile ['prəʊfaɪl] Profil; Beschreibung, Portrait V

profit ['prɒfɪt] Gewinn, Profit III

program ['prəʊgræm] *(AE)* Programm V

programme ['prəʊgræm] (Fernseh-) Sendung I

progress ['prəʊgres]:
1. **be in progress** im Gange sein VI 2 (39)
°2. Fortschritt(e)

project ['prɒdʒekt] Projekt II

promise ['prɒmɪs] versprechen IV

°**promote** [prə'məʊt] fördern, unterstützen

°**properly** ['prɒpəli] richtig, ordentlich, korrekt

pros and cons *(pl)* [prəʊz ənd 'kɒnz] Pro und Kontra; Für und Wider V

protect (from) [prə'tekt] (be)schützen (vor) V

protest [prə'test] protestieren IV

protest ['prəʊtest] Protest(demonstration) VI 2 (34)

proud (of) [praʊd] stolz (auf) I

prove [pruːv] beweisen; nachweisen VI 2 (36) **prove sb. wrong** beweisen, dass jd. Unrecht hat VI 2 (36)

provide [prə'vaɪd] (an)bieten, zur Verfügung stellen VI 1 (24)

pub [pʌb] Kneipe, Lokal III

public ['pʌblɪk] öffentlich VI 1 (11)

pull [pʊl] ziehen IV **pull back** sich zurückziehen, zurückweichen V **pull back your hair** sich die Haare zusammenbinden V **pull in** anhalten, an den Straßenrand fahren IV °**pull up** anhalten, an den Straßenrand fahren

pullover ['pʊləʊvə] Pullover I

punctual ['pʌŋktʃuəl] pünktlich V

punctuation [pʌŋktʃu'eɪʃn] Zeichensetzung VI 1 (17)

puppy ['pʌpi] (Hunde-)Welpe V

purple [pɜːpl] violett; lila I

°**purpose** ['pɜːpəs] Absicht, Zweck, Ziel

°**purse** [pɜːs] Portemonnaie, Geldbörse

push [pʊʃ] schieben, stoßen, drücken IV

put [pʊt], **put, put** *(etwas wohin)* tun, legen, stellen II **put sth. in** etwas einsetzen, eingeben II **put sth. on** etwas anziehen *(Kleidung)*; etwas aufsetzen *(Hut, Brille)* II **put sth. on** etwas einschalten VI 2 (42) **put sth. up** etwas aufhängen *(Bild etc.)* VI 2 (46) **put up one's hand** sich melden; seine/die Hand heben V °**put sth.** *(+ Adverb)* etwas *(auf eine bestimmte Art)* ausdrücken, formulieren °**put sth. off** etwas verschieben, hinauszögern

puzzle ['pʌzl] Rätsel IV

°**puzzled** ['pʌzld] verwirrt, verwundert

pyjamas *(pl)* [pə'dʒɑːməz] Schlafanzug II

Q

qualification [kwɒlɪfɪ'keɪʃn] (Schul-) Abschluss, Qualifikation V

qualified ['kwɒlɪfaɪd] qualifiziert; ausgebildet, mit Abschluss V

qualify ['kwɒlɪfaɪ] (sich) qualifizieren V

quality ['kwɒləti] Eigenschaft; Qualität V **personal qualities** persönliche Eigenschaften V

queen [kwiːn] Königin III

question ['kwestʃən]:
1. Frage I
ask questions Fragen stellen I
2. **question sb.** jn. befragen, verhören V

question mark ['kwestʃən mɑːk] Fragezeichen VI 1 (17)

questionnaire [kwestʃə'neə] Fragebogen IV

quick [kwɪk] schnell II

quiet ['kwaɪət] ruhig, still, leise I

quite [kwaɪt] ziemlich II

quiz [kwɪz] Quiz, Ratespiel I

quote [kwəʊt]:
1. Zitat VI 2 (46)
2. zitieren VI 2 (46)

R

rabbit ['ræbɪt] Kaninchen I
race [reɪs]:
1. (Wett-)Rennen V
2. rasen, schnell fahren V
race [reɪs] Volk, Stamm; Rasse V
racing ['reɪsɪŋ] Rennsport V
racism ['reɪsɪzəm] Rassismus V
racist ['reɪsɪst]:
1. Rassist/in V
2. rassistisch V
°**radar** ['reɪdɑː] Radar
°**radiation** [reɪdi'eɪʃn] Strahlung
radio ['reɪdiəʊ] Radio III
rain [reɪn]:
1. Regen II
2. regnen II
rainbow ['reɪnbəʊ] Regenbogen VI 1 (10)
°**rainforest** ['reɪnfɒrɪst] Regenwald
°**rainmaker** ['reɪnmeɪkə] Regenmacher
rainy ['reɪni] regnerisch II
raise money (for sth.) [reɪz] Geld sammeln, auftreiben (für etwas) VI 2 (39)
ran [ræn] *siehe* **run**
°**rand, *pl* rand** [rænd] Rand *(südafrikanische Währung)*
rang [ræŋ] *siehe* **ring**
ranger ['reɪndʒə] Ranger/in; (Park-)Aufseher/in II
rap [ræp] rappen I
rat [ræt] Ratte I
°**rate** [reɪt] bewerten, beurteilen
°**rates** *(pl)* [reɪts] Gebühren
rather than ['rɑːðə ðən] anstelle von, (an)statt VI 1 (15)
reach (sb./a place) [riːtʃ] (jn./einen Ort) erreichen V
react (to) [ri'ækt] reagieren (auf) III
reaction (to) [ri'ækʃn] Reaktion (auf) VI 1 (25)
read [riːd], **read, read** lesen I °**read out** (laut) vorlesen
read [red] *siehe read*
reader ['riːdə] Leser/in III
ready ['redi] bereit, fertig III **get ready (for)** sich fertig machen (für), sich vorbereiten (auf) I
real [rɪəl] echt, wirklich I
realistic [riːə'lɪstɪk] realistisch V
reality [ri'æləti] Wirklichkeit, Realität II
reality show [ri'æləti ʃəʊ] Realityshow II
realize sth. ['riːəlaɪz] etwas erkennen, sich einer Sache bewusst werden V
really ['riːəli], ['rɪəli] wirklich I
reason ['riːzn] Grund III **for lots of reasons** aus vielen Gründen III
°**reasonable** ['riːznəbl] vernünftig, angemessen
°**reblog** [ri'blɒg] Reblog
receipt [rɪ'siːt] (Kauf-)Beleg, Quittung, Kassenzettel VI 3 (67)
receive [rɪ'siːv] erhalten, empfangen VI 2 (46)
recent ['riːsnt] jüngst, aktuell VI 2 (37)
recently ['riːsntli] in letzter Zeit; vor Kurzem III
receptionist [rɪ'sepʃənɪst] Empfangschef/in III
recharge [riː'tʃɑːdʒ] (wieder) aufladen VI 3 (67)
recipe ['resəpi] (Koch-)Rezept I
recommend sth. (to sb.) [rekə'mend] (jm.) etwas empfehlen IV
recommendation [rekəmen'deɪʃn] Empfehlung V
record [rɪ'kɔːd] aufnehmen, aufzeichnen, dokumentieren V
°**record** ['rekɔːd] Rekord
recruitment [rɪ'kruːtmənt] Anwerbung, Einstellung *(von Personal)* VI 2 (46)
recycle [riː'saɪkl] wiederverwerten II
red [red] rot I
redness ['rednəs] Rötung, Röte V
reduce (by) [rɪ'djuːs] reduzieren, verringern (um) V
reef [riːf] Riff V
°**refer to** [rɪ'fɜː] sich beziehen auf, Bezug nehmen auf
reference ['refrəns] Referenz, Empfehlung; jd., der eine Referenz erteilt V
refugee [refju'dʒiː] Flüchtling VI 2 (38)
refund [rɪ'fʌnd] *(Kosten)* (rück)erstatten VI 3 (67)
refund ['riːfʌnd] Rückzahlung, (Kosten-)Erstattung VI 3 (67)
°**register to vote** [redʒɪstə tə 'vəʊt] sich in die Wählerlisten eintragen lassen
regular ['regjələ] regelmäßig, normal V
relationship [rɪ'leɪʃnʃɪp] Beziehung VI 1 (12)
relax [rɪ'læks] sich entspannen V
relaxing [rɪ'læksɪŋ] entspannend, beruhigend II
release sb. from sth. [rɪ'liːs] jn. (aus etwas) freilassen, befreien VI 1 (11)
relevant ['reləvənt] relevant, wichtig V
reliable [rɪ'laɪəbl] zuverlässig, verlässlich V
religion [rɪ'lɪdʒən] Religion VI 1 (10)
religious [rɪ'lɪdʒəs] religiös VI 1 (10)
religious building [rɪlɪdʒəs 'bɪldɪŋ] Sakralbau, Kirchengebäude VI 1 (10)
remarkable [rɪ'mɑːkəbl] bemerkenswert VI 2 (38)
remember [rɪ'membə]:
1. sich erinnern (an) I
2. daran denken; sich merken I
remind sb. (of sth.) [rɪ'maɪnd] jn. (an etwas) erinnern IV
°**remote control** [rɪməʊt kən'trəʊl] Fernbedienung
remove sth. [rɪ'muːv] etwas entfernen, beseitigen VI 1 (22)
rent [rent] mieten, leihen IV
repair [rɪ'peə]:
1. reparieren V
°2. Reparatur
repeat [rɪ'piːt] wiederholen V
°**repetition** [repə'tɪʃn] Wiederholung
°**replace** [rɪ'pleɪs] ersetzen, austauschen
°**replay sth.** [riː'pleɪ] etwas (vor dem inneren Auge) noch einmal Revue passieren lassen; sich etwas noch einmal vor Augen führen
reply [rɪ'plaɪ]:
1. Antwort VI 1 (15)
2. antworten VI 1 (15)
report [rɪ'pɔːt]:
1. Bericht IV
2. **report (on sth.)** (über etwas) berichten IV
3. **report sth. (to)** etwas melden, anzeigen (bei) *(z.B. bei der Polizei)* VI 1 (23)
reporter [rɪ'pɔːtə] Reporter/in III
represent [reprɪ'zent] repräsentieren, vertreten III
°**representative** [reprɪ'zentətɪv]: **class representative** Klassensprecher/in
request [rɪ'kwest] Wunsch, Bitte; Anfrage V
°**require** [rɪ'kwaɪə] erfordern, benötigen
rescue ['reskjuː]:
1. Rettung(sdienst) IV
2. retten VI 2 (47)
°**research** [rɪ'sɜːtʃ] Forschung(en), Recherche(n) **do research** recherchieren
reservation [rezə'veɪʃn] Reservierung III
respect [rɪ'spekt]:
1. respektieren, achten III
2. Respekt V
respectful [rɪ'spektfl] respektvoll V
respond [rɪ'spɒnd] reagieren, antworten VI 1 (21)
response [rɪ'spɒns] Reaktion, Antwort VI 1 (21)
responsible [rɪ'spɒnsəbl] verantwortungsbewusst; verantwortlich IV
rest [rest] (Erholungs-)Pause IV
restaurant ['restrɒnt] Restaurant I
restroom ['restruːm] *(AE)* Toilette, WC IV
result [rɪ'zʌlt] Ergebnis, Resultat III **as a result** folglich, demzufolge VI 1 (16)
°**retake** ['riːteɪk] Nachdrehen einer Szene *(Film)*
retell [riː'tel], **retold, retold** nacherzählen V
retold [riː'təʊld] *siehe* **retell**
°**retreat** [rɪ'triːt] sich zurückziehen
return [rɪ'tɜːn] zurückkehren, zurückkommen VI 1 (19)
°**reuse** [riː'juːz] wiederverwenden
review [rɪ'vjuː] Rezension, Besprechung, Kritik IV
revision [rɪ'vɪʒn] Wiederholung *(des Lernstoffs)* III

revolution [revəˈluːʃn] Revolution VI 2 (45)

°**rewrite** [riːˈraɪt], **rewrote, rewritten** noch einmal schreiben, neu schreiben

°**rewritten** [riːˈrɪtn] *siehe* **rewrite**

°**rewrote** [riːˈrəʊt] *siehe* **rewrite**

°**rhino,** *pl* **rhinos** [ˈraɪnəʊ] *(infml)* Nashorn

°**rhyme** [raɪm] (sich) reimen

°**rice** [raɪs] Reis

rich [rɪtʃ] reich V

rid [rɪd]: **get rid of sth.** etwas loswerden II

ridden [ˈrɪdn] *siehe* **ride**

ride [raɪd] Fahrt; Fahrgeschäft *(auf Volksfest, in Vergnügungspark)* III

ride [raɪd], **rode, ridden**:
1. reiten I
ride a pony auf einem Pony reiten I
2. fahren IV
ride a bike Rad fahren I

°**rider** [ˈraɪdə] Radfahrer/in

right [raɪt]:
1. rechts; nach rechts I
on the right rechts, auf der rechten Seite I
2. richtig I
all right gut; in Ordnung; OK IV
You're right. Du hast Recht. III
3. **right now** jetzt gerade; im Augenblick III
°**right behind him** direkt hinter ihm

right [raɪt] Recht V **civil rights** *(pl)* Bürgerrechte IV **have every right to do sth.** guten Grund / alles Recht haben, etwas zu tun V

°**ring** [rɪŋ] Ring

ring [rɪŋ], **rang, rung**:
1. läuten, klingeln I
2. anrufen III

ringtone [ˈrɪŋtəʊn] Klingelton III

rise [raɪz], **rose, risen** (an)steigen VI 3 (63)

risen [ˈrɪzən] *siehe* **rise**

risk [rɪsk]:
1. Risiko III
take risks Risiken eingehen III
2. riskieren, wagen V

risky [ˈrɪski] riskant V

river [ˈrɪvə] Fluss II

road [rəʊd] Straße *(Landstraße zwischen Orten, aber auch in Orten)* I

road trip [ˈrəʊd trɪp] Autoreise IV

°**rob** [rɒb] ausrauben, berauben

robber [ˈrɒbə] Räuber/in VI 2 (38)

robot [ˈrəʊbɒt]:
1. Roboter VI 3 (66)
°2. Ampel *(südafrikanisches Englisch)*

rock [rɒk]: Fels, Felsen II

rode [rəʊd] *siehe* **ride**

°**role** [rəʊl] Rolle

role model [ˈrəʊl mɒdl] Vorbild III

roll [rəʊl] rollen IV **roll over** sich überschlagen VI 2 (42) **roll sth. down** etwas herunterrollen IV **roll sth. up** etwas aufrollen, hochrollen, aufkrempeln IV

romance [rəʊˈmæns] Romanze IV

romantic [rəʊˈmæntɪk] romantisch; Liebes- IV

roof [ruːf] Dach V

room [ruːm], [rʊm] Raum, Zimmer I

°**root** [ruːt] Wurzel

rose [rəʊz] *siehe* **rise**

round [raʊnd]:
1. rund II
2. **do a paper round** Zeitungen austragen II

route [ruːt] Strecke, Route IV

routine [ruːˈtiːn] Routine IV

row [rəʊ] rudern VI 3 (64)

rowing boat [ˈrəʊɪŋ bəʊt] Ruderboot VI 3 (64)

rubber [ˈrʌbə]:
1. Radiergummi I
°2. Gummi

rubbish [ˈrʌbɪʃ] (Haus-)Müll, Abfall II
That's rubbish. *(infml)* Das ist Unsinn. / Das ist Quatsch. III

rucksack [ˈrʌksæk] Rucksack II

rude [ruːd] unhöflich, frech III

rug [rʌg] Teppich, Läufer I

rule [ruːl] Regel II

ruler [ˈruːlə] Lineal I

run [rʌn], **ran, run** rennen, laufen II
run a business / a hotel eine Firma / ein Hotel leiten, führen III **run a campaign** eine Kampagne durchführen VI 2 (46) **run after sb.** hinter jm. herrennen IV **run around** umherrennen; herumlaufen II **run out** knapp werden V **I often run out of money.** Mir geht oft das Geld aus. / Bei mir wird oft das Geld knapp. V

rung [rʌŋ] *siehe* **ring**

runner [ˈrʌnə] Läufer/in III

°**rush sb. to …** [rʌʃ] jn. auf dem schnellsten Weg nach …/zu … bringen

S

sad [sæd] traurig II

sadness [ˈsædnəs] Traurigkeit V

safari [səˈfɑːri] Safari VI 1 (14)

safe [seɪf] sicher; in Sicherheit III

safety [ˈseɪfti] Sicherheit II

said [sed] *siehe* **say**

salad [ˈsæləd] Salat *(als Gericht oder Beilage)* I

salami [səˈlɑːmi] Salami II

sale [seɪl] Verkauf; Schlussverkauf I
sales *(pl)* Verkauf V **for sale** zu verkaufen; zum Verkauf V

sales assistant [ˈseɪlz əsɪstənt] Verkäufer/in V

salesperson [ˈseɪlzpɜːsn] Verkäufer/in III

salt [sɔːlt] Salz V

same [seɪm]: **be the same** gleich sein II **the same** derselbe/dieselbe/dasselbe; dieselben I

°**sand tiger shark** [sænd taɪgə ˈʃɑːk] Sandtigerhai

sang [sæŋ] *siehe* **sing**

sat [sæt] *siehe* **sit**

Saturday [ˈsætədeɪ], [ˈsætədɪ] Samstag, Sonnabend I

sauce [sɔːs] Sauce V

sausage [ˈsɒsɪdʒ] Wurst, Würstchen II

save [seɪv]:
1. sparen (Geld, Zeit) II
2. retten III

savvy [ˈsævi] *(infml)* versiert, gewieft V

saw [sɔː] *siehe* **see**

say [seɪ]:
1. **say, said, said** sagen I
Say hi to everybody. Grüß alle. I
2. **say (in sth.)** Mitspracherecht (in/bei etwas) VI 2 (36)
have one's say die/seine Meinung äußern VI 2 (36)

°**scale** [skeɪl]: **internet-scale security** Internet-Sicherheit

scan a text [skæn] einen Text schnell nach bestimmten Wörtern/Informationen absuchen IV

°**scar** [skɑː]:
1. Narbe
2. **scar sb.** bei jm. Narben hinterlassen
scarred von Narben bedeckt

scare sb. [skeə] jn. erschrecken, jm. Angst machen II

scared [skeəd]: **be scared (of)** Angst haben (vor) II

scarf, *pl* **scarves** [skɑːf], [skɑːvz] Schal II

scary [ˈskeəri] unheimlich, gruselig II

scene [siːn] Szene I

school [skuːl] Schule I **leave school** von der Schule abgehen III

school bag [ˈskuːl bæg] Schultasche I

school subject [ˈskuːl sʌbdʒɪkt] Schulfach III

school yard [ˈskuːl jɑːd] Schulhof II

science [ˈsaɪəns] Naturwissenschaft I

scientist [ˈsaɪəntɪst] (Natur-)Wissenschaftler/in VI 3 (54/55)

scissors *(pl)* [ˈsɪzəz] Schere I

scone [skɒn] *kleines rundes Milchbrötchen, leicht süß, oft mit Rosinen* I

scrambled eggs [skræmbld ˈegz] Rühreier IV

°**scratch** [skrætʃ] (zer)kratzen, sich kratzen **scratch one's head** sich am Kopf kratzen

scream [skriːm] schreien II

°**screech** [skriːtʃ] kreischen; *(Reifen, Bremsen)* quietschen

screen [skriːn] Leinwand; Bildschirm IV

script [skrɪpt] Drehbuch VI 2 (47)

sea [siː] Meer I

sea lion [ˈsiː laɪən] Seelöwe IV

seagull ['si:gʌl] Möwe I
search [sɜ:tʃ]:
1. Suche V
2. **search for sth.** etwas suchen / nach etwas suchen V
search the internet for sth. das Internet nach etwas durchsuchen V
season ['si:zn] Jahreszeit II **high season** Hauptsaison VI 1 (10) **low season** Nebensaison VI 1 (10)
seat [si:t] (Sitz-)Platz I **take a seat** Platz nehmen *(sich hinsetzen)* VI 2 (39)
second ['sekənd] zweite(r, s) I
second ['sekənd] Sekunde IV
°**secondary school** ['sekəndri sku:l] weiterführende Schule, Sekundarschule
second-hand [sekənd 'hænd] gebraucht, aus zweiter Hand II
Secondly, … ['sekəndli] Zweitens … III
secret ['si:krət]:
1. geheim V
2. Geheimnis V
security [sɪ'kjʊərəti] Sicherheit; Sicherheits- III °**internet-scale security** Internet-Sicherheit
see [si:], **saw, seen** sehen I **See you around.** Bis dann. V **See you. / See you later.** Bis dann. / Bis später. I **I see.** Ach so. / Aha. / Verstehe. II **Let's see.** Mal sehen. / Mal abwarten. III
seem [si:m] scheinen *(anscheinend sein)* IV
seen [si:n] *siehe* **see**
segregate ['segrɪgeɪt] trennen *(nach Hautfarbe/Religion/Geschlecht)* VI 1 (11)
segregation [segrɪ'geɪʃn] Trennung *(nach Hautfarbe/Religion/Geschlecht)* IV
self-portrait [self 'pɔ:treɪt] Selbstporträt V
sell [sel], **sold, sold** verkaufen III
send [send], **sent, sent** schicken, senden I **send sth. out** etwas verschicken V
°**sense (of …)** [sens] Gefühl (von), (…-)Bewusstsein **sense of time** Zeitgefühl
°**sensible** ['sensəbl] vernünftig
sent [sent] *siehe* **send**
sentence ['sentəns] Satz II
September [sep'tembə] September I
series, *pl* **series** ['sɪəri:z] (Sende-)Reihe, Serie II
°**serious** ['sɪəriəs] ernst(haft)
serve [sɜ:v] servieren *(Essen, Getränke)*; bedienen *(Kunden)* III
service ['sɜ:vɪs] Dienst, Service II
°**session** ['seʃn] Sitzung, (Unterrichts-)Stunde **question and answer session** Fragestunde
set, set, set [set]: **set the table** den Tisch decken I °**set off** aufbrechen, losfahren/-fliegen °**be set (in)** spielen (in) *(Film, Geschichte)*
setting ['setɪŋ] Schauplatz *(z.B. Film/Geschichte)* V
settle ['setl] sich niederlassen, sich ansiedeln V
settler ['setlə] Siedler/in IV
seven ['sevn] sieben I
several ['sevrəl] mehrere, einige VI 3 (62)
shade [ʃeɪd] Schatten *(vor der Sonne geschützt)* V
shadow ['ʃædəʊ] Schatten *(Umriss)* V
°**shake** [ʃeɪk], [ʃʊk], ['ʃeɪkən], **shook, shaken** zittern; schütteln
°**shaken** ['ʃeɪkən] *siehe* **shake**
shame [ʃeɪm]: **a shame** ein Jammer; schade V
°**shameful** ['ʃeɪmfl] schändlich, beschämend
share a room with … [ʃeə] sich ein Zimmer mit … teilen I
shark [ʃɑ:k] Hai II
she [ʃi:] sie *(Singular)* I
shed [ʃed] Schuppen *(Hütte, Lagerraum)* VI 3 (63)
sheep, *pl* **sheep** [ʃi:p] Schaf I
shelf, *pl* **shelves** [ʃelf], [ʃelvz] Regal I
shift [ʃɪft] Schicht *(bei der Arbeit)* V **work shifts** im Schichtdienst arbeiten V
shine [ʃaɪn], **shone, shone** scheinen (Sonne) III °**shine a light on …** die Aufmerksamkeit lenken auf …
ship [ʃɪp] Schiff III
shirt [ʃɜ:t] Hemd I
shock [ʃɒk] schockieren V
shocked [ʃɒkt] schockiert V
shocking ['ʃɒkɪŋ] schockierend V
shoe [ʃu:] Schuh I
shone [ʃɒn] *siehe* **shine**
°**shook** [ʃʊk] *siehe* **shake**
°**shoot** [ʃu:t], **shot, shot** erschießen, schießen (auf)
shop [ʃɒp] Geschäft, Laden I
shop window [ʃɒp 'wɪndəʊ] Schaufenster VI 1 (19)
shoplift ['ʃɒplɪft] Ladendiebstahl begehen V
shoplifting ['ʃɒplɪftɪŋ] Ladendiebstahl V
shopper ['ʃɒpə] (Ein-)Käufer/in IV
shopping ['ʃɒpɪŋ]: **do the shopping** Einkäufe erledigen, einkaufen gehen V **go shopping** einkaufen gehen I
shopping centre ['ʃɒpɪŋ sentə] Einkaufszentrum I
shopping mall ['ʃɒpɪŋ mɔ:l] *(oft auch kurz:* **mall***)* Einkaufszentrum III
°**shore** [ʃɔ:] Ufer *(eines Sees)*
short [ʃɔ:t]:
1. kurz II
2. klein *(Person)* II
short story [ʃɔ:t 'stɔ:ri] Kurzgeschichte V
shorts *(pl)* [ʃɔ:ts] Shorts, kurze Hose IV
shot [ʃɒt]:
1. Schuss III
2. Aufnahme, Foto; *(Film)* Einstellung VI 1 (25)
°3. *siehe* **shoot**
should [ʃʊd]: **What should I do?** Was sollte ich tun? II
shoulder ['ʃəʊldə] Schulter I
shout [ʃaʊt]:
1. Ruf IV
2. rufen II
show [ʃəʊ], **showed, shown**:
1. zeigen II
°**show sb. (a)round (your town)** jn. (in deiner Stadt) herumführen
2. sich zeigen, sichtbar sein V
shown [ʃəʊn] *siehe* **show**
Shut up! [ʃʌt 'ʌp] *(infml)* Halt den Mund! I
shy [ʃaɪ] schüchtern, scheu II
sick [sɪk] krank V **I'm/I feel sick.** Mir ist schlecht/übel. V
side [saɪd] Seite III **side by side** Seite an Seite IV
sidewalk ['saɪdwɔ:k] *(AE)* Gehweg, Bürgersteig IV
°**sigh** [saɪ] seufzen
sight [saɪt] Anblick III
sights *(pl)* [saɪts] Sehenswürdigkeiten III
sightseeing tour ['saɪtsi:ɪŋ tʊə] Rundfahrt *(zur Besichtigung der Sehenswürdigkeiten)* III
sign [saɪn]:
1. Schild; Zeichen I
2. unterschreiben IV
sign up (for) sich anmelden (für) VI 3 (60)
°**sign language** ['saɪn læŋgwɪdʒ] Zeichensprache, Gebärdensprache
signal ['sɪgnəl] Signal III
signature ['sɪgnətʃə] Unterschrift VI 2 (34)
silence ['saɪləns] Stille, Schweigen IV
silent ['saɪlənt] still, ruhig; lautlos VI 1 (20) **fall silent** still werden, verstummen VI 1 (20)
silly ['sɪli] albern; blöd II **Silly me!** Bin ich blöd! II
similar (to sth./sb.) ['sɪmələ] (etwas/jm.) ähnlich IV
°**simile** ['sɪməli] Vergleich *(Stilmittel)*
simple ['sɪmpl] einfach, simpel V
°**simplicity** [sɪm'plɪsəti] Einfachheit, Schlichtheit
since [sɪns]:
1. seit III
since August / 12 o'clock seit August / 12 Uhr III
2. **since she'd lost …** seit(dem) sie … verloren hatte VI 3 (64)
3. seitdem, seither V
°4. weil, da
sincerely [sɪn'sɪəli]: **Sincerely yours** *(AE)* Mit freundlichen Grüßen *(Briefschluss)* V **Yours sincerely …** *(BE)* / **Sincerely, …** *(AE)* Mit freundlichen Grüßen *(Briefschluss)* IV

sing [sɪŋ], **sang, sung** singen I
singer ['sɪŋə] Sänger/in I
single ['sɪŋgl] ledig, alleinstehend II
single parent [sɪŋgl 'peərənt] Alleinerziehende(r) IV
single ticket [sɪŋgl 'tɪkɪt] einfache Fahrkarte IV
sir [sɜː] gnädiger Herr V **Dear Sir/ Madam** Sehr geehrte Damen und Herren V
siren ['saɪrən] Sirene VI 2 (42)
sister ['sɪstə] Schwester I
sit [sɪt], **sat, sat** sitzen; sich setzen I **sit down** sich hinsetzen III
site [saɪt] *(kurz für:* **website***)* Website IV
situation [sɪtʃu'eɪʃn] Situation V
six [sɪks] sechs I
size [saɪz] Größe IV
skateboard ['skeɪtbɔːd] Skateboard fahren I
skating ['skeɪtɪŋ]:
1. *(= ice skating)* Schlittschuhlaufen V
2. *(= roller skating)* Rollschuhlaufen V
skeleton ['skelɪtn] Skelett VI 3 (54/55)
ski [skiː] Ski laufen, Ski fahren II
skier ['skiːə] Skiläufer/in III
skill [skɪl] Fähigkeit, Fertigkeit V
°**skills file** ['skɪlz faɪl] Anhang mit Lern- und Arbeitstechniken
skim a text [skɪm] einen Text überfliegen *(um den Inhalt grob zu erfassen)* III
skin [skɪn] Haut IV
skinny ['skɪni] *(infml)* mager, dürr III
skirt [skɜːt] Rock I
skive [skaɪv] *(infml)* schwänzen *(Schule)* II
sky [skaɪ] Himmel IV **in the sky** am Himmel IV
skyline ['skaɪlaɪn] Skyline IV
skyscraper ['skaɪskreɪpə] Wolkenkratzer IV
slave [sleɪv] Sklave/Sklavin IV
slavery ['sleɪvəri] Sklaverei III
sleep [sliːp]:
1. Schlaf II
Go to sleep! Schlaf jetzt! I
2. **sleep, slept, slept** schlafen I
sleeping bag ['sliːpɪŋ bæg] Schlafsack I
sleepless ['sliːpləs] schlaflos VI 3 (56)
sleepover ['sliːpəʊvə] Schlafparty I
sleepy ['sliːpi] schläfrig III
slept [slept] *siehe* **sleep**
slide [slaɪd]:
1. Dia, Folie V
°2. Rutsche, Rutschbahn
°**slip** [slɪp] (aus)rutschen
°**slippery** ['slɪpəri] rutschig, glatt
slow [sləʊ]:
1. langsam II
°2. **slow down** (sich) verlangsamen, langsamer werden

small [smɔːl] klein I
smart [smɑːt] schick, smart; schlau, clever IV
smell [smel]:
1. riechen II
2. Geruch, Gestank IV
smile [smaɪl]:
1. lächeln III
2. *(das)* Lächeln II
smoke [sməʊk] rauchen IV
smoothie ['smuːði] Smoothie *(Getränk aus Fruchtpüree, evtl. mit Milchprodukten)* II
snake [sneɪk] Schlange I
sneaker ['sniːkə] *(AE)* Turnschuh IV
snow [snəʊ] Schnee II
snowy ['snəʊi] schneebedeckt; verschneit II
so [səʊ]:
1. also; deshalb, daher II
2. **so boring** so langweilig I
so far bis jetzt V **so that** sodass, damit IV **and so on** und so weiter VI 3 (66)
3. **I don't think so.** Das glaube/denke ich nicht. III
I think so. Ich glaube ja. III
soap [səʊ] Seife; *(infml auch:)* Seifenoper II
soccer ['sɒkə] Fußball IV
social ['səʊʃl] gesellschaftlich, sozial V
social media *(pl)* [səʊʃl 'miːdiə] soziale Medien/Dienste V
society [sə'saɪəti] (die) Gesellschaft V
sock [sɒk] Socke, Strumpf I
sofa ['səʊfə] Sofa II
software engineer ['sɒftweə endʒɪnɪə] Softwareentwickler/in VI 2 (46)
°**solar panel** [səʊlə 'pænl] Sonnenkollektor
sold [səʊld] *siehe* **sell**
soldier ['səʊldʒə] Soldat/in IV
solution (to a problem) [sə'luːʃn] Lösung (eines Problems) V
solve a problem [sɒlv] ein Problem lösen VI 2 (35)
some [sʌm], [səm] einige, ein paar; etwas I **Would you like some tea/ chips?** Möchtest du (etwas) Tee / (ein paar) Pommes frites? II
some day ['sʌm deɪ] eines Tages VI 1 (25)
somebody ['sʌmbədi] jemand II
somehow ['sʌmhaʊ] irgendwie VI 1 (19)
someone ['sʌmwʌn] jemand II
someplace ['sʌmpleɪs] irgendwo(hin) IV
something ['sʌmθɪŋ] etwas I **... or something** ... oder so was III
sometime ['sʌmtaɪm] irgendwann V
sometimes ['sʌmtaɪmz] manchmal I
somewhere ['sʌmweə] irgendwo; irgendwohin III
son [sʌn] Sohn III

song [sɒŋ] Lied, Song I
soon [suːn] bald I **as soon as** sobald, sowie III
sore [sɔː]: **a sore throat** Halsschmerzen II **I have a sore leg.** Mein Bein tut weh. I
sorry ['sɒri]: **Sorry. / I'm sorry.** Tut mir leid. / Entschuldigung. I **I'm sorry about yesterday.** Es tut mir leid wegen gestern. II **say sorry** sich entschuldigen V
°**sort** [sɔːt]: **that sort of thing** so etwas; dergleichen
sound [saʊnd]:
1. Geräusch; Klang, Laut; Ton I
2. klingen, sich *(gut/schrecklich/...)* anhören III
°**soundtrack** ['saʊndtræk] Filmmusik; Tonspur
soup [suːp] Suppe I
°**source** [sɔːs] Quelle *(z.B. Text)*
south [saʊθ] Süden; nach Süden II **south-east** Südosten; nach Südosten II **south-west** Südwesten; nach Südwesten II
southern ['sʌðən] südlich, Süd IV
space [speɪs] Platz I
°**spacecraft**, *pl* **spacecraft** [speɪskrɑːft] Raumfahrzeug, Raumschiff
spacesuit ['speɪssuːt] Raumanzug VI 3 (61)
speak [spiːk], **spoke, spoken** sprechen I
speaker ['spiːkə] Sprecher/in; Redner/in V
special ['speʃl] besondere(r, s) I **make sth. special** etwas zu etwas Besonderem machen III **What's special about ...?** Was ist das Besondere an ...? III
special offer [speʃl 'ɒfə] Sonderangebot I
°**specialist** ['speʃəlɪst] Spezialist/in, Fachmann/-frau
°**speciality** [speʃi'æləti] Spezialität
°**speculate** ['spekjuleɪt] spekulieren
°**sped** [sped] *siehe* **speed**
speech [spiːtʃ] Rede; Sprechweise V **give/make a speech** eine Rede halten V
°**speed** [spiːd]:
1. Geschwindigkeit
2. **speed, sped, sped** rasen, zu schnell fahren
°**speed hump** ['spiːd hʌmp] Bodenschwelle, Bremsschwelle *(zur Verkehrsberuhigung)*
spell [spel] buchstabieren I
spelling ['spelɪŋ] Rechtschreibung; Schreibweise IV
spend time/money (on) [spend], **spent, spent** Zeit verbringen (mit); Geld ausgeben (für) II
spent [spent] *siehe* **spend**
spider ['spaɪdə] Spinne V

spirit ['spɪrɪt] Geist, Stimmung IV **school spirit** Schulklima, Gemeinschaftsgefühl IV **team spirit** Teamgeist, Mannschaftsgeist IV
spite [spaɪt]: **in spite of** trotz VI 1 (14)
°**splash** [splæʃ] spritzen, platschen
spoke [spəʊk] *siehe* **speak**
spoken [spəʊkən] *siehe* **speak**
°**spokesperson,** *pl* **spokespersons** *or* **spokespeople** ['spəʊkspɜːsn] Sprecher/in
sport [spɔːt] Sport; Sportart I **do sport** Sport treiben I
sports car ['spɔːts kɑː] Sportwagen IV
sports hall ['spɔːts hɔːl] Sporthalle I
sportsman/-woman ['spɔːtsmən, -wʊmən] Sportler/in III
sporty ['spɔːti] sportlich II
spot [spɒt] Stelle, Ort; Fleck V
spot sth. [spɒt] etwas entdecken IV
°**spotter** ['spɒtə]: **shark spotter** Hai-Beobachter/in; jemand, der nach Haien Ausschau hält
spring [sprɪŋ] Frühling II
square [skweə] Platz *(in Stadt oder Dorf)* III
squat [skwɒt] (ein Haus/Grundstück) besetzen V
squatter ['skwɒtə] Hausbesetzer/in V
stadium ['steɪdiəm] Stadion II
staff [stɑːf] Personal, Belegschaft V
stage [steɪdʒ] Bühne VI 2 (38)
stairs *(pl)* [steəz] Treppe; Treppenstufen III
stamp [stæmp] Stempel II
stand [stænd]:
1. Standpunkt, Haltung VI 2 (32)
take a stand (on/against sth.) Stellung beziehen (zu/gegen etwas) VI 2 (32)
2. **stand, stood, stood** stehen; sich (hin)stellen III
stand out (from) sich abheben (von), herausragen (aus) III **stand up** aufstehen IV **stand up for** eintreten für, sich einsetzen für VI 2 (37)
standard ['stændəd]:
1. Norm, Standard V
2. normal, üblich, Standard- V
stank [stæŋk] *siehe* **stink**
star [stɑː]: Stern IV
stare [steə] starren IV
start [stɑːt]:
1. Start II
2. anfangen, beginnen I
start a business ein Geschäft/eine Firma gründen III **start off (as)** anfangen (als) V **get started** anfangen III **To start with, …** Erstens …; Zunächst …; Zuerst einmal … IV
°**start out** (zunächst) beginnen; am Anfang stehen
state [steɪt]:
1. Staat IV
°2. Zustand

statement ['steɪtmənt] Aussage II
station [steɪʃn] Bahnhof II
statistics *(pl)* [stə'tɪstɪks] Statistik IV
statue ['stætʃuː] Statue IV
°**status update** ['steɪtəs ʌpdeɪt] Statusaktualisierung *(bei sozialen Netzwerken)*
stay [steɪ]:
1. bleiben I
2. Aufenthalt III
steal [stiːl], **stole, stolen** stehlen V
step [step]:
1. Schritt II
step by step Schritt für Schritt V
2. Stufe IV
3. treten *(einen Schritt tun)* VI 1 (14)
stepbrother ['stepbrʌðə] Stiefbruder I
stepdad ['stepdæd] Stiefvater I
step-dancing ['stepdɑːnsɪŋ] Stepptanz IV
stepfather ['stepfɑːðə] Stiefvater I
stepmother ['stepmʌðə] Stiefmutter I
stepmum ['stepmʌm] Stiefmutter I
stepsister ['stepsɪstə] Stiefschwester I
stereotype ['steriətaɪp] Stereotyp, Klischee(vorstellung) VI 2 (46)
stick [stɪk], **stuck, stuck** (haften) bleiben VI 1 (25) **stick together** zusammenhalten III
still [stɪl] immer noch, noch immer II
still [stɪl]:
1. still, ruhig V
°2. **(film) still** Standbild *(Film)*
sting [stɪŋ]:
1. (Insekten-)Stich V
2. **sting, stung, stung** stechen *(Insekt)*; brennen V
stink [stɪŋk], **stank, stunk** stinken IV
stole [stəʊl] *siehe* **steal**
stolen ['stəʊlən] *siehe* **steal**
stomach ['stʌmək] Magen, Bauch IV
stomach ache ['stʌmək eɪk] Magenschmerzen II
stone [stəʊn] Stein II
°**Stone Age** ['stəʊn eɪdʒ] Steinzeit
stood [stʊd] *siehe* **stand**
stop [stɒp]:
1. Halt, Haltestelle IV
2. anhalten III
3. stoppen II
stop sth. mit etwas aufhören; etwas stoppen II **It stops with me.** Bei mir hört's auf. / Ich mache da nicht mit. V °**stop sb. doing sth.** jn. davon abhalten, etwas zu tun
store [stɔː] Geschäft, Laden III
°**storm** [stɔːm] stürmen
story ['stɔːri] Geschichte, Erzählung I
storyline ['stɔːrilaɪn] Handlung *(z.B. eines Films / einer Geschichte)* VI 2 (47)
°**straight** [streɪt]:
1. direkt, gleich
2. gerade
straight away [streɪt ə'weɪ] sofort V

straight on [streɪt 'ɒn] geradeaus (weiter) II
strange [streɪndʒ] seltsam, sonderbar II
stranger ['streɪndʒə] Fremde(r) VI 1 (19)
strategy ['strætədʒi] Strategie V
strawberry ['strɔːbəri] Erdbeere IV
°**stream** [striːm] strömen
street [striːt] Straße *(in Orten)* I
strength [streŋθ] Stärke, Kraft V
stress [stres]:
1. Stress, Belastung V
heat stress Hitzestress, Wärmebelastung des Körpers V
°2. betonen
stressed [strest] gestresst III
stressful ['stresfl] anstrengend, stressig IV
°**stretcher** ['stretʃə] Trage, (Trag-)Bahre
strict [strɪkt] streng I
°**strike** [straɪk] Streik
stroke [strəʊk] streicheln I
strong [strɒŋ] stark III
structure ['strʌktʃə]:
1. strukturieren, gliedern III
2. Struktur V
°**struggle** ['strʌgl] kämpfen, sich abmühen
stuck [stʌk] *siehe* **stick**
student ['stjuːdnt] Schüler/in; Student/in I
student card ['stjuːdnt kɑːd] Schülerausweis; Studentenausweis VI 1 (23)
studio ['stjuːdiəʊ] Studio I
study ['stʌdi] studieren; lernen V
stuff [stʌf] *(infml)* Zeug, Kram II
stung [stʌŋ] *siehe* **sting**
stunk [stʌŋk] *siehe* **stink**
°**stunt** [stʌnt] Stunt
stupid ['stjuːpɪd] dumm, blöd I
style [staɪl] Stil V
stylist ['staɪlɪst] Friseur/in; (Mode-)Stylist/in V
°**stylistic** [staɪ'lɪstɪk] stilistisch, Stil-
°**stylistic device** [staɪlɪstɪk dɪ'vaɪs] Stilmittel
subject ['sʌbdʒɪkt]:
1. Thema; *(in E-Mails)* Betreff II
2. Schulfach III
suburb ['sʌbɜːb] Vorstadt, Vorort VI 1 (12)
subway ['sʌbweɪ] *(AE)* U-Bahn IV
succeed [sək'siːd] Erfolg haben VI 3 (60)
success [sək'ses] Erfolg VI 3 (60)
successful [sək'sesfl] erfolgreich III
such (a) [sʌtʃ] so(lch) (ein/e) V
there's no such thing as … es gibt kein/e … V
such as ['sʌtʃ əz] wie zum Beispiel V
suck [sʌk]: **It sucks!** *(infml)* Es nervt! / Es ist Mist! III
°**sudden** ['sʌdn] plötzliche(r, s)
suddenly ['sʌdənli] plötzlich, auf einmal II

suffer (from) ['sʌfə] leiden (an), erleiden V
sugar ['ʃʊgə] Zucker II
sugary ['ʃʊgəri] süß(lich); zuckerhaltig II
suggest sth. (to sb.) [sə'dʒest] (jm.) etwas vorschlagen III
°**suggestion** [sə'dʒestʃən] Vorschlag
suit [su:t]:
1. (Damen-)Kostüm VI 3 (61)
2. (Herren-)Anzug VI 3 (61)
suitable ['su:təbl] geeignet, passend V
sum sth. up [sʌm 'ʌp] etwas zusammenfassen III **To sum up, ...** Um (es) zusammenzufassen, ... / Zusammenfassend kann man sagen, ... V
summarize ['sʌməraɪz] zusammenfassen IV
summary ['sʌməri] Zusammenfassung III
summer ['sʌmə] Sommer I
sun [sʌn] Sonne II
suncream ['sʌnkri:m] Sonnencreme, Sonnenschutzmittel II
Sunday ['sʌndeɪ], ['sʌndi] Sonntag I
sung [sʌŋ] *siehe* **sing**
sunglasses *(pl)* ['sʌnglɑ:sɪz] (eine) Sonnenbrille II
sunlight ['sʌnlaɪt] Sonnenlicht IV
sunny ['sʌni] sonnig II
sunshine ['sʌnʃaɪn] Sonnenschein IV
superhero, *pl* **superheroes** ['su:pəhɪərəʊ] Superheld/in VI 3 (69)
supermarket ['su:pəmɑ:kɪt] Supermarkt I
°**supply** [sə'plaɪ] Versorgung, Lieferung; Vorrat
support [sə'pɔ:t]:
1. unterstützen V
2. Unterstützung V
supposed [sə'pəʊzd]:
be supposed to be/do sth. etwas sein/tun sollen VI 3 (67)
sure [ʃʊə], [ʃɔ:] sicher I **for sure** ganz sicher, ganz bestimmt V **make sure that ...** sicherstellen, dass ...; darauf achten, dass ...; dafür sorgen, dass ... V
surf [sɜ:f] surfen, wellenreiten IV
surfing ['sɜ:fɪŋ] Surfing, Wellenreiten IV
surprise [sə'praɪz]:
1. Überraschung I
2. überraschen V
surprised [sə'praɪzd] überrascht II
surprising [sə'praɪzɪŋ] überraschend V
°**surround** [sə'raʊnd] umgeben
survey ['sɜ:veɪ] Umfrage II
survival [sə'vaɪvl] *(das)* Überleben VI 2 (38)
survive [sə'vaɪv] überleben VI 2 (38)
suspension bridge [sə'spenʃn brɪdʒ] Hängebrücke IV
suspicious [sə'spɪʃəs] verdächtig IV
sustainable [sə'steɪnəbl] nachhaltig, umweltverträglich; zukunftsfähig VI 3 (58)
swam [swæm] *siehe* **swim**
swamp [swɒmp] Sumpf IV
swap [swɒp] tauschen VI 1 (25) **swap places with sb.** mit jm. die Plätze tauschen VI 1 (25)
sweat [swet] Schweiß IV
sweatshop ['swetʃɒp] Ausbeutungsbetrieb VI 2 (45)
sweet [swi:t] süß IV
sweets *(pl)* [swi:ts] Süßigkeiten I
swerve [swɜ:v] *(das Auto/Steuer)* herumreißen, *(mit dem Auto)* ausweichen V
swim [swɪm], **swam, swum** schwimmen I
swimmer ['swɪmə] Schwimmer/in III
swimming pool ['swɪmɪŋ pu:l] Schwimmbad, Schwimmbecken I
°**swing** [swɪŋ], **swung, swung** schwingen
switch sth. on/off [swɪtʃ] etwas ein-/ausschalten III
swum [swʌm] *siehe* **swim**
°**swung** [swʌŋ] *siehe* **swing**
symbol ['sɪmbl] Symbol III
°**symbolic (of)** [sɪm'bɒlɪk] symbolisch (für)
°**synonym** ['sɪnənɪm] Synonym *(Wort mit gleicher oder ähnlicher Bedeutung)*
system ['sɪstəm] System VI 1 (11)

T

table ['teɪbl]:
1. Tisch I
°2. Tabelle
table tennis ['teɪbl tenɪs] Tischtennis II
°**tackle** ['tækl] *(Problem)* angehen; angreifen
tae kwon do [taɪ kwɒn 'dəʊ] Taekwondo I
tail [teɪl] Schwanz II
take [teɪk], **took, taken**:
1. nehmen; mitnehmen II
2. (weg-, hin)bringen IV
3. dauern, *(Zeit)* brauchen III
take a message (jm.) etwas ausrichten III **Take it easy!** *(infml) etwa:* Reg dich nicht auf. / Bleib mal locker. III **take notes** (sich) Notizen machen *(beim Lesen oder Zuhören)* III **take part in sth.** an etwas teilnehmen, bei etwas mitmachen III **take photos** fotografieren, Fotos machen II **take place** stattfinden VI 2 (39) **take risks** Risiken eingehen III **take sth. off** etwas abnehmen, absetzen *(Brille, Hut)*; etwas ausziehen *(Kleidung)* VI 3 (67) **take sth. on** etwas annehmen, übernehmen V **I'll take it.** Ich nehme es (ihn, sie). *(beim Einkaufen)* I °**take it easy** sich schonen °**take to sth.** sich flüchten zu/an *(einen Ort)*
takeaway ['teɪkəweɪ] Essen zum Mitnehmen V
taken ['teɪkən] *siehe* **take**
°**take-off** ['teɪk ɒf] Start *(Flugzeug)*
talent ['tælənt] Talent, Begabung III
talk [tɔ:k]:
1. Vortrag, Rede; Gespräch II
give a talk einen Vortrag halten II
2. **talk (to sb.)** sprechen, reden (mit jm.) I
°**talk sth. over (with sb.)** etwas (mit jm.) besprechen
talker ['tɔ:kə] Redner/in III
tall [tɔ:l] groß *(Person)*; hoch *(Gebäude, Baum)* II
target ['tɑ:gɪt]:
1. Ziel V
2. **target sb.** auf jn. zielen *(jn. als Zielgruppe haben/wählen)*, jn. ins Visier nehmen V
task [tɑ:sk] Aufgabe II
tattoo [tə'tu:] Tattoo, Tätowierung III
taught [tɔ:t] *siehe* **teach**
taxi ['tæksi] Taxi II
tea [ti:] Tee I
teach [ti:tʃ], **taught, taught** unterrichten, lehren III **teach sb. a lesson** jm. eine Lektion erteilen V
teacher ['ti:tʃə] Lehrer/in I
team [ti:m]: **the under-18s team** das Team der unter 18-Jährigen V
team spirit ['ti:m spɪrɪt] Teamgeist, Mannschaftsgeist IV
teamwork ['ti:mwɜ:k] Teamarbeit V
tear [tɪə] Träne IV
technique [tek'ni:k] Methode, Technik VI 1 (25)
technology [tek'nɒlədʒi] Technik, Technologie I
teen [ti:n] Teenager III
teen talk ['ti:n tɔ:k] *etwa:* Teenagergespräche II
teenage ['ti:neɪdʒ]: **a teenage girl** ein Mädchen im Teenageralter V
teeth [tu:θ] *Mehrzahl von* **tooth** IV
telephone ['telɪfəʊn] Telefon V
°**television** ['telɪvɪʒn] Fernsehen
tell (about) [tel], **told, told** erzählen (von), berichten (über) II **tell sb. (not) to do sth.** jn. auffordern, etwas (nicht) zu tun; jm. sagen, dass er/sie etwas (nicht) tun soll IV **tell sb. the way** jm. den Weg beschreiben II
temperature ['temprətʃə] Temperatur; Fieber II **have a temperature** Fieber haben II **take sb.'s temperature** (bei jm.) Fieber messen V
ten [ten] zehn I
tent [tent] Zelt II
term [tɜ:m] Trimester III
terrible ['terəbl] schrecklich, fürchterlich I

territory ['terətri] Gebiet, Territorium IV
°**terror** ['terə] (panische) Angst
terrorist ['terərɪst] terroristisch, Terror-; Terrorist/in IV
test [test]:
1. Test; Klassenarbeit II
2. (*kurz für:* **driving test**) Fahrprüfung, Führerscheinprüfung IV
text [tekst]:
1. SMS; Text I
2. **text a friend** einem Freund / einer Freundin eine SMS schicken I
text message ['tekst mesɪdʒ] (*kurz auch:* **text**) SMS I
than [ðən]: **more than** mehr als III **older than me** älter als ich II
thank you ['θæŋk juː] danke (schön) IV
Thanks. [θæŋks] Danke. I **Thanks very much.** Danke sehr. / Danke vielmals. II
Thanksgiving [θæŋks'gɪvɪŋ] Erntedankfest *(amerikanischer Feiertag am vierten Donnerstag im November)* IV
that [ðæt], [ðət]:
1. das (dort) I
that field das Feld (dort), jenes Feld I **that morning/afternoon/evening** an jenem Morgen/Nachmittag/Abend III **That's £159.** Das macht 159 Pfund. I **That's because ...** Das liegt daran, dass ... IV **That's us.** Das sind wir. IV **That's why ...** Deshalb ..., Darum ... II
2. der, die, das; die *(Relativpronomen)* III
3. dass IV
so that sodass, damit IV **they think that ...** sie glauben, dass ... II
the [ðə], [ði] der, die, das; die I **the 90s** die Neunzigerjahre II
theatre ['θɪətə] Theater I
their [ðeə] ihr/e *(Plural)* I
theirs [ðeəz] ihre/r, ihrs *(zu „they")* V
them [ðem], [ðəm] sie; ihnen I
theme [θiːm] Thema I
theme park ['θiːm pɑːk] Themenpark *(Freizeitpark mit Attraktionen zu einem bestimmten Thema)* V
themselves [ðəm'selvz] sich III
then [ðen] dann, danach I **(back) then** damals VI 1 (12)
there [ðeə] da, dort; dahin, dorthin I
there are ... es sind ... / es gibt ... I
there's ... es ist ... / es gibt ... I
over there da drüben, dort drüben V
°**therefore** ['ðeəfɔː] daher, deshalb
these [ðiːz] die, diese (hier) II
these days ['ðiːz deɪz] heutzutage VI 2 (34)
they [ðeɪ]:
1. sie *(Plural)* I
2. man *(die Leute)* VI 3 (64)

thief, *pl* thieves [θiːf], [θiːvz] Dieb/in VI 1 (22)
thin [θɪn] dünn IV
thing [θɪŋ] Ding, Sache I
think [θɪŋk], **thought, thought** denken, meinen, glauben I **think of sth.** an etwas denken, sich etwas ausdenken III **think of/about** halten von, denken über III **I don't think so.** Das glaube/denke ich nicht. III **I think so.** Ich glaube ja. III
third [θɜːd] dritte(r, s) I
Thirdly, ... ['θɜːdli] Drittens ... III
thirsty ['θɜːsti]: **be thirsty** durstig sein, Durst haben II
this [ðɪs] diese(r, s) I **This is ...** Dies ist ... / Das ist ... I **this morning/afternoon/evening** heute Morgen/Nachmittag/Abend II
those CDs [ðəʊz] die CDs dort; jene CDs II
though [ðəʊ]:
1. aber; allerdings; jedoch V
2. obwohl V
°**even though** auch wenn, obwohl *(betont)*
thought [θɔːt] *siehe* **think**
thousand ['θaʊznd] tausend III
three [θriː] drei I
threw [θruː] *siehe* **throw**
°**thrill sb.** [θrɪl] jn. begeistern, überwältigen
°**thrilling** ['θrɪlɪŋ] aufregend, spannend
throat [θrəʊt] Hals II **a sore throat** Halsschmerzen II
through [θruː] durch I
throw [θrəʊ], **threw, thrown** werfen III
thrown [θrəʊn] *siehe* **throw**
thunder ['θʌndə] Donner VI 3 (69)
Thursday ['θɜːzdeɪ], ['θɜːzdi] Donnerstag I
ticket ['tɪkɪt]:
1. Eintrittskarte I
2. Fahrkarte III
one-way ticket einfache Fahrkarte IV
ticket office ['tɪkɪt ɒfɪs] Kartenschalter II
tidy ['taɪdi]:
1. ordentlich, aufgeräumt III
2. aufräumen II
tidy (sth.) up (etwas) aufräumen III
tie [taɪ] Krawatte I
tiger ['taɪgə] Tiger I
tights *(pl)* [taɪts] Strumpfhose I
till [tɪl] bis V
time [taɪm]:
1. Zeit; Uhrzeit I
at all times jederzeit, ständig V **on time** pünktlich II **over time** im Laufe der Zeit VI 2 (43) **What's the time?** Wie spät ist es? I °**in time** rechtzeitig
2. Mal II

for the last time zum letzten Mal III
°**at a time** jeweils, ununterbrochen
timetable ['taɪmteɪbl] Stundenplan I
°**tiny** ['taɪni] winzig
tip [tɪp] Tipp II
tired ['taɪəd] müde I **be tired of sth.** die Nase voll haben von etwas VI 1 (20)
title ['taɪtl] Titel, Überschrift IV
to [tu], [tə]:
1. *(örtlich)* zu, nach I
to the cinema ins Kino I
2. bis I
from Monday to Friday von Montag bis Freitag I
3. um zu II
To start with, ... Erstens ...; Zunächst ...; Zuerst einmal ... IV
4. **He doesn't like to be lonely.** Er mag es nicht, allein zu sein. I
today [tə'deɪ] heute I
together [tə'geðə] zusammen I
toilet ['tɔɪlət] Toilette I
toilet roll ['tɔɪlət rəʊl] Rolle Toilettenpapier II
told [təʊld] *siehe* **tell**
tomato, *pl* tomatoes [tə'mɑːtəʊ] Tomate III
tomorrow [tə'mɒrəʊ] morgen II
tongue [tʌŋ] Zunge IV
tonight [tə'naɪt] heute Nacht, heute Abend III
°**tonne** [tʌn] Tonne *(= 1.000 kg)*
too [tuː]:
1. auch I
from Berlin too auch aus Berlin I
Me too. Ich auch. I
2. **too old/big/...** zu alt/groß/... I
took [tʊk] *siehe* **take**
°**tool** [tuːl] Werkzeug
tooth, *pl* teeth [tuːθ], [tiːθ] Zahn IV
toothpaste ['tuːθpeɪst] Zahnpasta IV
top [tɒp] obere Ende, Oberteil IV
at the top (of) oben; am oberen Ende (von), an der Spitze (von) II
topic ['tɒpɪk] Thema V
torch [tɔːtʃ] Taschenlampe; Fackel III
tornado [tɔː'neɪdəʊ] Tornado IV
total ['təʊtl] Gesamt-; total, völlig VI 1 (12) **totally free** völlig, total frei VI 1 (12)
touch [tʌtʃ]:
1. berühren, anfassen VI 3 (56)
°2. **get in touch with** (sich) in Verbindung setzen mit
tough [tʌf] (knall)hart IV
tour [tʊə] **a tour of the school** ein Rundgang durch die Schule I
tourist ['tʊərɪst] Tourist/in II
tourist office ['tʊərɪst ɒfɪs] Touristeninformation; Fremdenverkehrsbüro III
towards sb./sth. [tə'wɔːdz] auf jn./etwas zu IV
towel ['taʊəl] Handtuch III
tower ['taʊə] Turm III

town [taʊn] Stadt I **in town** in der Stadt I
township ['taʊnʃɪp] Township *(überwiegend von Schwarzen bewohnte Siedlung in Südafrika)* VI 1 (11)
toy [tɔɪ] Spielzeug II
track [træk]:
1. Pfad, (Feld-)Weg III
°2. (zurück-, nach)verfolgen, beobachten
tractor ['træktə] Traktor III
°**trade secret** [treɪd 'si:krət] Handels-/Branchengeheimnis
tradition [trə'dɪʃn] Tradition IV
traditional [trə'dɪʃənl] traditionell V
traffic ['træfɪk] Verkehr III
traffic lights *(pl)* ['træfɪk laɪts] Verkehrsampel II
trail [treɪl] Weg, Pfad IV
train [treɪn] Zug II
train sb. [treɪn] jn. trainieren, ausbilden III
trainee [treɪ'ni:] Auszubildende(r), Trainee V
trainer ['treɪnə] Trainer/in III
trainers *(pl)* ['treɪnəz] Turnschuhe I
training ['treɪnɪŋ] Training, Ausbildung I
tramp [træmp] Obdachlose(r), Stadtstreicher/in V
translate [træns'leɪt] übersetzen VI 1 (24)
°**translator** [træns'leɪtə] Übersetzer/in
transport ['trænspɔ:t] Verkehrsmittel; Transport(wesen) III
trapped [træpt] gefangen *(in einer Falle)* IV
trash [træʃ] *(AE)* Abfall, Müll IV
travel ['trævl]:
1. reisen; fahren, sich fortbewegen III **travel the world** die Welt bereisen VI 1 (12)
2. *(das)* Reisen V
travel costs *(pl)* ['trævl kɒsts] Reisekosten V
Travelcard ['trævlkɑ:d] *Ein- oder Mehrtagesfahrkarte (London)* III
traveller ['trævələ] Reisende/r VI 1 (15)
travel-sick ['trævlsɪk] reisekrank III
tree [tri:] Baum I
tribe [traɪb] (Volks-)Stamm IV
trick [trɪk] Trick, Kunststück III
trip [trɪp] Ausflug; Reise II
troll [trəʊl] Troll, Kobold; *(in Online-Medien)* Provokateur/in VI 2 (34)
trouble ['trʌbl]: **be in trouble** in Schwierigkeiten sein; Ärger kriegen I **get sb. into trouble** jn. in Schwierigkeiten bringen V
trousers *(pl)* ['traʊzəz] Hose I
truck [trʌk] Lastwagen; LKW IV
true [tru:] wahr I
truly ['tru:li] wahrhaft(ig), wirklich VI 1 (14)
trust [trʌst] trauen, vertrauen IV
truth [tru:θ] Wahrheit IV
try [traɪ] probieren, ausprobieren I **try hard** sich sehr bemühen, sich anstrengen IV
Tube [tju:b]: **the Tube** die U-Bahn (in London) III **on the Tube** in der (Londoner) U-Bahn III
Tuesday ['tju:zdeɪ], ['tju:zdi] Dienstag I
°**tunnel** ['tʌnl] Tunnel
turn [tɜ:n]:
1. sich umdrehen 4 (79)
turn around sich umdrehen 1 (21)
turn over (sich) umdrehen; *(Auto)* sich überschlagen 1 (16) **turn right/left** (nach) rechts/links abbiegen 2 (42)
turn sth. etwas umdrehen 3 (62)
turn to sich wenden an, gehen zu 2 (34) °**turn away** sich abwenden, sich wegdrehen °**turn sth. off** etwas ausschalten °**turn sth. on** etwas einschalten °**turn up** auftauchen, erscheinen °**turn yellow** gelb werden
2. **It's your turn.** Du bist dran. / Du bist an der Reihe. 2 (45)
°**a good turn** ein Gefallen
turning point ['tɜ:nɪŋ pɔɪnt] Wendepunkt IV
TV [ti:'vi:] Fernsehen, Fernsehgerät I
twelve [twelv] zwölf I
twice [twaɪs] zweimal III
twig [twɪg] (kleiner) Zweig IV
twin sister/brother [twɪn] Zwillingsschwester/-bruder V
twins *(pl)* [twɪnz] Zwillinge V
two [tu:] zwei I
type (of) [taɪp] Art, Sorte, Typ (von) V
typical (of) ['tɪpɪkl] typisch (für) VI 1 (18)
tyre ['taɪə] Reifen V

U

unattended [ʌnə'tendɪd] unbeaufsichtigt VI 1 (22)
uncle ['ʌŋkl] Onkel I
uncomfortable [ʌn'kʌmftəbl] unbequem VI 3 (67)
°**unconscious** [ʌn'kɒnʃəs] bewusstlos
uncool [ʌn'ku:l] uncool II
under ['ʌndə] unter I **the under-18s team** das Team der unter 18-Jährigen V
underground ['ʌndəgraʊnd]: **the underground** die U-Bahn III
°**underline** [ʌndə'laɪn] unterstreichen
understand [ʌndə'stænd], **understood, understood** verstehen I
understood [ʌndə'stʊd] *siehe* **understand**
unemployed [ʌnɪm'plɔɪd] arbeitslos III
unemployment [ʌnɪm'plɔɪmənt] Arbeitslosigkeit VI 1 (12)
unexpected [ʌnɪk'spektɪd] unerwartet VI 2 (36)
unfit [ʌn'fɪt] nicht fit II
unforgettable [ʌnfə'getəbl] unvergesslich IV
unfortunately [ʌn'fɔ:tʃənətli] unglücklicherweise, leider VI 3 (62)
unfriendly [ʌn'frendli] unfreundlich II
unhappy [ʌn'hæpi] unglücklich I
unhealthy [ʌn'helθi] ungesund II
uniform ['ju:nɪfɔ:m] (Schul-)Uniform I
uninteresting [ʌn'ɪntrəstɪŋ] uninteressant II
unique [ju'ni:k] einzigartig, einmalig VI 1 (14)
unit ['ju:nɪt]:
1. Kapitel, Lektion I
2. Abteilung *(z.B. im Krankenhaus)* VI 2 (43)
United Kingdom (UK) [junaɪtɪd 'kɪŋdəm] Vereinigtes Königreich III
unity ['ju:nəti] Einheit, (innere) Geschlossenheit V
university [ju:nɪ'vɜ:səti] Universität V
unknown [ʌn'nəʊn] unbekannt IV
unless [ən'les] es sei denn; außer (wenn) IV
unlikely [ʌn'laɪkli] unwahrscheinlich VI 1 (12)
unsure [ʌn'ʃʊə], [ʌn'ʃɔ:] unsicher II
until [ən'tɪl] bis *(zeitlich)* II
unwanted [ʌn'wɒntɪd] unerwünscht V
unwelcome [ʌn'welkəm] unerwünscht, unwillkommen II
up [ʌp]: **up the hill/wall** den Hügel/die Mauer hinauf III **be up for sth.** *(infml)* bei etwas dabei sein, mitmachen V
up to ['ʌp tə] bis (zu) V
upside ['ʌpsaɪd] gute Seite, Vorteil III
upside down [ʌpsaɪd 'daʊn] verkehrt herum, auf dem/den Kopf V
upstairs [ʌp'steəz] oben; nach oben I
us [ʌs], [əs] uns I
use [ju:z] benutzen, verwenden I
use [ju:s] Gebrauch, Verwendung VI 3 (54/55) **make use of** Gebrauch machen von, nutzen VI 3 (54/55)
used to ['ju:st tə]:
1. **be used to sth.** an etwas gewöhnt sein IV
get used to sth. sich an etwas gewöhnen IV
2. **where he used to play** wo er früher (immer) gespielt hat IV
useful ['ju:sfl] nützlich III
usual ['ju:ʒuəl] gewöhnlich, üblich III
usually ['ju:ʒuəli] meistens, normalerweise I

V

vacation [və'keɪʃn], [veɪ'keɪʃn] *(AE)* Ferien, Urlaub IV
vacuum cleaner ['vækjuəm kli:nə] Staubsauger V
vague [veɪg] vage, unbestimmt VI 3 (67)

vain [veɪn] eitel V
valley ['væli] Tal IV
value ['vælju:] Wert I **It's good value.** Es ist sein Geld wert. I
vamping ['væmpɪŋ] *spät in der Nacht noch aktiv sein* V
vampire ['væmpaɪə] Vampir V
van [væn] Transporter, Lieferwagen III
vegetables *(pl)* ['vedʒtəblz] Gemüse I
°**vegetarian** [vedʒə'teəriən] vegetarisch; Vegetarier/in
°**vegetation** [vedʒə'teɪʃn] Vegetation
vehicle ['vi:əkl] Fahrzeug III
°**vérité** [verɪ'teɪ]: **(cinema) vérité** Cinéma vérité *(bestimmte Technik des Dokumentarfilmens)*
°**verse** [vɜ:s] Vers, Strophe *(Lied)*
version ['vɜ:ʃn] Fassung, Version IV
very ['veri] sehr I **Thanks very much.** Danke sehr. / Danke vielmals. II
via ['vaɪə] über, durch, per VI 2 (34)
vicinity [və'sɪnəti] Umgebung V
victim ['vɪktɪm] Opfer V
video-chat ['vɪdiəʊ tʃæt] *sich per Videokonferenz unterhalten* V
view [vju:]:
1. Blick, Aussicht IV
2. Ansicht VI 3 (59)
in my/your/... view meiner/deiner/... Ansicht nach VI 3 (59) **point of view** Standpunkt III
viewer ['vju:ə] Zuschauer/in VI 1 (25)
village ['vɪlɪdʒ] Dorf I
violence ['vaɪələns] Gewalt; Gewalttätigkeit IV
violent ['vaɪələnt] gewalttätig; gewaltsam III
virtual ['vɜ:tʃuəl] virtuell V
virus, *pl* **viruses** ['vaɪrəs], ['vaɪrəsɪz] Virus V
vision ['vɪʒn] Vision; Vorstellung VI 3 (54/55)
visit ['vɪzɪt]:
1. besuchen I
2. Besuch IV
visitor ['vɪzɪtə] Besucher/in; Gast I
visitor pass ['vɪzɪtə pɑ:s] Besucherausweis IV
visuals *(pl)* ['vɪʒuəlz] *(kurz für:* **visual materials)** visuelle Materialien/Hilfsmittel V
vocabulary [və'kæbjələri]:
1. Wörterverzeichnis, Vokabelverzeichnis I
2. Wortschatz, Vokabular VI 1 (18)
voice [vɔɪs] Stimme II
voice-over ['vɔɪs əʊvə] Off-Stimme; (Film-)Kommentar VI 1 (25)
volleyball ['vɒlibɔ:l] Volleyball II
volunteer [vɒlən'tɪə]:
1. freiwillig/ehrenamtlich arbeiten *(unbezahlt)* IV
2. Freiwillige(r), Ehrenamtliche(r) IV
vote [vəʊt]:
1. abstimmen III
2. wählen, zur Wahl gehen VI 2 (36)
vote for sb. für jn. stimmen II
°**register to vote** sich in die Wählerlisten eintragen lassen

W

wage, *oft auch:* **wages** *(pl)* [weɪdʒ] Lohn, Gehalt VI 2 (45) °**minimum wage** Mindestlohn
wait (for) [weɪt] warten (auf) II **sb. can't wait to do sth.** jd. kann es kaum erwarten, etwas zu tun V
waiter ['weɪtə] Kellner III
waiting room ['weɪtɪŋ ru:m] Wartezimmer IV
waitress ['weɪtrəs] Kellnerin III
wake [weɪk], **woke, woken**:
1. wecken I
2. **wake up** aufwachen III
walk [wɔ:k]:
1. (zu Fuß) gehen I
walk around umhergehen; herumlaufen II **walk the dog** mit dem Hund rausgehen, den Hund ausführen IV °**walk sb. to ...** jn. nach .../zu ... begleiten; jn. nach .../zu ... bringen *(zu Fuß)*
2. Spaziergang II
go for a walk einen Spaziergang machen, spazieren gehen II
walker ['wɔ:kə] Spaziergänger/in; Wanderer/Wanderin III
walking boots *(pl)* ['wɔ:kɪŋ bu:ts] Wanderstiefel II
°**walkway** ['wɔ:kweɪ] Fußweg, Laufgang
wall [wɔ:l] Wand; Mauer II
wallet ['wɒlɪt] Brieftasche, Börse VI 1 (23)
want sth. [wɒnt] etwas (haben) wollen I **want to do sth.** etwas tun wollen I **We want you to go to ...** Wir möchten/wollen, dass du nach ... gehst. III
war [wɔ:] Krieg IV
wardrobe ['wɔ:drəʊb] Kleiderschrank I
warm [wɔ:m] warm II
warn sb. [wɔ:n] jn. warnen, jn. ermahnen V
warning ['wɔ:nɪŋ] Warnung IV
was [wɒz], [wəz]: **I/he/she/it was** *Vergangenheitsform von* **be** I
wash [wɒʃ] waschen II **wash up** abwaschen I
washing machine ['wɒʃɪŋ məʃi:n] Waschmaschine V
waste [weɪst]:
1. Verschwendung III
°2. Müll, Abfall
°**waste management** ['weɪst mænɪdʒmənt] Abfallwirtschaft
watch [wɒtʃ] Armbanduhr VI 3 (56)
watch sth. [wɒtʃ] sich etwas anschauen; etwas beobachten I **watch TV** fernsehen I
water ['wɔ:tə]:
1. Wasser I
2. gießen, (be)wässern IV
water sports *(pl)* ['wɔ:tə spɔ:ts] Wassersport III
°**waterfront** ['wɔ:təfrʌnt] Hafen(viertel)
°**waterless** ['wɔ:tələs] wasserlos, ohne Wasser
waterproof ['wɔ:təpru:f] wasserdicht, wasserfest, wasserundurchlässig V
wave [weɪv] Welle IV
wave (to sb.) [weɪv] (jm. zu)winken IV
way [weɪ]:
1. Weg 5 (98)
ask sb. the way jn. nach dem Weg fragen 2 (42) **by the way** übrigens 2 (45) **on the way to ...** auf dem Weg zu/nach ... 5 (98) **one way** einfache Fahrt 3 (57) **one-way ticket** einfache Fahrkarte 3 (57) **tell sb. the way** jm. den Weg beschreiben 2 (42)
2. Richtung 2 (41)
come sb.'s way auf jn. zukommen 2 (41) **the wrong way** (in) die falsche Richtung 2 (41) **this way** hier entlang/in diese Richtung 2 (41)
3. Art und Weise 2 (39)
way of life Lebensweise 1 (15) **in a different way** anders; auf andere Art und Weise 2 (39) **in some ways** in mancher Hinsicht 2 (48) **It's the way you do it.** So macht man das. 3 (64) **No way!** Auf keinen Fall! 1 (22)
4. **it's way cooler than ...** *(infml)* es ist viel cooler als ... 1 (17)
we [wi:] wir I
weak [wi:k] schwach III
weakness ['wi:knəs] Schwäche V
wear [weə], **wore, worn** tragen, anhaben *(Kleidung)* II
wearable ['weərəbl] tragbar *(Kleidung)* VI 3 (56)
weather ['weðə] Wetter II
weather forecast ['weðə fɔ:kɑ:st] Wettervorhersage II
Wednesday ['wenzdeɪ], ['wenzdi] Mittwoch I
°**wee** [wi:] *(infml, Kindersprache)* Pipi machen
week [wi:k] Woche I
°**weekday** ['wi:kdeɪ] Werktag, Wochentag
weekend [wi:k'end] Wochenende I **at the weekend** am Wochenende I
weeper ['wi:pə]: **Finders, keepers, losers, weepers.** Was man findet, darf man behalten. *(Redensart)* V
weigh [weɪ] wiegen VI 1 (14)

welcome ['welkəm]:
1. welcome sb. (to) jn. begrüßen (in), jn. willkommen heißen (in) III **Welcome to Plymouth.** Willkommen in Plymouth. I
2. You're welcome. Bitte, gern geschehen. / Nichts zu danken. I
°**welfare** ['welfeə] Wohl, Wohlergehen
Well, … [wel] Nun, … / Also, … / Na ja, … I
well [wel]: **Well done.** Gut gemacht! I **well paid** gut bezahlt IV **be well known** bekannt sein IV **I'm not feeling well.** Ich fühle mich nicht gut. II **work/speak well** gut funktionieren/sprechen I
°**well-heeled** [wel 'hi:ld] *(infml)* gut betucht, wohlhabend
well-known [wel 'nəʊn] bekannt V
went [went] *siehe* **go**
were [wɜ:], [wə]: **we/you/they were** *Vergangenheitsform von* **be** I °**If he were to …** Wenn/Falls er …
west [west] Westen; nach Westen II
western ['westən] westlich, West- IV
wet [wet] nass I
whale [weɪl] Wal IV
what [wɒt]:
1. was I
2. welche(r, s) I
What a pain! *etwa:* So ein Mist. / Es nervt! III **What about …?** Wie wär's mit …? I **What about you?** Und du? / Und was ist mit dir? I **What do you need money for?** Wofür brauchst du Geld? II **What kind of mistakes …?** Was für Fehler …? II **What page is it?** Auf welcher Seite sind wir? I **What would you like?** Was möchtest du? / Was hättest du gern? II **What's for homework?** Was haben wir als Hausaufgabe auf? I **What's going on?** Was ist los? / Was gibt's? IV **What's it like?** Wie ist es? / Wie sieht es aus? I **What's special about …?** Was ist das Besondere an …? III **What's the time?** Wie spät ist es? I **What's your name?** Wie heißt du? *(wörtlich: Was ist dein Name?)* I **What's the matter?** Was ist denn? / Was ist los? II **Like what?** Was (denn) zum Beispiel? III
wheel [wi:l] Rad IV
wheelchair ['wi:ltʃeə] Rollstuhl I
wheels *(pl)* [wi:lz] *(infml)* ein fahrbarer Untersatz *(Auto)* IV
when [wen]:
1. wann I
When's your birthday? Wann hast du Geburtstag? I
2. wenn I
3. als II
where [weə] wo; wohin I
°**wherever** [weər'evə] egal, wo(hin) / wo(hin) (auch) immer
°**whether** ['weðə] ob
which [wɪtʃ]:
1. Which club? Welcher Klub? II
2. der, die, das; die *(Relativpronomen)* V
while [waɪl]:
1. während IV
2. a while eine Weile, einige Zeit V
whisper ['wɪspə] flüstern II
whistle ['wɪsl] (Triller-)Pfeife II
white [waɪt] weiß I
who [hu:]:
1. wer I
Who are you? Wer bist du? / Wer seid ihr? I
2. wen II
Who did Adam meet? Wen hat Adam getroffen? / Wen traf Adam? II
3. wem II
Who did Mia talk to? Mit wem hat Mia gesprochen? / Mit wem sprach Mia? II **Who is the text about?** Von wem handelt der Text? III
4. der, die, das; die *Relativpronomen* III
whole [həʊl] ganze(r, s), gesamte(r, s) IV
°**whom** [hu:m] *(fml)*: **… whom you could trust.** …, wem man trauen konnte.
whose [hu:z]
1. wessen V **Whose are these?** Wem gehören die (hier)? V
°**2.** dessen, deren *(Relativpronomen)*
why [waɪ] warum I **that's why** deshalb, darum II
wide [waɪd] breit, weit V
wife, *pl* **wives** [waɪf], [waɪvz] Ehefrau IV
Wi-fi ['waɪ faɪ] WLAN VI 1 (22)
wild [waɪld]:
1. wild; wild lebend I
2. in the wild in freier Wildbahn VI 1 (14)
wildlife ['waɪldlaɪf] Tiere *(in freier Wildbahn)*, Tierwelt VI 1 (10)
will [wɪl]: **I'll have …** Ich nehme … *(beim Essen, im Restaurant)* II **it won't rain (= it will not rain)** es wird nicht regnen II **the weather will be good** das Wetter wird gut sein II **We'll find him.** Wir werden ihn finden. II
win [wɪn], **won, won** gewinnen I
wind [wɪnd] Wind II
window ['wɪndəʊ] Fenster I
windy ['wɪndi] windig II
winner ['wɪnə] Gewinner/in II
winter ['wɪntə] Winter II
wireless ['waɪələs] drahtlos, Funk- VI 3 (56)
wish [wɪʃ]: **I wish I could tell you …** Ich wünschte, ich könnte dir erzählen, … IV
wishes ['wɪʃɪz]: **Best wishes** Viele Grüße, … *(Briefschluss)* I
wishful thinking [wɪʃfl 'θɪŋkɪŋ] Wunschdenken VI 3 (62)
witch [wɪtʃ] Hexe II
with [wɪð] mit I **with Ellie** mit Ellie; bei Ellie I
within [wɪ'ðɪn] innerhalb (von), in VI 3 (67)
without [wɪ'ðaʊt] ohne II **do without sth.** ohne etwas auskommen VI 3 (66)
wives [waɪvz] *Mehrzahl von* **wife** IV
woke [wəʊk] *siehe* **wake**
woken ['wəʊkən] *siehe* **wake**
woman, *pl* **women** ['wʊmən], ['wɪmɪn] Frau II
won [wʌn] *siehe* **win**
wonder ['wʌndə] sich fragen; gern wissen wollen III
wonderful ['wʌndəfl] wunderbar VI 2 (40)
won't [wəʊnt]: **it won't rain (= it will not rain)** es wird nicht regnen II
wood [wʊd] Holz; Wald III
word [wɜ:d] Wort I
word building ['wɜ:d bɪldɪŋ] Wortbildung III
word field ['wɜ:d fi:ld] Wortfeld II
wore [wɔ:] *siehe* **wear**
work [wɜ:k]:
1. Arbeit I
2. arbeiten; funktionieren I
work hard hart arbeiten I **work on sth.** arbeiten an etwas V **work sth. out** etwas herausfinden, etwas herausarbeiten IV
work experience ['wɜ:k ɪkspɪəriəns] Praktikum/Praktika; Arbeitserfahrung(en) V
worker ['wɜ:kə] Arbeiter/in III
working hours *(pl)* [wɜ:kɪŋ 'aʊəz] Arbeitszeit(en) V
world [wɜ:ld] Welt I **the best of both worlds** das Beste von beidem I
worn [wɔ:n] *siehe* **wear**
worried (about) ['wʌrid] beunruhigt, besorgt (wegen) I
worry (about) ['wʌri] sich Sorgen machen (wegen, um) I
worse (than) [wɜ:s] schlechter, schlimmer (als) III
worst [wɜ:st] am schlechtesten, am schlimmsten III
worth [wɜ:θ] wert V **The film is worth watching.** Es lohnt sich, den Film anzuschauen. V
would [wʊd]: **Would you like some tea/chips?** Möchtest du (etwas) Tee / (ein paar) Pommes frites? II **I'd (= I would) like to go home.** Ich würde gern nach Hause gehen. II **I'd (= I would) love to come.** Ich komme sehr gern. / Ich würde sehr gern kommen. I **I'd (= I would) prefer …** ich würde … vorziehen; ich würde lieber … III **What would**

you like? Was möchtest du? / Was hättest du gern? II °**they would sit …** sie saßen (früher) immer …
would-be ['wʊd bi:] künftige(r, s), angehende(r, s) VI 3 (60)
write [raɪt], **wrote, written** schreiben I **write sth. down** (sich) etwas aufschreiben III
writer ['raɪtə] Schreiber/in; Schriftsteller/in III
written ['rɪtn] *siehe* **write**
wrong [rɒŋ] falsch I **go wrong** schiefgehen III **prove sb. wrong** beweisen, dass jd. Unrecht hat VI 2 (36) **You're wrong.** Du hast Unrecht. III
wrote [rəʊt] *siehe* **write**

Y

yard [jɑ:d] *(AE)* Garten IV **school yard** Schulhof II
year [jɪə] Jahr I
yellow ['jeləʊ] gelb I
yes [jes] ja I
yesterday ['jestədeɪ] gestern II
yet [jet]:
1. *(in Fragen)* schon IV
Have you had dinner yet? Hast du schon zu Abend gegessen? IV
2. **not … yet** noch nicht II
yogurt ['jɒgət] Jogurt III
you [ju], [ju:]:
1. du; ihr; Sie I
2. dich; dir; euch; Sie; Ihnen I
3. man VI 3 (64)
young [jʌŋ] jung I
your [jɔ:], [jə] dein/e; euer/eure; Ihr/e I
yours [jɔ:z]:
1. deiner, deine, deins I
2. eurer, eure, eures III
Yours sincerely, … [jɔ:z sɪn'sɪəli] Mit freundlichen Grüßen *(Briefschluss)* IV
yourself [jɔ:'self], [jə'self] dich III
yourselves [jɔ:'selvz], [jə'selvz] euch III
youth [ju:θ] Jugend, Jugend- III
yummy ['jʌmi] *(infml)* lecker II

Z

zoo [zu:] Zoo I

ENGLISH SOUNDS AND ALPHABET

English sounds

[i:]	green, he, sea
[ɑ:]	ask, class, car, park
[ɔ:]	or, ball, door, four, morning
[u:]	ruler, blue, too, two, you
[ɜ:]	early, her, girl, work, T-shirt
[ɪ]	in, big, expensive
[e]	yes, bed, again, breakfast
[æ]	animal, apple, black, cat
[ʌ]	mum, bus, colour
[ɒ]	song, on, dog, what
[ʊ]	book, good, pullover
[ə]	again, today, a sister
[i]	happy, monkey
[eɪ]	name, eight, play, great
[aɪ]	I, time, right, my
[ɔɪ]	boy, toilet, noise
[əʊ]	old, no, road, yellow
[aʊ]	now, house
[eə]	where, pair, share, their
[ɪə]	here, dear
[ʊə]	tour
[b]	bike, table, verb
[p]	pen, paper, shop
[d]	day, window, good
[t]	ten, letter, at
[g]	go, again, bag
[k]	kitchen, car, back
[m]	man, remember, mum
[n]	no, one, ten
[ŋ]	wrong, young, uncle, thanks
[l]	like, old, small
[r]	ruler, friend, sorry
[w]	we, where, one
[j]	yes, you, uniform
[f]	family, after, laugh
[v]	very, seven, have
[s]	six, poster, yes
[z]	zoo, quiz, his, music, please
[ʃ]	she, station, English
[ʒ]	usually, revision, garage
[tʃ]	child, teacher, watch
[dʒ]	job, German, project, orange
[θ]	thing, three, bathroom, both
[ð]	the, father, with
[h]	house, who, behind

The English alphabet

a	[eɪ]
b	[bi:]
c	[si:]
d	[di:]
e	[i:]
f	[ef]
g	[dʒi:]
h	[eɪtʃ]
i	[aɪ]
j	[dʒeɪ]
k	[keɪ]
l	[el]
m	[em]
n	[en]
o	[əʊ]
p	[pi:]
q	[kju:]
r	[ɑ:]
s	[es]
t	[ti:]
u	[ju:]
v	[vi:]
w	['dʌblju:]
x	[eks]
y	[waɪ]
z	[zed]

infinitive	simple past	past participle	
be	*I/he/she/it* **was**; *you/we/you/they* **were**	**been**	sein
beat	**beat**	**beaten**	schlagen, besiegen
become	**became**	**become**	werden
begin	**began**	**begun**	beginnen, anfangen
bite [aɪ]	**bit** [ɪ]	**bitten** [ɪ]	beißen
bleed	**bled**	**bled**	bluten
blow	**blew**	**blown**	blasen, pusten; wehen *(Wind)*
break	**broke**	**broken**	brechen; zerbrechen
bring	**brought**	**brought**	bringen, mitbringen
build	**built**	**built**	bauen
burst	**burst**	**burst**	bersten, platzen
buy	**bought**	**bought**	kaufen
catch	**caught**	**caught**	fangen, erwischen
choose [uː]	**chose** [əʊ]	**chosen** [əʊ]	(sich) aussuchen, (aus)wählen
come	**came**	**come**	kommen
cost	**cost**	**cost**	kosten
creep up (on)	**crept**	**crept**	sich heranschleichen (an)
cut	**cut**	**cut**	schneiden; *(Rasen)* mähen
deal with	**dealt** [e]	**dealt** [e]	umgehen mit, fertigwerden/klarkommen mit
do	**did**	**done** [ʌ]	tun, machen
draw	**drew**	**drawn**	zeichnen
drink	**drank**	**drunk**	trinken
drive [aɪ]	**drove**	**driven** [ɪ]	*(mit dem Auto)* fahren; (an)treiben
eat	**ate** [et, eɪt]	**eaten**	essen
fall	**fell**	**fallen**	fallen, hinfallen
feed	**fed**	**fed**	füttern
feel	**felt**	**felt**	fühlen; sich fühlen
fight	**fought**	**fought**	kämpfen; bekämpfen
find	**found**	**found**	finden
fly	**flew**	**flown**	fliegen
forget	**forgot**	**forgotten**	vergessen
freeze	**froze** [əʊ]	**frozen** [əʊ]	(ge)frieren; erstarren
get	**got**	**got**	bekommen; holen, besorgen; werden; gelangen, (hin)kommen
give	**gave**	**given**	geben
go	**went**	**gone** [ɒ]	gehen
grow	**grew**	**grown**	wachsen; anbauen, anpflanzen, (allmählich) werden
hang	**hung**	**hung**	hängen
have	**had**	**had**	haben
hear [ɪə]	**heard** [ɜː]	**heard** [ɜː]	hören
hide [aɪ]	**hid** [ɪ]	**hidden** [ɪ]	verstecken; sich verstecken
hit	**hit**	**hit**	schlagen; treffen; prallen/stoßen gegen/auf
hold	**held**	**held**	halten
hurt	**hurt**	**hurt**	verletzen; wehtun
keep	**kept**	**kept**	behalten; halten; aufbewahren
know [nəʊ]	**knew** [njuː]	**known** [nəʊn]	wissen; kennen
leave	**left**	**left**	abfahren; (weg)gehen; verlassen; zurücklassen
lend sb. sth.	**lent**	**lent**	jm. etwas leihen
let	**let**	**let**	lassen

infinitive	simple past	past participle	
lie [aɪ]	**lay**	**lain**	liegen
light	**lit**	**lit**	anzünden
lose [uː]	**lost** [ɒ]	**lost** [ɒ]	verlieren
make	**made**	**made**	machen
mean [iː]	**meant** [e]	**meant** [e]	bedeuten; meinen, sagen wollen
meet	**met**	**met**	treffen; sich treffen; kennenlernen
overspend (on)	**overspent**	**overspent**	zu viel Geld ausgeben (für)
overtake	**overtook**	**overtaken**	überholen
pay	**paid**	**paid**	bezahlen
put	**put**	**put**	*(etwas wohin)* tun, legen, stellen
read [iː]	**read** [e]	**read** [e]	lesen
retell	**retold**	**retold**	nacherzählen
rewrite	**rewrote**	**rewritten**	noch einmal schreiben, neu schreiben
ride [aɪ]	**rode**	**ridden** [ɪ]	reiten; *(Rad)* fahren
ring	**rang**	**rung**	läuten, klingeln; anrufen
rise	**rose**	**risen**	(an)steigen
run	**ran**	**run**	rennen, laufen
say [eɪ]	**said** [e]	**said** [e]	sagen
see	**saw**	**seen**	sehen
sell	**sold**	**sold**	verkaufen
send	**sent**	**sent**	schicken, senden
set the table	**set**	**set**	den Tisch decken
shake	**shook**	**shaken** [eɪ]	schütteln
shine	**shone** [ɒ]	**shone** [ɒ]	scheinen *(Sonne)*
shoot	**shot**	**shot**	erschießen, schießen (auf)
show	**showed**	**shown**	zeigen
shut up	**shut**	**shut**	den Mund halten
sing	**sang**	**sung**	singen
sit	**sat**	**sat**	sitzen
sleep	**slept**	**slept**	schlafen
speak	**spoke**	**spoken**	sprechen
speed	**sped**	**sped**	rasen, zu schnell fahren
spend	**spent**	**spent**	ausgeben *(Geld)*; verbringen *(Zeit)*
spread	**spread**	**spread**	verbreiten *(z.B. Krankheit)*
stand	**stood**	**stood**	stehen; sich (hin)stellen
steal	**stole**	**stolen**	stehlen
stick	**stuck**	**stuck**	(haften) bleiben
sting	**stung**	**stung**	stechen *(Insekt)*; brennen
stink	**stank**	**stunk**	stinken
swim	**swam**	**swum**	schwimmen
swing	**swung**	**swung**	schwingen
take	**took**	**taken**	nehmen; mitnehmen; (weg-, hin)bringen; dauern, *(Zeit)* brauchen
teach	**taught**	**taught**	unterrichten, lehren
tell	**told**	**told**	erzählen, berichten
think	**thought**	**thought**	denken
throw	**threw**	**thrown**	werfen
understand	**understood**	**understood**	verstehen
wake	**woke**	**woken**	wecken
wear [eə]	**wore** [ɔː]	**worn** [ɔː]	tragen, anhaben *(Kleidung)*
win	**won** [ʌ]	**won** [ʌ]	gewinnen
write	**wrote**	**written**	schreiben

First names (Vornamen)

Adana [ə'dɑːnə]
Akhia [æ'kiə]
Alex ['ælɪks]
Alice ['ælɪs]
Amar [ə'mɑː]
Amy ['eɪmi]
Andre ['ɒndreɪ]
Andrew ['ændruː]
Anita [ə'niːtə]
Apache [ə'pætʃi]
Arav ['eərəv]
Asandiswa [ʌ'sʌndɪswʌ]
Avril ['ævrɪl]
Baz [bæz]
Benjamin ['bendʒəmɪn]
Beth [beθ]
Brode ['brəʊdə]
Buyi ['buːɪ]
Buyisiwe [bʊjɪ'siːwə]
Cathy ['kæθi]
Chris [krɪs]
Cooper ['kuːpə]
Danny ['dæni]
Dominique [dɒmɪ'niːk]
Ea [iː]
Elizabeth [i'lɪzəbəθ]
Emma ['emə]
Fanie ['fʌni]
Florence ['flɒrəns]
Gary ['gæri]
Hannah ['hænə]
Idris ['ɪdrɪs], ['aɪdrɪs]
Indira ['ɪndɪrə]
Jake [dʒeɪk]
James [dʒeɪmz]
Jamilia [dʒə'mɪliə]
Jamilla [dʒə'mɪlə]
Jeff [dʒef]
John [dʒɒn]
Johnny ['dʒɒni]
Jon [dʒɒn]
Jonathan ['dʒɒnəθən]
Julia ['dʒuːliə]
Kate [keɪt]
Katy ['keɪti]
Leitah ['laɪtə]
Lindokuhle [lɪndəʊ'kuːlə]
Lucy ['luːsi]
Luke [luːk]
Lukie ['luːki]
Lwazi [lə'wɑːzi]
Lyca ['laɪkə]
Marcus ['mɑːkəs]
Mark [mɑːk]
Martin ['mɑːtɪn]
Matthew ['mæθjuː]
Maya ['maɪə]
Naomi ['neɪəmi], [neɪ'əʊmi]
Natalie ['nætəli]
Natasha [nə'tæʃə]
Nazma [nʌz'mɑː]
Nelson ['nelsn]
Pete [piːt]
Peter ['piːtə]
Reuben ['ruːbən]
Richard ['rɪtʃəd]
Richart ['rɪtʃət]
Robin ['rɒbɪn]
Sarah ['seərə]
Shane [ʃɑːn], [ʃeɪn]
Shiva ['ʃiːvə]
Sienna [si'enə]
Simon ['saɪmən]
Simoshile [sɪ'məʊʃɪleɪ]
Stef [stef]
Tahiat ['tɑːhiət]
Teboho ['tiːbəhəʊ]
Teresa [tə'riːzə], [tə'reɪzə]
Tess [tes]
Vanessa [və'nesə]
Vincent ['vɪnsnt]
Vulu ['vuːluː]
Winnie ['wɪni]
Yi-Ling ['jiː lɪŋ]
Zoe ['zəʊi]

Family names / Surnames (Familiennamen)

Begum ['beɪgəm]
Bluhm [bluːm]
Bond [bɒnd]
Callebaut ['kʌləbaʊt]
Dube [djuːb]
Fletcher ['fletʃə]
Ghandi ['gændi]
Gunther ['gʌntə]
Hinton ['hɪntən]
Mabalane ['mʌbəleɪn]
Mahboob [mə'buːb]
Mandela [mæn'delə]
Mosley ['məʊzlɪ]
Sedgwick ['sedʒwɪk]
Smith [smɪθ]
Sowa ['səʊə]
Tambo ['tæmbəʊ]
Thun [tuːn]
Turk [tɜːk]
Viljoen [fi'jɜːn]
Wenger ['veŋə]
Wills [wɪlz]
Zephaniah [zefə'naɪə]

Place names (Ortsnamen)

Agra ['ɑːgrə]
Alabama [ælə'bæmə]
Amazon ['æməzən]
Balule [bel'juːl]
Birmingham ['bɜːmɪŋəm]
Boulders Beach [bəʊldəz 'biːtʃ]
Brittany ['brɪtni]
Brussels ['brʌslz]
Cambridge ['keɪmbrɪdʒ]
Camden ['kæmdən]
Cape Town ['keɪp taʊn]
Capilano Suspension Bridge [kæpɪlɑːnəʊ sə'spenʃn brɪdʒ]
Delhi ['deli]
East Ham [iːst 'hæm]
Exeter ['eksɪtə]
False Bay [fɔːls 'beɪ]
Heathrow ['hiːθrəʊ]
Highdown ['haɪdaʊn]
Huntsville ['hʌntsvɪl]
Jamshedpur [dʒɑːm'ʃedpə]
Jersey ['dʒɜːzi]
Johannesburg [dʒəʊ'hænəzbɜːg]
Joyxee Island [dʒɔɪgsiː 'aɪlənd]
Kruger National Park [kruːgə næʃnəl 'pɑːk]
Liverpool ['lɪvəpuːl]
Maine [meɪn]
Melbourne ['melbən], ['melbɔːn]
Mvezo [m'vezɒ]
Norwich ['nɒrɪdʒ]
Rana Plaza [rænə 'plɑːzə]
Robben Island [rɒbən 'aɪlənd]
San Francisco [sæn frən'sɪskəʊ]
Soweto [sə'wetəʊ]
Sydney ['sɪdni]
Vancouver [væn'kuːvə]
Waterberg Mountain ['wɔːtəbɜːg maʊntən]
Waterworld ['wɔːtəwɜːld]
Westphalia [west'feɪliə]

Other names (Andere Namen)

Afrikaans [æfrɪ'kɑːns]
Bloukrans River [bluːkræns 'rɪvə]
Blue Moon Hostel [bluː 'muːn hɒstl]
braai [braɪ]
Chatwin ['tʃætwɪn]
Childline ['tʃaɪldlaɪn]
dal [dɑːl], [dæl]
Floodland ['flʌdlənd]
Fly-Hi [flaɪ 'haɪ]
Ford [fɔːd]
isiNdebele [ɪsin'debələ]
isiXhosa [ɪsi'kɔːsə]
isiZulu [ɪsi'zuːluː]
Lilypad ['lɪlipæd]
NASA ['næsə]
Ngiyabonga [nəgiə'bɒŋgaː]
Nobel Peace Prize [nəʊbel 'piːs praɪz]
ROBOTECH ['rəʊbəʊtek]
roti ['rəʊti]
Sawubona [saʊ'bəʊnə]
Sepedi [sə'pedi]
Sesotho [sɪ'suːtuː]
Setswana [sət'swɑːnə]
siSwati [si'swɑːti]
Taj Mahal [tɑːdʒ mə'hɔːl]
Tshivenda [tʃiː'vendə]
UNICEF ['juːnɪsef]
XiTsonga [ʃi'tsɒŋgʌ]
Zulu ['zuːluː]

Country/Continent	Adjective	Person	People
Florence is from **Canada**.	*Hockey is* **Canadian**.	*Florence is* **a Canadian**.	**Canadians love** *Hockey*.
Afghanistan [æf'gænıstæn] *Afghanistan*	**Afghan** ['æfgæn]	**an Afghan**	**the Afghans**
Africa ['æfrıkə] *Afrika*	**African** ['æfrıkən]	**an African**	**the Africans**
Albania [æl'beıniə] *Albanien*	**Albanian** [æl'beıniən]	**an Albanian**	**the Albanians**
America [ə'merıkə] *Amerika*	**American** [ə'merıkən]	**an American**	**the Americans**
Asia ['eıʃə, 'eıʒə] *Asien*	**Asian** ['eıʃn, 'eıʒn]	**an Asian**	**the Asians**
Australia [ɒ'streıliə] *Australien*	**Australian** [ɒ'streıliən]	**an Australian**	**the Australians**
Austria ['ɒstriə] *Österreich*	**Austrian** ['ɒstriən]	**an Austrian**	**the Austrians**
Belarus [ˌbel'ruːs] *Weißrussland*	**Belarusian** [ˌbel'ruːsiən]	**a Belarusian**	**the Belarusians**
Belgium ['beldʒəm] *Belgien*	**Belgian** ['beldʒən]	**a Belgian**	**the Belgians**
Bosnia and Herzegovina ['bɒzniə ən ˌhɜːtsəgə'viːnə] *Bosnien und Herzegowina*	**Bosnian** ['bɒzniən]; **Herzegovinian** [ˌhɜːtsəgə'vıniən]	**a Bosnian; a Herzegovinian**	**the Bosnians; the Herzegovinians**
Botswana ['bɒtswɑːnə] *Botswana*	**Botswanan** ['bɒtswɑːnən]	**a Motswana**	**the Batswana**
Brazil [brə'zıl] *Brasilien*	**Brasilian** [brə'zıliən]	**a Brasilian**	**the Brasilians**
Bulgaria [bʌl'geəriə] *Bulgarien*	**Bulgarian** [bʌl'geəriən]	**a Bulgarian**	**the Bulgarians**
Canada ['kænədə] *Kanada*	**Canadian** [kə'neıdiən]	**a Canadian**	**the Canadians**
China ['tʃaınə] *China*	**Chinese** [tʃaı'niːz]	**a Chinese**	**the Chinese**
Croatia [krəʊ'eıʃə] *Kroatien*	**Croatian** [krəʊ'eıʃn]	**a Croatian**	**the Croatians**
the Czech Republic [tʃek rı'pʌblık] *Tschechien, die Tschechische Republik*	**Czech** [tʃek]	**a Czech**	**the Czechs**
Denmark ['denmɑːk] *Dänemark*	**Danish** ['deınıʃ]	**a Dane** [deın]	**the Danes**
England ['ıŋglənd] *England*	**English** ['ıŋglıʃ]	**an Englishman/-woman**	**the English**
Estonia [e'stəʊniə] *Estland*	**Estonian** [e'stəʊniən]	**an Estonian**	**the Estonians**
Europe ['jʊərəp] *Europa*	**European** [jʊərə'piːən]	**a European**	**the Europeans**
Finland ['fınlənd] *Finnland*	**Finnish** ['fınıʃ]	**a Finn** [fın]	**the Finns**
France [frɑːns] *Frankreich*	**French** [frentʃ]	**a Frenchman/-woman**	**the French**
Germany ['dʒɜːməni] *Deutschland*	**German** ['dʒɜːmən]	**a German**	**the Germans**
(Great) Britain ['brıtn] *Großbritannien*	**British** ['brıtıʃ]	**a Briton** ['brıtn]	**the British**
Greece [griːs] *Griechenland*	**Greek** [griːk]	**a Greek**	**the Greeks**
Holland ['hɒlənd] *Holland, die Niederlande*	**Dutch** [dʌtʃ]	**a Dutchman/-woman**	**the Dutch**
Hungary ['hʌŋgəri] *Ungarn*	**Hungarian** [hʌŋ'geəriən]	**a Hungarian**	**the Hungarians**
Iceland ['aıslənd] *Island*	**Icelandic** [aıs'lændık]	**an Icelander** ['aısləndə]	**the Icelanders**
India ['ındiə] *Indien*	**Indian** ['ındiən]	**an Indian**	**the Indians**
Iran [ı'rɑːn] *Iran*	**Iranian** [ı'reıniən]	**an Iranian**	**the Iranians**
Ireland ['aıələnd] *Irland*	**Irish** ['aırıʃ]	**an Irishman/-woman**	**the Irish**
Italy ['ıtəli] *Italien*	**Italian** [ı'tæliən]	**an Italian**	**the Italians**
Jamaica [dʒəmeıkə] *Jamaika*	**Jamaika** [dʒəmeıkən]	**a Jamaican**	**the Jamaicans**
Japan [dʒə'pæn] *Japan*	**Japanese** [dʒæpə'niːz]	**a Japanese**	**the Japanese**
Kosovo ['kɒsəvəʊ] *Kosovo*	**Kosovan** ['kɒsəvən]	**a Kosovan**	**the Kosovans**
Latvia ['lætviə] *Lettland*	**Latvian** ['lætviən]	**a Latvian**	**the Latvians**
Lebanon ['lebənən] *Libanon*	**Lebanese** [lebə'niːz]	**a Lebanese**	**the Lebanese**
Lesotho [lə'suːtuː] *Lesotho*	**Basotho** [bə'suːtuː]	**a Mosotho**	**the Basotho**
Lithuania [ˌlıθju'eıniə] *Litauen*	**Lithuanian** [ˌlıθju'eıniə]	**a Lithuanian**	**the Lithuanians**
Mozambique [məʊzæm'biːk] *Mosambik*	**Mozambican** [məʊzæm'biːkən]	**a Mozambican**	**the Mozambicans**

Luxembourg ['lʌksəmbɜːg] *Luxemburg*	**Luxembourg**	**a Luxembourger** ['lʌksəmbɜːgə]	**the Luxembourgers**
Macedonia [ˌmæsə'dəʊniə] *Mazedonien*	**Macedonian** [ˌmæsə'dəʊniən]	**a Macedonian**	**the Macedonians**
Malta ['mɔːltə] *Malta*	**Maltese** [mɔːl'tiːz]	**a Maltese**	**the Maltese**
Mexico ['meksɪkəʊ] *Mexiko*	**Mexican** ['meksɪkən]	**a Mexican**	**the Mexicans**
Moldova [mɒl'dəʊvə] *Moldawien*	**Moldovan** [mɒl'dəʊvən]	**a Moldovan**	**the Moldovans**
Montenegro [ˌmɒntɪ'niːgrəʊ] *Montenegro*	**Montenegrin** [ˌmɒntɪ'niːgrɪn]	**a Montenegrin**	**the Montenegrins**
Namibia [nə'mɪbiə] *Namibia*	**Namibian** [nə'mɪbiən]	**a Namibian**	**the Namibians**
the Netherlands ['neðələndz] *die Niederlande, Holland*	**Dutch** [dʌtʃ]	**a Dutchman/-woman**	**the Dutch**
New Zealand [njuː 'ziːlənd] *Neuseeland*	**New Zealand** [njuː 'ziːlənd]	**a New Zealander**	**the New Zealanders**
North America [ˌnɔːθ‿ə'merɪkə] *Nordamerika*	**North American** [ˌnɔːθ‿ə'merɪkən]	**a North American**	**the North Americans**
Northern Ireland [ˌnɔːðən‿'aɪələnd] *Nordirland*	**Northern Irish** [ˌnɔːðən‿'aɪrɪʃ]	**a Northern Irishman / a Northern Irishwoman**	**the Northern Irish**
Norway ['nɔːweɪ] *Norwegen*	**Norwegian** [nɔː'wiːdʒən]	**a Norwegian**	**the Norwegians**
Pakistan [pækɪ'stæn] *Pakistan*	**Pakistani** [pækɪ'stæni]	**a Pakistani**	**the Pakistani**
Poland ['pəʊlənd] *Polen*	**Polish** ['pəʊlɪʃ]	**a Pole** [pəʊl]	**the Poles**
Portugal ['pɔːtʃʊgl] *Portugal*	**Portuguese** [pɔːtʃu'giːz]	**a Portuguese**	**the Portuguese**
Romania [ru'meɪniə] *Rumänien*	**Romanian** [ru'meɪniən]	**a Romanian**	**the Romanians**
Russia ['rʌʃə] *Russland*	**Russian** ['rʌʃn]	**a Russian**	**the Russians**
Scotland ['skɒtlənd] *Schottland*	**Scottish** ['skɒtɪʃ]	**a Scotsman/-woman, a Scot** [skɒt]	**the Scots, the Scottish**
Serbia ['sɜːbiə] *Serbien*	**Serbian** ['sɜːbiən]	**a Serb** [sɜːb]	**the Serbs**
Slovakia [slə'vækiə] *die Slowakei*	**Slovak** ['sləʊvæk]	**a Slovakian** [slə'vækiən]	**the Slovakians**
Slovenia [slə'viːniə] *Slowenien*	**Slovene** ['sləʊviːn]	**a Slovenian** [slə'viːniən]	**the Slovenians**
Somalia [sə'mɑːliə] *Somalien*	**Somali** [sə'mɑːli]	**a Somali**	**the Somali**
South America [ˌsaʊθ‿ə'merɪkə] *Südamerika*	**South American** [ˌsaʊθ‿ə'merɪkən]	**a South American**	**the South Americans**
Spain [speɪn] *Spanien*	**Spanish** ['spænɪʃ]	**a Spaniard** ['spænɪəd]	**the Spaniards**
Swaziland [swɑːzilænd] *Swasiland*	**Swazi** [swɑːzi]	**a Swazi**	**the Swazis**
Sweden ['swiːdn] *Schweden*	**Swedish** ['swiːdɪʃ]	**a Swede** [swiːd]	**the Swedes**
Switzerland ['swɪtsələnd] *die Schweiz*	**Swiss** [swɪs]	**a Swiss**	**the Swiss**
Syria ['sɪriə] *Syrien*	**Syrian** ['sɪriən]	**a Syrian**	**the Syrians**
Tunisia [tju'nɪziə] *Tunesien*	**Tunisian** [tju'nɪziən]	**a Tunisian**	**the Tunisians**
Turkey ['tɜːki] *die Türkei*	**Turkish** ['tɜːkɪʃ]	**a Turk** [tɜːk]	**the Turks**
Ukraine [juː'kreɪn] *die Ukraine*	**Ukrainian** [juː'kreɪniən]	**a Ukrainian**	**the Ukrainians**
the United Kingdom (the UK) [junaɪtɪd 'kɪŋdəm, juː'keɪ] *das Vereinigte Königreich (Großbritannien und Nordirland)*	**British** ['brɪtɪʃ]	**a Briton** ['brɪtn]	**the British**
the United States of America (the USA) [junaɪtɪd steɪts‿əv‿ə'merɪkə, juː‿es‿'eɪ] *die Vereinigten Staaten von Amerika*	**American** [ə'merɪkən]	**an American**	**the Americans**
Vietnam [ˌviːet'næm], [ˌviːet'nɑːm] *Vietnam*	**Vietnamese** [viːˌetnə'miːz]	**a Vietnamese**	**the Vietnamese**
Wales [weɪlz] *Wales*	**Welsh** [welʃ]	**a Welshman/-woman**	**the Welsh**
Zimbabwe [zɪm'bɑːbwi] *Zimbabwe*	**Zimbabwean** [zɪm'bɑːbwiən]	**a Zimbabwean**	**the Zimbabweans**

Titelbild
Shutterstock/Dudarev Mikhail

Illustrationen
Carlos Borrell Eiköter, Berlin (Umschlaginnenseite 2; S. 8/9 *Hintergrund*; S. 85 *unten* (u. S. 97 *unten*)); **Michael Fleischmann**, Waldegg (S. 17 *oben*; S. 28; S. 92; S. 105); **Klein & Halm**, Berlin (S. 16; S. 26 *flags*; S. 51 *Mitte*; S. 54 (u. 55) Blasen (M); S. 117); **David Norman**, Meerbusch (S. 43 *unten*; S. 45; S. 48; S. 63 (u. S. 130); S. 64 (u. s. 130); S. 131 *oben*; S. 154; S. 159); **Dorina Teßmann**, Berlin (*alle Hantel-Icons*, S. 81 u. S. 96).

Bildquellen
action press (S. 70 *oben*: REX FEATURES LTD./Vincent Callebaut Architectures); **Alamy Images** (S. 14 *unten*: Murray Clarke; S. 106 *unten*: Ingram Publishing); **CartoonStock** (S. 180 *oben*: Richard Dall, *unten li.*: Kresten Forsman, *unten re.*: Ralph Hagen); **www.colourbox.de** (S. 66 *(E)*; S. 75 *oben*: JuNiArt); **Corbis** (S. 29 *re.*: Frederic Soltan); **ddp images** (S. 11 *Mitte*: CAMERA PRESS/Martine Velon; S. 26 *oben*: 360°/ CAMERA PRESS/Chad Chapman/Gallo Images S. 52; S. 60 *oben*; S. 71 *re.*); **epd-bild** (S. 27: Henner Frankenfeld); **F1online digitale Bildagentur** (S. 102 *re.*: UpperCut Images/B); **Fotolia** (S. 4 *oben „English"*: relif, *Mitte re.*: Papa Bravo, S. 6 *oben li. großes Bild*: ra2 studio, *oben li. kleines Bild*: Artur Marciniec, *oben re.*: Syda Productions, *unten*: jannoon028; S. 8 Reuben: Daniel Ernst; S. 9 *oben Taj Mahal*: jool-yan, *Yi-Ling*: kentoh, *Jamilla*: Mayer Riccardo, *unten Kaptstadt*: michaeljung; S. 10 *unten*: demerzel21; S. 11 *Elefant*: gallas, *Leopard*: Michael Wick, *Büffel*: VOLODYMYR BURDYAK; S. 15 *Baz*: Joachim Martin, *Capetowngirl*: Papa Bravo, S. 17 *unten*: zooco; S. 22 *oben*: Jacques PALUT, *(A)*: mindscanner; S. 23: Samuel Borges; S. 48 *oben (u. S. 123 oben)*: milosducati, *unten Tablet*: koosen; S. 51 *oben*: Zffoto; S. 54 *(B)*: mipan, *(E) li.*: ra2 studio, *re.*: Artur Marciniec; S. 58 *(C)*: destina; S. 60 *DrSpock*: photo-nuke; S. 66 *(A)*: higyou; S. 68: Oleksandr Delyk; S. 73 *Werkzeug*: romvo; S. 74: Tom Wang; S. 76 (1A): andrej pol, (1B): shaunwilkinson, (1C): vinbergv, (3B): aruba2000, (3C): Elnur, *unten*: WavebreakmediaMicro; S. 79: Maridav; S. 82 *oben*: Serj Siz`kov; S. 83 *li.*: zmiter, *re.*: trokerr; S. 85 *oben*: IEGOR LIASHENKO, S. 86: didecs; S. 89 *unten (u. S. 99 unten Mitte)*: Dan Race; S. 90 *Partner A*: Felix Pergande, *beach holiday (u. S. 99)*: Romolo Tavani, *city visit (u. S. 99)*: vitaliyvill; S. 91 *oben li. (u. S. 99 unten re.)*: highwaystarz, *oben Mitte*: Sachs500, *oben re.*: Dan Race, *Mitte li.*: Lisa F. Young, *Mitte 2. von li.*: Delphotostock, *Mitte re.*: Klaus Eppele; S. 94: Maridav; S. 125 *Weltkugel*: Romolo Tavani, *unten re.*: floya7; S. 134 *Bundesverfassungsgericht*: Klaus Eppele; S. 144: Andrey Kuzmin; S. 152: Chris Hinkley; S. 154 *li.*: Daniel Ernst; S. 155 *unten*: Daniel Ernst; S. 156: Daniel Ernst; S. 158 *re.*: Marina Lohrbach; S. 159 *unten*: Dirk Vonten; S. 165: Monkey Business; S. 169: jesadaphorn; S. 171: JPC-PROD; S. 183 *unten*: www.miriamdoerr.com); **Prince EA** (S. 59: "Sorry" from "Dear Future Generations"); **GlowImages** (S. 55 *(C)*: ScienceFaction; S. 73 *oben*: Imagesource); **Julia Gunther** (S. 31); **Image Source** (S. 38 *re.*: Brock Jones; S. 62 *re.*: Petra Weitz; S. 170 *unten*: J. Geoffrey Canon); **interfilm** (S. 25 u. 100 *unten*: Amar/PILGRIM FILMS PRODUCTION S. 47: Walk or Fly/It's My Shout Productions LTD; S. 69 u. S. 133 oben: The Red Thunder/Seariders Entertainment); **interfoto e. k.** (S. 8 *unten Straße*: Martin Moxter); **laif** (S. 50: Polaris; S. 72: Reporters/Merlin Meuris; S. 100 *oben*: hemis.fr/Emmanuel Berthier; S. 136 *unten*: Le Figaro Magazine/Martin); **mauritius images** (S. 8 *oben Schlittenhunde*: Alamy/Rubens Abboud; S. 9 *Mitte Singapur*: robertharding/Gavin Hellier, S. 14 *2. von oben*: Bluegreen Pictures, *2. von unten*: Alamy/ AfriPics.com; S. 19: Alamy Stock Photo/Alex Segre; S. 28 *oben*: age/Melba; S. 29 *li.*: Alamy/Naomi Bailey; S. 34 *re.*: Alamy/Wendy White; S. 43 *oben*: Wavebreakmedia, S. 45 *oben*: Alamy/zakir hossain chowdhury zakir; S. 49: Alamy/Ian Shipley IND; S. 51 *(3)*: Alamy/Jochen Tack; S. 58 *(E)*: Alamy/Thomas R. Fletcher; S. 70 *unten (u. S. 133 unten)*: Alamy/classic/ Roger Cracknell 01; S. 71 *li.*: nature picture library/ Mark Taylor; S. 91 *Mitte 2. von re. (u. S. 99 unten li.)*: Juice Images/Ian Lishman; S. 93 *unten*: Alamy/Angela Hampton Picture Library; S. 106 *oben*: Alamy Stock Photo/Alex Segre; S. 125 *unten li.*: Alamy/PE Forsberg; S. 137 *oben*: Alamy/TRVL/Horizons WWP; S. 179: Onoky/Eric Audras; S. 182 *oben*: UrbanImages/Alamy); **One Login** (S. 46 *Mitte*: Isis Wenger Ashalee, *oben*); **panthermedia** (S. 46 *(C)*: justtscott; S. 55 *(G)*: Harvepino; S. 55 *(H) unten*: opicobelloz; S. 76 *(2A)*: GeoImages; S. 77 *unten*: iophoto; S. 80 *oben (u. S. 95 unten)*: kjpargeter); **Picture-Alliance** (S. 34 *li.*: AP; S. 54 *(A)*: dpa, *(F)*: AP Photo; S. 55 *(D)*: dpa; S. 82 *unten*: dpa; S. 137 *2. von oben*: abaca); **Rockfinch** (S. 184: Claire Cunningham); **Jan Scannell** (S. 13) **Shutterstock** (S. 4 *Mitte li.*: michaeljung, *unten li.*: abeadev, *unten re.*: Pixsooz; S. 8 *Florence*: Tracy Whiteside; S. 9 *Arav*: ZouZou; S. 10/11 *unten Hintergrund*: Andrzej Kubik, Regenbogen: Don Pablo, *Rand (u. S. 11)*: wikki; S. 11 *Löwe*: Deborah Kolb, *Hippo*: Anton_Ivanov, *unten*: michaeljung; S. 14 *oben*: HPH Image Library; S. 15 *AP*: Samuil Levich, *Vulu*: Volt Collection, *Stef*: bluedarkat, S. 20: Monkey Business Images; S. 22 *(B)*: graphic stocker, *(C)*: argus; S. 24 *re.*: Jorg Hackemann; S. 26 *unten*: Shane Gross; S. 35: Akhenaton Images; S. 38 *li.*: jtairat, *Mitte*: Armin Staudt; S. 40 *oben re.*: Claudia Paulussen, *unten*: Doin Oakenhelm; S. 44 *oben*: LianeM, *unten*: abeadev; S. 46 *(A)*: Blend Images, *(B)*: CURAphotography, *(D)*: RobinE; S. 48 *Mitte*: symbiot; S. 51 *(1)*: Kzenon, *(2)*: Christian Draghici; S. 54/55 *Hintergrund*: Willyam Bradberry; S. 55 *(H) oben*: angelo sarnacchiaro, *re.*: angelo sarnacchiaro; S. 56 *oben*: Kostsov, *unten*: Ralwel; S. 57: Aleksandra Suzi; S. 58 *(D)*: Zhao jian kang; S. 60 *Mars*: Vadim Sadovski, *Spacecadet*: Reginast777; S. 65: isak55; S. 66 *(B)*: Pavel Ignatov, *(C)*: ColorsArk, *(D)*: Eric Isselee; S. 71 *unten*: jesadaphorn; S. 75 *unten*: ZouZou; S. 76 (2B): Matej Kastelic, (2C): kurhan, S. 76 (3A): Patricia Hofmeester; S. 77 *oben*: Avatar_023; S. 80 *unten (u. S. 95 oben)*: SpeedKingz; S. 88 (u. 98): Martin Novak; S. 89 *oben li.*: Yulia Grigoryeva, *oben re.*: John Gomez; S. 90 *hiking (u. S. 99)*: Sharon Freeman, *boat trip*: NEILRAS, *cycling tour*: Gabi Wolf; S. 91 *unten li.*: Reno Martin; S. 93 *oben*: Avatar_023; S. 101 *li.*: Sebastian Duda,

Mitte: Axel Bueckert; S. 102 *li.*: Monkey Business Images; S. 107: Monkey Business Images; S. 123 *re. (u. S. 123 re.)*: symbiot; S. 129: PathDoc; S. 131 *unten*: isak55; S. 134 *oben li.*: XiXinXing, *oben re.*: Bobb Klissourski, *Bundestag*: Sergey Kelin, *Schloss Bellevue*: bofotolux, S. 134 *unten li.*: Elpisterra, *Kanzleramt*: Sergey Kohl; S. 135: Photographee.eu; S. 136 *Karte*: Sergey Pomogayev, 2015, *Biber*: Dolimac, *Eisbären*: GUDKOV ANDREY; S. 137 *2. von unten*: Becky Stares, *unten*: satori.artwork; S. 138: LUSTOCKPHOTO; S. 139 *Gateway of India*: saiko3p, *Queenstown*: ChameleonsEye, *Ocho Rios*: Susan Santa Maria, *Lagos*: Bill Kret;. 140 *li.*: J Main, *Mitte*: Zack Frank, *re.*: Adam Parent; S. 149: art4all; S. 150: Constantin Stanciu, S. 153: Pinar Ince; S. 154 *re.*: Robert Kneschke; S. 155 *oben*: Robert Kneschke; S. 157: Robert Kneschke; S. 158 *li.*: Daniel M Ernst; S. 159 *oben*: Frolphy; S. 163: dotshock; S. 164: Lorelyn Medina; S. 167: Blend Images; S. 170 *oben*: Jesus Sanz; S. 172: Tharakorn; S. 175: Monkey Business Images; S. 178: l i g h t p o e t; S. 182 *Flaggen (u. S. 203)*: Christopher Poliquin; S. 183 *oben*: Artisticco; S. 210: Solaie; S. 211 *oben*: Blan-k, *unten*: Artisticco; S. 212 *oben*: Henrique Daniel Araujo, *unten*: John Carnemolla; S. 214 *oben*: Rudchenko Liliia, *Mitte*: suwatpatt, *unten*: AlexMaster; S. 215: Nightman1965; S. 216 *oben li.*: Victoria Kurylo, *oben re.*: saknakorn, *Mitte li.*: Gouraud Studio, *Mitte re.*: Misha Beliy, *unten*: Camilo Torres; S. 217: ChrisVanLennepPhoto; S. 219: Elena Noeva; S. 220: Zerbor; S. 221 *oben*: Vertes Edmond Mihai, *unten li.*: Arcady, *unten re.*: phoelixDE; S. 222 *oben li.*: kulyk, *oben re.*: Earl Wilkerson, *Mitte li.*: Dja65, *Mitte re.*: Early Spring, *unten*: STILLFX; S. 223 *oben li.*: AlexRoz, *oben re.*: Petr Malyshev, *unten*: Robert Crum; S. 224 *oben li.*: Neil Mitchell, *oben re.*: StockCube, *speed hump*: nulinukas, *scar*: ArtStudia Group, *junction*: Weenee; S. 225 *oben*: Tyler Olson, *Mitte*: Minerva Studio, S. *unten li.*: Hriana, *unten re.*: Fer Gregory; S. 226 *oben*: Blablo101, *unten*: wavebreakmedia; S. 227 *oben*: Christopher Elwell, *unten*: Slavoljub Pantelic; S. 228 *oben*: AlexRoz, *Mitte*: Maksym Bondarchuk, *unten*: Ivonne Wierink; S. 229: Liudmyla Marykon; S. 230 *oben li.*: Neda Sadreddin, *oben Mitte*: wizdata1, *oben re.*: HIRO-Lab, *unten*: grace21; S. 231: tektur; S. 232 *oben*: Punyaruk Baingern, *Mitte*: Ints Vikmanis, *unten*: Microgen; S. 233 *oben li.*: Patrick Foto, *oben re.*: pavel dudek, *Mitte*: Marbury, *unten*: CTR Photos; S. 234: Zadiraka Evgenii; S. 236 *oben*: Ricardo Reitmeyer, *unten*: BPTU; S. 237: Rafal Kulik; S. 276/277: Angela Jones); **The Independent** (S. 30: Julia Gunther 2015); **TopicMedia** (S. 90 *Partner B*: imageBROKER/hkp); **Trócaire** (S. 84 (u. S. 97 *oben*); **Gary Turk** (from „It's your future": S. 36; S. 37 (u. S. 115); **UNICEF** (S. 32; S. 33); **Vincent Callebaut Architectures** (S. 58 *(A)*), **Visum** (S. 101 *re.*: A. Vossberg); **Volunteering Solutions/Marloes Reinders** (S. 24 *li.*); **Alexia Webster** (S. 12); **WILDLIFE** (S. 91 *unten re.*: S. Muller); **YourPhotoToday** (S. 82 *Mitte*).

Textquellen

S. 12 Berichte von Asandiswa, Brode, Akhia, Teboho, Lindokhule aus: "Born Frees and the Confidence of Youth". Alexia Webster 2014;
S. 19–21 u. **S. 106–107** u. **S. 108–109** "Returned". Aus: Fanie Viljoen: "Scarred Lions". Ransom Publishing, Winchester 2013; S. 10–57 (Auszüge);
S. 30 "The Lion Queens". Aus: Kate Wills: "Power Rangers – The Lion Queens" The New Review. 27.09.2015, S. 20–21;
S. 36 u. **S. 115** "It's Your Future", Gary Turk (2015);
S. 41–43 u. **S. 121–122** Benjamin Zephaniah: "Face". © 1999 by Benjamin Zephaniah. Published by Bloomsbury Publishing Children's Books, U.S.A., New York 2004, S. 45–65;
S. 52 Jon Snow: "My shameful dilemma": http://blogs.channel4.com/snowblog/my-shameful-dilemma/1715 (25.06.2009);
S. 63–64 u. **S. 130–131** Marcus Sedgwick: "Floodland". Orion children's books (imprint of Hodder & Stoughton, reissue 2010). First published in Great Britain as a Dolphin paperback (2000), S. 3–8;
S. 80–81 u. **S. 95–96** Ann Angel: "The Bracelet". Aus: "Sudden Flash Youth". 65 Short-short stories, ed. by Christine Perkins et al. Persea Books Inc, New York, 2007, S. 154–157;
S. 84 u. **S. 97** "Climate change challenge weekend". Trócaire 2015;
S. 86 Daniel Handler: "Principals and principles". Aus: "Guys write for guys read". Edited by Jon Scieszka. Viking 2005, S. 112–113;
S. 79 u. **S. 94** „I am European" Wettbewerb 2013/ youthreporter.eu;
S. 112 "Interview with Film-maker Andrew Hilton". Tahiat Mahboob. Asia Society 2012;
S. 126 "Sorry". Aus: Prince Ea: "Dear Future Generations: Sorry" (2015);
S. 142–144 Brent Hartinger: "The Question: A Play in One Act" copyright © Brent Hartinger, 2007. Aus: "21 Proms". Edited by David Levithan & Daniel Ehrenhaft. Scholastic children's books, London 2015, S. 136–149;
S. 146–149 Malorie Blackman: "Searching for a two-way street". Aus: "Stories celebrating Human Rights". Amnesty International. Walker Books Ltd, London 2009, S. 136–142;
S. 151 Hanna Bottomy Voskuil: "Currents". Aus: "Sudden Flash Youth". 65 Short-Short Stories. Edited by Christine Perkins-Hazuka, Tom Hazuka, and Mark Budman. Persea Books, New York 2011, S. 28–29.

TYPICAL EXAM INSTRUCTIONS

General	Allgemein
Read the tasks carefully.	Lies die Aufgaben sorgfältig.
You now have 60 seconds to read the tasks.	Du hast ab jetzt 60 Sekunden zum Lesen der Aufgaben.
Now do the tasks.	Nun bearbeite die Aufgaben.
Tick the correct box / the correct boxes.	Setze ein Häkchen (✓) in das / die richtige(n) Kästchen.
Tick the right statements. (There's only one possible answer per statement.)	Setze ein ✓ bei den korrekten Aussagen. (Pro Aussage ist nur eine Antwort möglich.)
Complete the sentences (with not more than three words per gap / … than two words each).	Vervollständige die Sätze (mit bis zu drei Wörtern pro Lücke/mit je bis zu zwei Wörtern).
Fill in the information / the missing words.	Füge die Information / die fehlenden Wörter ein.
Fill in suitable words / the correct numbers.	Füge passende Wörter / die korrekten Zahlen ein.
Fill in only one detail per box.	Füge nur ein Detail pro Kästchen ein.
Complete these sentences.	Vervollständige diese Sätze.
There is only one possible answer.	Es gibt nur eine mögliche Antwort.
There are two more words than you need.	Es gibt zwei Wörter mehr als du benötigst.
Choose the correct options and fill in the blanks.	Wähle die korrekten Varianten und fülle die Lücken aus.
Mark *true* or *false*.	Markiere (z.B. mit einem ✗) *wahr* oder *falsch*.
There is an example at the beginning.	Am Anfang steht ein Beispiel.
You have a choice here. Choose one of the following tasks: …	Hier hast du die Wahl. Wähle eine der folgenden Aufgaben aus: …

Listening	Hörverstehen
You are going to hear a story / an interview about …	Du wirst eine Geschichte / ein Interview über … hören.
Listen to the interview.	Höre dir das Interview an.
Listen to these people talking about … Who thinks what? Tick the correct letters.	Höre dem Gespräch dieser Personen über … zu. Wer denkt was? Setze ein ✓ bei den korrekten Buchstaben.
You will hear five short conversations.	Du wirst fünf kurze Gespräche hören.
You will hear each conversation twice.	Du wirst jedes Gespräch zweimal hören.
While you are listening, tick the correct box / …	Während du zuhörst, setze ein ✓ in das richtige Kästchen.
At the end you will hear the story / interview again.	Am Ende hörst du die Story / das Interview nochmal.
Now listen to the story and do the tasks.	Höre dir jetzt die Geschichte an und löse die Aufgaben.
Which word group completes the sentence best?	Welche Wortgruppe vervollständigt den Satz am besten?
Mark the correct option to complete the sentences.	Markiere die jeweils korrekte Vervollständigung der Sätze.
Complete the table using two to five words.	Vervollständige die Tabelle mit zwei bis fünf Wörtern.

Reading and Writing	Leseverstehen und Schreiben
First read the text. Then read the sentence beginnings and tick the correct ending.	Lies zuerst den Text. Dann lies die Satzanfänge und setze ein ✓ beim jeweils korrekten Satzende.
First read the information about the people, then look at the job / holiday / … offers. In each case find two options the person could choose.	Lies zuerst die Informationen über die Personen, dann schau dir die Job-/ Ferien-/ …-Angebote an. Finde für jede Person zwei Möglichkeiten, die sie wählen könnte.
You need not write complete sentences.	Du musst keine vollständigen Sätze schreiben.
Quote from the text.	Zitiere aus dem Text.
Find the correct parts of Mr Miller's quote.	Finde die korrekten Teile aus Mr. Millers Zitat.
Match each of these headings with a suitable paragraph from the text. (Some paragraphs don't match.)	Ordne jede dieser Überschriften einem passenden Textabsatz zu. (Zu einigen Absätzen passt keine Überschrift.)
Match the correct sentence parts. (Write down the letter in the box.)	Ordne die passenden Satzteile einander zu. (Schreibe den Buchstaben in das Kästchen.)
Match 1–4 to the information given in A–G. Some information doesn't fit.	Ordne 1–4 den Informationen in A–G zu. Einige Informationen lassen sich nicht zuordnen.
Answer the questions below. Give short answers.	Beantworte die unten stehenden Fragen kurz.
Answer the questions in complete sentences.	Beantworte die Fragen mit vollständigen Sätzen.
You can't find the answers to the following questions directly in the text.	Du wirst auf die folgenden Fragen keine direkten Antworten im Text finden.
The following words have more than one meaning. Which of the meanings is the one used in the text?	Die folgenden Wörter haben mehr als eine Bedeutung. Welche Bedeutung ist im Text gemeint?
Write down the German meaning as used in the text.	Schreibe die im Text gemeinte deutsche Bedeutung auf.
Complete the following sentences with suitable phrases from the text (with not more than five to seven words per gap).	Vervollständige die folgenden Sätze mit passenden Wendungen aus dem Text (max. fünf bis sieben Wörter pro Lücke).
Finish the sentences using information from the text.	Beende die Sätze mit Informationen aus dem Text.
Decide whether the following statements are right or wrong.	Entscheide, ob die folgenden Aussagen wahr oder falsch sind.
Find out whether the following statements are true, false or not given in the text. Tick the correct box.	Sind die folgenden Aussagen wahr, falsch oder nicht im Text gegeben? Setze ein ✓ in das korrekte Kästchen.
Scan paragraph A. Name two examples …	Scanne Absatz A. Nenne zwei Beispiele …